Revitalization of Waqf for Socio-Economic Development, Volume I

"Waqf has historically played significant role in the Islamic social sector. After long periods of colonization and intellectual drought, its revival is essential. Waqf's impact on achieving SDGs can enhance by integration with finance e.g. through Qard to have-nots to reduce vulnerability and increase resilience, thus adding productive economic activities, yet with sustenance to the institution. AAOIFI, accordingly, initiated a comprehensive Waqf project Shari'ah, governance and accounting standards, believing that Islamic finance shall integrate the SDGs, through utilizing the institution of Waqf. I believe the anthology of scholarly papers offers comprehensive knowledge about this important aspect of Islamic social finance."

—Omar Mustafa Ansari, *Secretary General, AAOIFI*

"While focusing on the revitalization of waqf and its implication in the socio-economic development of modern societies, this book does not only address aspects of waqf management and poverty alleviation, it also critically analyzes the value of waqf in structuring sukuk and Islamic bank products. This unique dimension to the overarching discourse on revitalization of waqf provides the reader with an invaluable reference on the role of waqf in deepening socio-economic development in selected jurisdictions."

—Umar Oseni, *Islamic Finance Scholar, Malaysia*

"Islamic social finance-waqf, zakat, sadaqah, microfinance- is a link for socio-economic development of the masses. An efficient Waqf management helps to preserve assets either in the form of cash or non-cash earned from voluntary but permanent distribution of wealth in an Islamic society. A Waqf institution transforms this value to enhance socio-economic contributions of Muslims and Islamic entities in a Shari'ah compliant way. Waqf stands as one of the most significant contributions of Islam to the world. This book is a must read for those who are interested in knowing the Islamic social justice framework to develop a society."

—Professor Azmi Omar, *President, INCEIF, Malaysia*

Khalifa Mohamed Ali · M. Kabir Hassan ·
Abd elrahman Elzahi Saaid Ali
Editors

Revitalization of Waqf for Socio-Economic Development, Volume I

Editors
Khalifa Mohamed Ali
Islamic Research and Training
Institute
Islamic Development Bank
Jeddah, Saudi Arabia

M. Kabir Hassan
Department of Economics
and Finance
University of New Orleans
New Orleans, LA, United States

Abd elrahman Elzahi Saaid Ali
Islamic Research and Training
Institute
Islamic Development Bank
Jeddah, Saudi Arabia

ISBN 978-3-030-18444-5   ISBN 978-3-030-18445-2   (eBook)
https://doi.org/10.1007/978-3-030-18445-2

This Palgrave Macmillan imprint is published by the registered company Springer Nature
Switzerland AG
The registered company address is: Gewerbestrasse 11, 6330 Cham, Switzerland

FOREWORD

Waqf has been historically a major source of support for socio-economic development in the Islamic world. The Islamic Development Bank is leading the revival of waqf to contribute toward the Sustainable Development Goals in our member countries.

This book comprises of research papers analyzing and proposing innovative applications of waqf. The book highlights the role of waqf management in socio-economic development, poverty alleviation, and the role that waqf institutions might potentially play in expediting inclusive and sustainable growth.

On behalf of the Islamic Research and Training Institute, I thank the authors and editors who made this book a reality. We hope such efforts contribute to better understanding and creative formulations of waqf to meet the challenges of the twenty-first century.

Jeddah, Saudi Arabia

Sami Al-Suwailem
Acting Director General
Islamic Research and Training
Institute (IRTI)

ACKNOWLEDGEMENTS

The two volumes of *Revitalization of Waqf for Socio-Economic Development* book result from an International Workshop on *Revival of Waqf for Socio-Economic Development* held at Pan Pacific Sonargaon in Dhaka, Bangladesh on 4–5 November 2017, under the auspices of Islamic Research and Training Institute (IRTI), Jeddah, Islami Bank Bangladesh Limited (IBBL) and Center for Zakat Management (CZM). We want to thank all workshop paper presenters, participants, session chairs, and paper reviewers for their timely and valuable contribution for the realization of this international workshop. The thought-provoking engagement of Islamic scholars in the two-day international workshop generated innovative ideas, new dimension and dynamics enabling waqf to mobilize resources for facilitation of health, education, poverty reduction, and other social services. This may open up a new source to shoring the resource gap for SDG goals and targets within the stipulated time frame.

The workshop was planned when Professor Dr. Azmi Omar was the DG of IRTI, and Arastoo Khan was the Chairman of the Board of Directors of Islami Bank Bangladesh Limited (IBBL). Niaz Rahim, Chairman of Center for Zakat Management (CZM), joined this effort with open arms. The book publishing was approved with Palgrave Macmillan when Dr. Humayon Dar was the DG of IRTI.

We want to thank the Honorable President of Bangladesh, His Excellency Md. Abdul Hamid for officiating this conference at Hotel Pan Pacific Sonargaon. We also want to thank the Governor of Bangladesh His Excellency Fazle Kabir, the Honorable Chairman of

IBBL Board His Excellency Arastoo Khan and Chairman, Center of Zakat Management, His Excellency Niaz Rahim for contributing to the success of this international conference.

Our special thanks go to Dr. Miah Muhammad Ayub and Mr. Arastoo Khan who played critical role at each stage of the workshop from original idea to completion of this conference. Without their much needed timely intervention and active engagement, this conference would not have been possible. Our sincere thanks are to Mr. Mohammad Habibur Rahman of IBBL International Wing for connecting us all across continents and different time zones in the world. We also thank Md. Abdul Hamid Miah, Ex-MD of IBBL and Md. Mahbubul Alam, ex-AMD and current MD of IBBL for their financial and logistical support for this international workshop.

We want to thank Eman Ahmed Adam of IRTI and Sydul Karim of University of New Orleans for editorial and formatting assistance. We want thank Dr. Mamun Rashid, now at University of Brunei Darussalam, Dr. Mizanur Rahman of Islamic Bank Training and Research Academy (IBTRA), Dr. Mahmood Ahmed, DG of IBTRA, Abdul Awwal Sarker, GM of Bangladesh Bank, Professor Muhammad Muzahidul Islam of Dhaka University, Professor M. Kabir Hassan of University of New Orleans, Dr. Khalifa Mohamed Ali and Dr. Abd elrahman Elzahi Saaid Ali of IRTI for reviewing papers for this conference.

We want to thank Professor Dr. Md. Nazmul Hassan, current IBBL Chairman, Professor Dr. M. Shamsher Ali, Professor Emeritus, Southeast University, Mr. Salahuddin Kasem Khan, Executive Chairman, SEACO Foundation, Dr. Mohammad Ayub Miah, CEO, Center for Zakat Management, Mr. Abdul Muyeed Chowdhury, Former Secretary of Government of Bangladesh, Mohammed Humayun Kabir, Director, IBBL, and Dr. Muhammad Abdul Mazid, Former Secretary of the Government of Bangladesh for chairing different sessions of the workshop.

We also want to thank Dr. Hafizur Rahman, former Waqf Administrator of Government of Bangladesh, Dr. Monzur-e-Elahi, Professor Mokhtar Ahmed, Asian University of Bangladesh, Professor Muzahidul Islam of Dhaka University, Dr. Sheikh Abdur Rashid, former Additional Secretary of Government of Bangladesh, Dr. Zubair Mohammad Ehsanul Hoque, Dhaka University, Professor Dr. Mohammad Main Uddin of Rajshahi University, Professor Dr. Mahbubur Rahman of North South University, Professor

Dr. Farid A. Sobhani of Daffodil University, AMM Nasiruddin, Former Secretary, Government of Bangladesh, Professor Dr. Syeda Sultana Razia of BUET and Dr. Shariful Alam, Chairman of ASEAB and Md. Shahidul Islam of the Office of Bangladesh Waqf Administrator for discussing papers in the different workshop sessions. We also want to thank the diplomats, high officials, bankers, industry leaders, and civil society for their participations and deliberations at the conference.

Finally, we want to thank Tula Weis, Senior Editor of Palgrave Macmillan for her support gracious support for publishing this book and Jacqueline Young for helping us through the production process for this book.

Khalifa Mohamed Ali
M. Kabir Hassan
Abd elrahman Elzahi Saaid Ali

CONTENTS

NOTES ON CONTRIBUTORS

Dr. Mustapha Abubakar is a Senior Lecturer in the Department of Banking and Finance of Ahmadu Bello University Business School, Zaria-Nigeria. Prior to joining the academic community in 1999, he worked as a banking officer in Union Bank of Nigeria for nearly three years from 1996 to 1999.

He obtained a Diploma in Accounting, B.Sc. Business Administration, M.B.A., M.Sc. Business Administration, and Ph.D. all from Ahmadu Bello University, Zaria-Nigeria in 1989, 1993, 1995, 2010, and 2017, respectively. He has participated in many academic conferences as a paper presenter in conventional and Islamic finance, banking, and economics areas in Nigeria, Malaysia, Saudi Arabia, and Bangladesh. He has also published papers in academic journals and book chapters in Nigeria and abroad and reviewed a number of academic papers for seminars, journals, theses, and books in areas of Islamic banking, economics, and finance. This is in addition to other numerous supervision works of undergraduate and postgraduate students he undertook.

Dr. Abu Umar Faruq Ahmad is currently an Associate Professor at Islamic Economics Institute (IEI), King Abdulaziz University, Jeddah, Saudi Arabia. He has a significant number of published peer-reviewed refereed journal articles, books, chapters in edited books, conference proceedings, and other intellectual contributions to his credit on Shari`ah compliance of Islamic banks' products and structures, the opportunities and challenges of Islamic finance, case studies of Islamic banks and financial institutions, Islamic insurance and reinsurance, Islamic microfinance, *Sukuk*, and dispute resolution in Islamic banking and finance, among others. He has presented over 50 scholarly research papers at international conferences held in the USA, Ireland, Australia, UAE, Saudi Arabia, Turkey, Brunei, Qatar, Sudan, Nigeria, Malaysia, Indonesia, Bangladesh, and Pakistan. His current editorial roles include serving as founding editor, senior editor, editorial advisory board member of a plethora of internationally reputed refereed journals including some of those published by Emerald Group Publishing, UK.

Abd elrahman Elzahi Saaid Ali currently works at the Research & Advisory Services Department, The Islamic Research and Training Institute. Abd elrahman does research in Financial Economics, Econometrics and Behavioural Economics. Their current project is 'Enhancing Women's Capability and Financial Inclusion in Sudan, Yemen, Comoros and Morocco'.

Dr. Khalifa Mohamed Ali is a Senior Research Economist at the Islamic Research and Training Institute(IRTI), Islamic Development Bank (IsDB), the leaders in promoting Islamic economics banking and finance and in knowledge dissemination. Before joining IRTI, he worked as assistant and associate Professor of Economics at the United Arab Emirates University and awarded merits of distinction (two times) for his outstanding contribution to the development of academic life in the University. Dr. Khalifa holds undergraduate degree in Economics and Statistics (with honors) from the University of Khartoum, Sudan and a graduate degree in Islamic Economics and Banking from The Islamic University, Sudan. He received his M.A. and Ph.D. in Economics from Iowa State University, USA, where he taught economics. Dr. Khalifa is the editor of the Islamic Economic Studies Journal, which one of IRTI's flagship publications, his research and books are published by some of the world leading publishers such as Springer, Wiley, Taylor & Francis Group and IRTI. Dr. Khalifa has developed several publications for teaching Islamic banking and finance at various levels, which are currently used to create Massive Open Online Courses for IRTI on line learning program with edX.

Prof. Dr. Rosni Bakar is a Professor in the School of Business Innovation and Technopreneurship at Universiti Malaysia Perlis. She is currently the Director of the Center for International Affairs of

Universiti Malaysia Perlis. She received her bachelor's degree and master's degree from the Eastern Illinois University, USA and the doctoral degree from the University of Exeter, England. She has authored a book titled *Making Micros into Millions in Agro-Based Food and Beverages (F & B) Industry in Sarawak* and is a co-author of a few other books. She is very active in her research activities and publications, both locally and internationally. She has been a lead researcher for numerous projects and written chapters for few books. Her recent research has spanned issues related to Higher Education, International Student Mobility, Green Technology, Entrepreneurship Education, Knowledge Management, Youth Employment and Unemployment, and Economics.

Dr. Mohd Fazlul Karim received his Ph.D. on waqf studies. His Ph.D. research, focusing on legal and administrative management of awaqf in Bangladesh, has been one of the groundbreaking researches at Ph.D. level as far as waqf research on Bangladesh is concerned. He has authored a number of chapters in books published by renowned publishers from India, Malaysia, and the UK. He has also published research papers in international and peer-reviewed journals that include journals listed in SCOPUS. Dr. Karim is privileged to have co-authored a number of publications with award-winning authors including Prof. M. Kabir Hassan, the winner of '*The 2016 IDB Prize in Islamic Banking and Finance*'. He has also presented numerous research papers in international conferences and chaired sessions and panel discussions in them. A major segment of his total publications is focused on waqf and aspects of Islamic Finances in relation to their relevance to waqf and waqf-based applications. He has extensive teaching experience and has taught in prestigious institutions like International Islamic University Malaysia (IIUM) and the Multimedia University (MMU) in Cyberjaya Malaysia. Dr. Karim is currently based in Canada and has recently earned a professional degree on global corporate law from the University of Toronto, Canada.

Prof. M. Kabir Hassan is Professor of Finance in the Department of Economics and Finance in the University of New Orleans. He currently holds two endowed Chairs-Hibernia Professor of Economics and Finance, and Bank One Professor in Business in the University of New Orleans. *Professor Hassan is the winner of the 2016 IDB Prize in Islamic Banking and Finance*. Professor Hassan received his B.A. in Economics and Mathematics from Gustavus Adolphus College, Minnesota, USA, and M.A. in Economics and Ph.D. in Finance from the University of

Nebraska-Lincoln, USA, respectively. Professor Hassan is a leading authority on empirical Islamic finance scholarship and published Islamic finance papers in top academic journals. Professor Hassan has over 300 papers published in refereed academic journals. Dr. Professor Hassan is the Editor *International Journal of Islamic* and *Middle Eastern Finance and Management* (Scopus and SSCI). He has guest edited special Issues of Islamic finance for a number of leading academic journals. He has published a number of book on Islamic finance, law and entrepreneurship by Edward Elgar, John Wiley, Palgrave Macmillan, Routledge, Pearson, and Emerald publishing company. Professor Hassan has won several awards for his outstanding teaching and research accomplishments by USA and international bodies.

Mr. Basharat Hossain is the Assistant professor of economics at the Department of Business Administration in the International Islamic University Chittagong, Bangladesh. He also worked as a junior research fellow in the Islamic Economics Research Bureau (IERB), Dhaka, Bangladesh. Mr. Hossain successfully completed the Bachelor of social science (Honors) and Master of social science in economics from the department of economics, University of Dhaka, Bangladesh. He is also a candidate of Master of Philosophy (M.Phil.) in the same university. He achieved scholarship at primary, secondary, higher secondary, honors, and M.Phil. level. Mr. Hossain is concerned about national economic issues and published twenty articles in national newspapers and magazines. He has an academic interest in public & monetary economics, development economics, economies of third world countries, and Islamic economics and finance. Ten of his research articles were published in the internationally reputed academic journal and more seven research articles are under review. He participated and presented papers in six international conferences.

Assoc. Prof. Md. Aminul Islam, Ph.D. is an Associate Professor in the School of Business Innovation and Technopreneurship at Universiti Malaysia Perlis. He received his bachelor's degree from the International Islamic University Malaysia. His M.B.A. and the doctoral degree from the Universiti Sains Malaysia. Prior to this, he has completed advanced diploma in teaching in higher education from the Nottingham Trent University. An award-winning teacher, he received the *Raffles Education Founder's Award* for being the most deserving academic staff of Olympia College Malaysia 2006, *Excellent Academic Support Award 2009*, and

Anugerah Pendidik Cemerlang (the best lecturer Award) 2010 at Universiti Malaysia Perlis. He also won '*The Best Thesis Award 2011*' for the outstanding Ph.D. dissertation at Universiti Sains Malaysia. He is an Advisory Board Member of the Australian Academy of Business Leadership (AABL) Sydney, Australia, a member of Asian Academy of Management and an associate member of Malaysian Finance Association. He is a visiting Professor of Northern University Bangladesh and an External Academic Advisor of Sentral Technology College Penang, Malaysia. He is the Chief Editor of the *Australasian Journal of Islamic Finance and Business (AJIFB)*. He is an editorial board member of number of journals, i.e., *Business Review, Australian Academy of Accounting and Finance Review, Australasian Journal of Accounting, Economics and Finance, International Journal of Ethics in Social Science,* and the founder Chief Editor of *International Journal of Business and Technopreneurship.* He has co-authored three books titled: (i) *SMEs in Malaysia: An Industry Research on the Green Technology Sector,* (ii) *Corporate Social Responsibility: A Consumer-Based Research on CSR in Malaysia,* and (iii) *Myanmar: The Catalyst to Bridge ASEAN and SAARC.* He has authored and co-authored about 126 research papers which include 83 papers published in international peer-reviewed Journals and 43 papers published in international conference proceedings. His recent research has spanned issues related to Entrepreneurship, IPO underpricing, Earning Management, Islamic Banking and Sukuk. Born in Ishurdi, Bangladesh, Dr. Md. Aminul Islam is married with two children.

M. Sydul Karim is a Ph.D. student of Finance in the Department of Economics and Finance at the University of New Orleans (UNO). He has more than 8 years of banking and private equity experience where he played significant roles in each of the organizations he worked for. His professional career journey started with the Management Trainee position at AB Bank Limited, one of the largest banks in Bangladesh. Credit risk management is the area of his specialization in banking. Prior to the joining to the UNO Ph.D. program, he was the Chief Investment Officer of a private equity firm at Bangladesh. Within the short span of his career, Karim has traveled from the very entry-level position to the top C-suite level and learned how to maximize the value of a firm.

Mohammad Masuduzzaman is a Deputy General Manager in the Research Department at Bangladesh Bank, the central bank of Bangladesh. He earned his bachelor degree with honors and master degree in economics from University of Dhaka, Bangladesh. His major areas of interest to research are central banking, monetary policy, money market, capital market, Islamic finance, SME finance, enterprise development with profit/loss sharing mode of finance, international trade, labor migration and inflow of foreign remittances, and investment, employment, and economic growth. He has participated in several surveys at home and abroad on SME finance, women entrepreneurship development and remittances. He is a lead author of a book entitled *Terms of Trade and Its Implications: Bangladesh Perspective* published by Lambert Academic Publishing, Germany. He has published five articles in refereed journals and presented several papers on different economic and financial areas at national and international workshops and conferences.

Mr. Abdul Awal Miah is a Development Consultant working with different international and national development and financing organizations including World Bank, Asian Development Bank, International Fund for Agricultural Development, Palli Karma Sahayak Foundation, Rahimafrooz Bangladesh Ltd (CZM), and Muslim Aid UK-BFO. Mr. Miah is a development leader turned Specialist. Besides being a thinker, planner, and organizer of development projects, Mr. Miah has been involved with writing, editing, and translating books and journals of different organizations of national and international repute including Bangladesh Institute of Islamic Thought-BIIT, Islamic Foundation Bangladesh, OSDER Publications, Muslim Aid UK, The Citizen Trust Bangladesh and so on. Obtaining his bachelor and master degrees in English from the University of Dhaka, Mr. Miah did his graduation in Law and M.Phil. (I) in Public Administration from the same University. As a Training Specialist, Mr. Miah received and imparted trainings in many disciplines of development arena and participated in over 100 workshops, seminars, conferences home abroad. His compilation, editing, and translation works include: *Genocide in Bangladesh, Tawhid and Science, Scientific Indications in the Holy Quran, Struggle of Muslim Women, Islam in Daily Life, Knowing Allah, Influence of Persian on Bengali, Imam Khomeini as viewed by Bangladesh Newspapers are mentionable.*

Dr. Murniati Mukhlisin, M.Acc. earned her degrees in Islamic accounting from International Islamic University of Malaysia (undergraduate), University of Indonesia (postgraduate), and University of Glasgow, UK (doctoral). She was awarded with distinguished scholarships to support her studies. Murniati has working experiences in banking, financial, and IT services, i.e., Unibank—Jakarta, Ernst & Young—Kuala Lumpur, and ANSI Berhad—Selangor, Malaysia. Murniati then started her career as a lecturer in Islamic Accounting and Finance in 2002, and she is currently Islamic accounting certified. She became Affiliate Staff at University of Glasgow after completing her Ph.D. in 2014 and then joined Essex Business School, University of Essex, Colchester, UK from 2015 to 2017. She sits on Editorial Advisory Board for an *Emerald Journal of Islamic Accounting and Business Research*—UK, *Journal of Muamalat and Islamic Finance Research*—Malaysia, and *Turkish Journal of Islamic Economics*. For research, Murniati works on critical perspective of research in the areas of financial reporting, Islamic accounting, Islamic banking and finance, and Islamic financial literacy. Murniati is currently a Rector, Tazkia University College of Islamic Economics, Bogor, Indonesia. She is also a team head at Islamic Accounting Compartment—Indonesian Institute of Accountants and a researcher for Bank Indonesia and Financial Services Authority. She is also a Shariah Expert at BRI Corporate University, board member of Indonesian Economist Association, and Advisor to Indonesian Association of Islamic FinTech. Murniati is also a public speaker and motivator. Together with her husband, Dr. Luqyan Tamanni, Murniati authored an inspirational book called Sakinah Finance that concerns about Islamic personal and family finance. They conduct several talk shows and trainings based on Sakinah Finance in several countries. She is also an active columnist both in national and in international media.

Rifka Mustafida is Research Assistant in LPPM Tazkia. She is currently studying Master of Islamic Banking and Finance in International Islamic University Malaysia. Before that, in 2016, she graduated summa cum laude from Tazkia University College of Islamic Economics—established in 2000, pioneer University in Islamic Economics—and studied Islamic Economics in the Faculty of Islamic Economics. In 2015 and 2016, she was finalist call for paper of Islamic economic and finance research forums held by Indonesian Financial Services Authority (OJK), and she also awarded the best researcher in call for paper of Redenomination held by Bank of Indonesia. She has conducted some researches including Branchless Banking: Toward The Role Of Sharia Banking In Reaching Financial Inclusion, Analysis of National Political and Social Readiness in the Application of Redenomination in Indonesia, Contribution of

Islamic Microfinance Studies in Achieving SDGs, Implanting Islamic FinTech in GCC Member Countries; Crowd-investment vs. Peer-to-Peer Lending and Two Words in Islamic Accounting Research; Accountability and Sustainability. Some of her papers already were presented in international forum.

Md. Golzare Nabi is a Deputy General Manager (research) working at Research Department in Bangladesh bank, Central Bank of Bangladesh. He earned bachelor degree in economics with Honors and Master in economics from University of Dhaka, and M.S. in economics with major in international finance from North South University, Bangladesh. He is also a Ph.D. (finance) candidate at School of Business Innovation and Technopreneurship of Universiti Malaysia Perlis (UniMAP). Besides, his regular search works at Bangladesh bank, he teaches at different universities in Bangladesh as visiting faculty. His major research areas include money and banking, capital market, Islamic finance, Islamic microfinance, Islamic endowment (waqf), conventional microfinance, rural finance, industrial finance, mobile financial services and remittances. As a professional researcher, he has actively participated in research projects on different economic and financial areas in Bangladesh which include capital market, remittances, Islamic banking, Islamic microfinance, agricultural credit, personnel finance, mobile financial services, green banking, infrastructure finance, international finance, money laundering and terrorist financing risk. Moreover, he has published more than 15 articles in reputable refereed journals. He has also presented several papers on different economic and financial areas in Bangladesh at national and international conferences.

Dr. Nosratollah Nafar received his Ph.D. in Industrial Economics from Gothenburg University, Sweden in 1997. He is currently the Lead Economist in Islamic Development Bank (IsDB). From July 2009 to April 2016, he served as a Manager for Economic Research and Policy Development Department. He led various technical research teams to undertake applied research on topical economic issues relevant to the mandate of IsDB, participate in policy dialogue with policy makers in member countries, and conduct economic analysis to support the informed decision in the Bank. He joined IsDB in July 2002 as a Senior Economist and conducted a number of policy-oriented studies to identify the core developmental needs of IsDB member countries. Before joining IDB, he served as an assistant Professor of Economics in Allame

Tabatabuee University, Iran. He has published several papers in international journals and was invited in many international conferences to share his views on relevant economic issues.

Dr. M. Mizanur Rahman is an economist received his Ph.D. from Imperial College, University of London, UK. Dr. Rahman has also completed Postgraduate Diploma in Islamic Banking and Insurance (PGDIBI) from IIBI, London. He started his career in 1987 as an economist with a Government Research Institute. During his service, he completed his M.S. with Government Scholarship and later completed Ph.D. with World Bank funded Scholarship and also completed PGDIBI. In 2006, Dr. Rahman moved to Islami Bank Training and Research Academy (IBTRA) as Research Director. In 2013, Dr. Rahman was deputed to Jaiz Bank in Nigeria as Director Training and worked there until 2016 and later backed to Islami Bank Training and Research Academy. During his 30 years long career he published 40 papers in different National and International Journals. Dr. Rahman also has presented 50 scientific papers in different National and International seminars in 30 countries across the world. He has published 5 books on Islamic Economics and Banking from Germany and 2 books from Bangladesh. Dr. Rahman is the associated editor of two scientific journals and also frequently review scientific articles sends from different National and International Journals. Dr. Rahman also conducts training classes on different issues of Islamic Economics, Finance and Banking in IBTRA.

Abdul Awwal Sarker is a General Manager of Research Department at the Central Bank of Bangladesh (Bangladesh Bank). Mr. Sarker is well known for his research works on an ongoing basis for providing guidelines for policymaking of the higher authority and to help formulate country's monetary policy in the context of economic growth, balance of payments position and government fiscal stance with a view to stabilizing inflation. He has more than 50 articles published in the reputed journals. He is considered as of one the key Islamic finance scholars in Bangladesh. His published articles have more than 685 citations with h-index 12 and i10 index-13. Mr. Sarker is also a member of the Islami Bank's Journal Editorial Board—one of the prominent Islamic finance journals of the country.

Mr. Edib Smolo has extensive experience in fields of Islamic banking and finance. He was the International Islamic Finance Manager at Tosan.

He worked as the Islamic Finance Manager at Islamic Banking Practice Unit, Indra Technology Solutions Malaysia, and also as the Shari'ah Coordinator at International Islamic Liquidity Management Corporation (IILM). Prior to that, he worked at the International Shari'ah Research Academy (ISRA) for Islamic Finance as a researcher and coordinator of the Islamic Capital Market Unit. He is also regular speaker and trainer-cum-consultant on various topics within the Islamic finance. At the same time, he was Assistant Professor at Faculty of Economics, Sarajevo School of Science and Technology, B&H.

Mr. Smolo authored and co-authored several chapters in books and papers in refereed journals on Islamic microfinance, economics, and finance. Recently, Mr. Smolo published the book *Introduction to Islamic Economics and Finance: Theory and Practice* in Bosnian language. His interests include Islamic banking and finance, microfinance, fiqh muamalat, takaful (Islamic insurance) and Islamic capital market products, among others. Mr. Smolo is a Ph.D. candidate at the International Centre for Education in Islamic Finance (INCEIF), the Global University of Islamic Finance, Malaysia. Mr. Smolo received his double degree, Bachelor of Economics (Honors) and Bachelor of Islamic Revealed Knowledge and Heritage (Honors), as well as Master of Economics from International Islamic University Malaysia (IIUM), Malaysia.

Mr. M. Nurul Islam Sohel is a Researcher and Faculty Member at Islami Bank Training and Research Academy (IBTRA). Mr. Sohel had been working in a private university for two years soon after completing his Bachelor of Business Administration (B.B.A.) and Master of Business Administration (M.B.A.) in Accounting from the University of Rajshahi. In 2011, he joined Islamic Bank Bangladesh Limited as a Probationary Officer and had been involved in operational banking at branch level for two years. After joining in banking profession, he started writing in the leading English dailies on contemporary banking, marketing, and business education issues. In 2013, he moved to the Research and Development Division where he undertook a range of applied banking research activities such as managing banking industry database, analyzing economy and financial market, and developing products. He completed his second M.B.A. from the Institute of Business Administration, University of Dhaka with marketing major in 2016. He has presented four research papers on Islamic finance and Sustainable Development Goals (SDGs) in international conferences.

Dr. Etsuaki Yoshida is Project Associate Professor at Kyoto University, Graduate School of Asian and African Area Studies, Japan. He also teaches Islamic finance at the Graduate School of Business and Finance, Waseda University. Dr. Yoshida received his B.A. in Commerce from Hitotsubashi University in Tokyo, after attending Harvard University, USA, as a visiting undergraduate majoring in Economics. He later earned his Ph.D. from Kyoto University. He started his career at Bank of Japan, the nation's central bank, where he spent twelve years doing economic research, foreign exchange intervention, setting international financial regulation, and working as the secretariat of the Policy Board. Etsuaki moved to the government-owned Japan Bank for International Cooperation and was engaged in various deals toward Africa and the Middle East. Dr. Yoshida is concurrently in charge of economic research on Asia and MENA regions as Director and Senior Economist. His publication includes five books in Japanese, as well as book chapters published by World Scientific, Springer, and Wiley. He is a frequent speaker at many international conferences on Islamic finance for practitioners, including World Islamic Banking Conference and was a member of a couple of task forces of the Islamic Financial Services Board.

LIST OF FIGURES

LIST OF TABLES

PART I

Role of Waqf Management
in Socio-Economic Development

CHAPTER 1

Introduction

Khalifa Mohamed Ali, M. Kabir Hassan
and Abd elrahman Elzahi Saaid Ali

The two volumes on waqf result from a workshop on the "Revival of Waqf for Socio-Economic Development," jointly organized by the Islamic Research and Training Institute (IRTI) of the Islamic Development Bank (IBD) Group, Islami Bank Bangladesh Limited (IBBL), and the Center for Zakat Management (CZM), in Dhaka, Bangladesh during November 4–5, 2017.

Socio-economic development, as the name suggests, consists of two dimensions: social and economic. The social development aspect signifies a transition from the traditional way of living to a modern and more

K. M. Ali · A. E. E. S. Ali
Islamic Research and Training Institute,
Islamic Development Bank, Jeddah, Saudi Arabia
e-mail: khalifaali@isdb.org

A. E. E. S. Ali
e-mail: aelzahi@isdb.org

M. K. Hassan (✉)
Department of Economics and Finance,
University of New Orleans, New Orleans, LA, United States
e-mail: mhassan@uno.edu

© The Author(s) 2019   3
K. M. Ali et al. (eds.), *Revitalization of Waqf*
for Socio-Economic Development, Volume I,
https://doi.org/10.1007/978-3-030-18445-2_1

progressive one. The primary concern of social development is to invest in people by providing inclusive access to education, health, and other social welfare programs. Thus, the people's development is wholly achievable through social justice. There are many competing definitions of social development. Nobel Laureate Amartya Sen sees social development as the creation of social opportunities for all. Social development includes economic development and encompasses all aspects of collective development in society in broader perspective and human welfare through improving the quality of life and sharing cultural and material goods equally.

The other dimension, economic development, is one of the most frequently used terminologies of the last two centuries. Very often economic growth is wrongly equated with economic development. According to Amartya Sen, economic development is, conceptually, broader than economic growth. It discusses how to develop the economic wealth of a community, region, or country for the citizen's well-being. A community's economic welfare and living standard can be significantly enhanced through various economic policies such as job creation, income generation, and redistribution through tax and other means.

Socio-economic development consists of a society inclusively and progressively improving its standard of living and quality of life. It relates to the sustainable well-being of all members of a society through increasing the stocks of physical as well as human capital (IGI global, Web site). Hence, any program that ensures people get access to the economy sustainably can be considered socio-economic development (sociology index, Web site). The literature of development economics abounds with examples of important factors of socio-economic development, among them education, health, gender parity, employment creation, preventing dowries and child marriage, income equality, etc.

Socio-economic development in the Islamic perspective, according to Mandal (2000), can be defined as "a process leading to a substantial and sustainable enhancement of the material and spiritual welfare of the Muslim population in the world." Gauging socio-economic development by statistics such as GNP growth or purchasing power is ultimately fruitless unless an equitable distribution of the income and wealth derived from an equitable ownership of the wealth of Allah is ensured. Hence, ecological and environmental balance must be maintained, and the government of a Muslim state must be competent enough to act as true agents of Allah. This means that the safety and security of life and property must be ensured and the basic needs for people's material prosperity must be fulfilled without placing barriers on their spiritual prosperity.

Mandal (2000) identifies nine objectives of socio-economic development from an Islamic perspective as follows: (1) Tawhid or the Oneness of Allah must be promoted; (2) material opulence and welfare are considered a mere intermediate objective, helpful to achieve the ultimate goal—maximization of spiritual prosperity and welfare; (3) balance between the material and spiritual spheres must be maintained while optimizing welfare; (4) the state should enforce regular prayers and compulsory charity and encourage voluntary sharing of wealth and income; (5) activities that upset ecological and environmental balance must be avoided; (6) peace and harmony at the interregional and international levels must be maintained; (7) the institution of brotherhood; (8) the promotion of faith, keeping in mind the reality of Doomsday and the Resurrection; and (9) appointments of nations to run world affairs on a fixed term basis.

Iqbal (2005) summarizes the Islamic perspective on distributive justice in three compelling goals: firstly, the guaranteed fulfillment of the basic needs of everyone; secondly, the establishment of personal income equity; and thirdly, the removal of any form of extreme inequalities of wealth and income. Quranic texts and the hadiths of the Prophet (PBUH), juristic agreement, and examples set by the Caliphs clearly endorse the guarantee of people's basic needs.

The United Nations' paradigm shift to Sustainable Development Goals (SDGs) paves the way for Islamic finance to excel because its models focus on societal well-being and environmental protections through Maqasid al Shariah realization. The models of Islamic banking and finance have been linked with the institutional and welfare concept of sustainability aimed at providing for the long-term solvency of financial institutions as well as the well-being of society. Islamic social finance—waqf, zakat, microfinance—is an ideal channel for the socio-economic development of the masses. The waqf-based financial activities in various Muslim countries across the world have huge potential to play quite a significant role in expediting welfare and development initiatives. It is time to revitalize the classical concept of waqf by discovering new tools and techniques to make possible those welfare activities aimed at covering a wider horizon and improving the socio-economic conditions of the impoverished segment of society. An all-embracing awareness program is a must to persuade the rich to voluntarily come forward in joining welfare programs through establishing various waqf-oriented financial enterprises.

In light of the above aspirations, the workshop aimed at exploring waqf regulation in IDB member countries, its modernization and relationship to Shariah, understanding the strategies and models to promote waqf related activities for greater socio-economic development, enhancing good governance practices through the formulation of policies for waqf projects, and understanding the confluence of waqf, zakat, charity, Islamic microfinance for impacting socio-economic development.

In its pursuit of distributive justice, Islam does not insist on perfect income equality. Islam recognizes that there are differences among human beings in terms of ability and their talent. Hence, it is justifiable in Islam to espouse differences in earnings based on personal ability and contribution to the production process or marginal productivity. Islam tolerates interpersonal income differences only when everyone's basic needs are satisfied. Extreme inequalities will cease to exist in a proper Islamic system, one that is based not only on justice but also on mutual love and kindness (Iqbal 2005).

The availability of natural resources and their exploration play a crucial role in the socio-economic development of any country through enhancement of the wealth base. Islam explicitly requires a long-term approach to stewardship of natural resources. Ahmed (2004) states that it is the responsibility of every Muslim to ensure that resources remain available for succeeding generations. To protect the rights of future generations, Islam prohibits the private ownership of certain types of natural resources. Public ownership is encouraged for two categories of productive assets: public utilities and natural resources.

Regarding consumption, production, and distribution, Islam preaches moderation. Goods and services that harm human health or damage social relations are prohibited. Producers are encouraged to produce the appropriate amount of a good so as to not create an imbalance in the supply and demand relationship. As for distribution, Islam does not encourage people to give away all of their belongings in the name of Allah; rather, people should give to charity according to their ability. Again, balance is the key. A balanced pattern of consumption, production, and distribution in society can be achieved through practicing these Islamic norms which lead to meaningful socio-economic development (Iqbal 2005).

Chapter 2 by Abdul Awwal Sarker analyses why the introduction of Cash Waqf Deposits (CWD) in the banking sector of Bangladesh. CWD accounts play a beneficial role in the socio-economic development of Bangladesh. Participation in these accounts has grown dramatically, from BDT 250 million in 2010 to BDT 1.056 trillion in 2016. The goal of making Bangladesh a middle-income country by 2021 is achievable if proper policies are formulated and major stakeholders such as the Waqf administration of the Government, National Board of Revenue, and Bangladesh Bank create an incentivized marketplace such that Bangladesh's socio-economic infrastructure is able to grow further.

Chapter 3 by Mustapha Abubakar conducts a study on the effect of waqf Islamic philanthropy, using Maqasid al Shariah principles, on the socio-economic development of orphans. This study uses data from a survey of orphans at the Aytam Orphanage Foundation in Zaria, Northern Nigeria. A total of 214 orphans, half the population of the orphanage, was selected through stratified random sampling. The respondents had previously received waqf assistance at the school dedicated to orphans, which was the first of its kind. Using the Maqasid al Shariah multi-dimensional poverty index, the survey questionnaire is assessed according to five dimensions: health services, access to education, practice of religion, pursuance of economic activities, and inclusion in social activities. The study finds that the socio-economic conditions of orphans regarding the dimensions of health services and access to education have increased significantly after receiving support from waqf institutions.

Chapter 4 by Etsuaki Yoshida discusses how FinTech, financial services augmented by the use of information and communication technologies (ICT), can improve the capability of cash waqf, especially in the context of social finance. Waqf has always played a role in social finance throughout Islamic history. With the ongoing rapid progress of ICT along with the increasing reach of personal communication devices such as cell phones, smartphones, and computers, the stage is set for cash waqf to create immense social value as it incorporates ICT. This development, which the author of this paper calls "FinTech-enabled cash waqf," is already becoming a reality. The author proposes that expanded forms of FinTech-enabled cash waqf, including microfinance, can be socially valuable financial systems. The paper also seeks to serve as a reference for policy makers and social venture entrepreneurs by discussing the practical and legal conditions necessary for such waqf to thrive. It then delves into the academic implications of FinTech-enabled cash waqf, engaging with the potential criticism of such waqf that may be levied by theory-based scholars of Islamic finance. The paper acknowledges that FinTech-enabled cash waqf is more than a social form of financial transaction—it indeed has academic and religious significance and can contribute considerably to socio-economic development.

Chapter 5 by M. Kabir Hassan, M. Fazlul Karim, and M. Sydul Karim argues that Islam holds that poverty alleviation can be achieved through both market and non-market means and should be based on the principles of justice and equitable distribution of wealth. This paper presents an alternative view of waqf as component of the traditional economic system. Waqf increases aggregate consumption, expenditure, and national income. This paper provides a cross-country review of the current state of waqf practices. The comparative analysis allows for a comprehensive understanding of the challenges and pressing issues facing waqf globally. The puzzle of why waqf is underutilized in Muslim-majority countries even though it is a superior social capital model becomes clearer when realizing that there is a lack of trust in waqf managers and institutions. There is much evidence that financial greed causes a fear of permanent loss among the endowers. Furthermore, waqf funds are not well-diversified or invested in a way to generate sufficient income to support waqf assets. To remedy this, alignment of waqf funds and stakeholders is necessary at the institutional level. This paper concludes by recommending a thorough legal framework to address the various financial, agency, and governance issues of waqf. A legal environment that is waqf-friendly, along with preferential tax treatment for the endowed funds, is fundamental for waqf to be a successful vehicle for the achievement of Islamic finance goals.

Chapter 6 by Edib Smolo states that there are many verses in the Qurān that encourage social entrepreneurial ventures and impart the spiritual guidance needed to engage in trade. Islamic Social Entrepreneurship (ISE), in particular, is vital for Muslims to attain sustainable community empowerment as well as social and economic justice. Waqf is a vehicle for financing ISE. The waqf-ISE model, showcased in this paper, mobilizes resources to provide a platform that caters to socio-economic development. The waqf-ISE model has been developed entirely from the ground up based on Islamic principles, without resorting to imitation of any Western model. It delivers an opportunity to solve many of the urgent societal issues afflicting Bosnia, especially in the areas of poverty alleviation and socio-economic development.

Chapter 7 by Md. Golzare Nabi, Md. Aminul Islam, Rosni Bakar, and Mohammad Masuduzzaman argues that waqf (voluntary Islamic endowment) has played a vital role in the socio-economic development of Muslims all over the world. Though waqf lay dormant during the colonial era, Muslim scholars and policy makers have recently begun to recognize that the revival of waqf as a strong social institution can be a catalyst to fund social projects and alleviate poverty in poor Muslim-majority countries. As the third largest Muslim-majority country in the world, Bangladesh in particular should explore waqf as a means of increasing socio-economic development, generating employment, and improving education and health services. Unfortunately, mismanagement and lack of proper structuring and innovation have heretofore limited the effectiveness of waqf in Bangladesh. However, with proper structuring and administration, waqf can emerge as an effective tool for managing and financing social projects. The present paper examines the current status of waqf and outlines its immense potential to help achieve SDGs in Bangladesh. The paper also makes policy recommendations to ensure that waqf can bring sustainable benefits for both Muslim and non-Muslim members of the community.

Chapter 8 by M. Mizanur Rahman and M. Nurul Islam Sohel explains why cash waqf as an innovation in waqf concept that holds immense promise in resolving some of the shortcomings of traditional waqf. According to the 1986 census of waqf estates in Bangladesh, there were thousands of such estates that were languishing under poor management, underdeveloped, and lacking any plan for development. These waqf properties were being leased or sold for paltry sums, realizing only a fraction of their potential value. Cash waqf is now well-established, with twelve commercial banks (six Islamic and six conventional) in Bangladesh channeling funds to the educational, social, and cultural development of the country. This study explores the Mudarabah Cash Waqf Deposit Product and Certificate and its contribution toward the socio-economic development of Bangladesh. Both qualitative and quantitative data are collected from secondary sources and through interviewing the clients and beneficiaries by using a semi-structured schedule. As a case study, the operational thrust of the banks is reviewed to provide real-life evidence of the process of floating a cash waqf Bank Deposit Product and its Certificate. This study shows that this voluntary sector savings and investment mobilization can help Islamic banking stimulate the economic development of the country. The study also reveals that the cash waqf

Bank Deposit and Certificate has been monetizing the Islamic voluntary sector, thus accumulating social capital and national wealth, promoting socio-economic development, and alleviating poverty. While the indirect tax system of Bangladesh is favorable to its growth, political will is needed for the continued success of this form of waqf.

Chapter 9 by Murianti Mukhlesin and Rifka Mustafida discusses the possibility of issuing sukuk based on waqf assets in Indonesia. Waqf assets in Indonesia have not been managed optimally nor productively, a fact reflected in a survey that states that 74% of waqf managers (nadzir) are unable to maximize the benefit from waqf due to the limitation on their ability to innovate, to develop, and to sustain waqf assets. At the same time, the Indonesian government has suffered from high foreign debt and seeks a source of alternate financing. Sukuk issuance can potentially be the link between the undermanaged waqf assets and the government's high debt demand. It utilizes interviews with respondents consisting of experts, regulators, and practitioners. It adopts the research method of benefit, opportunity, cost, and risk from the standpoints of both the issuer and the investor. Using a two-floor level Analytic Network Process, the results show that the priority of the Benefit aspect is to secure alternative sources of financing. The main priority of the opportunity aspect is to develop more innovative Islamic finance products. The priority of the cost aspect is to have nonprofessional management of waqf funds, while the priority of the risk aspect is the dispute of endowment assets. For both the short-term and the long-term strategies, the main priority is on creating partnerships with other institutions. The main contribution of this paper is to inform regulators on the legal ramifications of waqf assets being used for sukuk financing, particularly on the issue of foreign debt.

Chapter 10 by Abu Umar Faruq Ahmad and Md. Fazlul Karim argues that the huge amount of national waqf assets in Bangladesh, a significant portion of which consists of underutilized funds, has enormous potential to contribute to its socio-economic development. The key objective of this paper is to explore the areas that require a fresh look at the revival and consumption of waqf funds to foster sustainable economic development and social progress in Bangladesh. Thus, this study seeks to (1) examine the issues and challenges of waqf management in Bangladesh; (2) identify the role of waqf in stimulating socio-economic development of the country; and (3) suggest legal, institutional, and functional reforms in the waqf sector for its continued development and to rejuvenate the economy of Bangladesh. If the assets held by waqf estates in Bangladesh were to be utilized more efficiently, poverty would be eliminated through making the necessary changes in waqf management to cater to the needs of the times. The study recommends using innovative Islamic finance products and empowering the poor through waqf funds in ways that would make the poor segments of the country an integral part of the development process. Waqf administration should consider its primary goal to be engaging the poor in the country's socio-economic development activities. The paper also includes some specific policy recommendations that deserve serious consideration for waqf development in Bangladesh.

Chapter 11 by Abdul Awal Miah explains why in order to properly uphold the microfinance industry's poverty alleviation approach, an Islamic microfinance approach has to be developed integrating Shariah-approved charity funding sources like zakat, sadaqah, and awaqf as well as and Shariah-compliant tools like Mudarabah, Musharakah, Bai-Muajjal, etc., all geared toward ensuring sustainable socio-economic development of the poor. Furthermore, the paper outlines how the CZM has been working mainly with zakat and awaqf funds toward the socio-economic development of the poor and extreme poor for the last nine years. During this time, the organization gained formidable experience and developed a model zakat-based poverty alleviation approach. The successes they achieved and the challenges they faced as an organization working with zakat and awaqf funds can provide an important lesson for all who favor the integration of zakat and awaqf as an effective step toward the socio-economic development of the poor and extreme poor in Bangladesh and elsewhere in the world.

Chapter 12 by Khalifa M. Ali Hassanain shows how the framework practiced by various multilateral development banks (MDBs), particularly the International Development Association (IDA), can be leveraged to establish a global waqf fund. The framework revolves around the IDA's operations, such as replenishments, allocation of funds by implementing specific formulas, and the determination approach, which is mainly used to monitor the effectiveness of the earlier processes. The study proposes integrating the Islamic vision of development based on Maqasid al Shariah with IDA principles for the allocation of funds for a potentially global waqf fund. The objective is to create a more effective approach for the raising and using of resources for a global waqf fund.

Chapter 13 by Basharat Hossain presents a model to initiate an Islamic microfinance and rehabilitation program that uses waqf funds for the slum and floating population in Muslim countries. The paper collects primary data from Bangladesh and secondary data from various national and international sources. It recommends that waqf funds, in addition to zakah and sadaqah, can be used to introduce Islamic finance to the slum population and rehabilitate them. This model will be implemented by founding an independent Waqf Management Institution by joint venture of the government of the respective countries as well as national and international Islamic agencies such as the IDB. The implementation will proceed through five stages: revival and registration of waqf estates; accumulation of funds; initiating Islamic microfinance; rehabilitation of the slum population; and forward linkage that may help the slum population engage in and make contributions to society.

Chapter 14 by Nosratollah Nafar explains there are three major constraints that hinder the effectiveness of waqf funds in adequately meeting the financial needs of IDB member countries: (i) inadequate awareness about the role of waqf in addressing socio-economic difficulties in many IDB member countries; (ii) lack of widely accepted Shariah-compliant products to integrate Islamic redistributive institutions such as waqf and zakat into inclusive development; and (iii) lack of innovative products to use waqf funds under certain programs, such as Poverty Entrepreneurship Schemes that can be used for creating employment opportunities. At the country level, governments need to play a critical role in mobilizing resources generated by waqf endowments. Specifically, they need to develop a supportive legal and regulatory framework and proactive policy targets on usage, access, and quality of waqf and zakat. At the IDBG level, the bank needs to play a more active role in supporting the efforts of its member countries in exploring the relevant policy, legal, regulatory, and institutional interventions necessary to expand the function of Islamic redistributive institutions in generating new sources of finance for socio-economic infrastructure development. Specifically, the bank may consider (i) creating a common platform to enhance dialogue among member countries to promote knowledge and increase awareness on the role of waqf in socio-economic infrastructure development; (ii) identifying successful case studies and good Islamic redistributive income practices throughout the world and having an exchange of visits and technical cooperation among member countries in the form of reverse linkage initiatives; and

(iii) supporting the development of widely accepted Shariah-compliant products related to Islamic redistributive institutions including waqf and zakat to support inclusive development.

REFERENCES

Ahmed, H. (2004). *Role of Zakah and Awqaf in poverty alleviation* (Occasional Paper No. 8). Jeddah: Islamic Development Bank, Islamic Research and Training Institute, Jeddah.

Iqbal, M. (Ed.). (2005). *Islamic Perspectives on Sustainable Development*. New York: Palgrave Macmillan.

Mandal, M. S. (2000). *Socioeconomic Development and Human Welfare: An Interdisciplinary Approach*. Rajshahi, Bangladesh: Uttoron Offset Press.

CHAPTER 2

Role of Cash Waqf Deposit (CWD) as an Instrument for Socio-Economic Development: Bangladesh Perspective

Abdul Awwal Sarker

1 INTRODUCTION

The institution of awaqf (waqf) is among several instruments allowed by the Islamic Shariah for socio-economic development. Awaqf may also be used for developing material infrastructure and can play a genuine source of revenue for enhancing social welfare activities. Basically, waqf in general sense denotes as a voluntary act of charity which continuously generate to fulfill targeted objectives. In the same manner, concept of waqf has been transmitted to the financial institution as "cash waqf" (CW). Cash waqf system was prominently used as an alternative

A. A. Sarker (✉)
Islamic Banking Cell, Research Department,
Bangladesh Bank, Dhaka, Bangladesh
e-mail: awal.sarkar@bb.org.bd

© The Author(s) 2019
K. M. Ali et al. (eds.), *Revitalization of Waqf
for Socio-Economic Development, Volume I*,
https://doi.org/10.1007/978-3-030-18445-2_2

15

to interest-based financing for the disadvantaged sections of people of society. "Cash waqf as a money-based type of waqf is capable of assisting the grass-root in securing interest free loan for small businesses, and also, subject to the purview of the mutawalli some of the grass-roots may also get no-refund financial assistance to start up a business. Cash waqf is capable of promoting entrepreneurship in the world with interest free loans from the cash waqf institutions."[1] The former Ottoman Empire successfully practiced cash waqf for a very long period and the positive impact in the alleviation of the poverty was felt. So also the city of Fes, Morocco, practiced cash waqf for lending and borrowing without additional premium to the principal during repayment. At present, many countries have proven this capability of cash waqf to be a vibrant alternative to interest-bearing loan. In the Middle East, for example, countries like Kuwait, Oman, UAE, and Saudi Arabia have been practicing cash waqf over a relatively long time and the practice has stood the test of time. In Asia, cash waqf has also gained acceptance. For example, the Malaysian National Fatwa Council passed the fatwa that permits cash waqf in 2007.[2] The huge cash waqf fund collected by the Selangor State Religious Council (SSRC) gives numerous advantages in developing the Islamic economy, loans in financing small and medium industry business, settling of debts, such as houses, investment in property for the Muslims as property will be rented to generate profits.[3]

1.1   Objectives of the Paper

The main objective of the paper is to assess the concept and operational methodology of Cash Waqf Deposits (CWD) maintained by the Islamic banks in Bangladesh. Secondly, to review the associated issues and problems with CWD and thirdly to suggest some pragmatic way out to popularize the CWD among the people since it has direct impact on socio-economic development of the country.

---

[1] Mahadi Ahmad. (2015). Cash Waqf: Historical Evolution, Nature and Role as an Alternative to Riba-Based Financing for the Grass Root. *Journal of Islamic Finance, 4*(1), 63–74. IIUM Institute of Islamic Banking and Finance. ISSN 2289-2117 (O) / 2289-2109 (P).

[2] Yayasan Waqaf Malaysia, 5 July 2014.

[3] Amir et al. (2010) in Ibrahim et al. (2013).

1.2 Organization of the Paper

We have organized the paper to encapsulate the concept of Cash Waqf Deposits and methodology to use the proceeds by the banks for socio-economic development of the country. Therefore, the paper has been divided into five sections. Section 1 deals with the definition of CWD as practiced by the Islamic banks in Bangladesh. Section 2 highlights the role of the Islamic banks in mobilization and management of CWD while Section 3 delineates the issues and problems of CWD management. Section 4 presents future directions for better management of Cash Waqf Deposits in Bangladesh. Finally, the paper concludes with some final remarks and recommendations.

2 Definition of Cash Waqf Deposits (CWD)

We find that cash waqf for mosques building contributions has been practiced in Singapore since the 1970s. This fund, also known as mosque Building and Mendaki Fund MBMF, is meant to redevelop all mosques in Singapore. This mode of finance is meant to engage all Muslim employees to contribute to the development of all mosques in Singapore through an automatic check off-system based on their monthly gross income. The deducted amount from their monthly salaries will then be channeled through the Central Provident Fund CPF to the MUIS where it will be channeled directly to redevelopment all the mosques in Singapore.[4] According to A. Karim, there are 175,000 Muslim employees in Singapore who contributed to this fund amount to S$6 million annually. Until 2010, 22 mosques have been redeveloped from this fund. This shows that this type of cash waqf is a powerful financial instrument, which will enable all mosques to have a continuous income for the maintenance and sustenance of all the mosques in Singapore (Abdul Karim 2010).[5]

---

[4] Abdul Karim, Shamsiah. (2010). Contemporary Shariah Structuring for the Development and Management of Waqf Assets in Singapore. *Kyoto Bulletin of Islamic Area Studies* 3–2, 143–164. From Magda Ismail Abdel Mohsin, et al. (2016). Financing the Development of Old Waqf Properties Classical Principles and Innovative Practices Around the World. *Palgrave Studies in Islamic Banking, Finance, and Economics.* New York: Palgrave.

[5] Magda Ismail Abdel Mohsin, et al. (2016). Financing the Development of Old Waqf Properties Classical Principles and Innovative Practices Around the World. *Palgrave Studies in Islamic Banking, Finance, and Economics.* New York: Palgrave.

2.1   Takaful Waqf Model

This is one of the recent modes of finance that has been developed in Muslim minority countries due to the urgent need for special funds and for specific reasons. Modus Operandi: The following is the modus operandi for Takaful Mode, as seen in Fig. 1.

Al-Tasuli in his commentary of Tuhfat al-Hukkam defined the meaning of cash waqf in the Maliki School, "as the process of dedicating cash as waqf for the purpose of lending it to those designated as the beneficiaries without interest" (Al-Tasuli 1998, v.2, p. 369).[6] Also, Zufar Ibn Al-Huzail (110AH–158AH) of the Hanafi School defined it "as the process of dedicating cash as waqf and investment of same so that the profits are used for the waqf's stipulated charitable deeds" (Ibn Nujaym, n.d., v. 5, p. 219).[7] In the same vein, Cizacka (2004)[8] defines cash waqf as "a charitable endowment established with cash capital." Cash waqf is getting a certain amount of money from founder and dedication of its usufruct according to founder's condition for the welfare of the society. Al-Tasuli's definition explains the objective of cash waqf, which is administering of a revolving loan without interest. The defect of the definition is that it did not touch on the method of making the fund sustainable; as only lending without investing the fund makes it prone to credit risk that would be further aggravated by default payment and so, the fund would crunch. However, the definition is a sample of one of the primary objectives of cash waqf. That is lending of money by the cash waqf institution to the poor beneficiaries without engaging them in mudarabah agreement with the cash waqf institution. This is what the above Zufar's definition clarifies by saying that the cash is invested "so that the profits are used for the waqf's

---

[6]Al-Tasuli, A. I. (1998). *Al-Bahjah Fi Sharh al-Tuhfah* (Muhammad AbdulQadir Shahun, Ed.). Lebanon: Dar Al-Kutub Al-Ilmiyyah. From Cash Waqf: Historical Evolution, Nature and Role as an Alternative to Riba-Based Financing for the Grass Root, by Mahadi Ahmad.

[7]Ibn Nujaym. (n.d.). *Al-Bahr Al-Raiq Sharh Kanz Al-Daqaiq v. 5*. Cairo: Dar Al-Kitab Al-Islami. From Cash Waqf: Historical Evolution, Nature and Role as an Alternative to Riba-Based Financing for the Grass Root, by Mahadi Ahmad.

[8]Cizacka, M. (2004). *Incorporated Cash Waqfs and Mudarabah, Islamic Non-bank.* Paper submitted during the International Seminar on Non-bank Financial Institutions, Kuala. From Cash Waqf: Historical Evolution, Nature and Role as an Alternative to Riba-Based Financing for the Grass Root, by Mahadi Ahmad.

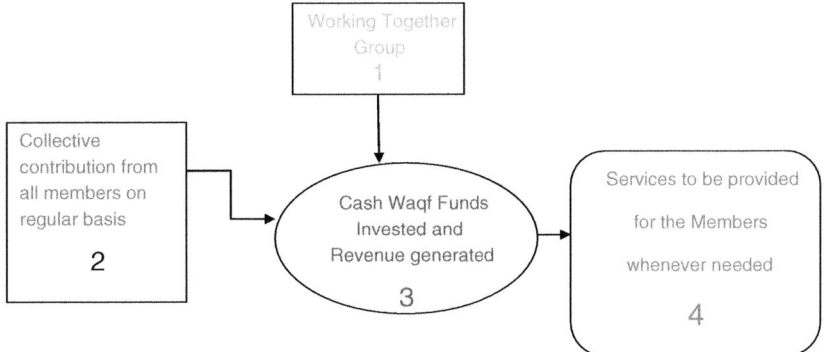

Fig. 1   Modus operandi for Takaful Model

stipulated charitable deeds." These two classical definitions complement each other to inform the exact nature of cash waqf. The two definitions though do not expressly prevent establishment of mudarabah-mudarib's relationship between the cash waqf and the poor beneficiary, but it is inferred that they have impliedly prevented it.

3   ROLE OF ISLAMIC BANKS IN MANAGEMENT OF CASH WAQF DEPOSITS IN BANGLADESH

3.1   *Cash Waqf Deposit Management by the Islamic Banks in Bangladesh*

The name of Islami Bank Bangladesh Limited's (IBBL's) Cash Waqf Deposits is Mudarabah Waqf Cash Deposit Account (MWCDA) introduced on July 1, 2004. This is a savings deposit taken on the mode of mudarabah which is perpetual in nature. It somehow boosts up the deposit base of the participatory banks since it is a non-cost deposit, encouraging deploying fund in a profitable way. The profit generated by cash waqf deposit is used for the welfare activities or sadaqah as directed by waqif. Al-Arafah Islami Bank Limited (AIBL) has started to mobilize deposits under cash waqf program from May 2006. The management methodology of cash waqf scheme is to collect permanent deposit at a time or installment basis from the depositors as a social capital for welfare works as per Islamic Shariah for the people of the country in the age-long from the profit of the deposits as per direction of the depositor (Waqif) or by the decision of the caretaker (mutawalli).

In the process of organizing Social Capital Market operations in the Voluntary sector, Social Islami Bank Limited (SIBL) has for the first time in the history introduced Cash Waqf Deposit scheme in 1997 in Bangladesh. This bank had played a pioneering role in conceptualizing and introducing CWD in the financial system of Bangladesh. As corporate objective, SIBL defined its operation in three different sectors—formal, non-formal, and voluntary. While formal sector deals with general commercial activities as a scheduled bank, non-formal sector aims at "Empowering Family" by creating investment opportunities for micro- and SME-clients. Its voluntary sector offers Cash Waqf Certificate Scheme (CWCS) in 1997 which is an innovative financial product in Bangladesh's financial marketplace aimed at socio-economic development. Initially, the CWDs are converted into income-generating units and the income so derived is utilized as per instruction of the Wāqif or in the absence of such instructions, on the basis of Islamic Shariah. The SIBL also collects cash waqf fund under mudarabah principle and kept in the investment fund which operates on the basis of Bai, Izara, and Shirkat mode of investment. Then the profit is spent by the bank/Waqif in the list of purposes determined by the bank or any other purpose(s) determined by Waqif permitted by the Shariah.

Shahjalal Islami Bank Limited (SJIBL) has started to mobilize deposits under cash waqf program in 2007. The cash waqf fund is collected under mudarabah principle and kept in the investment fund which operates on the basis of Bai, Izara, and Shirkat mode of investment. Income from cash waqf fund is used in different religious and development purpose of the society. Bank has made a range of purposes, while the Waqif has the right to choose the purpose(s) permitted by the Shariah as for (a) family rehabilitation, (b) education and culture, (c) health and sanitation, (d) social utility services, etc. Trust Bank Limited also introduced CW deposit account in 2014. As usual, the principal amount of CW deposit remains intact and only the profit amount is spent for the purpose(s) specified by the waqif. Bank has selected the sector-wise list of institutions eligible to receive assistance from the CW fund. The sectors eligible for CW assistance are—(a) mosques, (b) religious schools and institutions, (c) family or needy people empowerment projects/Qard/assistance, (d) human resource development, and (e) health, sanitation and social utility services or any other purpose(s) permitted by Shariah or the Waqif. The Bank Asia started cash waqf deposit mobilization in 2013. Two management methodologies for opening cash waqf deposit are maintained by the bank as (a) Onetime Cash Waqf Deposit: A Waqif (Depositor) can waqf at least Tk.1.00 Lac at a time. (b) Monthly/Quarterly Cash Waqf Deposit: A Waqif can deposit his/her waqf amount on monthly installment basis. Minimum waqfed amount is Tk.1.00 lac only. Other Islamic banks more or less follow the same line of operational framework in opening and managing the CW deposits.

3.2 Parties to a Cash Waqf

As discussed earlier, based on modality of managing cash waqf deposits, the parties to a cash waqf are three namely:

1. The waqifun (donors), who intend to get rewarded by Allah by offering part of their hard-earned income as assistance to the poor through the cash waqf deposit.
2. The banks, the cash waqf's investees, who invests the fund for the purpose of generating profit.
3. The beneficiaries of the CWD or the management (mutawallis) of different institutions/socio-economic sectors.

3.3 The Investment Strategy of Cash Waqf Deposits

The Islamic banks investment procedure in banks is mudarabah in respect of the waqif. Bank deploys the fund in any of its profitable lucrative mode in trading or project or industries. Some of the banks invest Cash Waqf Deposits against long-term investment, and profit is distributed for (a) poor rehabilitation, (b) education and culture, (c) health service, and (d) social development as per direction of the depositor (Waqif) or by the decision of the caretaker (mutawalli).

The investment strategy of Cash Waqf Fund of SIBL is: "The more the waqf investment return, the more mawquf 'alaih benefit from waqf fund" is the basis of investment. The investment decision is made on the following principles:

1. Waqf fund is invested under the principal of Islamic Shariah.
2. Attracts benefits to waqf, its beneficiaries.

3. Consistent with public interest and is according to the conditions of the donor.
4. Has advance strategic investment and financial planning with consultation with Shariah and management professionals.
5. Applying waqf fund in new and traditional investment projects such as the profit will maximize.
6. Keeping waqf fund perpetual (daimumah) so that its income is generated continuously.
7. Allocate some of the collected fund as profit sharing-based investment to selected development of housing estates, commercial buildings, securities and others small businesses. Technical and managerial assistance are required to accompany this investment.

3.4   Profit Distribution Framework of CWD

1. CWD gets priority weightage of the banks for calculation of profit.
2. Provisional profit under the CWD scheme is payable to the respective sector(s) determined by the Waqif on Monthly Basis/ Anniversary Basis which is also adjusted after declaration of final rate of profit of the bank.
3. The waqf amount may not remain intact as the fund is operated as per mudarabah principle. To be mentioned that the profit amount only will be spent for the purpose(s) specified by the Waqif. Unspent profit amount will automatically be added to waqf amount and earn profit to grow over the time. As per mudarabah principle, if any loss is incurred in course of business the loss is to be realized through deduction of the waqf deposit.
4. As a general principle, the Waqif may withdraw his deposits and donate for major works in other endowments, if he desired so.

It is evident from Table 1 that out of 8 full-fledged Islamic banks, 5 banks are engaged with the CWD management and out of 17 conventional banks having Islamic banking branches and windows 4 banks have these CWD operations which are very minimal compared to full-fledged ones. However, IBBL stood 1st position to manage CWD followed by SIBL. AIBL and EXIM Bank also exerted their effort but still below the double-digit level. But the growth trend indicates that BDT 250 million in 2010 had increased to BDT 1056 million in 2016. It reflects the growing participation of the people to the socio-economic activities (Fig. 2).

Table 1 Management of Cash Waqf Deposits by the Islamic banks and branches/windows of the conventional banks (BDT in crore)

S/L	Name of the bank	2010	2011	2012	2013	2014	2015	2016
1	Islami Bank Bangladesh Limited	20.400	26.100	36.700	43.590	53.300	65.850	75.260
2	Social Islami Bank Limited	4.100	5.350	6.890	8.460	9.930	17.880	23.690
3	Al-Arafah Islami Bank Limited	0.330	0.380	0.490	0.540	0.760	1.710	1.880
4	EXIM Bank Limited	0.000	0.460	0.910	1.210	1.620	2.470	3.560
5	Shahjalal Islami Bank Limited	0.190	0.260	0.290	0.300	0.330	0.360	0.390
6	AB Bank Limited	0.000	0.000	0.020	0.250	0.000	0.010	0.600
7	Agrani Bank Limited	0.000	0.000	0.000	0.000	0.000	0.010	0.010
8	Trust Bank Limited	0.000	0.000	0.000	0.010	0.002	0.075	0.077
9	Bank Asia Limited	0.000	0.000	0.000	0.000	0.120	0.160	0.170
	Total	25.020	32.550	45.300	54.360	66.062	88.525	105.637

Source Individual banks' data/information

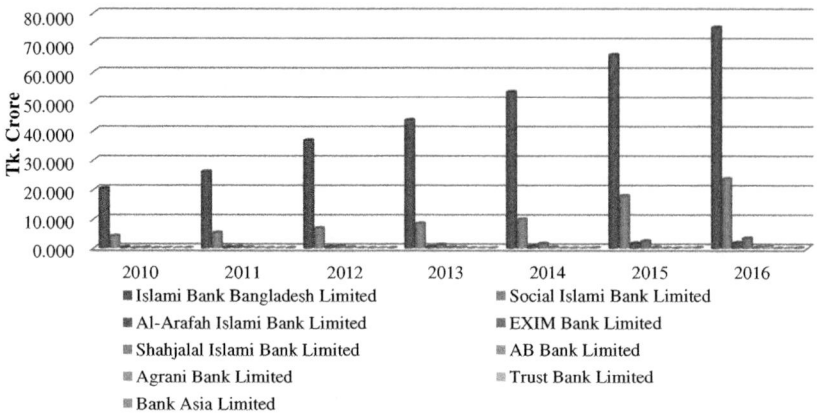

Fig. 2   Cash Waqf Deposits of Islamic banks

Table 2   Bank-wise Cash Waqf Deposits of Islamic banks in 2016 (figure in TK. crore)

S/L	Name of the bank	BDT in crore	% of share
1	Islami Bank Bangladesh Limited	75.260	71.244
2	Social Islami Bank Limited	23.690	22.426
3	Al-Arafah Islami Bank Limited	1.880	1.780
4	EXIM Bank Limited	3.560	3.370
5	Shahjalal Islami Bank Limited	0.390	0.369
6	AB Bank Limited	0.600	0.568
7	Agrani Bank Limited	0.010	0.009
8	Trust Bank Limited	0.077	0.073
9	Bank Asia Limited	0.170	0.161
Total		105.64	100.00

Source Individual banks' data/information

It is seen from Table 2 that on count of % share IBBL captured 71% among all Islamic banks and Islamic banking branches/windows of 17 conventional banks followed by the SIBL. The success factors of these two banks tell that their management and employees are fully committed to achieve the goals of the Shariah through voluntary works to raise the rate of socio-economic development. They follow special type of strategy to attract the people for participating in this type of voluntary

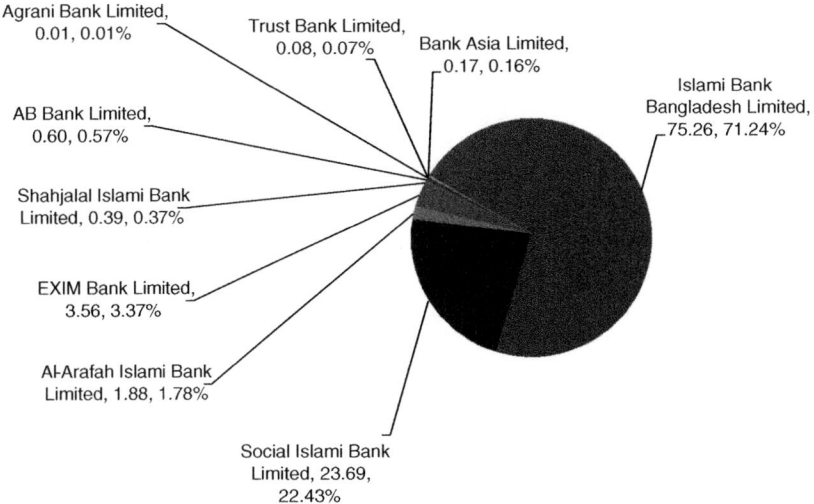

Fig. 3   Cash Waqf Deposits in 2016

activities. These two banks fix targets for their employees to help open at least one CWD account in each month. They have the programs to mobilize the rich clients of the bank to participate in this CWD program (Fig. 3).

It is seen from Table 3 that as compared to bank's total deposits, amount of CWD is at a very negligible level. IBBL mobilized only 0.04% of its total deposits as CWD followed by SIBL by 0.01%. It reflects that there are many scopes to enhance this CWD. If appropriate policies are followed the amount of CWD will grow manifold.

Strategies Followed by the Banks to Popularize the Cash Waqf Deposits
The Islamic banks have taken different initiatives to popularize CW deposits among the people of the country. The principal initiatives are:

1. Allocation of individual target for the officers of the bank to open at least one CWD Account in every month.
2. Special campaign launched every year to increase the amount of CW deposit through increasing the number of Cash Waqf Deposits Accounts.

Table 3 Cash Waqf Deposits of Islamic banks as % of total deposits (figure in TK. crore)

S/L	Name of the bank	2016			
		Total deposit	Cash Waqf Deposits		% of share with total deposit
		TK. crore	TK. crore	% of share	
1	Islami Bank Bangladesh Limited	67,978.160	75.260	71.244	0.0401
2	Social Islami Bank Limited	17,347.040	23.690	22.426	0.0126
3	Al-Arafah Islami Bank Limited	21,945.510	1.880	1.780	0.0010
4	EXIM Bank Limited	23,196.190	3.560	3.370	0.0019
5	Shahjalal Islami Bank Limited	12,440.980	0.390	0.369	0.0002
6	AB Bank Limited	407.120	0.600	0.568	0.0003
7	Agrani Bank Limited	98.790	0.010	0.009	0.0000
8	Trust Bank Limited	1381.910	0.077	0.073	0.0000
9	Bank Asia Limited	1087.860	0.170	0.161	0.0001
10	All others Islamic banks	41,811.340	0.000	0.000	0.0000
Total		187,694.90	105.64	100.00	

Source Individual banks' data/information

3. Banks make list of the rich persons or clients and approach them for opening the CWD accounts and regular follow-up is done.
4. To popularize the Cash Waqf Deposits among the people, the management of the banks offered special campaign during the Service Month declared in each year. Bank officers also do direct personal contact with the potential client.
5. Vigorous initiative had been taken by the management of the banks to motivate the employees for increasing Cash Waqf Deposit Account by encouraging and enhancing awareness about the benefit of cash waqf among the people.
6. Beside this, Special Cash Incentive also offered by some of the banks' management to the employees individually that is awarded based on the highest amount and Number of CWD accounts.
7. To popularize the Cash Waqf Deposits of the bank, some banks arrange client get-together wherein Chairman/Vice Chairman/

members of Shariah Supervisory Boards inspired the mass people about the benefits of CWD.

8. Several banks exhibits banner, festoon, Poster, X-festoon at their branch premises to aware the people about the benefits of the CWD.

9. Some banks distribute leaflet for direct marketing and advertise in different print and electronic media to promote the Cash Waqf Deposit among the religious-minded customers.

4 ISSUES AND PROBLEMS IN MANAGEMENT OF CASH WAQF DEPOSITS IN BANGLADESH

Among the problems associated with Cash Waqf Deposits, it is prominent that deduction of advance income tax, excise duty, and other bank charges reduces the profit of the accounts and affects welfare activities. The other issues are:

1. Lack of central cash waqf administration at government level to monitor and take positive role in enhancing the CWD accounts that require new innovative avenues.

2. Lack of positive guidelines/directions on CWD by the regulatory authority.

3. Lack of propagation among the people about the benefit of cash waqf.

4. No initiative has yet been taken from the Office of the Waqf administration in Bangladesh to introduce and nurture cash waqf practices in the country.

5. Lack of innovative research, seminar, conference, workshop, etc. for progression of CWD.

6. Lack of incentive from the Government for CWD Account holders (like exemption of tax, etc.).

7. Lack of proper publicity from banks, Islamic Scholars, Media to encourage the people/clients to open Cash Waqf Deposit accounts.

8. Lack of participation by other banks to mobilize CWD which is absolutely no-cost deposits.

5   FUTURE DIRECTIONS FOR BETTER MANAGEMENT OF CASH WAQF DEPOSITS

Not only banks every stakeholder in the financial system has to think about their role for socio-economic development. Since Bangladesh has to achieve middle-income Country status by the year 2021, we have to work on many fronts to raise the level of standard of life of the people especially of the disadvantaged people of the country. Cash waqf is an excellent measure to minimize the rich-poor gap by providing them basic needs and improving the socio-economic infrastructure. Therefore, every conscious citizen of the country should come up with the innovative ideas and programs to boost the development path.

Many measures can be undertaken to make the CWD as a poverty reduction tool. Among others, following issues may be considered by the bankers and economist on an urgent basis:

1. Regular campaign, monitoring, and follow-up of the CWD activities by the individual employees/branches to open and manage should be given utmost priority.
2. Banks may arrange conference, seminar, and symposium at Divisional/District level to grow awareness among the people.
3. The Central Bank may take initiative to make a common policy/guideline on Cash Waqf Deposits for Islami Banks, Islamic Banking Branches/Windows in Bangladesh.
4. Islami Banks may take initiatives to include CWD as a financial inclusion tool and arrange nation-wide seminar/symposium on Cash Waqf Deposits with proper guidance of the Central Bank.
5. In order to ensure the participation of the general public, it is an important prerequisite to educate them on the importance and potential role of cash waqf in socio-economic development. To achieve this, government may use its machinery to mobilize the people. Government may establish a central cash waqf administration to oversee the development in this regard.
6. The clients of the banks may be motivated to invest the profit of Cash Waqf Deposit accounts in productive sectors/income generating activities of the distressed people.

7. Proper channel should be innovated to mobilize the profits generated through CWD to increase the productiveness and capabilities of the poor and needy.
8. Modern and innovative approach toward awqāf in general and cash waqf in particular is needed drawing lessons from selected countries including Bahrain, Indonesia, Kuwait, Malaysia, Singapore, and Turkey.
9. A comprehensive and uniform legal framework for cash waqf management affairs may be thought of.
10. Incentive may be given for Cash Waqf Account holders (like exemption of tax, etc.).
11. Central Bank may give incentives in many forms to the Institutions (Banks and NBFIs) who are maintaining a large amount of Cash Waqf Deposit.

6   Final Remarks and Recommendations

Cash waqf deposit has been growing increasingly in Bangladesh. The trend would be more contributory to socio-economic development if the banks utilize the CWD fund to create some visible investment areas which would attract the potential donors to come ahead to serve the purpose. Many real sector investments like building modern shopping malls, markets, hospitals, and universities, etc. may be undertaken through CWD which would inspire others to come forward for creating CWD in the banks.

There is no alternate to research and innovation. This area should be taken into consideration by the bank managements. Central Bank should also come up with the necessary policies/guidelines to nurture this type of noble initiatives of the banks which ultimately adds value in enhancing financial inclusion at large. The Waqf administration of the country should also come up with policies to boost up this sector and National Board of Revenue (NBR) may also shed their positive look into the tax regime related to CWDs of the banks.

Acknowledgements The author is grateful to Mr. Rezaul Islam, Assistant Director; Research Department, Bangladesh Bank for the assistance provided by him in preparing the tables and figures.

REFERENCES

Abdul Karim, S. (2010). Contemporary Sharia'h Structuring for the Development and Management of Waqf Assets in Singapore. *Kyoto Bulletin of Islamic Area Studies* 3–2, 143–164. From Mohsin, M. I. A., et al. (2016). Financing the Development of Old Waqf Properties Classical Principles and Innovative Practices Around the World. *Palgrave Studies in Islamic Banking, Finance, and Economics*. New York: Palgrave.

Ahmad, M. (2015). Cash Waqf: Historical Evolution, Nature and Role as an Alternative to Riba-Based Financing for the Grass Root. *Journal of Islamic Finance*, 4(1), 63–74. IIUM Institute of Islamic Banking and Finance. ISSN 2289-2117 (O) / 2289-2109 (P).

Al-Tasuli, A. I. (1998). *Al-Bahjah Fi Sharh al-Tuhfah* (Muhammad AbdulQadir Shahun, Ed.). Lebanon: Dar Al-Kutub Al-Ilmiyyah. From Cash Waqf: Historical Evolution, Nature and Role as an Alternative to Riba-Based Financing for the Grass Root, by M. Ahmad Amir, et al. (2010) in Ibrahim et al. (2013).

Cizacka, M. (2004). *Incorporated Cash Waqfs and Mudaraba, Islamic Non-bank*. Paper submitted during the International Seminar on Non-bank Financial Institutions, Kuala. From Cash Waqf: Historical Evolution, Nature and Role as an Alternative to Riba-Based Financing for the Grass Root, by Mahadi Ahmad.

Ibn Nujaym. (n.d.). *Al-Bahr Al-Raiq Sharh Kanz Al-Daqaiq v. 5*. Cairo: Dar Al-Kitab Al-Islami. From Cash Waqf: Historical Evolution, Nature and Role as an Alternative to Riba-Based Financing for the Grass Root, by Mahadi Ahmad.

Mohsin, M. I. A., Dafterdar, H., Cizakca, M., Alhabshi, S. O., Razak, S. H. A., Sadr, S. K., et al. (2016.) Financing the Development of Old Waqf Properties Classical Principles and Innovative Practices Around the World. *Palgrave Studies in Islamic Banking, Finance, and Economics*. New York: Palgrave.

CHAPTER 3

Waqf Philanthropy and Orphans' Socio-Economic Development in Northern Nigeria Based on Maqasid al Shariah Principles

Mustapha Abubakar

1 INTRODUCTION

The word philanthropy is derived from the Latin word philanthropia, which in Greek means kindliness, humanity, benevolence, love to mankind extended from gods, men, or things. The adjective of the word, which is philanthropos connotes being loving mankind, being useful to man (Ismail et al. 2016). This is due to the fact that it is derived from phil- "loving" (see philo-) + anthropos "mankind" (see anthropo-).

Philanthropy was not a familiar term in the early period of Islam. However, viewed from conventional perspective, the word philanthropy has a different meaning from the tradition of Islam. In conventional perspective, philanthropy is interpreted in a sense oriented by the "love of man" with moral motivation, propelled voluntarily and devoid of any element of obligation from Allah (Subhanahu Wa Ta'ala, i.e., the most glorified, the highest). This clearly is at variance with what obtains in

M. Abubakar (✉)
Department of Business Administration,
Ahmadu Bello University, Zaria, Nigeria

© The Author(s) 2019
K. M. Ali et al. (eds.), *Revitalization of Waqf*
for Socio-Economic Development, Volume I,
https://doi.org/10.1007/978-3-030-18445-2_3

Islam, where the philosophical basis is the "obligation" to succumb to "Allah" to achieve social justice. This understanding may thus result in unity between the love of the human, moral motivation, and the obligations to Allah (the most glorified, the highest) to achieve social justice in this world.

Among the most vulnerable strata of all human societies are the orphans. Orphans in Islamic perspective are both male and female children who lose their male parents before they attain maturity. Sahl b. Sa'd (radiyallaahu 'anhu) said: Allaah's Messenger (salallaahu 'alaihi wassallam) said:

> "Me and who sponsors the orphan will be like this in Paradise." Then he indicated with his index and forefinger, separating between them. (Al-Bukhaaaree no 5304)

According to Shaikh Muhammad b. Saalih al-'Uthaimeen (rahimahullaah):

> There is a limit to which an orphan remains so and that is when he attains adolescence. Therefore, when a child attains adulthood, then he ceases to remain an orphan. But prior to attaining adolescence, he remains an orphan where his father has died. But where it is a situation in which his mother has passed away whilst his father is alive, then he cannot be seen to be an orphan. (Explanation of Riyaadus-Saaliheen, 1/645)

Consequently, the orphans' plight should occupy front burners in discourses and actions and anything short of that is both reprehensible and inadequate. However, an exact number of children that are orphans are difficult to come by in Nigeria. The orphans have encountered different albeit unpleasant experiences due to varying courses including but not limited to death of fathers from diseases, through sudden accidents or in cases of war and violence. Needless to state the multitudes of thought-provoking unpleasant life experiences which the orphans go through which have numerous negative implications to their well-being, livelihood, and to the society in general. Such experiences by orphans, border around poverty, lack of education, unattended and deteriorating health conditions, insecurity, and a general likelihood of falling victims to mischief makers in igniting violence in the society. All these, which are down payments for moral decadence, are without doubt, at variance with Maqasid al Shariah. This therefore generates the imperative for an institution of efforts such as the waqf instrument to complement in tackling the scourge of neglected orphans in Northern Nigeria.

When Nigeria returned to democratic governance on May 29, 1999, this resulted in the re-invigoration of several agitations for the re-enactment and conscious implementation of Shariah (the legal system recognized as the valid one in Islam) across many states in Northern Nigeria. Consequently, twelve states: Bauchi, Borno, Gombe, Jigawa, Kaduna, Kano, Katsina, Kebbi, Niger, Sokoto, Yobe, and Zamfara all keyed into the Shariah legal system and put in place certain key arrangements and institutions such as Shariah commissions, da'awah committees, the Hisbah groups as well as the zakat and waqf [endowment] bodies. Accordingly, the Aytam foundation school (where the researcher undertook a voluntary one year teaching) was established by an individual as a charitable endowment under waqf philanthropy and started operation in the 2011/2012 academic session, being managed by a board of governors, with only 50 students drawn and admitted through a clear selection process from all walks of life in Northern Nigeria. These students formed the pioneer class in this remarkable unprecedented effort and have graduated at the end of 2016/2017 session.

Against the foregoing discourse therefore, this study undertook an assessment of the waqf philanthropy effort on the social and economic developments of the orphans in accordance with the Maqasid al Shariah guidelines and principles.

2   Islamic Philanthropy Concept

The term "Philanthropy" was an alien one in the early period of Islam but which in recent times saw some Arabic words being used as its synonym. Hence the term Philanthropy is sometimes translated as *al-'ata' al-ijtima'i* (social gift) as well as *al-takaful al-insani* (humanitarian solidarity), *'ata khayri* (gift for good deeds), *al-birr* (good deeds) or *sadaqah* that is charity. It is noteworthy that the last two terms are familiar ones even in the early era of Islam.

The term Islamic philanthropy, which in Islam includes charity or sadaqah refers to generosity, social justice, sharing, and mutually reinforcing, is indeed a contemporary one even though Islam has an inbuilt philanthropic spirit. This is manifest in several verses in the Holy Quran as well as in the Prophet's tradition (*hadith*) that seek to encourage/

instruct Muslims to extend charity in different forms to the less privileged members of the society. For example, in chapter *Al Baqarah* verse 215, Allah mentioned that: "They ask you, [O Muhammad], what they should spend." Say, "*Whatever you spend of good must be for parents and relatives and orphans and the needy and the wayfarer, and whatever you do of good deeds, truly, Allah knows it well.*"

In similar narration in the Sunnah, the Holy Prophet said in an occasion:

> Good deeds become a barrier for bad matters, concealed charity can prevent Allah's anger, silaturrahim i.e. keeping ties can lengthen age and every good deed is sadaqa/charity. Owner of goodness in the world is owner of goodness in hereafter, and owner of badness in the world is the owner of badness in hereafter, and the first comer in the paradise is the owner of goodness. (Recorded by Thabrani)

3   Waqf

Waqf is defined as the locking up of the title of an owned asset from disposition and allotment of its benefits for a specific purpose or purposes (Sadeeq 2002). Thus, an asset delivered for waqf cannot be disposed of and therefore its title cannot be transferred. Purposes for which an asset is delivered in waqf must be within the confines of permitted activities under Shariah.

Waqf is a voluntary activity that requires perpetuity. Waqf is a charitable endowment which involves donating lands and buildings for education, health, orphanages, businesses, mosques, graveyards, roads, and other public goods. The objective of the institution of waqf in Islam is to take care of the needy members of the society, this does not mean though, that waqf can be instituted for general public use. Waqf also serves as a mechanism for income generation in situations where the devoted asset is turned around for income generation. In the long run, such an institution will serve as a vehicle for regeneration of the people.

The word waqf which is originated from Arabic language is a masdar form or derivative form from the verb (*fi'il madhi*) of *waqafa*. The word waqf is a synonym with the word habs (hold). The Prophet Muhammad used this word to Umar bin al Khattab: "*in syi'ta habbasta ashlaha wa tashaddaqta biha,*" therefore, waqf could be defined as stop, stopping, or holding.

A related Quranic verse that commands us to create shadaqah (endowment) is in *surah Ali Imran* verse 92 below: *By no means shall ye attain righteousness unless ye give (freely) of that which ye love; and whatever ye give of a truth Allah knoweth it well.*

According to the majority of scholars, waqf means holding of some quantity of useful assets and not reducing its *'ain* (original form/ matter). However, to the Hanafi jurists, waqf entails holding some quantity of property which remains in ownership of a man who donates waqf and gave away the benefit from it to the society at large.

Waqf has different names in different places; it is referred to as boniyad in Iran and habs in North and West Africa (Chowdhury et al. 2012). Nonetheless, its import means to hold and also guard assets of endowment or philanthropy used strictly for the specified purpose as stated in aqd and which cannot be traded.

Furthermore, Chowdhury opines that waqf could be applied on durable assets, and thus its derived benefit is utilized and devoid of depletion. Common examples of these waqf assets are lands, buildings, books, livestock, cash money, etc. Land is the most important waqf asset because of its productivity. Recent developments however have made cash waqf as another important type of waqf on account of its productivity just like land.

4   MAJOR CONCEPTS AND CATEGORIZATIONS IN MAQASID AL-SHARI'A

The concept of Maqsid (in plural form: Maqasid) connotes objective, a clear intention, an aim, a guide, an end goal or a goal. Thus, the concept of Maqasid al Shariah is accordingly defined in literal terms as intents, guides, aims, purposes as well as outcomes behind the many divine laws made by Allah (Ashur 2006). Some scholars are of the opinion that the concept of Maqasid al Shariah is associated with attaining what is in conformity with human societies' interests. It is therefore clear that all these perceived interpretations have broader meaning against an ordinarily literal perception and thus reflects "interest for humanity" in the meaning of Maqasid al Shariah (Auda 2008). But it must be recognized here that interests of people must reflect Shariah injunctions.

It is essential to note that Maqasid al Shariah is usually categorized in accordance with hierarchies in the maslahah, thus identifying first from the fundamentals (daruriyyah), followed by the legitimate needs (hajiyyah) and finally the non-essential luxuries (tahsiniyyah). Accordingly, the fundamentals that border on essentials or those of primary interest can be defined as things in life that are non-negotiable as far as human existence and their survival as well as their well-being is concerned, to the extent that elimination, obliteration, and any form of undermining has negative effects on smooth running of human life. This is closely followed by such needs that border on attaining secondary interests are relevant to elimination of severe or uncomfortable difficulties which are not fundamentally destructive to sound and normal state of human life. However, the luxurious aspects (tahsiniyyah) pertain to issues that relate to attaining the refinement, enjoying lust and reaching perfect state in human activities at every level of achievements (Kamali 2008). Here, it is noteworthy to indicate the three milestones in the historical development processes of Maqasid principles (Kasri 2012).

First is the early maqāṣid era that was pioneered by scholars within the first to the fourth centuries in the Islamic calendar during which time, the focus of scholars was on attempting to survey as well as establish rationale right from the scriptures for the various injunctions. Thus, no considerations were given to human well-being objectives. In the second era, which lasted for another four years and perceived to be a golden period, the attention of scholars focused on coming up with relevant ways that establish bases for Maqasid guidelines, which recognized human well-being as well as poverty issues (Kasari and Ahmed 2015). Then comes the final period where the contemporary period is characterized with further considerations beyond just the conservative guides of Maqasid and which recognized the changing time and thus prescribes new needs in human social and economic spheres of life.

5   METHODOLOGY

In this study, copies of questionnaire were administered in a survey. The questionnaire contained questions that seek to obtain data on socio-demographic profiles of respondent orphans as well as their perceptions about the level of changes in their respective economic conditions after receiving waqf assistance for periods ranging from one to six years. The study population is the total number of registered students in the orphanage foundation school in the junior secondary school (JSS) and the senior secondary school (SSS) sections, which stood at

428 as at the end of 2016/2017 school session, made up of 271 males and 157 females. Stratified sampling technique using 50% for each stratum was in the opinion of the researcher, the appropriate technique for determining the sample size. Thus, 214 of this which stands at 50% of the entire population were served with copies of the questionnaire of which 199 were found valid. The responses from copies of questionnaire were analyzed in respect of five dimensions which are: health services, access to education, practice of religion, pursuance of economic activities, and inclusion in social activities which were operationally measured by twenty-one Maqasid- based multi-dimensional poverty measures. To measure the perceptions of the respondents, a rating scale itemized from 1 to 6 was used. Thus, items were scored from 1 to 3 and categorized as recording negative changes (too far worse, worse, and mildly worse) whereas scores from 4 to 6, depict improved changes (slightly better, better, and extremely better) (Kasri and Ahmed 2015). To aid the analysis, the study adopted a Maqasid al Shariah Multidimensional Poverty Index (MSMPI) advanced by Kasari and Ahmed (2015) expressed in the following equation:

$$\text{MSMPI} = 1/n \sum H + \text{Ed} + \text{R} + \text{Ec} + \text{S}$$

where n is the value of each indicator and is considered to be similar for all the indicators (i.e., $n = 1/5$); H, Ed, R, Ec, and S are the weighted average value/score of poverty/well-being in health services, access to education, practice of religion, pursuance of economic activities, and inclusion in social activities respectively. Uniform values were assigned to each of the indicators in the absence of valid justification to do otherwise (Kasri and Ahmed 2015). It should be noted here that this approach has been utilized in past studies that relate to human development index (Kasri and Ahmed 2015).

6 ANALYSIS AND FINDINGS

From Table 1, a total of 214 copies of questionnaires were distributed of which 201 were retrieved while 199 were found valid for analysis. The response rate indicated a valid response that ranges from 832 to 100% which is sufficient for reliable and generalized statistics (Stevens 2002; Tabachnick and Fidell 2007). The response rate attained can be

Table 1   Statistics for questionnaire administration and response rate

Class	No of questionnaires administered (male)	No of questionnaires administered (female)	No of filled and returned questionnaires	Percentage of response	Valid questionnaires
JSS 1A	21	–	20	95	20
JSS 1C	–	20	20	100	20
JSS 2A	13	–	12	92	12
JSS 2B	12	–	10	83	10
JSS 2C	–	13	13	100	12
JSS 3A	12	–	12	100	12
JSS 3B	12	–	10	83	10
JSS 3C	–	18	16	88	16
SSS 1A	14	10	20	83	20
SSS 1B	13	5	18	100	17
SSS 2A	12	4	16	100	16
SSS 2B	8	3	11	100	11
SSS 3A	10	3	12	92	12
SSS 3B	9	2	11	100	11
Total	136	78	201		199

Source Researcher's computation from output

as a result of the data collection strategy adopted: self-administration of questionnaire. Many previous studies on survey of customers' perceptions and knowledge that utilized similar procedure have recorded reasonable response rates. A response rate of 30% is acceptable for surveys.

Descriptive statistics on respondents' religion, gender, age, and class are shown in Table 2. From Table 2, it is seen that all the respondents are Muslims and this is not far from the fact that the school is situated in the Muslim dominated part of Northern Nigeria. In addition to this, Muslims are the target recipients of waqf.

The estimated figure for the MSMPI is seen in Table 3. In the average, the estimated figure shows a value of 3.979. Even though the value is slightly lower than four, it can be interpreted to mean that the well-being of the orphans has recorded mild increase after enjoying the waqf assistance. In other words, the orphans' poverty has decreased due to the contributions of the waqf effort put in place.

Table 2 Respondents' profile (orphans waqf beneficiaries)

	Frequency	Percent	Cumulative percent
Religion			
Islam	199	100	100
Gender			
Male	126	63.3	63.3
Female	73	36.7	100
Total	199	100	
Age			
10–12	40	20.1	20.1
13–14	34	17.1	37.2
15–16	40	20.1	57.3
17–18	64	32.2	89.4
18–19	21	10.6	100
Total	199	100	
Class			
JSS1	40	20.1	20.1
JSS2	34	17.1	37.2
JSS3	40	20.1	57.3
SSS1	37	18.6	75.9
SSS2	27	13.6	89.4
SSS3	21	10.6	100
Total	199	100	

Source Result from spss version 16 output

Table 3 Findings on the Maqāṣid-based Multidimensional Poverty Index (MSMPI)

Dimension of poverty/ well-being	Observation	MSMPI	Std. deviation	Minimum	Maximum
Health	199	4.191	.231	4	6
Education	199	4.106	.192	4	6
Religion	199	3.955	.196	3	6
Economic	199	4.216	.289	3	6
Social	199	3.429	.198	3	6
Average		3.979			

Source Results from spss version 16 outputs 2017

Table 4 Clear specific changes in multidimensional poverty measure

Poverty measure/indicator	N	Negative changes (declined improvement/poorer)		Positive changes (better/less poor)	
		Frequency	Percentage	Frequency	Percentage
Health dimension					
Food consumption	199	–	–	199	100
Access to health service	199	–	–	199	100
Health awareness	199	–	–	199	100
Quality of health	199	–	–	199	100
Average					100
Education dimension					
School access	199	–	–	199	100
School attendance	199	–	–	199	100
Literacy	199	–	–	199	100
School achievement	199	–	–	199	100
Average					100
Religious/spiritual dimension					
Praying and fasting	199	–	–	199	100
Islamic/Quranic study	199	–	–	199	100
Charity	199	–	–	199	100
Hajj	199	59	29.6	140	70.4
Average			7.4		92.6
Economic dimension					
Skill	199	107	53.8	92	46.2
Employability	199	–	–	199	100
Income	199	87	43.7	112	56.3
Purchasing power	199	–	–	199	100
Savings	199	–	–	199	100
Average			19.5		80.5
Social dimension					
Future	199	–	–	199	100
Harmony	199	–	–	199	100
Anti-social behavior	199	–	–	199	100
Community activity	199	130	65.3	69	34.7
Average	199		16.33		83.67

Source Researcher's computation spss output 2017

It is shown that the orphans, on aggregate terms, have benefitted a mildly higher well-being in other words a mildly lower poverty, with respect to four of the five dimensions as the MSMPI values are all but one higher than the threshold points of four. The result shows that the highest point of welfare improvement is recorded with respect to pursuance of economic activities dimension (value 4.216) and is followed by health services dimension (value 4.191) and then access to education dimension (value 4.106). The score for religion dimension is approximated to 4 (3.955). However, the lowest poverty reduction is seen in respect of social dimension (value 3.429).

Details on assessment of each of the socio-economic well-being dimensions are presented in summarized form in Table 4. It is clear from Table 3 that the highest well-being improvement was experienced in the health services and access to education dimensions. On average, around 100% of the respondents mentioned that the orphans' well-being in those dimensions had increased significantly after the receipt of support from the waqf institutions although at varying levels. These are followed by a religious/spiritual dimension with 92.6%, social dimension with 83.67% while economic dimension recorded 80.5%.

In contrast, specific, negative changes were recorded in religious, economic, and social dimensions as indicated by not too large proportions of average negative changes of 7.4, 19.5, and 16.33% respectively. This can be explained by the fact that the respondents are not fully grown up to learn about Hajj, obtain sufficient skills and earn income, as well as partake in economic activities.

7 CONCLUSIONS AND RECOMMENDATION

This study is an attempt at showcasing the existence of waqf philanthropy as it impacts on orphans' socio-economic development in Northern Nigeria based on Maqasid al Shariah. The findings however are from a limited waqf philanthropic effort with a success story that needs to be further improved upon. This is achievable through establishment of more institutions in the medicare, skill acquisition, and other life endeavours. From policy perspective, the findings imply that declining changes (i.e., increased poverty) in each indicator serves as a clarion call to nebulous institutions such as government and other relevant institutions to work more at improving their outings. In the same vein, positive changes indicate that activities in the areas represent the right tonic that needs to be consolidated. To this end, advocacy and sensitization programmes should be further encouraged to bring the importance of waqf as a complementary poverty tackling mechanism in poverty ravaged Muslim societies across the world.

REFERENCES

Auda, J. (2008). *Maqāṣid al-Sharī'ah: A Beginner's Guide*. London: International Institute of Islamic Thought.

Ashur, I. (2006). *Treatise on Maqāṣid al-Sharī'ah*. London: International Institute of Islamic Thought.

Chowdhury, M. S. R., et al. (2012). Problems of Waqf Administration and Proposals for Improvement: A Study in Malaysia. *Journal of Internet Banking and Commerce, 17*(1), 1–8.

Islamic Solidarity Fund for Development. (2016). *Fighting Poverty, Improving Lives, Restoring Dignity ISFD Strategy 2016-2025 1.*

Ismail, A., Zaenal, M. H., & Taufiq, U. (2016). *Can Islamic Philanthropy Increase Financial Inclusion?* (IRTI Working Paper 1437-02).

Kamali, M. (2008). *Maqāṣid al-Sharī'ah Made Simple*. Herndon: International Institute of Islamic Thought.

Kasri, R. A. (2012). *Can Financial and Social Performance of Zakāh Institution Be Assessed by Using the Maqāṣid al-Sharī'ah Approach?* 5th Kyoto-Durham International Workshop in Islamic Economics and Finance "New Horizons in Islamic Economics: Critical Perspectives on the Financial and Social Performance of Islamic Finance", Kyoto, Japan.

Kasri, R., & Ahmed, H. (2015). Assessing Socio-Economic Development Based on Maqāṣid al-Sharī'ah Principles: Normative Frameworks, Methods and Implementation in Indonesia. *Islamic Economic Studies, 23*(1), 73–100.

Sadeq, A. M. (2002). Waqf, Perpetual Charity and Poverty Evaluation. *International Journal of Social Economics, 29*(1/2), 135–151.

Stevens, J. P. (2002). *Applied Multivariate Statistics for the Social Sciences*. London: Lawrence Erlbaum Associates Publishers.

Tabachnick, B. G., & Fidell, L. S. (2007). *Using Multivariate Statistics*. New York: HarperCollins.

CHAPTER 4

FinTech-Enabled Cash *Waqf*: Effective Intermediary of Social Finance

Islamic Social Finance

Etsuaki Yoshida

1 Introduction

This paper tries to explore how "FinTech," or financial services enhanced by high utilization of information and communication technologies (ICT), can enable potential capability of cash *waqf*, especially in the context of social finance. It is also intended to shed light on effectiveness the FinTech-enabled cash *waqf* as one of the financial intermediaries of Islamic social finance.

Whilst growth of Islamic finance was evident not just in its market volume but in product development as well, the industry has often been criticized by academic scholars that the current practice of Islamic finance is not in the direction of pursuing its objective of the religion or *Maqasid al Shariah*. Now, the industry offers Islamic derivatives, Islamic project finance, Islamic asset management services using highly sophisticated financial engineering techniques, to name just a few, but those

E. Yoshida (✉)
ASAFAS, Kyoto University, Tokyo, Japan

© The Author(s) 2019
K. M. Ali et al. (eds.), *Revitalization of Waqf for Socio-Economic Development, Volume I*,
https://doi.org/10.1007/978-3-030-18445-2_4

scholars are not satisfied with functions and outcomes of Islamic financial services, as discussed later. In this context, *waqf*, as explained later, is considered as one of the few Islamic financial transactions that contribute to more financially equal society through its income redistribution function.

Meanwhile, a wave of development in information and communication technology has completely reached the huge continent of the financial industry, and financial services highly enhanced by ICT are recently called "FinTech." Originally, money is conceptual existence and notes and coins theoretically contain no value by themselves under the current fiat money standard. Due to these natures, financial services are well-harmonized with ICT that deals with data processing, and we can expect infinite varieties of forms of financial services even in the near future.[1]

Under these circumstances, a phenomenon of "FinTech-enabled cash *waqf*" has emerged, as depicted later in this paper, and shows the sign of further growth. So far, preceding studies on the theme are very limited, and a quick search by the Google Scholar in English came up with only 1 result.[2] Sifa (2016), the only result by the search, proposes ICT-based cash *waqf* transaction system, including its collection and management. However, it only proposes a potential scheme of the *waqf* transaction. This paper, on the contrary, provides a more comprehensive framework to make the FinTech-enabled *waqf* come true and discusses academic and religious significance of it.

Or, just to discuss the issue in a broader scope of view, "Islamic FinTech" is also considered to be a very limited topic for academic research so far, with only one relevant result in the similar search by the Google Scholar.[3] Rather, a section in the Islamic Financial Services Industry Stability Report 2017 (IFSB 2017, pp. 114–113) provides a comprehensive landscape of Islamic FinTech. It appears as one of the two emerging issues in Islamic finance and wraps up Shariah compliance and regulatory aspects of Islamic FinTech. Not much attention is paid to *waqf* itself.

---

[1] Kuroda (2017) argues that "It is not at all surprising that such new information technologies are expected to be utilized in various financial services, considering that the basic function of finance is information processing."

[2] Accessed on September 18, 2017. The number includes the paper with the direct linkage of "FinTech" and "*waqf*", and excludes one with just coexistence of the two words.

[3] Lajis (2017). This only refers to the "Islamic Fintech Alliance," which is a group of Islamic FinTech companies in Malaysia, and again, provides no fundamental insights on Islamic FinTech itself.

With this status quo as the background of academic research on the FinTech-enabled cash *waqf*, this paper intends to sort out how FinTech-enabled *waqf* will best contribute to an Islamic community in a practical manner, and academic and religious significance of it.

2 Overview of *Waqf* and the "FinTech-Enabled Cash *Waqf*"

2.1 Overview of Waqf *and the Scope of This Paper*

As mentioned earlier, while Islamic finance has achieved generally acceptable growth in its practice in terms of its penetration into the consumers' and professionals' community, product development, and global expansion to even Muslim-minority countries, some academic scholars make criticisms against the current practice of Islamic finance. One of the major criticisms is that the current practice is just for economic profit of the industry, leaving the benefit of society such as mitigating the income disparity. Hence, it is natural that more socially beneficial finance should attract the attention, or just to put it more shortly, Islamic social finance should play a bigger role.[4]

Waqf should show up on the main stage as a matter of course when we talk about social finance in an Islamic context. Although *waqf* transactions were popular in older days such as the Ottoman Empire periods, they also enjoy modern popularity, not just as a practice that was continuously conveyed from the past, but also as an effective financial tool and mechanism that will enhance economic equality in a society, as seen in past works such as Ahmed (2007) and Nagaoka (2013).

Waqf, as one of the traditional methods of income redistribution in Islam, is generally considered as a transaction of asset in the form of real estate or cash, donated by the owner (*waqif*) of the asset. The *waqif* in the beginning specifies an asset (*mawquf*) for the *waqf* transaction, with its purpose and the recipients of the benefits (*mawquf 'alay-hi*) and a trustee (*mutawalli*).

---

[4] In this regard, international financial organizations have showed significant efforts in enlightening and providing information. See World Bank and IDB (2016) and IRTI (2014, 2015). Also, ADB and IFSB (2015) pick up financial inclusion for inclusive growth in the region.

Waqf can be theoretically categorized, as a snapshot of its forms in the current practice, by two kinds of dimensions. One dimension is the beneficiary (*mawquf 'alay-hi*), the designated (*mu'ayyan*)[5] or the undesignated (*majhul*). The other dimension is the nature of the endowed assets (*mawquf*), real estates, or chattels (movables).[6] Among these types, traditionally there have been a lot of debates regarding the permissibility under *Shariah*, especially regarding cash *waqf* and family *waqf*, but the paper does not mention much on it, as the focus is set on cash waqf, which is efficiently utilized by the use of ICT, as FinTech.

2.2   Overview of the "FinTech-Enabled Cash Waqf"

FinTech recently enjoys growing interests in the financial industry all over the world. The word itself did not even exist ten years ago, but we are sure that it will give a huge change on shapes of financial transactions in coming ten years or even shorter.

Islamic finance also enjoys benefit of this growing FinTech. Just a quick look at several stories depicts how Islamic FinTech is recently seen as a significant element that will cause a big change in contents of Islamic financial transactions.

- The 22nd World Islamic Banking Conference held in 2015 in Bahrain picked up FinTech as one of the sessions of this prestigious industry event with the longest tradition among others.
- At the Global Islamic Finance Forum held in Malaysia in 2015, Governor of Bank Negara Malaysia, Datuk Muhammad bin Ibrahim, mentioned FinTech as one of the three key issues of Islamic finance in his keynote speech.
- In 2016, the Islamic FinTech Alliance was established in Malaysia by firms providing Islamic FinTech services including crowdfunding platform providers. Led by "Ethis Ventures," other firms such as "blossom," "FundingLab," "easi," "narwi," "LaunchGood," "KapitalBoost," "Skolafund" joined the Alliance.[7]
- RedMoney launched the "IFN Fintech" newsletter and held "IFN Fintech Forum," both in 2017.

---

[5] This can include an organization (*jiha*).

[6] This includes cash, which is the main theme of this paper.

[7] See IFT (2016).

- Several cities in the Middle East are making efforts to become an Islamic FinTech hub, as described in Economist (2017).
- Islamic Development Bank Group is now calling for business ideas of Islamic FinTech under the project called "FinTech Islamic Finance Challenge." The project is in collaboration with Spain's IE Business School and the Islamic Banker magazine. The project invites business ideas until November this year.

Note that FinTech is a general and collective term and it has many varieties of financial services practiced now. A research firm called Venture Scanner categorized FinTech companies into 13 groups by their businesses: (1) lending, (2) personal finance, (3) payments, (4) equity financing, (5) remittances, (6) retail investing, (7) institutional investing, (8) security, (9) infrastructure, (10) business tools, (11) crowdfunding, (12) online banking, and (13) research and data.[8] This implies that we need to look at concrete forms of financial services among various types, when we talk about the actual transaction.

Based on these backgrounds, FinTech will be able to increase the efficiency of financial transactions in a *waqf* scheme, and with its increased efficiency, it may be able to create additional values on the *waqf* transaction. The author calls this new type as the "FinTech-enabled cash *waqf*." As indicated earlier, technologies are utilized in various aspects of financial transactions, so we can expect various forms of expansion of the FinTech-enabled cash *waqf*.

Before moving on to countless forms of the FinTech-enabled cash *waqf*, here is one of the basic forms of FinTech, which is generally called "crowdfunding" (Fig. 1). A platform on the internet provides information on each project for the sake of potential investors. If an individual decides to invest certain amount of money on the project he/she would like to support, he/she does so by clicking a relevant button on the website or the application software. The funds are provided typically in four ways: (1) donation, (2) reward (physical products such as manufactured goods), (3) loan, and (4) equity[9] (Massolution 2015). For collection of funds from the public, FinTech can play a huge role with extremely high efficiency of acquiring information and payment from the viewpoint of potential provider of funds.

---

[8] See Venture Scanner (2016).

[9] For more comprehensive and analytical discussion on Islamic equity crowdfunding, see Yoshida (2016). For more theoretical and conceptual approach, see Ng et al. (2015).

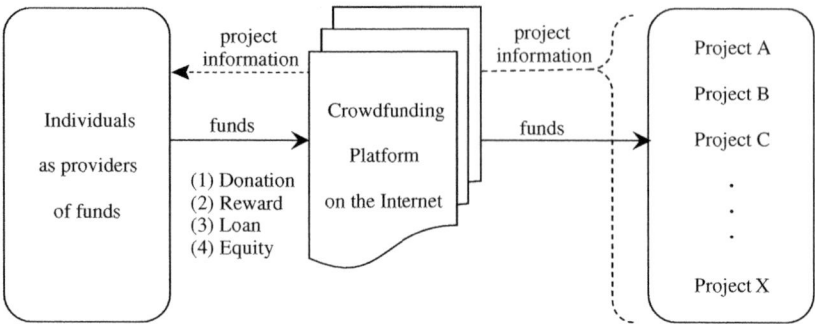

Fig. 1 Crowdfunding mechanism (*Source* Author's own)

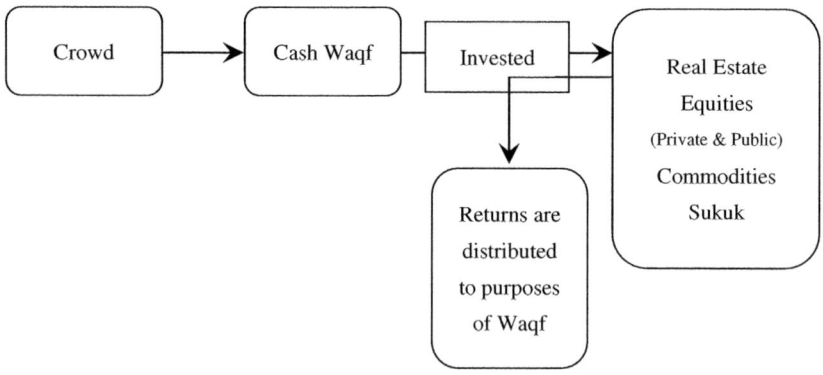

Fig. 2 Waqf World (*Source* Depicted by the author based on Waqf World)

Figure 2 shows a basic and good example of the FinTech-enabled cash *waqf*, which is called the "Waqf World," of the FinTech-enabled cash *waqf*. It is based on, again, crowdfunding mechanism, which is considered to be one of the major business models of FinTech services. This example shows that the FinTech-enabled cash *waqf* is not just a conceptual dream, but the reality.

A potential donator (*waqif*) of cash *waqf* will go to the Web site of the Waqf World and provide details of *waqf* amount and the *waqif* him/herself. The collected funds will be invested into real estates, equities (private and public), commodities, *sukuk*, to name just a few, in a Shariah-compliant manner, and in the form of crowdfunding. The profit gained from those investments will be distributed to the people in need, as a typical form of social finance. Operation of this platform, including technological aspects, is carried out by Ethis Ventures, which usually offers Islamic equity crowdfunding platform.

The initiative was taken by Tun Abdullah Badawi, the ex-Prime Ministry of Malaysia, and launched at the 12th World Islamic Economic Forum held in Jakarta in August 2016. The idea was reportedly first presented by Research Center for Islamic Economics and Finance (EKONIS) of National University of Malaysia (UKM) at a forum held by IRTI in January 2016.

3   Practical Forms of the FinTech-Enabled Cash *Waqf*

3.1   Prerequisites for Practice

FinTech, not limited to *Islamic* FinTech but including the conventional equivalent in general, has just started its substantial growth, and of course, institutional developments and other arrangements in many aspects will be necessary in order for the business area to grow in a sustainable manner. Below are typical preconditions that may be required in many jurisdictions.

(a) Legal accommodation

One big issue in a jurisdiction will be legal treatment to accommodate with the existing system. The crowdfunding mechanism in general may be interpreted as fund-raising mechanism from many and the unidentified people, and this may require additional treatments in law. For example, the equity-based crowdfunding deals in US required legal amendments, because the party that intends to raise funds is required to register with the Securities and Exchange Commission (SEC), with preparing required disclosure documents, under the Securities Act of 1933, and the registration with the SEC means continuous disclosure under the Securities Exchange Act of 1934. Amendment of exemption of these requirements was made, to escape from a lot of regulations intended for transparency and disclosure upon each and every single one of individual investors. More precisely, the government prepared in 2012 a new law called "Jumpstart Our Business Startups Act," or JOBS Act. The Act has six topics, one of which is about crowdfunding. In this Act, if the fund-raising size is not larger than 100 million USD and other conditions are met, the broker (the party that manages crowdfunding platform) is exempted from registration procedures.

(b) Shariah screening

Shariah screening will be essential. The developer of a FinTech-enabled cash *waqf* fund, for example, should acquire fatwa for the whole transaction in order to avoid ex-post troubles in terms of Shariah compliance. If the fund manager is not a party from financial industries (e.g., Internet technology companies, governmental entities and nonprofit organizations), it may be able to consider retaining a third-party consulting firm with the function of a Shariah board, or it may want to collaborate with financial institutions with expertise of offering Islamic financial services including.

Sometimes, absence of Shariah screening process in recent Islamic crowdfunding firms is reported, but this *waqf*-based scheme is solely Islamic and it should be in line with the doctrine. So far, there is no standardized process of Sharia screening among Islamic FinTech ventures, but hopefully it will be accomplished as they acquire bigger presence in the market.

(c) Public awareness

Public awareness, or through marketing of a key FinTech service, such as crowdfunding platform, will also be a big challenge. If there are not enough people that know and can potentially participate in this scheme, this idea will not make any sense. One possible solution is that the government shall be an operating body as a catalyst, so that many can be aware of it. Another idea will be that major banks can offer these services using its high creditworthiness and popularity among the residents in a country. Riding on a major SNS would be a good idea as well.

(d) Securities

The more ICT is used in a financial transaction, the bigger the risk of ICT securities grows. Every stakeholder must be cautious, while seeking no risk will result in no growth in the business. There is not an easy solution, but it must come along with the FinTech business.

3.2   Potential Forms of FinTech-Enabled Cash Waqf

With full utilization of ICT and social entrepreneurs' imagination and invention, cash *waqf* can take countless types of forms of financial transactions. Below are just a couple of examples to show its flexibility and variety in forms.

(a) Platform of Poverty Alleviation Projects (PPAP) Model (Fig. 3)

As a typical crowdfunding, which is part of FinTech, a *waqif* of cash *waqf* can find a project on a platform, which he/she would like to donate. People may want to assist a mosque that is near their house, a *madrasa* to which their sons go, or just put the money into a general *waqf* fund. It is quite important that a *waqif* is satisfied with the usage of the money, knowing the usage in advance, and feeling that they are contributing to the community.

(b) Microfinance-based Dual Social Finance Model (Fig. 4)

Microfinance is known as a typical form of social finance since it provides loans to financially challenged people, to which banks seldom provide

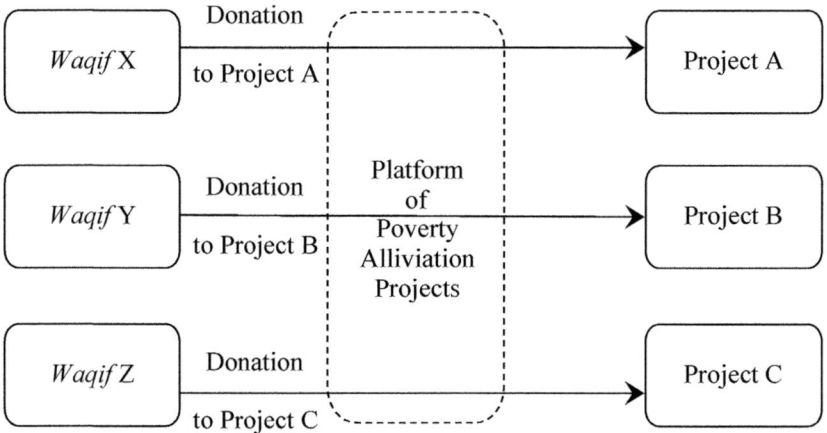

Fig. 3   Platform of Poverty Alleviation Projects (PPAP) Model

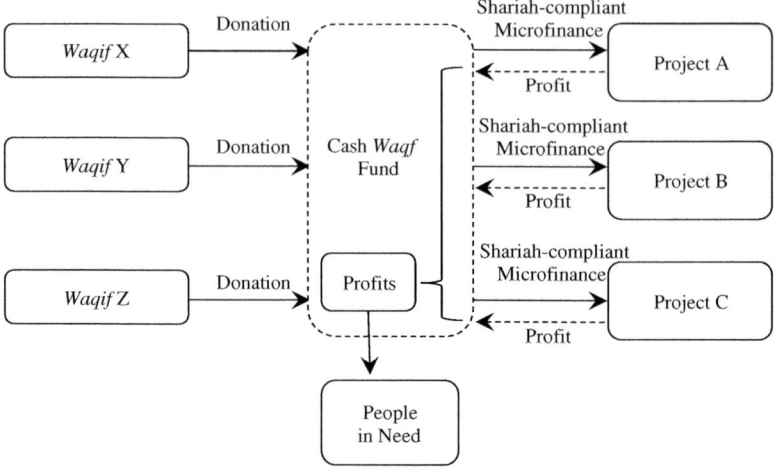

Fig. 4   Microfinance-based dual social finance model

finance. This model is, not just for those who will benefit from acquiring the microfinance loans, but also for people who must depend on donations from the fund, the source of which is profits generated through the microfinance business using the donated funds. ICT can facilitate collection of cash and provision of information on the microfinance projects for potential *waqif*. Also, there can be an automatic system, enhanced by ICT, to transfer a certain portion of the profits to those who are in need.

(c) Leveraging Social Venture Model (Fig. 5)

Social finance is not just for charity, but can include business-oriented natures. If a crowdfunding platform opens the door for both social venture capitalists and potential *waqif*'s, the equity investment for a social business project is leveraged using the collected funds of *waqf*.

Of course, all these are just intuitive and indicative schemes of how FinTech-enabled cash *waqf* will be structured. It may require a lot of challenges when they develop those ideas into practical, but at least this section can conclude the concept of FinTech-enabled cash *waqf* has a big potential.[10]

---

[10]A more conceptual but comprehensive analysis of waqf's potential is seen in Masyita (2005), although it does not refer to FinTech as it is somewhat an older work.

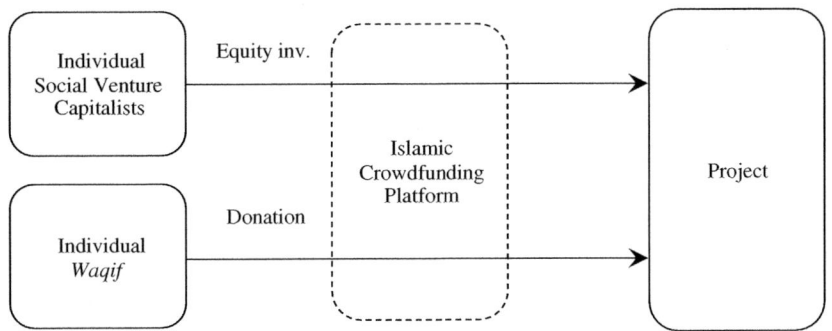

Fig. 5 Leveraging social venture model

4   Significance of FinTech-Enabled Cash *Waqf* in Product Development

4.1   Criticism Against the Current Form of Product Development

Although the Islamic finance industry has shown remarkable growth, the current situation is not necessarily welcomed by Islamic economists.[11] A debt-oriented aspect is one thing, as seen in the phrase of criticism, "*Murabaha* Syndrome," which is a terminology by Tarik M. Yousef (2004). Chapra (2007) argues that the share of equity-based transactions should increase in the current financial system, while that of the debt-based ones should decrease substantially. However, little attention on the aspect of social finance, including poverty alleviation, would be a more serious problem than that of little equity-based financial assets, especially from the viewpoint of people who puts emphasis on religious values.

Hasan (2010) criticized that the industry does not care enough about the objective of Islamic finance, and hence, there is a mismatch between structure and objective of the religious economic behavior. El-Gamal (2003) described the current situation as "Islamic finance quickly turned to mimicking the interest-based conventional finance." In addition, Hamoudi (2007) called the current situation as "Jurisprudential Schizophrenia" and De Lorenzo (2007) bantered it as

---

[11] In this paper, the definition of "Islamic Economists" is simply scholars that deal with economic issues in consideration of religious values of Islam.

"Shariah-conversion technology." Habib Ahmed (2011) observed the situation in a more objective manner, saying "contemporary practice of Islamic finance has been criticized for not fulfilling the *maqasid*." Also, Dr. Wahbah Al-Zuhayli (2001) says, "the primary goal of Islamic financial institutions is not profit-making, but the endorsement of social goals of socio-economic development and the alleviation of poverty." This situation is called the crossroads of Islamic finance.[12]

Practitioners (and some of other Islamic economists) tend to consider that their idea on product development as in the current practice is natural, implying that social finance is not realistic. Gainor (2000) describes this recognition in a very concise manner, saying "Much of the research and development that has worked its way into existing products in the marketplace has been generated from adapting conventional products. It may follow that if a product was successful in the conventional marketplace, then if successfully engineered as to not be inconsistent with Islamic Sharia, it should be successful in the Islamic marketplace." Thus, there is a cognitive dichotomy on product development of Islamic finance between practitioners and Islamic economists.

4.2   FinTech-Enabled Cash Waqf Can Contribute

FinTech may be able to provide a significant solution to the above-mentioned controversy. Conceptually, use of ICT will make redistribution of income from the rich to the lower-income group in a much more efficient manner, because it can enhance cash *waqf*, social investments, microfinance, and other types of social finance. Of course, the efficiency for the rich to find opportunities and project details is essential.

5   Conclusion

This paper picked up the FinTech-enabled cash *waqf*, a part of the emerging trends of Islamic FinTech, and considered its application to financial products which are more Islamic, and discussed religious significance of it.

---

[12] This appears as an opening remark of the second half in the Thunderbird International Business Review's special edition on Islamic finance. The edition has Chapra (2007), and many other meaningful papers with critical views on the current practice of Islamic finance.

Use of ICT in financial services is expected to create huge changes, and so is to Islamic finance as well. Especially, FinTech will reduce the cost related to supply and consumption of financial services, but there is more than that. This paper focused on transparency and networking opportunities realized by the high use of ICT and imagination of business developers. This will surely enhance poverty alleviation, which is the objective of social finance, and the *Maqasid al Shariah*.

The second Caliph, Umar, is considered to have said, if he were to live longer, he would see to it that even a shepherd on the Mount San'a' received his share from his wealth, according to Bukhari.[13] In the context of the FinTech-enabled cash *waqf*, the story can be interpreted as follows: if the Caliph lived longer enough until the days when smartphone is available to everybody and donation is easily done on the palm, a shepherd in the Mount San'a' could have received the donation from the Caliph living in Madinah through the FinTech-enabled cash *waqf* mechanism.

The voyage with FinTech has just begun. It is a big challenge for the human society whether we can fully utilize the powerful tool for qualitative development of financial system in terms of Shariah, and more income equality as part of *maslahah* (public interest), or we just end with having more efficient financial transactions.

REFERENCES

Ahmed, H. (2007, March 6–7). *Waqf-Based Microfinance: Realizing the Social Role of Islamic Finance*. A Paper Written for the International Seminar on "Integrating Awqaf in the Islamic Financial Sector", Singapore.

Ahmed, H. (2011). Maqasid al-Shari'ah and Islamic Financial Products: A Framework for Assessment. *ISRA International Journal of Islamic Finance, 3*(1), 149–160.

Asian Development Bank (ADB) and Islamic Financial Services Board (IFSB). (2015). *Islamic Finance for Asia: Development, Prospects, and Inclusive Growth*.

Bank Negara Malaysia. (2014). *Financial Stability and Payment Systems Report 2014*.

Chapra, M. U. (1979). *Objectives of the Islamic Order*. Leicester, UK: The Islamic Foundation.

---

[13] The saying was cited from Chapra (1979).

Chapra, M. U. (2007). The Case Against Interest: Is It Compelling? *Thunderbird International Business Review, 49*(2), 161–186.

Chapra, M. U. (2017). The Looming International Financial Crisis: Can the Introduction of Risk Sharing in the Financial System as Required by Islamic Finance, Play a Positive Role in Reducing Its Severity? *Islamic Economic Studies, 25*(2), 1–13.

Dar, H. (Ed.). (2010). *Global Islamic Finance Report 2010.* London: BMB Islamic U.K.

De Lorenzo, Y. T. (2007). *The Total Returns Swap and the "Shariah Conversion Technology".* Dinar Standard: Stratagem.

Diaw, A., Hassan, S., & Ng, A. B. K. (2010). Performance of Islamic and Conventional Exchange Traded Funds in Malaysia. *ISRA International Journal of Islamic Finance, 2*(1), 131–149.

Economist. (2017). *The Race to Become Islamic Banking's Fintech Hub.*

El-Gamal, M. A. (2003). "Interest" and the Paradox of Contemporary Islamic Law and Finance. *Fordham International Law Journal, 27*(1), 108–149.

Feller, J. (2016). *100+ Fintech Startups in MENA: 3 Initial Findings.*

Gainor, T. (2000). *A Practical Approach to Product Development.* A Paper Prepared for the Fourth Harvard University Forum on Islamic Finance.

Hamoudi, H. A. (2007). Jurisprudential Schizophrenia: On Form and Function in Islamic Finance. *Chicago Journal of International Law, 7*(2), 605–622.

Hasan, Z. (2005). Islamic Banking at the Crossroads: Theory Versus Practice. In M. Iqbal & R. Wilson (Eds.), *Islamic Perspectives on Wealth Creation* (pp. 11–25). Edinburgh: Edinburgh University Press.

Hasan, Z. (2010, March 17). *Islamic Finance: Structure-Objective Mismatch and Its Consequences.* A Paper Presented at the Workshop on Islamic Finance at the Business School Strasbourg University, France.

IFSB (Islamic Financial Services Board). (2017). *Islamic Financial Services Industry Stability Report 2017.*

IFT (Islamic FinTech Alliance). (2016). *Islamic FinTech Industry Snapshot Report 2016.*

Iqbal, M., & Molyneux, P. (2005). *Thirty Years of Islamic Banking: History, Performance and Prospects.* New York: Palgrave Macmillan.

Islamic Research and Training Institute (IRTI). (2014). *Islamic Social Finance Report 2014.*

Islamic Research and Training Institute (IRTI). (2015). *Islamic Social Finance Report 1436H (2015).*

Kayed, R. N., & Hassan, M. K. (2010). *Islamic Entrepreneurship. Durham Modern Middle East and Islamic World.* New York: Routledge.

Kuroda, H. (2017). *AI and the Frontiers of Finance: Remarks at the Conference on AI and Financial Services/Financial Markets.* Bank of Japan.

Lajis, S. M. (2017). Risk-Sharing Securities: Accelerating Finance for SMEs. *Islamic Economic Studies, 25*(2), 35–55.

Lewis, M. K., & Algaoud, L. M. (2001). *Islamic Banking.* Cheltenham: Edward Elgar.

Massolution. (2015). *2015 CF: The Crowdfunding Industry Report.*

Masyita, D. (2005, July 17–21). *A Dynamic Model for Cash Waqf Management as One of the Alternative Instruments for the Poverty Alleviation in Indonesia.* A Paper Presented at the 23rd International Conference of the System Dynamics Society, Sloan School of Management, MIT, Boston.

Nagaoka, S. (2012). Critical Overview of the History of Islamic Economics: Formation, Transformation, and New Horizons. *Asian and African Area Studies, 11*(2), 114–336.

Nagaoka, S. (2013, September 10). *Revitalization of the Traditional Islamic Economic Institutions (Waqf and Zakat) in the Twenty-First Century: Resuscitation of the Antique Economic System or Novel Sustainable System?* A Paper Presented at the 9th International Conference in Islamic Economics and Finance, Growth, Equity and Stability: An Islamic Perspective, Turkey.

National Board of Zakat (BAZNAS) and Bank Indonesia. (2014). *Towards an Establishment of an Efficient and Sound Zakat System: Proposed Core Principles for Effective Zakat Supervision.* Background Paper for the Working Group of Zakat Core Principles.

Ng, A., Mirakhor, A., & Ibrahim, M. H. (2015). *Social Capital and Risk Sharing: An Islamic Finance Paradigm.* New York: Palgrave Macmillan.

al-Rifai, T. (1999). *Islamic Equity Funds: A Brief Industry Analysis.* Failaka International Inc.

Sifa, E. N. (2016). E-Waqf as an Alternative Solution for Infrastructure Development Based on Crowdfunding. In *Proceeding of the First International Conference on Law, Economics and Education,* Muhammadiyah University of Metro, Indonesia.

Venture Scanner. (2016). *Financial Technology Market Overview.*

World Bank, Islamic Development Bank, and Islamic Research and Training Institute. (2015). *Leveraging Islamic Finance for Small and Medium Enterprises (SMEs).* Joint WB-IDB Policy Report.

Yoshida, E. (2016). *Islamic Crowdfunding: A New Tool for SME Financing and Its Religious Significance.* A Paper Presented at the 2nd Annual Symposium on Islamic Economics Finance 2016 by World Bank, Islamic Research and Training Institute (IRTI) and Guidance Financial Group.

Yousef, T. M. (2004). The Murabaha Syndrome in Islamic Finance: Laws, Institutions and Politics. In C. M. Henry & R. Wilson (Eds.), *The Politics of Islamic Finance* (pp. 63–80). Edinburgh: Edinburgh University Press.

World Bank and Islamic Development Bank Group. (2016). *Global Report on Islamic Finance: Islamic Finance: A Catalyst for Shared Prosperity.* Washington, DC. https://doi.org/10.1596/978-1-4648-0926-2.

al-Zuhayli, D. W. (2001). *Islamic Jurisprudence and Its Proofs* (M.A. El-Gamal, Trans.). Damascus: Dar al-Fikr.

Zulkhibri, M., Ismail, A. G., & Hidayat, S. E. (Eds.). (2016). *Macroprudential Regulation and Policy for the Islamic Financial Industry: Theory and Applications.* Springer.

CHAPTER 5

Experiences and Lessons of Cash *Waqf* in Bangladesh and Other Countries

M. Kabir Hassan, Mohd Fazlul Karim and M. Sydul Karim

1 INTRODUCTION

Today, cash *waqf* is recognized in the whole Muslim world as one of the most effective mechanisms in realizing the socio-economic and welfare objectives of the institution of *waqf*. Imam Zufar first introduced the concept of cash *waqfs* in the eighth century. He formulated the concept of cash *waqf* based on two key principles: (a) *mudarabah* should be the investment vehicle for pooled cash endowment; (b) investment

---

This is the keynote address given at the 2017 Waqf Conference in Dhaka on November 4, 2018, at Hotel Sonargaon.

M. K. Hassan · M. S. Karim (✉)
Department of Economics and Finance,
University of New Orleans, New Orleans, LA, United States
e-mail: mhassan@uno.edu

M. F. Karim
University of Toronto, Toronto, ON, Canada

© The Author(s) 2019
K. M. Ali et al. (eds.), *Revitalization of Waqf for Socio-Economic Development, Volume I*,
https://doi.org/10.1007/978-3-030-18445-2_5

59

returns should be spent for social welfare and charity (Cizakça 2009). If we look beyond Muslim era, we see the existence of cash *waqf* in some of the primitive civilizations such as Mesopotamia, Roma, and Greece. For example, the Ottoman Empire approved the practice of cash *waqf* in the early fifteenth century. The concept of cash *waqf* gained huge popularity among the people of Anatolia and rapidly spread all over its European provinces (Ottoman Cash *Waqf* Revisited: The Case of Bursa 2004). By the end of sixteenth century, cash *waqf* accounted for more than half of all the newly created waqf in the Ottoman Empire.

A renewed enthusiasm toward cash *waqf* is now visible in many Muslim majority countries including Bangladesh, which is the 4th largest Muslim population in the world (Stencel et al. 2009). Compared to the standard traditional concept of dedicating immovable properties as *waqf*, cash *waqf* is a favorite to many Muslims, affluent or otherwise for its built-in value propositions that meet Shariah objectives with mobility and liquidity. Bangladesh is one of the densely populated countries where land and similar tangible properties are becoming increasingly scarce every day even for agriculture and housing sector. Therefore, cash *waqf* is a futuristic alternative that is gaining popularity and acceptance to the people who are willing to get involved in welfare-oriented activities within the framework of Islam.

2   DEFINITION OF CASH *WAQF*

Cash *waqf* has been defined by many scholars. Al-Tasuli from Maliki School defines cash *waqf* as "the process of dedicating cash as *waqf* for lending it to identified borrowers without interest." Similarly, Zufar from Hanafi School defines cash *waqf* as investing money endowed as *waqf* and distributing the profit earned from investments to the specific charitable works. Despite slight variations in the definitions, there is a unanimous fatwa among classical scholars that cash *waqf* is permissible. With minor variations, however, their definitions come to a common point that cash *waqf* is a benevolent endowment fund formed with cash corpus, which is permanently dedicated to charitable activities and privately (Cizakça 2009) owned by a Muslim, or a group of Muslims, or a corporate body governed according to Shariah with perpetual dedication (Magda 2009) of its usufruct to be spent on any purpose recognized by Shariah. The definition of *waqf* in section 2 of the Waqfs Ordinance 1962 defines cash *waqf* as an endowment or grant fund that falls under the broader definition of *waqf* for the purposes mentioned in the Ordinance, as such cash *waqf* is deemed to be covered by the definition of *waqf*. Section 2(10) of the *Waqfs* Ordinance 1962 defines *waqf* as both movable and immovable assets dedicated for any purpose that falls within the Islamic jurisdictions. This definition includes any kind of benevolent endowment and/or grant provided by Muslim or non-Muslim and the endowment can be used for the creation of a *waqf*.

3   Main Features of Cash *Waqf*

The distinguishing features of cash *waqfs* are as follows:

Liquid Fund as Corpus: In a "cash *waqf*," the main corpus is a "cash capital" as opposed to standard immovable waqfs in which the corpus is usually a "real estate." Cizakca argues that irrespective of the debate on the legality of the cash *waqf* that started as early as sixteenth century, the fact remains that "cash *waqfs*" are being endowed worldwide and it is gaining acceptance and popularity to a wider audience. Any *corpus* should be *Waqf* able, as long as it gives some usufruct for others to benefit from it. In Bangladesh, many *waqf* lands have perished and disappeared by river erosion—nothing is non-perishable—an argument supports the propositions of cash *waqf*. Everything on the face of the earth is perishable (The Holy Quran, Surah Ar-Rahman:25). Simply by being perishable, a corpus does not lose its eligibility of being *Waqf* able so long Shariah approves it.

Immediate Usufruct: Unlike real estate, benefit from cash *waqf* follows almost immediately after creating it. An immovable property such as a piece of land may be worth millions but unless it is developed into an income generating project, it is unable to give any consistent benefit. Even a small amount of cash *waqf* may start generating income through investment right from its inception.

Affordability and Convenience: Buying real property and dedicating it as *waqf* is only affordable to the rich people. With cash *waqf*, it is much easy and affordable compared to real estate due to high expense and scarcity of immovable properties. Many Muslims who wish to contribute to the society through waqf cannot afford to buy an immovable property, i.e., land or real estate property because such properties are both expensive and scarce. Cash *waqf* brings that opportunity even to not-so-rich people who are willing to donate but have resource constraints.

Remarkable Mobility of Cash Waqf: It enables transfer of *waqf* capital across economic sectors simply by redirecting investments from one set of borrowers to another. This makes a huge difference in how we see *waqf* as a source of welfare for the poor. The core objective of creating a waqf, cash or otherwise, is to do a good deed by helping others. This objective is better achievable by cash *waqf*.

Benefits from Cash: *Waqf* can be delivered to various activities such as education, food, social, and religious services. When the *waqf* is in the form of cash corpus and such corpus is invested to grow, a regular usufruct can be earned and be spent for any welfare purposes. Such flexibility is not available when the *waqf* property is an immovable property such as land, particularly if the land is not being utilized and not producing regular harvests or otherwise earning a steady income from rentals, etc. If a land-based *waqf* is not at its best in terms of its location, size, and productivity, it is unable to be a steady source of regular usufruct and the land, despite its current value, lies worthless.

4   ECONOMIC VALUES OF CASH *WAQF*

The institution of a *wqāf* in general and the cash *waqf*, in particular, has brought multidimensional economic benefits to many Muslim nations throughout the Islamic history. Many essential services, which otherwise would have been an economic responsibility and burden on the state, were provided to the citizens at no cost to the state. The cash *waqf* makes charitable donations convenient for not only the affluent class of the society but also the middle and lower middle class who can only afford to donate a small amount of cash. As more people can contribute to cash *waqf* easily to build collective fund corpus or single fund, the objective of social welfare can be achieved faster with cash *waqf* than general *waqf*. This aspect of cash *waqf* acts as a helping hand by sharing some of the expenses of government that directly links to social safety net programs for the poor. In other words, cash *waqf* reduces both government expenditures and interest rate by taking care of some of the expenditures that government would have to spend under social safety program in the absence of cash *waqf*. Thereby, a cash *waqf*-based system can reduce and even eliminate riba by providing services. Cross-country experiences show that cash *waqf* significantly assists the government in economic development (Sanusi and Shafiai 2015).

In Bangladesh, one of the pioneers in Islamic banking is Islami Bank Bangladesh Limited (IBBL). IBBL introduced "Mudaraba *Waqf* Cash Deposit Account (MWCDA)" with special features that fulfill the specific purpose of a cash waqf without compromising Shariah values. This list of purposes is made readily available to the *wāqif* who can choose any specific purpose from the list or may request the bank to include a Shariah permitted specific purpose missing in the list. The list of purposes includes the following areas (IBBL Circular No. BCD/836 2004).

Family Rehabilitation: Individuals and institutions can create a cash *waqf* fund corpus for rehabilitating poor, homeless, and physically handicapped people who are ignored and hardly get any kind of support from the government.

Education and Culture: The purpose of this cash waqf is to provide formal and informal education for orphans and poor, development of proper education for skill development, support physical and vocational trainings, provide scholarship to the deserving students, conduct *da'wah* activities, patronage religious education and research, and establish educational chair.

Health and Sanitation: Health and sanitation purposes provide supports to improve sanitation conditions among the rural and urban slum dwellers. Health care services extend to underprivileged segment who do not have ability or access to standard health care services. Acute shortage of pure drinking water is one of the main causes of more than 200 diseases in Bangladesh. In the rural areas, the government has taken very limited initiatives that provide pure drinking water to the poor people; cash waqf has identified this purpose and allows to establish fund corpus that would support people to get drinking water. cash waqf fund also provides support to conduct research of any contagious disease, establish rural community clinic, provide free medical services, and distribute free medicines among the disadvantaged people.

Social Welfare Service: This includes providing legal aid for the deserving people in dispute settlement and assisting the marriage of poor girls. Newly converted Muslims can get support to cope with the transition process. Social welfare is not confined to the Muslim community; there are many projects to help non-Muslims who need financial, legal, and any other permissible assistance. Some cash waqf corpus such as tree plantation, urban beautification, developing public utility services, and discouraging anti-social activities have overall social welfare impact. The services mentioned above provided by IBBL through its cash waqf programs would have been otherwise the government's responsibility. These services through *aWqāf* would reduce the economic burden on the government.

5   CURRENT PRACTICES OF CASH *WAQF* IN BANGLADESH

The emergence of cash *waqf* in Bangladesh is an encouraging trend, and the degree of awareness on cash *waqf* in recent years in Bangladesh has been remarkable. Few Islamic banks in Bangladesh lead cash *waqf* practices. After the government of Bangladesh enacted the Private University Act of 1992, many private universities and higher learning institutions have been established in the country, a few of which are financed by cash *waqf*. One such institution is the Social Science Institute (SSI). SSI has an endowment fund which is a cash *waqf*. The cash *waqf* fund is kept in the investment fund of an Islamic bank, which operates based on *mudarabah*. Profits from mudarabah are spent for fulfilling some Islamic objectives laid down in the constitution of SSI. This is an encouraging trend for the rich segment of Muslims who may come forward and pool their fund to create cash *waqf* to help the disadvantageous population of the country. In this way, cash *waqf* may add a new dimension to the charity activities in the country.

6   CASH *WAQF*—AN ALTERNATIVE ISLAMIC FINANCING MODEL IN BANGLADESH

Islamic banks are the key providers of cash *waqf* services in Bangladesh. Many Islamic banks offer both conventional finance and microfinance services to people as per the Shariah laws. For instance, Social Islamic Bank Limited, in addition to its conventional Islamic banking activities, has developed special programs to manage the *waqf* and other religious institutions. SIBL started its operation in 1995 with clearly defined corporate objectives to operate in three different sectors—formal, non-formal, and voluntary. While formal sector deals with general commercial activities as a scheduled bank, non-formal sector aims at "Empowering Family" by creating investment opportunities for micro and SME clients. Its voluntary sector offers Cash *Waqf* Certificate Scheme which is an innovative financial product aimed at social welfare. The *waqf* properties are converted into income generating units and the income so derived is utilized as per instruction of the *Wāqif* or in the absence of such instructions, based on Islamic Shariah.

"*Mudaraba Waqf* Cash Deposit Account" (MWCDA) system is one of the key schemes of IBBL that directly promotes cash *waqf* services in the country. In this scheme, the deposited money is invested and the profit is spent in accordance with the will and wishes of the *wāqif* (IBBL Circular No. BCD/836 2004). The main objectives of the MWCDA scheme are as follows:

- to design and implement banking services that facilitate management of cash waqf;
- to create a platform that allows to pool savings from people and deposit it in a cash; waqf with a defined successor planning. This helps to augment the family bonding, especially among the family members of the well-off class of the society;
- to create sustainable social capital is one of the objectives of cash waqf. Cash waqf encourages people in social investments without expecting any monetary return from their investments except social well-being;
- to develop a resource distribution system that only cascades down to the poor benefiting them financially and socially;
- to make the rich segment of the society aware of its responsibilities and liabilities to the poor;
- to channel alternative sources of fund to the capital market through new investment vehicles; and
- to support the macro-level development initiatives of the government and integrate among different efforts that aim to bring together social security and social justice.

6.1 Operational Guidelines of Cash Waqf-Based Products Adopted by Some Islamic Banks in Bangladesh

Cash *waqf* deposit accounts have long been introduced by many Islamic banks in the country. All these banks have guidelines for operating these types of accounts that are convenient, customer-friendly, and motivational in promoting good deeds.

Cash Waqf-Based "Mudarabah Deposit Account"
IBBL, Exim Bank, Shahjalal Islami Bank, and Social Islami Bank—all have introduced "Mudaraba Cash *Waqf* Deposit" as a product that creates an opportunity for the wealthy people to invest in socially beneficial projects such as establishing educational institutions to increase literacy rate, arranging training programs to increase workforce skills,

providing free medical facilities to poor people. Income generated from the cash *waqf* fund is spent for different purposes chosen by the *Wāqif*.

The Objectives of Cash Waqf *Mudarabah Deposit Accounts (CWMDA)*

The following are the objectives for the cash *waqf*-based mudarabah deposit accounts:

- To assist the government in its overall development initiatives by establishing linkages among different parts and phases of development programs that would be otherwise difficult for the government to integrate due to resources constraint.
- To help people contributing to benevolent cash corpus by sharing expertise and developing knowledge. The ultimate objective is to establish a sustainable social capital platform that is transparent to all and dedicated to social capital stronger.
- To create a social investment ecosystem to alleviate poverty from the society.
- To motivate and remind the affluent group of the society about its responsibility and importance of its proactive engagement for overall social well-being.
- To establish links among different social initiatives so that social security does not become separated from social welfare.
- To give people necessary financial support to organize different religious events that increase morality of the participants.

Cash Waqf *in Perpetuity and Mutawalli's Discretions*

These Cash *Waqf* Mudarabah Deposit Accounts (CWMDA) are created in Perpetuity where cash is received from the *Wāqif* as an endowment fund and deposited the same in a mudarabah account. Banks get the authority to manage the cash *waqf* for the *Wāqif*. The *Wāqif* or the bank is not allowed to withdraw the principal deposit from the mudarabah account—principal deposit withdrawal is restricted. The *Wāqif* has the discretion to transfer the account or may nominate another bank to manage the cash waqf fund without compromising Shariah norms.

In his/her lifetime, the *Wāqif* is the mutawalli of cash *waqf*. A mutawalli has the authority and privilege to select the nominees and request the bank in writing about his/her decision. Mutawalli is not allowed to withdraw *waqf* deposit amount after the death of *Waqif*.

CWMDA Created with Lump Sum Amount or by Installments
Wāqif has a choice to create cash *waqf* with a lump sum amount given at once or on an installment basis. If the *Waqif* decides to deposit in cash *waqf* in multiple installments, he may initiate the *mudarabah* account by depositing the initial amount and thereafter may make the deposits in equal regular installments. If a *Waqif* decides to make all or part of the committed amount through advance installment, he may request the bank to accept such amount. If the *wāqif* fails to deposit one or more installments, under normal circumstances, he can deposit the past due installments. For calculating profit, banks use the total deposit received in the account till date. If a *Wāqif* fails to deposit for more than five times, the bank will not accept further deposit from him.

Issuance of CWMDA Certificate and Receipt
Wāqif deposits cash *waqf* amount using a specific endowment form. Once the bank receives the full amount of cash corpus from the *Wāqif*, it issues a certificate for the full amount. If a *Wāqif* decides to reduce the size of committed cash *waqf* corpus, or unable to deposit future installments, he may inform the bank about his pacific situation and declare his final size of the fund. The bank upon reviewing his application may decide to issue a certificate for the total amount credited to his mudarabah account till date.

How CWMDA Operates
CWMDA is a *mudarabah* account established under the legal contract between the depositor and the bank. The depositor is known as *Wāqif*/ owner of the fund and the bank is known as the business organizer or agent.

Investment in Conformity with Shariah
The bank is empowered to make all investment decisions of the cash *waqf* corpus at its own discretion ensuring Shariah compliance. The *waqif* has no rights to dictate or influence any investment decisions of the bank.

High Rate of Investment Income
The *Wāqif* gets up to 65% of the investment profits. Normally, profit sharing varies among cash *waqf* accounts. Bank decides the percentage of allocation based on weightage allocation of the deposit.

Distribution of Usufruct to the Beneficiaries
Banks use provisional profit rate to calculate and credit monthly profits into mudarabah accounts. Once the banks declare annual final profit rates, adjustments may be made to previous monthly profits to reflect actual annual profit percentage. Profit amounts can be withdrawn and spent for the purposes mentioned in the cash *waqf* contract. Only the designated persons can withdraw profits from the accounts and utilization of the profit amount must be per Shariah compliance. If any amount of profit remains unspent or unutilized, such amount will be accumulated with principal *waqf* amount. The *Wāqif* can give standing instruction to the bank to transfer specified installment from his/her account maintained with the branch. In such cases, the bank charges a minimal service charge from the *wāqif's* account.

Profit–Loss Sharing
Mudarabah account does not guarantee the protection of principal. As the account runs on profit–loss sharing basis, profit increases principal deposit amounts, and loss decreases the principal deposit amount.

Cash Waqf *Management Committee*
A special *Waqf* Management Committee comprising of the officials of the bank manages the cash *waqf* fund. The *waqf* management committee addresses all concerns, complaints, suggestions regarding the *waqfs* received from *Waqif* and or any other persons. The decision of the Committee is final.

Readily Available List of Purposes
The *Wāqif* can select any purpose from the list of purposes or may request the bank to create a new purpose which is Shariah permitted.

Family Rehabilitation
This includes providing lifesaving stuff to the people who are in a displaced situation and who need rehabilitation most. Lifesaving stuff includes food, water, shelter, medicine, and restoration of handicapped people.

Education, Sports, Da'wa and Culture
This includes providing education facilities to the orphans, such as supplying books, development of technical education for skill development

and vocational education in general, providing scholarships to deserving students and descendants, financing research and establishing educational chairs. Conducting Dawah activities by promoting Islamic culture and heritage. Celebrating different Islamic Festivals.

Health and Sanitation

This includes providing low-cost or free medical supports to the poor people who cannot afford to pay medical bills. The medical assistance to the poor is provided through specialized hospitals and community clinics established with cash *waqf*. Sanitation is a key concern for spreading many life-threatening diseases in rural areas and urban slums. Cash *waqf* fund provides financial support for proper sanitation and for the research in sanitation-related diseases.

Social Service

This includes providing legal aid to the poor and deserving people. Providing assistance to dowry-free marriage(s) to poor girls and their families, planting and preserving trees on street sides. Helping converted reverted Muslims with rehabilitation during their transition periods. Giving legal, financial, and social supports to people from other religions and races. Initiating participatory social awareness programs to make people aware of the bad impacts of drugs, gambling, child abuse, woman rights. Assist the government in the smooth delivery of social welfare services.

Arrangement After Serving the Specific Purpose or Death of Wāqif

When a *waqf* achieves its goal, the mudarabah account profit may be distributed as per the purpose mentioned in the *waqf* account. In the absence of any clearly defined profit allocation instruction, the matter may be taken to *Waqf* Management Committee for further guidance and final decision. If *Wāqif* dies, profit of the *waqf* account will be distributed as per the instructions of *Waqif*. If there is any doubt about how to spend the profit amount or in case there is any opaqueness, *Waqf* Management Committee will make the final decision. If there is any shortfall of the declared waqf amount, the family members and successors may deposit the gap amount.

Liabilities and Rights of the Bank

The banks carry limited liability in *waqf* management. The bank does not bear any loss arises due to any reason that is uncontrollable and cannot be resolved with proper due diligence and reasonable care. The examples of such events are electrical problems, mechanical issues, riots, acts of God, natural calamities, cybercrimes, civil wars, etc. The operation of *waqf* accounts is subject to the compliance of the Money Laundering Prevention Act, 2012, Anti-Terrorism Act, 2009 (including amendments in 2013), Shahriah guidelines, and other rules and regulations as presided by the regulatory authorities from time to time. All account-related charges such as VAT, Tax, excise duties, and other charges and fees are deducted as per the published schedule of charges of the banks.

Banks maintain the privacy and confidentiality of all accounts. Banks do not disclose any waqf account information, transaction profile to the third party unless asking third party is one of the following entities:

a. Regulatory agencies with authority to seek account-related information from banks.
b. Court orders the banks to disclose information to an authorized person.

7   Cross-Country Review of Cash *Waqf*

Cash *waqf* practice has been flourished in different parts of the world. To highlight the learning points from those countries, some of the countries are being briefly evaluated in this paper that includes Bahrain, India, Indonesia, Kuwait, Malaysia, Singapore, South Africa, Sudan, Turkey, and UK. Besides, World *Waqf* Fund under IDB and OPEC *Waqf* Fund will also be discussed briefly.

7.1   *Bahrain*

The Central Bank of Bahrain in collaboration with the Islamic Financial Institutions (IFIs) of Bahrain established the first cash *waqf* fund in 2006

Objectives of the Waqf *Fund*
The main objectives of this cash *waqf* fund are to provide support in the field of financial research, increase the quality of finance education, train people in Islamic finance, and create Islamic scholars. The fund has been actively contributing to industrial development and shaping the ways the markets should perform.

Contributors of Waqf *Fund*
The major banks and financial institutions of Bahrain contributed to establishing the *waqf* fund. The *waqf* corpus was collected from the participating institutions. The fund is invested through Shariah permitted money market instruments and profits earned on investments are distributed to meet the purposes of the Fund.

A Waqf Fund Sponsored Programs
Ever since its establishment, the *waqf* fund has been active in sponsoring some important flagship initiatives that include:

Human Capital Development in Islamic Finance
There is an acute global shortage of Islamic scholars who have a profound understanding of both the conventional and Islamic finance. To take the movement of Islamic finance forward, a clear understanding of Islamic principles and different Shariah laws is crucial. To address these issues, *waqf* fund of Bahrain distributes its profit in Islamic scholar development programs which train people to lead the way of Islamic finance. The Accounting and Auditing Organization for IFIs is one such organization that operates Certified Islamic Professional Accountant (CIPA) and has been successful in its endeavor to create some quality Islamic scholars who are now very respected both in the field of Islamic finance and in the field of conventional finance.

Besides, the Fund has also been instrumental in organizing various other human capital development programs that include launching a training program for the senior management officials to qualify them as Islamic finance leaders. *Waqf* fund also holds Corporate Governance Workshop for CEOs and Directors.

Research and Collaboration with Other Nations
As part of its support for Islamic finance training, education, and research, the *waqf* fund hosts and sponsors regular dialogue, monthly conferences, and special sessions with leading Shariah and Islamic finance scholars. The *waqf* fund sponsors government collaboration with other Muslim and non-Muslim nations in the field of Islamic finance.

Curriculum Development
The *waqf* fund is playing a crucial role in developing the curriculum for Islamic financial services sector. The Fund in collaboration with the

University of Bahrain has launched a Shahriah-based bachelor degree program in banking and finance and providing financial assistance to the students. To the create skilled personnel for the Shariah internal revenue department, the fund is planning to initiate a diploma program.

7.2   Indonesia

A nonprofit organization under the Ministry of Religious Affairs in Indonesia has turned the concept of cash *waqf* into a movement. A group of Indonesian journalists established the nonprofit organization named Dompet Dhuafa Republika (DDR) to raise a pool of fund for the welfare of the poor through *zakat, Infaq, Sadaqah, and Waqf* (ZISWAF). Though informally established in 1993, DDR was registered in October 2001 with the government as National Zakat Institution (Lembaga Amil Zakat) under the auspices of the Ministry of Religious Affairs.

DDR Cash Waqf Fund

DDR then created a waqf fund named Indonesian *waqf* fund (Tabung Wakaf Indonesia) with a four-layer network of welfare program, that includes Health care, Education, Economy, and Social Development.

Health Care

DDR has established several health care institutions to serve the poor patients. Under this program, they have a hospital named Rumah Sehat Terpadu (RST) equipped with inpatient and outpatient services including surgery and intensive care units. Located in Bogor, West Java this hospital provides health care services free of charge for the poor who are unable to afford adequate health care. This hospital serves more than 50,000 patients a year.

They have also established a free clinic named "Layanan Kesehatan Cuma Cuma" that provides medical services to the poor patients who do not need to be admitted to hospital. Many Muslim doctors give voluntary services to this clinic.

Education

DDR helps deserving Indonesian children to pursue their education and provide them regular stipend under scholarship programs. Under this division, several training schools and business schools are run, such as "Sekolah SMART Ekselensia Indonesia" and "Umar Usman Business School" which has a campus named Prophetic Entrepreneur Campus where they introduced a special entrepreneurship program. Their training schools also offer "Character Building Trainings."

Economic Empowerment and Social Welfare
DDR has various empowerment programs to reduce poverty in Indonesia and create entrepreneurs who are otherwise less privileged. In return, these entrepreneurs are gaining the ability to contribute to the social development later by themselves. DDR works on disaster management migrant workers welfare, da'wah activities, free funeral services, and many other voluntary services.

7.3 Kuwait

In Kuwait, the *waqf*, whether cash or non-cash, is aimed at contributing to the efforts intended to serve the revitalization of the *waqf* practice and tradition by putting forward developmental projects in Islamic forms to fulfill the needs of the society. This aim is usually achieved by requesting the people to donate cash funds or to other norms of assets as *waqf*. These *waqf* funds are managed and overseen by Kuwait *AWqāf* Public Foundation (KAPF) to meet the social as well as developmental needs as addressed by various action programs. These action programs grant waqf authority an allowance for achieving the highest developmental return and to help achieve the connection among the *waqf* projects. In addition to the projects run by the *AWqāf* Public Foundation (KAPF), there are many other *waqf* projects undertaken by the Government Agencies and the Associations of Public Benefit.

Objectives of Kuwait AWqāf *Public Foundation (KAPF)*
The KAPF has set several objectives of *waqf* funds, which are outlined below:

- to restore and revitalize the practice and tradition of *waqf* by calling for projects which are closer to the hearts of the people and more responsive to their needs,
- to renew and modernize the developmental role of the *waqf*,
- to advance the charity work by introducing a new model to be followed as an example,

- to meet the needs of the society and the citizens in the domains, which are not properly subsidized,
- to create a balance between external charity work and the internal one,
- to bring into effect the popular participation in the call for waqf and managing its projects, and
- to start off the waqf work through an "Organization" that fulfills flexibility as well as disciplinary requirements at the same time.

Waqf *Fund Board of Directors*

Cash *waqf* funds in Kuwait are governed by Board of Directors consisting several popular and eminent persons chosen by the President of *Waqfs* Affairs Council. This council is permitted to add representatives of some Government Agencies interested in the areas of work of the fund. The Board is appointed for two years with the possibility of further renewal of term. The Board shall choose a Chairman and two Vice-Chairmen from the members. The Board of Directors is assisted by a fund manager, who is appointed by the Secretary-General. The Secretary-General is chosen from the general staff of the KAPF. He must be an ex-officio member of the Board of Directors and would act as the Secretary of the Board. An assistant to the Director may be appointed, according to the needs of the project.

7.4   Malaysia

Malaysia practices both general *waqf* and cash *waqf*. The *waqf* management process in Malaysia is to some extent different from other countries. *Waqf* fund in Malaysia is controlled by several regulations. The Islamic Religious Council, which consists of 13 states as well as several federal territories, mainly controls the *waqf* and cash *waqf* funds (Mashitoh Mahamood, *Waqf* in Malaysia: Legal and Administrative Perspective 2006). Due to differences in state laws, fund management regulations vary from fund to fund, which creates the standardization, uniformity, and comparability issues.

Public Response to Cash Waqf *in Malaysia*

Studies reveal that cash *waqf* is not yet a popular financial vehicle in Malaysia (Ismail Abdel Mohsin 2009). Study of Mohsin shows that people are not fully aware and responsive of cash *waqf* even though the size of cash *waqf* is quite big. That means a small group of people and institutions are aware of cash waqf in Malaysia. Many people believe that cash *waqf* fund managers engage the fund in leverage activities and to buy immovable property through both the acceptability and public response to cash *waqf* concept and its management have increased in recent years, still, considerable efforts are required to further strengthen practices of *waqf* in the Islamic economic system. On the other hand, the study of Arshad (2011) on Malaysian waqf and perception of people about the concept finds that most of the people still believe cash *waqf* is a way of collecting fund for construction of mosque and donation of land for graveyard. The concept of cash *waqf* is narrowly understood by most of the Malaysian. The study of Laldin (2005) was quite similar to the study of Arshad. Laldin also finds that donors of Malaysia hardly understand any differences among *waqf, zakat,* and *sadaqah.* However, subsequent developments, as discussed in the following paragraph, suggest otherwise and this author is of the view that the future of cash *waqf* in Malaysia looks very promising.

Potential for Cash Waqf in Malaysia
Some studies find the future of cash *waqf* in Malaysia very promising. For example, Salleh and Muhammad (2008) found that the amount of cash *waqf* in a given year would be RM4.3billion, if each Malaysian muslin donates only RM1 a day for consecutive 30 days. They further revealed that the Penang state is most likely to do better in cash *waqf* in the long run because it has developed the strategic goals and integrated the value propositions with the goals.

Another research (Sayyin and Suyurno 2006) stated that shares schemes of Selangor *waqf* can significantly contribute to the development of cash *waqf* system in Malaysia. The study of Siti Mashitoh Mahamood presents the cash *waqf* scenario in Malaysia from popularity aspects. He concludes that it is not yet a very popular concept in the country (Mahamood 2007).

Cash Waqf Shares and the State Islamic Religious Council (SIRC)
Most of the State Islamic Religious Council support cash *waqf* concept in Malaysia. Out of the nine councils, only two have reservations about the practice of cash *waqf* (Ismail Abdel Mohsin 2009). Shares and stocks are the most popular instruments through which majority of the cash *waqf* transactions happen in Malaysia. Buyers of the cash *waqf* shares buy the shares and

give those shares to councils as *waqf*. If the council wants, it may sell cash waqf shares of existing assets or potential assets to the interested buyers who will then endow purchased shares to the council (Mahamood 2006).

7.5   Singapore

Syed Omar Aljunied who came to Singapore from Indonesia established the first cash *waqf* fund in the country. In 1905, the first *waqf* legislation was enacted in Singapore under both the Muslim and Hindu endowments rules. In fact, philanthropists like Syed Omar Aljunied created not only mosques but also revenue stream to ensure that these mosques have income generating sources for their maintenance and religious activities. These philanthropists had developed a socioreligious enterprise model, which is now becoming a new trend in charity and nonprofit enterprises.

Cash Waqf by Salary Deduction

However, *waqf* in the form of cash is found to be unique here in Singapore, and the cash *waqf* fund there included mostly the Mosque Building Fund. Under this kind of cash *waqf* philosophy, every Muslim employee donates a fixed amount to the fund on a regular interval. As of July 1, 2005, cash *waqf* funds received a donation from around 175,000 Muslims. Their contribution was deducted from their monthly salary by their employer and then channeled it through the Central Provident Fund.

As of the same date as mentioned earlier, the fund received an estimated $6 million contribution annually from those Muslim employees. This fund has enabled *waqf* authority to build 22 mosques with an accumulated amount of $130 million. In fact, the act of creating a *waqf* from a pool of fund to build mosques is proven to be excellent instruments. These instruments have been used to generate income streams to meet the mosques related operational costs.

7.6   Turkey

The concept of *waqf* has always been widely diversified in Turkey. During the fifteenth and sixteenth centuries, the Ottoman Courts first approved a special type of cash endowment fund dedicated to fulfilling social purposes (Cizakça 2004). Most of the *waqf* funds in turkey is backed by land property, which ensures continuous charity of the *waqf* and reduces uncertainty. Later, many movable properties backed *waqf* funds were created.

Public Facilities Supported by Cash Waqf

It was the Ottoman period when Turkey had its golden period in *waqf* and cash *waqf*. Most of the public services including education, social welfare, public utility, religious activities were supported by cash *waqf*. As a result, the government could concentrate on other areas for development knowing that many of the public works would be taking care of by the *waqf* funds. To make a comparison between the current situation of *waqf* with that of Ottoman period, we can say that most of the educational expenses of modern Turkey are directly supported by the government whereas in Ottoman period educational services were met from *waqf* funds.

Financial Services Provided by Cash Waqf

Cash *waqf* acted as a reliable source of fund that kept the credit flow alive and eased many of the intricate financial services. The study conducted by Cizakça estimated that around 10% of the population of Bursa city took financial services or borrowed money from cash *waqf* funds. Every cash *waqf* had defined purposes which directly contributed to the greater social well-being as well as had a lasting impact on the society. Some of the most recognized purposes of cash *waqf* were spending money to support education, supplying food and water to the poor, providing medical services to the disadvantaged people, giving legal assistance, making payments to bail someone from jail.

Revenue Earned by Cash Waqf

The way cash *waqf* practiced in Turkey raised many questions regarding cash *waqf's* validity under the jurisdiction of Shariah law. Many scholars argued that profit earning scheme of cash *waqf* is very much like usurious piety—activity that supports usury in the name of Shariah (Islahi 2007)! For example, in Turkey earning profit from cash *waqf* money became primary and social well-being became a secondary objective of cash *waqf*.

Cash Waqf and the Debate on Interest

There are many arguments that cash *waqf* is against the law of Islamic Shariah as it's directly involved in money making business. There are many instances of cash *waqf* being used as an instrument for usury under the veil of Islam. Proponents of cash *waqf* did not deny the allegation of riba business opportunity in cash *waqf*, but defended that as per Shariah law there is nothing harmful in cash *waqf* and if we properly follow the Shariah law, it should not conflict with Islamic economic system—it's all about how an individual manages the cash *waqf* and the purpose he wants to achieve with cash *waqf*.

8   ROLE OF CASH *WAQF* IN POVERTY ALLEVIATION

Since the concept of *waqf* is similar to trust and endowments of cash resources, cash *waqf* has widespread usability. Unfortunately, like most people of Malaysia, the concept of cash *waqf* has been narrowly understood in Bangladesh. At present, most of the *waqfs* are real estate backed, which gives people the sense of tangible permanence. There were instances in history when cash *waqf* concept had widespread acceptability. The example of Ottoman Empire provides sufficient evidences about the considerable impact of cash *waqf* on the social systems. Cash *waqf* is very liquid and can quickly fulfill the needs of the target group. Cash *waqf* can be tailored to meet many types of needs including addressing of the special situations which are not possible to address by real estate backed *waqf* due to time constraint. The cash *waqf* concept is very interesting but requires specified purposes and strict compliance to avoid any deviation from Islamic Shariah. Arguably, there is a slim distance between business profit from cash *waqf* and *riba* from loans. Therefore, the controller and manager of cash *waqf* must apply proper care to ensure full of the compliance with Shariah laws.

9   RECOMMENDED CASH *WAQF* MODEL FOR BANGLADESH

The cash *waqf* concept can be applied to achieve numerous social objectives that are Shariah allowed and that fall within the jurisdiction of Islamic economic systems. The aspect of liquidity is the main strength and weakness of cash *waqf*. The sensitivity of cash *waqf*, which can be turned into riba business or speculation if profit motive gets priority over social welfare. Though cash *waqf* fund does not belong to the *Waqif* or to the person who manages it, sometimes financial greed overtakes our moral values and transgressions happen. *Waqif* assets should be preserved in a way that maximizes social welfare. To avoid conflict of interest, we

Fig. 1   Existing path of cash waqf

Fig. 2   Recommended path of cash waqf

recommend the presence of an independent line of authority between *Waqif* and *waqf* manager for capital market and private investment to make the entire process more transparent. As of today, we have not seen any dedicated cash *waqf* for the capital market, private equity, and venture capital investment in Bangladesh. Although different countries have already applied cash *waqf* in several areas including microcredit, SME (Mohd Thas Thaker et al. 2016). Cash *waqf* in Bangladesh is mainly a banking product and a money market instrument limited within few Islamic banks and the conventional banks with their Islamic banking wings. To get most out of the cash *waqf* fund, we recommend inclusion of other institutions in the management of the *waqf*. One study in Jordan finds that developing cash *waqf* into a financial instrument for microfinance is more effective to finance small projects, which play important role in alleviation of unemployment (Alani et al. 2016). Figures 1 and 2 presented in recommendation sections show the existing and proposed channels of cash *waqf* flow.

Recommendation 1: We recommend creation of additional paths for more diversified flow of cast *waqf* to fulfill its purposes. Mobilizing cash *waqf* fund using different investment vehicles will increase the acceptability of cash *waqf*. To create more cash *waqf* investment channels, it is important that reputed institutions should come forward and regulatory authorities should develop a legal framework that addresses the trust issue of the prospective *Waqifs* (Johari et al. 2015).

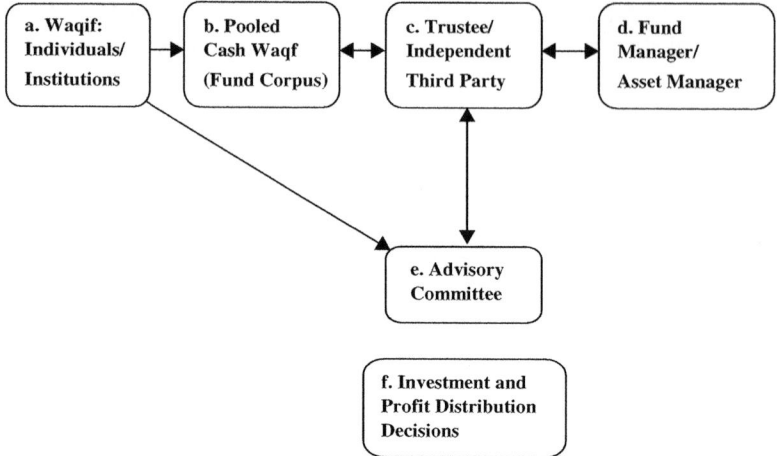

Fig. 3   Cash waqf governance model

Recommendation 2: Governance model of cash *waqf* recommends monitoring of the fund through Trustee/Independent third party. Implementation of efficient collection method and distribution strategies of *waqf* determine the success of cash *waqf* management (Sanusi and Shafiai 2015). We recommend this step especially for capital market and alternative investments. Banks use mudarabah deposit accounts to accept cash *waqf* fund from different sources, make their own investment decisions, and mobilize fund from pooled deposits to the selected sectors. The process of making investment decision of a bank is widely accepted unless there are any special circumstances that make the presence of trustee inevitable, there is generally no need of a trustee for a cash *waqf* if the fund flows through banks and financial institutions. Figure 3 shows the governance mechanism of capital market and alternative investment cash *waqf* funds;

   a. **Waqif: Individuals/Institutions**—At the invitation of fund manager/asset manager who is authorized by the Securities and Exchange Commission of Bangladesh to collect cash waqf fund from eligible persons/entities capital market/alternative, Waqif commits to give money in cash waqf corpus. Fund manager clearly prescribes the purposes of the fund, portfolio selection process, and provides other relevant information in the information memorandum (IM) of cash waqf fund.

b. **Fund Corpus**—The realized individual subscriptions and commitment together form the fund corpus. Whether a cash waqf fund is open ended or closed ended must be declared in the IM.

c. **Trustee/Independent Third Party**—The subscription money will be collected through a Trustee/Independent third party who is also the custodian of the fund corpus. The trustee will maintain the fund in a dedicated bank account and only disburse fund to the purposes that meet the terms of the contract between Waqifs and fund manager.

d. **Fund Manager/Asset Manager**—The fund manager will select and analyze the portfolio companies and forward their selection decisions to the advisory committee for approvals. Depending on the nature of investments, the committee may give blanket approval to fund manager. For example, for mutual fund operations, obtaining decisions on a daily basis is hardly possible. In such case, the committee may review their blanket approval at a regular interval.

e. **Advisory Committee**—Advisory committee will be acting like a Shariah committee who will not only approve the portfolio proposals of Fund manager but also make full compliance with Islamic laws. An advisory committee can be formed with a combination of the Waqifs, Islamic scholars, and capital market experts.

f. **Investments and Profit Distribution Decisions**—Once investment portfolios generate profits, fund manager distributes the realized profits to the cash waqf and advisory committee make the allocation of the profits to the intended purposes.

10   CONCLUSION

It has been regretfully observed that there is no initiative at all from the Office of the *Waqf* administration in Bangladesh to introduce and nurture cash *waqf* practices in the country. As such this research has focused on private and non-government initiatives for cash *waqf* developments in the country. Some of the private Islamic banks have come up with some products on cash *waqf*. However, these products are not enough to bring this practice to the doorsteps of the greater audiences who are willing to donate are not aware of cash *waqf* concept at all. This paper has discussed the current situations of cash *waqf* in Bangladesh and argued for the need of modern and innovative approach toward *a Wqāf* in general and cash *waqf* in particular reviewing lessons from selected countries including Bahrain, Indonesia, Kuwait, Malaysia, Singapore, and Turkey. A brief discussion of the role of cash *waqf* in poverty alleviation is also provided in the later section of this paper.

The purpose of this paper was by no means to deal with cash *waqf* comprehensively because the scope of this research does not warrant that. This research attempts to show where does the country stand in terms of cash *waqf* practices and to draw lessons from those countries as cash *waqf* holds a lot of potential for an overpopulated country like Bangladesh where the prospects for creating land-based *waqf* have been narrowed down substantially.

Our cross-country review of cash *waqf* practices represents a combination of countries with different demographics, such as an overpopulated country like Indonesia; Muslim-minority countries like Singapore; and affluent Muslim nations like Bahrain, Kuwait, Malaysia, and Turkey. Our finding shows that cash waqf practices in these countries address different welfare needs of the deserving sections of population and sectors of these countries. We also find the examples of cash *waqf*-based projects from these nations that irrespective of a country's economic and demographic standing; cash *waqf* can play its role of welfare not only for the poor and unprivileged population segment but also for the affluent segment of the population.

References

Alani, A., Algodah, M. T. S., & Alshwaiyat, M. S. (2016). Role of Waqf (Endowment) Funds in Financing Small Projects. *Global Business and Management Research: An International Journal, 8*(2), 14L.

Cizakça, M. (2004). *Incorporated Cash Waqfs and Mudaraba, Islamic Non-bank Financial Instruments from the Past to the Future.* Istanbul, Turkey: Bahcesehir University.

Cizakça, M. (2009). *Incorporated Cash Waqfs: Islamic Non-banking Financial Instruments From the Past to the Future.* INCIEF, 16.

IBBL Circular No. BCD/836. (2004). Dhaka: Islami Bank Bangladesh Limited.

Islahi, A. A. (2007). Cash Waqf: Is It a Usurious Piety? *Hiwar al-Arba'a', 27–30.

Ismail Abdel Mohsin, M. (2009). *Cash Waqf a New Financial Product* (p. 16.). Petaling Jaya, Selangor: Prentice Hall.

Johari, F., Alias, H., Shukor, S. A., Wahab, K. A., Aziz, R. A., Ahmad, N., et al. (2015). Factors That Influence Repeat Contribution of Cash Waqf in Islamic Philanthropy. *Malaysian Accounting Review, 14*, 55–78.

Magda. (2009). *Cash Waqf: A New Financial Product*. Petaling Jaya, Selangor: Prentice Hall.

Mahamood, S. M. (2006). *Waqf in Malaysia: Legal and Administrative Perspective* (p. 36). Kuala Lumpur, Malaysia: University of Malaya Press.

Mahamood, S. M. (2007). Pembentukan Dana Wakaf Menurut Perspektif Syariah Undang Undang Serta Aplikasinya di Malaysia. *Jurnal Syariah, 15*(2), 61–83.

Mohd Thas Thaker, M. A. B., Mohammed, M. O., Duasa, J., & Abdullah, M. A. (2016). The Behavioral Intention of Micro Enterprises to Use the Integrated Cash Waqf Micro Enterprise Investment (ICWME-I) Model as a Source of Financing. *Gadjah Mada International Journal of Business, 18*(2), 111–130.

Ottoman Cash Waqf Revisited: The Case of Bursa. (2004). Foundation of Science Technology and Civilization (FSTC).

Salleh, S., & Muhammad, S. (2008). Waqf Development in Malaysia Issues and Challenges. *Jurnal Pengurusan Jawhar, 2*, 13–37.

Sanusi, S., & Shafiai, M. H. (2015). The Management of Cash Waqf: Toward Socio-Economic Development of Muslims in Malaysia. *Jurnal Pengurusan, 43*, 3–12.

Sayyin, B., & Suyurno, S. (2006). *Pengenalan Kepada Konsep Wakaf dalam Islam* (p. 46). Kuala Lumpur: Ampang Press Sdn Bhd.

Stencel, S., Useem, A., Miller, T., & Tisdale, S. (2009). *Mapping the Global Muslim Population*. Washington, DC: Pew Research Center.

The Holy Quran. (n.d.). Surah Ar-Rahman:25.

CHAPTER 6

The Role of *Waqf* (Endowment) in Economic Development of Bosnia and Herzegovina: A Historical Overview and Future Prospects

Waqf and Socio-Economic Development

Edib Smolo

1   INTRODUCTION

Quran does not mention *waqf* (endowment) in specific terms. However, a number of verses encourage Muslims to do good deeds and promote charitable activities. This was also promoted by the Sunnah (sayings and actions) of the Prophet (p.b.u.h.). In fact, the institution of *waqf* was established by the Prophet (p.b.u.h.) by which a Muslim is seeking Allah's pleasure. In general, *waqf* is a form of charity (*sadaqah*) that is encouraged in Islam. The Prophet (p.b.u.h.) especially encouraged people to invest in what is called "perpetual charity" or "*sadaqah jari-yyah*." Abu Hurayrah (r.a.) reported: The Messenger of Allah (ﷺ) said, "*When a man dies, his deeds come to an end except for three things:*

E. Smolo (✉)
SARAYCON—Saray Consultancy for Socially Responsible
and Ethical Finance, Sarajevo, Bosnia and Herzegovina

© The Author(s) 2019   85
K. M. Ali et al. (eds.), *Revitalization of Waqf*
for Socio-Economic Development, Volume I,
https://doi.org/10.1007/978-3-030-18445-2_6

Sadaqah Jariyah (perpetual charity); a knowledge which is beneficial, or a virtuous descendant who prays for him (for the deceased)."[1]

His *ashab* (companions) implemented this practice of *waqf* and passed it to next generations. According to some documents, there was no companion of the Prophet (p.b.u.h.) that did not form a *waqf* in one way or the other. This practice continued to live among Muslims ever since and until these days countless number of *awqāf* properties exist in the world.

The *waqf* institution was most central in financing socioreligious and public welfare systems during the early days of Islam. More importantly, the contribution of philanthropic *waqf* effectively sponsored and maintained the social welfare of the Muslim Ummah in general. Gradually, however, the creation of this type of *waqf* degenerated and today, by and large, the *waqf* consists of religious kind (Mahmud and Shah 2009).

When it comes to Bosnia and Herzegovina, the *waqf* institution was introduced to the local community with the arrival of the Ottomans in the fifteenth century. The local population accepted Islam as their religion and implemented its teachings in their everyday life. Consequently, the *waqf* propertied became widely spread and used for the socio-economic development of the country. In this paper, we will try to briefly discuss the establishment and development of the *waqf* institution in Bosnia and Herzegovina and shortly elaborate different historical and sociopolitical phases that it went through up until now.

The paper consists of five sections including the introduction. Section 2 briefly defines the term *waqf* and provides its general classification. Section 3 discusses in more details the institution of *waqf* and its emergence in Islam. Section 4 is the main section of the paper as it focuses primarily on the *waqf* institution in Bosnia and Herzegovina. Finally, Sect. 5 is reserved for concluding remarks.

2   DEFINING *WAQF* (ENDOWMENT)

Literally, *waqf* (plural *awqāf*) means to stop, to hold, to restrain, to detain, or to prevent, such as saying "preventing from disposition" (al-Zuhayli 2007, p. 133). The term *habs* (plural *ahbas*) and its infinitive *tahbīs* is also used in the same sense, i.e., devoting in the way of Allah

---

[1] Reported in *Sahih Muslim*, see El-Munziri (2004, p. 951).

(fi sabil Allah). Hence, in Arabic a ministry of endowments would be called *vazīrah al-awkāf*. However, in Morocco, for example, this ministry is called *vazīrah al-ahbās* (see Ibn Ābidīn, pp. 357–358; Tuhmaz 1424/2003, p. 413).

In Islamic law, *waqf* refers to an irrevocable confinement of a wealth or a property (movable or immovable) by a founder(s) and dedication of its usufruct in perpetuity to the public or to the family with the overriding objective of getting closer to Allah. In other words, the term *waqf* refers to assets that are donated, bequeathed, or purchased for the purpose of being held in perpetual trust as ongoing charity (*sadaqah jāriyah*) or for a general or specific cause that Islam regards as socially beneficial. This condition of perpetuity has led over the years to a considerable accumulation of societal wealth such that *awqāf* has become an important sector dedicated to the social and economic improvement of the Muslim society (Abdul Kader and Dahlan 2009; Dafterdar 2009).

Although there are several types of *waqf*, usually they can be classified into following three categories, namely:

a. *waqf khayri* or public *waqf*;
b. *al-waqf al-ahli* or family *waqf*; and
c. *al-waqf al-mushtarak* or a combination of a public and a family *waqf* (Abdel Mohsin 2009).

3   The Institution of *Waqf* in Islam

The institution of *waqf* was first founded and became known with the advent of Islam as it was not known to the Arabs of the *Jahiliyyah* period (period of ignorance and before Islam). It is considered as a *sunnah* of the Prophet (p.b.u.h.) by which a Muslim is seeking Allah's pleasure. In general, *waqf* is a form of charity (*sadaqah*) that is encouraged in Islam. The Prophet (p.b.u.h.) especially encouraged people to invest in what is called "perpetual charity" or "*sadaqah jariyyah*." Abu Hurayrah (r.a.) reported: The Messenger of Allah (ﷺ) said, "*When a man dies, his deeds come to an end except for three things: Sadaqah Jariyah (perpetual charity); a knowledge which is beneficial, or a virtuous descendant who prays for him (for the deceased).*"[2]

---

[2] Reported in *Sahih Muslim*, see El-Munziri (2004, p. 951).

Although the term *waqf* is not directly mentioned in the text of the Holy Quran, *waqf* derives its validity from the general directives of the Quran exhorting Muslims to be benevolent and charitable toward the social causes. For instance, the Quran says: "*What you can spare of your wealth as should benefit the parents, the relatives, the orphans, the needy, the wayfarers for Allah is not unaware of the good deeds that you do.*"[3] In another verse, it states: "*By no means shall you attain right-eousness unless you give of that which you love; and whatever you give, of a truth God knows it well.*"[4] In addition, the following verse further encourages Muslims to give what of the good things they have when it says: "*O you who believe! Give of the good things which you have law-fully earned ...*"[5]

Furthermore, a proof of its Shariah validity can be found in the Sunnah (practice) and hadith (saying or tradition) of the Prophet (p.b.u.h.) who is considered as the best example (*uswatun hasanatun*) for the Ummah (Muslim community). Leading by example, he started building social infrastructure on the basis of *waqf*. For instance, he erected the first mosque (Quba') in Madinah, on a parcel of land made *waqf* by two orphans. These two pioneers in making Islamic *waqf*, in spite of the Prophet's insistence on paying them for their land, refused it and stated that that they would claim its reward from Allah in the next world. This mosque now stands on the same plot with a new and enlarged structure. In addition, in his last will the Prophet (p.b.u.h.) dedicated all his belongings to the Muslim Ummah and forbade his legal heirs from inheriting anything after his death. He only left small portions (sustenance) needed for their everyday life.

His *ashab* (companions) followed his example. As a result, a number of *waqf* properties have been established during the Prophet (p.b.u.h.) lifetime, and this practice continued even after his demise. Among the first *ashab* that created a *waqf* property was 'Umar (r.a.). In a hadith reported in Sahih al-Bukhari and narrated by Ibn 'Umar (r.a.) is stated: "When 'Umar got a piece of land in *Khaibar*, he came to the Prophet (ﷺ) saying, "I have got a piece of land, better than which I have never got. So what do you advise me regarding it?" The Prophet (ﷺ) said,

---

[3] Al-Baqarah: 215.

[4] Al-i-'Imran: 92.

[5] Al-Baqarah: 267.

"*If you wish you can keep it as an endowment to be used for charitable purposes.*" So, Umar gave the land in charity (i.e. as an endowments on the condition that the land would neither be sold nor given as a present, nor bequeathed (and its yield) would be used for the poor, the kinsmen, the emancipation of slaves, Jihad, and for guests and travelers; and its administrator could eat in a reasonable just manner, and he also could feed his friends without intending to be wealthy by its means."[6]

Sahih al-Bukhari reported another hadith narrated by Enes (r.a.), which states: "Abu Talha had the greatest wealth of date-palms amongst the Ansar in Medina, and he prized above all his wealth (his garden) Bairuha, which was situated opposite the Mosque (of the Prophet (ﷺ))". The Prophet used to enter it and drink from its fresh water. When the following Divine Verse came: "*By no means shall you attain piety until you spend of what you love,*" (3.92) Abu Talha got up saying. "O Allah's Messenger (ﷺ)! Allah says, '*You will not attain piety until you spend of what you love,*' and I prize above all my wealth, Bairuha' which I want to give in charity for Allah's Sake, hoping for its reward from Allah. So you can use it as Allah directs you." On that the Prophet (ﷺ) said, "*Bravo! It is a profitable (or perishable) property. (Ibn Maslama is not sure as to which word is right, i.e. profitable or perishable.) I have heard what you have said, and I recommend that you distribute this amongst your relatives.*" On that Abu Talha said, "O Allah's Messenger (ﷺ)! I will do (as you have suggested)." So, Abu Talha distributed that garden amongst his relatives and cousins."[7] This was the first family *waqf* in the Muslim history.[8]

---

[6] See El-Buhari (2009), Sahih al-Bukhari, Hadith No. 2772 (p. 614).

[7] See El-Buhari (2009), Sahih al-Bukhari, Hadith No. 2769 (p. 612).

[8] Similar examples have been realized from the creation of the companions of the Prophet (p.b.u.h.) as has been documented by Al-Humaidi, *shaykh* of al-Bukhari, who gave the names of the companions, their endowments, and their beneficiaries. He stated that Caliph Abu Bakr endowed his house to his children, 'Omar b. al-Khatab endowed his land at Thamgh to his children, Sa'd ibn Abu Waqqas his house in Madinah and Egypt for his children, and al-Zubair ibn al-'Awwam his houses in Makkah and Egypt and his money in Madinah for his children, 'Omar b. al-'As his house in Makkah for his children, and Hakim b. Hizam his houses in Makkah and Madinah to his children. Moreover, most of the wives of the Prophet (p.b.u.h.) had created family *waqf*, for example, 'Aisha, Umm Salamah, Umm Habibah, Safiah and Hafsah created their own *waqf* for the benefit of their kin (see Abdel Mohsin 2009).

The above *hadith*, as pointed out by Abdel Mohsin (2009), lists down a number of rules related to the *waqf*. First, once the property becomes a *waqf*, it must not be sold or inherited or given away as a gift. Second, it is up to the founder to specify beneficiary(ies), either person(s) or institution(s) he feels need it more, i.e., either to the public or to his family. In this case, Caliph 'Umar devoted it to both public and family. Third, the administration of the *waqf* is also clarified since the founder, he himself administers his own *waqf* and at the same time he can benefit from it in a reasonable manner as long as he lives.

Hence, the institution of *waqf* is a *sunna* established by the Prophet (p.b.u.h) that played a remarkable role in the socio-economic development of Muslim societies: for centuries and in assisting them in providing all the essential services such as financing and supporting health and educational sectors; supplying basic infrastructures such as roads, water canals, and bridges; financing and sustaining mosques, schools, universities, hospitals, and other public utility charitable institutions; creating jobs; enhancing commercial and business activities; providing food for the hungry and shelter for the poor and the needy; and supporting agricultural and industrial sectors. On top of that, all these services by *waqf* properties and institutions were carried out without any cost to the government (Abdel Mohsin 2009; Čajlaković 2009; Esmaeili 2009; Saleem 2009).

Historically speaking, the nonprofit institution of *waqf* soon became a model for socio-economic development of Muslim societies throughout the world wherever Islam was introduced and accepted by people. In fact, the *waqf* institution offered many services that the modern welfare state today strives to offer. However, over the years and especially since the end of the nineteenth century, the role of the *waqf* as an effective tool for socio-economic development had been deteriorated, neglected, and often forgotten. This can be attributed to a number of reasons including, but not limited to the legacy of colonization of Muslim countries, centralization, confiscation, and abolishment of *waqf* properties by both Muslim and non-Muslim governments, just to name a few. As a result, creation of new *waqf* properties is almost nonexistent as very few are donated nowadays. In addition, we can witness a dormant nature of many *waqf* assets. Over the years, "a large number of *awqāf* properties were expropriated, lost, or remained undeveloped or under-utilized and the latent wealth of *awqāf* remains largely untapped" (Abdel Mohsin 2009; Dafterdar 2009).

4 THE ROLE OF *WAQF* IN ECONOMIC DEVELOPMENT OF BOSNIA AND HERZEGOVINA

Historically speaking and as mentioned briefly above, the institution of *waqf* played a very important role in the socio-economic development of the Muslim world. The same is true when we consider Bosnia and Herzegovina. As the institution of *waqf* was introduced by the Prophet (p.b.u.h.), its spread over the world followed the conquests of Muslim state and dissemination of Islamic teachings. Bosnia and Herzegovina is but an example how Islam, with all its teachings and principles, contributed to the socio-economic development of the country. In the following pages, we will discuss the historical phases through which the institution of *waqf* went through (and still going through) and indicate its contributions to the socio-economic development of the country.[9]

4.1   Phase I—The Ottoman Period

The institution of *waqf* in Bosnia and Herzegovina was introduced in fifteenth century with the Ottoman's conquest of that region. Namely, in 1463 Maḥmūd Pasha, under the direction of Sultan Muḥammad II the Conqueror (r. 1444–1446 and 1451–1481), led the Ottoman armies to victory over hostile forces in Bosnia. The conquest started much earlier and by the year 1492, the rest of Herzegovina came under Ottoman rule as well.[10] During that period, the territory of B&H was occupied by local people who called themselves Bosniaks and were also known by the Roman Church as the *Bogomils*.[11] It is reported that the Bogomils,

---

[9] Please note that we will not discuss much about the history of Bosnia and Herzegovina as this is not the main focus of the study. Rather, we will focus directly on the institution of *waqf* and its relevance for the socio-economic development of Bosnia and Herzegovina.

[10] Bosnia and Herzegovina (B&H) was initially knows as Kingdom of Bosnia. Later on, its name was changed to Bosnia and Herzegovina where "Bosnia" refers to northern and central parts of the modern territory of B&H and "Herzegovina" to south parts. Nowadays, when we refer to Bosnia we mean B&H as a whole.

[11] The Bogomils were a Gnostic religio-political sect founded in the First Bulgarian Empire by the priest Bogomil during the reign of Tsar Peter I in the tenth century. It most probably arose in what is today the region of Macedonia as a response to the social stratification that occurred as a result of the introduction of feudalism and as a form of political movement and opposition to the Bulgarian state and the church. The Bogomils called for a return to early Christianity, rejecting the ecclesiastical, and their primary political tendencies were resistance to the state and church authorities. This helped the movement

due to similarities between their beliefs and rituals with Islamic tradition, accepted Islam *en masse* and the Ottoman rule over the territory. This is contrary to overwhelming opinion that Islam was spread "by the sword" including the B&H territory and people (Abid 2017; Trakić 2012).

B&H was under the Ottoman Empire's rule for 415 years, since 1463 until 1878 and during this period, all issues related to the *waqf* institutions were addressed according to Islamic teachings, namely according to the Holy Quran and the Sunnah of the Prophet (p.b.u.h.). These two, the Quran and the Sunnah, were the basic sources of Ottoman law since the fourteenth century until the beginning of the twentieth century. Legal gaps have been completed by passing a series of regulations that were largely contained in the laws (*kānūn*) and the imperial orders (*farmān*). During the nineteenth century, a number of laws were adopted. The Law on the *Waqf* administration was passed in 1863 and the Law on the Order of Succession of the *ijāratayn*[12] *waqf* in 1870. In other laws passed during this period, we can find regulations on *waqf* properties, especially in the Ottoman Land Law from 1858 and the Ottoman Civil Code, better known as *Majallah*, whose regulations were gradually passed from 1869 to 1876. At that time, a great deal of attention was given to the institution of *waqf* as it had a great and importance for the whole society. During that period, the state controlled the administration, the army, and the authorities in general while almost all other social activities were based on the *waqf* institution (Begović 1963, p. 5). It should be noted, however, that even during that period there were many issues related to the *waqf* institution and properties. Documents

---

spread quickly in the Balkans, gradually expanding throughout the Byzantine Empire and later reaching the Kievan Rus, Bosnia and Herzegovina, Dalmatia, Italy, France, and England. The Bogomils were dualists in that they believed the world was created not by the Abrahamic God, but by an evil demiurge—the Devil. They did not use the cross nor build churches, preferring to perform rituals outdoors (for details see Obolensky 2004; as mentioned in Trakić 2012).

[12] *Ijāratayn* means leasing waqf property under two leases (rentals). According to Shariah principles, when it is found that the *waqf* property has no money that can be used for renovation of its properties, for instance rebuilding a demolished house or a shop, and when there is no one willing to do so using his/her own resources, in that case Shariah allows this practice of *ijāratayn*. A person that is looking for a rent, *ijāratayn*, is required to pay two prices: (i) a price that is approximately equal to the value of the property; and (ii) a smaller price that would be payable at the end of every year and it was called ijarah mujallah (see Balagija 1933, pp. 19–21; as mentioned in Čajlaković 2009, p. 244).

show many mismanagements and abuses of *waqf* properties which indicate that it did not functioned completely well even then.

The first *waqf* in B&H was founded in the fifteenth century. In 1537, under the direction of the regional Ottoman governor, Gazi Husrev Beg (d. 1541), the first major *madrasa* was established in Sarajevo. The aim of this new *madrasa* was the complete integration of the latest sciences of the time, such as mathematics, literature, and natural sciences, plus the traditional religious sciences such as Islamic theology, *tafsīr* (Qurānic exegesis), *hadīth* (prophetic traditions), and *uṣūl al-fiqh* (principles of Islamic jurisprudence) (Trakić 2012). At that time, only what was fully owned (*mulk*) could have been a subject matter of a *waqf*. The *waqf* institution in B&H reached its pinnacle in the period from sixteenth century to eighteenth century when over two thousand *waqf* properties were founded. Numerous *vakufnama*[13] (*waqfnāmes* or *waqf* certificates), as living witnesses of the *waqf* institution and its history in B&H, remained attached to the *waqf* properties or were kept by founders themselves, which is why, in most cases, they were lost.

During the Ottoman period, the *waqf* institution was a powerful factor in promoting and maintaining the then state-political concepts, which was of particular importance for the then government. This was the reason why the state administration insisted on the early establishment of *awqāf* and the construction of *waqf* properties. The presence of *waqf* in the newly conquered territory meant the ideological and political strengthening of the regime, the guarantee of its stability, and thus the security of the defense of the Bosnian soil, whose strategic and political importance in the Ottoman Empire was great (Čajlaković 2009).

Living for hundreds of years with *waqf* and from the income generated out of *waqf* properties—an institution that provided conditions for undisturbed religious life, and which, during the Ottoman administration, was responsible for education and social care of the Muslim population as well as a founder of new urban and economic milieu and facilities[14]—Muslims

---

[13] *Vakufnama* or *waqfnāmes* simply represent a certificate of a *waqf* which list down all matters related to the administration and utilization of the particular *waqf* property.

[14] Up until October 8, 1966, there was no hospital in B&H. In that year, upon the incentive of then protector, Sharif Osman-Pasha, a *waqf* Hospital was build and opened at Kovači, in the street Halilbašića 16. The construction of this hospital was founded from the revenues generated out of the Gazi Husrev Beg's *waqf* properties. In the beginning, the hospital had: a manager, a doctor, a pharmacist, several servers, and thirty-two beds.

in B&H have accepted *waqf* as an integral part of their daily social life. Thus, *waqf* became a kind of national institution (Čajlaković 2009; Čaušević 1983).

Mutawallīs (managers) managed *awqāf.* Due to a process of a general decline of the power of the Ottoman Empire, this inevitably led to weakening and various misuse of the *waqf* management. Along with the weakening of the supervisory authority, consisting of a Shariah judge (*qādi*) and a supervisor (*nāzir*), the influence and the power of *mutawallīs* increased tremendously. As a result, *mutawallīs* increased their personal wealth unjustly and at the expense of *awqāf* (Durmišević 2002; Handžić 1983).

At the end of the nineteenth century, the Ottoman Empire began with reforms. A unique central authority, a ministry of *waqf* that was in charge of *awqāf* was established in Istanbul, with a sole objective of preventing selfishness and misuse of *mutawallīs.* The above ministry assumed the surveillance of *waqf* revenues. Unfortunately, nothing, in essence, has changed. However, this reform led to a creation of *awqāf* directory, which contributed to the preservation of the most important information about them (Čajlaković 2009).

In short, the establishment of *waqf* in B&H started with the official arrival of the Ottomans as shown briefly above. How much the *waqf* institution meant for the development of B&H and the emergence of urban, and therefore political, economic, cultural, and religious centers, the most illustrative is the fact that the names of some cities in B&H have in their names the word *waqf* (or its Bosnian equivalent "*vakuf*") indicating that these cities and towns were founded upon a *waqf* property(ies). These cities are, for example, Kulen-Vakuf, Skender-Vakuf, Gornji Vakuf, Donji Vakuf and many others. In addition to these, for some cities it is known that they used to have the word "*vakuf*" in their own name. Thus, today's Mrkonjić-Grad was once called Varcar-Vakuf, and today's Sanski Most was only called Vakuf and the like.

Patients received treatments regardless of their religious denominations and they were treated, most often, for free. *Waqf* was covering the costs of the hospital.

At the beginning of 1882, the State Government took over this hospital. Over time, this hospital became too crowded that led to a construction of the State Hospital, which began in 1894. That year the *Waqf* Hospital was turned into an Institute for mental illness, which functioned until the construction of a modern hospital for mental illness within the complex of the National Hospital (Talić 1996).

Most of the old cities in B&H are somehow related to the establishment and/or development of a certain *waqf*, that is, to a person who founded that particular *waqf*. Thus, for example, the following cities are related to the establishment of a *waqf* and its *waqif* (benefactor), namely:

a. Sarajevo—Isa-beg Ishaković and Gazi Husrev Beg[15];
b. Tuzla—Turali-beg;
c. Mostar—Karađoz-beg and Koski Mehmed-pasha;
d. Tešanj—Ferhad, son of Skenderov;
e. Maglaj—Kalavun Yusuf-pasha;
f. New Kasaba—Musa-pasha, a *vazir* from Budim;
g. Banja Luka—Ferhad-pasha Sokolovic and Sophie Mehmed-pasha;
h. Gradačac—Captain Gradaščević: Osman, Murat and Husein;
i. Foča—Mehmed-pasha Kukavica;
j. Mrkonjić-Grad—Kizlar-aga Mustafa;
k. Rogatica—Hussein-beg, son of Ilijaz-beg;
l. Višegrad and Rudo—Kara Mustafa-pasha;
m. Čajniče—Gazi Sinan-beg;
n. Gračanica—Ahmed-pasha Budimlija.

From the list shown, it can be seen that the vast majority of the *wākifs* (benefactors) came from the domestic population who played significant political and military functions within the Ottoman state governing the territory of B&H. These are: *vazirs, pashas, bays, agas, gāzis,* captains, and others.[16] However, this does not mean that *vakifs* were only rich members of the Bosnian community. Rather, *vākifs* that *vākifs* came from all social classes as numerous data indicate. Thus, many traders, craftsmen, cadavers, *mufti, 'ulema* and *imams,* men and women contributed to the creation of various *awqāf* in B&H (Štulanović 2004; Vakufska direkcija 2010, 2011).

4.2 Phase II—The Habsburg Monarchy

Bosnia and Herzegovina fell under Austro-Hungarian rule in 1878 when the Congress of Berlin approved the occupation of the Bosnia *Vilayet*,

---

[15] *Beg* or *Bay*—a title used on territories controlled by the Ottoman Empire.

[16] Different names and titles given to various roles played by administrative people within the Ottoman Empire.

which officially remained part of the Ottoman Empire. Knowing the significance of the *waqf* institution, Austro-Hungarian authorities took over the control of it. This has been a long-lasting issue and a dispute between the new government and Muslims in B&H. On one hand, Muslims demanded that Austro-Hungarian government leave the management and control over the *waqf* institutions in their hands referring to the convention of April 21, 1879 between the Ottomans and Austria-Hungary. On the other hand, Austro-Hungarian, made every step possible to keep the *waqf* institutions under its control.

The newly established government found the *waqf* institution in a very bad shape and immediately began with the state of affairs and the introduction of orders. The initial steps came from the Muslims themselves that resulted in issuance of the first order, three years after the occupation, in 1881. Consequently, the government passed several orders related to the organization *waqf* property.[17] The government agreed that the administration of the *waqf* would be entrusted upon a Muslim. Thus, on March 15, 1883, the *Provincial Waqf Commission* (*Zemaljsko Vakufska Komisija*) was established. This commission, among other things, was tasked with registering all *waqf* properties in the country, to control their expenditure, and to carry out new regulations regarding the *Waqf* administration. The PWQ was composed of the President, Inspector, Secretary, four members of the council of Muslim clerics (*majlis al-"ulamā"*), two High *Sharī'ah* Court judges, and two prominent Muslims from each of Bosnia's six districts (Trakić 2012). In this commission, the government was represented by a special official in the capacity of a government commissioner. Without his presence and consent, no significant *waqf* work could have been done. Thus, the government controlled all *waqf* jobs and directly interfered with their management (Čajlaković 2009).

In addition, the *Provincial Waqf Board* (*Zemaljsko Vakufsko Ravnateljstvo*) was established. It was an *executive* body whose main duty was to assist the PWQ with the fieldwork and gathering of any information in relation to *Waqf* administration in every district. The PWB was composed of the President, Inspector, and Secretary of the PWQ, with

---

[17] The first order issued in 1881 was followed by orders from 1883, 1884, 1885, and 1894. In general, all orders left the Austro-Hungarian government's influence on the *Waqf* administration. These orders introduced a uniform and stable administration of *waqf* affairs (see Čajlaković 2009; Trakić 2012).

necessary clerical staff. In the districts, these *waqf* boards were headed by *Sharī'ah* judges. Unfortunately, the members of those bodies were appointed by the Habsburg administration, a circumstance which left considerable space for the misuse of *awqāf* for purposes other than those which are permitted by Islamic law (Trakić 2012).

The Muslims in Bosnia were not happy with the existing situation. Already heated situation culminated with an incident that happened in Herzegovina. Namely, in 1899, an underaged Muslim girl from the town of Mostar—Fata Omanović—was taken away by Catholic nuns, converted to Christianity, and secretly sent to Austria to marry an Austrian officer. This event caused outrage among the local Muslim community. Demonstrations were led by Ali Fehmi Dzabić (1853–1918),[18] the *muftī* of Mostar, who submitted demands to the Habsburg administration demanding the reorganization of Muslim religious affairs, in particular the *waqf* and educational sectors (Karcić 1999). All this resulted in the creation of a movement for *religious and waqf-educational autonomy* (*vjerska i vakufsko-mearifetska samouprava*). The movement demanded the reshaping of the *Waqf* administration in such a way that members of *waqf* bodies would be elected by the Muslims themselves. Dzabic was the leader of this movement until his visit to Ottoman Istanbul, when the Habsburg administration prohibited him from returning back to Bosnia and Herzegovina.

As a result of the constant pressure by Bosniaks, Vienna accepted most of the movements' demands pertaining to the administration of Islamic affairs. *The Statute for the Autonomous Administration of Islamic Religious and Waqf-Educational Affairs in Bosnia and Herzegovina* (*Statut za autonomnu upravu islamsko-vjerskih i vakufsko-mearifskih poslova u BiH*) was adopted on April 15, 1909. By virtue of this statute, the autonomy and election of an authority administering the *waqf* were granted. The said Statute has determined that all movable and immovable *waqf* property is the property of a *waqf* itself; to be governed by Shariah; to be governed by the bodies that Muslims chose; and that it serves exclusively for the religious and educational purposes of Muslims. The consequences of this struggle were multiply significant both internally and internationally,

---

[18]Ali Fehmi Dzabić was the *muftī* of the town of Mostar. He was also known under the name of 'Alī b. Shākir Fahmī Jābirzāde al-Mustarī and had an excellent knowledge of Arabic, literature, and geology. He wrote a number of works such as *Ḥusn al-ṣiḥābah fī sharḥ al-ṣaḥābah and Ṭilbat al-ṭālib fī sharḥ Lāmiyyah Abī Ṭālib*.

because this statute was the basis of all subsequent resolutions about *waqf*, regardless of the change in the government in BiH, until 1945 (Begović 1963; Čajlaković 2009; Karcić 1983; Mulalić 2001; Trakić 2012).

4.3   Phase III—The Kingdom of Serbs, Croats, and Slovenes (SHS)

With the collapse of the Austro-Hungarian Monarchy, in 1918, there was internationalization of the *waqf* issue. Namely, with the creation of the Kingdom of SHS, the state of Muslims deteriorated further. However, the Kingdom of SHS was forced to sign Saint-Germaine peace agreement on September 10, 1919. Article 10 of that agreement states: *"The state of Serbs, Croats and Slovenes is committed to ensuring the protection of mosques, cemeteries and other Muslim religious institutions. All necessary facilities and permits will be provided to Muslim endowments (awqāf) and religious charities; the government of the Serbs, Croats and Slovenes will not deprive any of the necessary reliefs for the establishment of new religious and charitable institutions"* (Bojić 2001, p. 163).

In 1929, the kingdom was renamed "Yugoslavia." During the "Kingdom of Yugoslavia" period, the Muslims claimed an autonomous administration over the *waqf* properties which was disputed by the authorities. For the Muslims, the situation only worsened by the introduction of the Sixth January dictatorship that took place on January 6, 1929, by King Aleksandar I Karađorđević (r. 1918–1934). On January 31, 1930, the King abolished the *Statute for the Autonomous Administration of Islamic Religious, Waqf, and Educational Affairs* and subsequently in 1936 introduced the *Law on the Islamic Community*.[19] Accordingly, the *Waqf and Educational Affairs* did not fall under the jurisdiction of the Islamic Community but were placed under the direct authority of the Ministry of Justice of the Kingdom of Yugoslavia (Čajlaković 2009; Trakić 2012).

---

[19] In the middle of 1930, the government of the Kingdom of Yugoslavia removed *raisu-l-ʿulama* Džemaludin Čaušević and sent him into early retirement. The reason for early retirement was his advocacy for Muslim rights and the protection of their properties. At the time, there were about two million Muslims in the Kingdom of Yugoslavia. However, many did not see their future in that country, so they migrated in large numbers. Since the creation of the Kingdom of SHS until December 1931 about 45,000 Muslims moved to Turkey (see Bojić 2001, p. 175).

4.4 Phase IV—The Socialist Federal Republic of Yugoslavia (SFRY)

The Constitution of the Federal National Republic of Yugoslavia (FNRY) was passed on January 31, 1946 and the Law on the Legal Position of Religious Communities was passed on July 13, 1953. New Yugoslavia maintained the principle of separation of religion from the state, so the state left the *Waqf* administration to the Islamic community of B&H. Furthermore, on May 16, 1959 the state is adopted a general law on the protection of cultural monuments. This law placed many *waqf* objects, such as mosques, *darwish* houses (*"tekije"*), *madrasas*, and cemeteries, were placed under the state protection. The Constitution of the SFRY issued on April 7, 1963 gave the Islamic Community rights over the *waqf* property so that it can govern and use it in the spirit of Shariah and within the boundaries of State laws (Begović 1963, pp. 9–10). However, this time witnessed the nationalization of *waqf* and Muslim properties in general. Hence, this period is considered as the most difficult period for the *waqf* institution in B&H. The conditions of the *waqf* institution during this period are further explained by Trakić (2012) in the following lines:

> The extraordinarily harsh attitude of communist regime toward the *waqf* at this particular time culminated in the year 1958 when the *Laws on Nationalisation of Leased Buildings and Land* was legislated. The purpose of this piece of legislation was to take the last breath of the *Islamic Community*. By this piece of legislation, the Islamic Community was left overnight without any immovable property – except the mosques.26 The *waqf* land, the forests, and the buildings – the financial skeleton of the *Islamic Community* for its maintenance and very existence – were simply taken away.27 Subsequently, on 13 July 1959, there was an emergency meeting of the *Islamic Community* in which a new constitution had been adopted which abolished the existence of the organs and administration of *waqf* because the new legislation on the nationalisation of *waqf* had caused it to slip out of its control. As a purely religious organisation, the *Islamic Community* remained secluded from any active participation in the lives of Muslims in Bosnia and Herzegovina. The mosques were maintained from the alms and financial contributions of Muslim families on a purely individual basis. (Trakić 2012, p. 344)[20]

---

[20]Only in Sarajevo, about 24 mosques were destroyed during the Socialist Yugoslavia. At the same time, 204,000m^2 of Muslim cemeteries were used for various purposes. A significant number of waqf shops were demolished with a useful surface of 2571m^2.

Even though the *waqf* institution was nationalized after the World War II and during the period of the SFRY, its significance did not vanish. The *waqf* institution remained connected to mosques and other properties that remained under the ownership of the Islamic Community. Besides, a number of new *waqf* formations were recorded during this period that, although much more modest, were equally important for the economic development of B&H as the old ones (Dobrača 1976, p. 45).

4.5   Phase V—Pre- and Post-Dayton Peace Accord

During the aggression on B&H that took place between 1992 and 1995, the *waqf* properties suffered massive losses and damages. Aggressors on both sides—the Serbs on east and north and the Croats on south and west of B&H—endangered, killed, and destroyed not only hundreds of thousands of lives of citizens of B&H, but destroyed a large number of Bosniaks' religious and cultural objects.[21]

During the aggression period, two important laws were legislated with an aim to protect and prevent the sale of *waqf* properties and other religious properties nationalized by previous regimes, namely:

Over 103,707 m^2 of waqf houses, courtyards and construction sites for houses were demolished. Expropriation and nationalization resulted in the seizure of more than 536,023 m^2 of waqf gardens, orchards, meadows, arable land, and other properties. This is only a brief overview of the suffering of the material and culture objects of Muslims in Sarajevo, as well as the properties that were used to sustain those facilities (see Begić 2000; Koštović 1995, p. 11).

[21] During the aggressor's march on B&H and the Bosniaks, the most important objects of Islamic architecture in BiH were not spared of their destructive and ill intentions. During the three-year aggression, more than 600 mosques were completely destroyed and more or less the same amount of mosques were partially demolished. Some of the examples are: the Gazi Husrev-beg mosque (1532); Careva mosque (1565); Baščaršijska (1529); Ali-pasha mosque (1561); Magribiya (1766) in Sarajevo; Aladža (1551) and Careva mosque (1483) in Foča; Sultan Esme Mosque (1745) in Jajce; Karađoz-beg mosque (1570) in Mostar; Ferhadija (1579) and Arnaudija (1595) in Banja Luka (destroyed on May 7, 1993); Emin Turhan-bey's mosque in Ustikolina (1449), which is the oldest mosque in BiH, as well as many others. Most of them were under the protection of UNESCO (see Ćeman 2007, 2008; Omerdić 1999, p. 15).

   i. *Laws on the Prohibition of the Sale of Common Property on which the Right Was Established Through Lease*[22]; and
  ii. *Laws on the Special Protection of Sacred Objects and Places.*[23]

As of today, there are no specific laws and no particular ministry that govern the *waqf* institution in B&H. In fact, as pointed out by Trakić (2012) "there is not even any specific law which mentions the name *waqf*. The word which indicates *waqf* is the word 'foundation'. In English the word 'foundation' can be defined as "an organisation that is established to provide money for a particular purpose, for example for scientific research or charity."[24] Therefore, the protection of *waqf* in the legal documentations of Bosnia and Herzegovina is done through the word 'foundation' ... Since the 'foundations' enjoy constitutional recognition, parliament, as a legislative body, was pressured to pass laws to govern and protect them. As a result, in 2001 the Parliament of the Federation of Bosnia and Herzegovina passed a statute called the *Law on Associations and Foundations.*[25] This piece of legislation was of great importance to all non-governmental organisations in Bosnia and Herzegovina, including 'foundations'. Thus, this law has legislated indirectly on the protection and legal recognition of *waqf*, since *waqf* has been regarded as a 'foundation'" (Trakić 2012, p. 346).

He goes further by stating:

> At present, *waqf* is mentioned and explained in the *Constitution of the Islamic Community* of 1998. There are a few articles explicitly explaining the matters relating to *waqf*. Article 28, for instance, says that "the property of the Islamic Community is comprised of *waqf*, as well as other things like monetary founds." Article 31 states that "every person, individual, or company (legal personality) can in accordance with *sharī'ah* laws leave his property as *waqf*." The Presidency of the Islamic Community, based on constitutional jurisdiction dealing with the *waqf* affairs, has

---

[22] *Official Gazette of the Socialist Republic of Bosnia and Herzegovina*, No. 4 (17 February 1992), 100.

[23] *Official Gazette of the Socialist Republic of Bosnia and Herzegovina*, No. 13 (June 1993), 324-25.

[24] See *Oxford Advanced Learner's Dictionary* ("Oxford," 2007)

[25] *The Law on Associations and Foundations* was passed by the Parliament of the Federation of Bosnia and Herzegovina in both Houses in 2002 (No. 01-3-02-3-46/02). It was also passed by the Parliament of Bosnia and Herzegovina on 5 October 2001.

come out on 22 May 1999 with the *Statute of the Waqf Directorate* which observes that other organs that are entrusted with jurisdictional powers to deal with *waqf* affairs are the local Islamic community, special judicial *waqf* bodies, and *mutawallīs*.[26] By virtue of Article 32 of the *Constitution of the Islamic Community in Bosnia and Herzegovina*, the *Waqf Directorate* manages the property of endowments. Therefore, the management of *waqf* in Bosnia and Herzegovina should be entrusted to the *Waqf* Directorate which would be assisted and consulted by three previously mentioned organs.[27] Furthermore, according to information provided by the former Director of the *Waqf* Directorate of Bosnia and Herzegovina, Nezim Halilović Muderris, by 24 October 2007 the *waqf* sector in Bosnia and Herzegovina consisted of 1,144 mosques, 570 *masjids*, 1,030 shopping lots, 3,027 graveyards, 1,570 houses and apartments, 886 buildings, and 4,829 parcels of land.[28] (Trakić 2012, p. 347)

Ever since the end of the aggression on B&H and the signing of the Dayton peace accord, attempts have been made by various groups from B&H (primarily by the representative of the Islamic Community) to restitute the *waqf* properties. An initial step was taken in December 1996 by the team of experts on matters pertaining to privatization in the Federation of Bosnia and Herzegovina whereby they drafted the *Bill on Restitution*. If the return of *waqf* property is not possible, then monetary compensation of equal value was to be paid. This battle for the restitution of the *waqf* properties is an ongoing challenge before the Government of B&H as the issue is yet to be settled.[29]

5   Conclusions

Waqf represents an Islamic financial institution that bases its foundation on the Quran and the Sunnah. *Awqāf* institutions played an invaluable role in the socio-economic, cultural, and religious development of Muslim societies and economies. The same is true for Bosnia and

---

[26] See Salikić (2001, p. 352).

[27] See Hrvačić (2000).

[28] See Ćeman (2007).

[29] For more details about the restitution of waqf properties in B&H.

Herzegovina. The emergence of *waqf* properties in B&H started with the arrival of the Ottomans and the introduction of Islam and its acceptance by the domicile people known as Bogomils.

Since the very adoption of Islam in the middle of the fifteenth century, the Muslims in B&H have acknowledged and promoted the institution of *waqf* by founding their own *waqf* properties for public and family uses. By doing so, the Muslims of B&H followed in the footsteps of the Prophet Muhammad (p.b.u.h.) and the first generations of Muslims who wanted to achieve Allah's pleasure by bequeathing what they dear the most in this world. Throughout the Balkans, and especially in B&H, an impressive number of *awqāf* properties were created. The exact number of *awqāf* properties is difficult to determine as it is difficult to clearly indicate their contributions to the economic development of any countries where they can be found, including B&H. It is suffice to say that they played a tremendous role in the socio-economic development and in most cases plays supplementary role to the government agencies in providing various social services that, otherwise, may not be available.

However, throughout the centuries and especially during the last hundred years B&H went through a number of different and something conflicting regimes. First, it migrated from the Oriental-Islamic to the Western-European civilization. Second, it passed through several state-legal frameworks, from monarchies to communist regimes witnessing a number of military conflicts including two World Wars and the aggression of 1990s. All these instances played a significant part in the *waqf* institution, and as pointed out briefly in the paper, a large number of *awqāf* properties were seized and/or destroyed.

Although attempts are made to restitute the *waqf* institution in B&H, remains to be seen whether the existing government in B&H will return the *awqāf* properties to the Islamic Community, as the only legal and legitimate owner.

References

Abdel Mohsin, M. I. (2009). *Family Waqf: Its Origin, Law Prospects.* Paper Presented at the Waqf Laws and Management: Reality and Prospects, Kuala Lumpur.

Abdul Kader, S. Z. S., & Dahlan, N. H. M. (2009). *Current Legal Issues Concerning Awqaf in Malaysia.* Paper Presented at the Waqf Laws and Management: Reality and Prospects, Kuala Lumpur.

Abid, S. (2017). *Europe's Endangered Species: Yugoslavia's Forgotten Muslims: A Survey of the Indigenous Muslims of Bosnia and Herzegovina Past History—Current Situation—Future Prospects*. Available Online at http://www.cyberistan.org/islamic/yugoslavia1.htm. Retrieved 22 September 2017.

al-Zuhayli, W. (2007). *Al-Wasaya wa al-Waqf fi al-Fiqh al-Islami*. Dimashq: Dar al-Fiqr.

Balagija, A. (1933). *Uloga vakufa u verskom i svetovnom prosvećivanju naših muslimana*. Beograd: Štamparija Drag. Gregorića.

Begić, M. (Ed.). (2000). *Zemljovlasnici Bosne: vlasnicke pravne norme od disolucije (31.12.1991) ex-Jugoslavije do potpisivanja Dejtonskog sporazuma (14.12.1995)* [Landlords of Bosnia: Legal Norms of Ownership from the Dissolution (31 December 1991) of Ex-Yugoslavia Until the Signing of the Dayton Peace Agreement (14 December 1995)]. Sarajevo.

Begović, M. (1963). *Vakufi u Jugoslaviji*. Beograd: SANU.

Bojić, M. (2001). *Historija Bosne i Bošnjaka (XVII–XX vijeka)*. Sarajevo: Šahinpašić.

Čajlaković, M. (2009). Nastanak i razvoj institucije vakufa s posebnim osvrtom na vakuf u BiH. *Glasnik, June* (3–4), 239–256.

Čaušević, H. (1983). Pravni i sociološki aspekti institucije vakufa-zaklade, s posebnim obzirom na njen razvoj u BiH. *Anali GHB biblioteke* (Vol. IX–X). Sarajevo: GHB biblioteka.

Ćeman, S. (2007). *Komparativna studija o polozaju vakufa i fondacija u serijatkom pravu i pozitivnim zakonima propisanim u Bosni i Hrcegovini* [Comparative Study of Waqfs and Foundations Under Sharīʿah Law and Positive Law Legislated in Bosnia and Herzegovina] (MA). University of Sarajevo, Sarajevo.

Ćeman, S. (2008). Vakufi i fondacije u svijetu i kod nas (sličnosti i razike). *Glasnik, December* (7–8), 627–641.

Dafterdar, H. (2009). *Towards Effective Legal Regulations and Enabling Environment for Awqaf*. Paper Presented at the Waqf Laws and Management: Reality and Prospects, Kuala Lumpur.

Dobrača, K. (1976). Vakufname u GHB biblioteci. *Anali GHB biblioteke* (Vol. IV). Sarajevo: GHB biblioteka.

Durmišević, E. (2002). *Uspostava i pravni položaj Rijaseta Islamske zajednice u Bosni i Hercegovini: 1882–1899*. Sarajevo: Magistrat.

El-Buhari, M. I. I. (2009). *Sahihu-l-Buhari: Buharijeva zbirka hadisa* (E. Ljevaković, H. Popara, M. Mehanović, Š. Ramić, H. Mehanović, & A. Adilović, Trans., Vol. 2). Sarajevo: Visoki saudijski komitet.

El-Munziri. (2004). *Muslimova zbirka hadisa: sažetak* (M. Mrahorović, M. Prljača, N. Karaman, J. Karaman, & A. Mujezin, Trans.). Sarajevo: El-Kalem.

Esmaeili, H. (2009). *The Relationship Between the Waqf Institution in Islamic Law and the Rule of Law in the Middle East*. Paper Presented at the Waqf Laws and Management: Reality and Prospects, Kuala Lumpur.

Handžić, A. (1983). Husrev-begov vakuf na prelazu iz XVI u XVII stoljeće. *Anali GHB biblioteke* (Vol. IX–X). Sarajevo: GHB biblioteka.

Hrvačić, E. (2000, December). *Restitucija i njeno pravno utemeljenje* [Restitution and Its Legal Origins], [Tuzla, Bosnia and Herzegovina]. *Hikmet 9–12*, 265.

Ibn Ābidīn. *Radd al-Muhtār alā al-Durr al-Mukhtār* (Vol. 3). Beirut: Dār al-Maktab al-Ilmiyyah.

Karcić, F. (1983). Međunarodnopravno regulisanje vakufskih pitanja u jugoslovenskim zemljama [Solving the Issues of Waqf by International Law in the States of Yugoslavia]. *Anali GHB biblioteke* (Vol. IX–X, pp. 141–154). Sarajevo: GHB biblioteka.

Karcić, F. (1999). *The Bosniaks and the Challenges of Modernity, Late Ottoman and Hapsburg Times*. Sarajevo: El-Kalem.

Koštović, N. (1995). *Sarajevo između dobrotvorstva i zla*. Sarajevo: El-Kalem.

Mahmud, M. W., & Shah, S. S. (2009). *Optimization of Philanthropic Waqf: The Need for Maqasid-Based Legislative Strategies*. Paper Presented at the Waqf Laws and Management: Reality and Prospects, Kuala Lumpur.

Mulalić, H. M. (2001). *Institucija vakufa u BiH*. Sarajevo: Svjetlost.

Obolensky, D. (2004). *The Bogomils: A Study in Balkan Neo-Manichaeism*. Cambridge: Cambridge University Press.

Omerdić, M. (1999). *Prilozi izučavanju genocida nad Bošnjacima (1992–1995)*. Sarajevo: El-Kalem.

Oxford Advanced Learner's Dictionary (7th ed.). (2007). Oxford: Oxford University Press.

Saleem, M. Y. (2009). *Towards Institutional Mutawallis for the Management of Waqf Properties*. Paper Presented at the Waqf Laws and Management: Reality and Prospects, Kuala Lumpur.

Salikić, M. (2001). *Ustavi islamske zajednice* [Constitutions of the Islamic Community]. Sarajevo: El-Kalem.

Štulanović, M. (2004). *Urf: običaj kao pomoćni izvor šerijatskog prava, s osvrtom na BiH*. Bihać: IPA.

Talić, Š. (1996). Stotinu trideset godina vakufske bolnice. *Preporod, 14*(597), 6.

Trakić, A. (2012). A Legal and Administrative Analysis of Inalienable Muslim Endowments (Awqaf) in Bosnia and Herzegovina. *Islamic Civilizational Review (ICR), 3*(2), 337–354.

Tuhmaz, A. A.-H. M. T. (1424/2003). *Hanefijski fikh* [Fiqh of Abu Hanifah] (A. Purdić, Z. Hasanović, & M. Mehanović, Trans., Vol. 2). Sarajevo: Haris Grabus (Translated from Arabic by Ahmed Purdić, Zuhdija Hasanović, & Muhamed Mehanović).

Vakufska direkcija. (2010). *Vakufi u Bosni i Hercegovini: historijat, trenutno stanje i perspektive*. Sarajevo: Islamska zajednica u BiH – Vakufska direkcija Sarajevo.

Vakufska direkcija. (2011, 22. juni). *Naučni skup Vakufi u Bosni i Hercegovini*. Sarajevo.

CHAPTER 7

Using Waqf for Socio-Economic Development in Bangladesh: Potentials, Challenges, and Policy Directions

Md. Golzare Nabi, Md. Aminul Islam, Rosni Bakar and Mohammad Masuduzzaman

1 Introduction

Waqf an Islamic voluntary endowment has played important roles in the socio-economic spheres of Muslim people all over the world since advent of Islam. A growing number of literatures reveal that waqf has worked as an effective tool for improving socio-economic condition of Muslim communities across the world from the early period of Islam till most Muslim countries came under colonial powers (Çizakça 2000; Ahmed 2004; Kahf 2003; Chapra 2008). Waqf as social institution became dormant in Muslim majority countries during colonial era as it could not function properly due to undue interferences in waqf management

---

Views expressed in the paper are authors' own; they do not reflect necessarily the views of the institutions in which they work.

M. G. Nabi (✉) · M. Masuduzzaman
Research Department, Bangladesh Bank,
Dhaka, Bangladesh

© The Author(s) 2019
K. M. Ali et al. (eds.), *Revitalization of Waqf for Socio-Economic Development, Volume I*,
https://doi.org/10.1007/978-3-030-18445-2_7

by colonial powers and decline in economic activities operated by Muslim communities (Çizakça 1998; Kahf 2003; Khalid 2011). The end of colonial rule and emergence of independent Muslim states in the middle of twentieth century have paved the ways to formulate and implement the socio-economic policy as per Islamic Shariah. As results, Islamic financial industry has started to groom in Muslim majority countries since early 1970s with the establishment of Islamic Development Bank (IDB) in 1975. Now Islamic finance industry with total assets of USD 2.293 trillion is gaining popularity due to its resilient and risk sharing feature and offering Islamic financial services in 70 countries, both in Muslim and non-Muslim countries (GIFR 2017). Despite rapid success in growth, profitability, and resiliency, some scholars opine that Islamic finance could not incorporate social goals in its operations as directed by Islamic Shariah and it has underserved the majority poor Muslim people following much practices of trade-/lease-based mode of investments, low investment in sharing modes like musharakah and mudarabah and minimum investment in social sectors like agriculture, micro-enterprises, and essential services such as education and health (Siddiqi 2006; Asutay 2007; Ayub 2007; Asutay and Zaman 2009). In order to achieve full potential of Islamic finance, waqf may be developed and managed alongside mainstream Islamic resources such as Islamic bank, capital markets, zakat, and microfinance. Given this, revival and expansion of Islamic social sector based on waqaf, zakat, and sadaqah has become imperative to cater the demands of 700 million poor living in the Muslim countries. Rashid S. Khalid (2011) mentions that at least one million awaqf (plural of waqf) exist in Muslim countries out of millions of awaqf which possess enormous potentials for developing socio-economic condition of the Ummah, particularly in the field of poverty alleviation. Many Muslim scholars and policy makers have also realized that using waqf as a strong social institution can act as catalyst in mobilization of funds in poor Muslim majority countries for financing social projects including

M. G. Nabi · M. A. Islam · R. Bakar
School of Business Innovation and Technopreneurship,
Universiti Malaysia Perlis (UniMAP), Arau, Malaysia
e-mail: amin@unimap.edu.my

R. Bakar
e-mail: rosni@unimap.edu.my

much-needed poverty alleviation (Sadeq 2002; Ahmed 2007; Kahf 2008; Shirazi et al. 2013; Haneef et al. 2015).

Practicing regular charity occupies an important chapter in the Islamic way of life and civilization. Many verses of the Holy Quran laid down utmost importance on charity for attaining countless rewards from Almighty Allah. We can mention three verses: (i) "By no means shall ye attain righteousness unless ye give (freely) of that which ye love; and whatever ye give, of a truth Allah knoweth it well" (Al-Quran-3:92); (ii) "And be steadfast in prayer; practise regular charity; and bow down your heads with those who bow down (in worship)" (2:43); and (iii) "It is not righteousness that ye turn your faces towards East or West; but it is righteousness- to believe in Allah and the Last Day, and the Angels, and the Book, and the Messengers; to spend of your substance, out of love for Him, for your kin, for orphans, for the needy, for the wayfarer, for those who ask, and for the ransom of slaves; to be steadfast in prayer, and practice regular charity..." (Al-Quran-2:177). Similarly, there are many hadith on importance of charity. For example, Abu Hurairah (Allah be pleased with him) reported Allah's Messenger Hazrat Mohammad (p.b.u.h) as saying: When a man dies, his acts come to an end, except three things, recurring charity, or knowledge (by which people benefit), or pious offspring, who prays for him (Sahih Muslim). Majority of Muslim jurists opine that recurring charity serves as the basis of waqf, Islamic endowment (Ahmad 2015a).

As the third largest Muslim majority country in the world, Bangladesh can explore waqf as an effective tool in social development such as poverty alleviation, employment generation, and improvement in education and health services. Though a large number of waqf exists in Bangladesh during over few centuries, they could not play effective roles following mismanagement and lack of proper structuring and innovation. With proper structuring and administration, waqf can be a boon for Bangladesh, a natural resource poor country blessed with 160 million people with 24% poor people.[1] As Bangladesh lags behind key social development indicators in terms of poverty alleviation, inequality, education and health services, waqf may emerge as an effective tool in managing and financing social projects. Waqf may help in achieving some Sustainable Development Goals (SDGs) in Bangladesh especially for no poverty (SDG1), zero hunger (SDG2), good health and well-being (SDG3), quality education (SDG4), reduced in equalities for households

[1] Bangladesh Economic Review, 2017, Ministry of Finance, Government of Bangladesh.

(SDG10), and shared economic growth (SDG8). Given this, the present paper would analyze present status of waqf and provides policy directions for using waqf as a policy tool toward achieving socio-economic development in Bangladesh.

The remaining portion of the paper would be organized as follows: Following introductory first section, Sect. 2 contains research methodology. Review of literatures is made in Sect. 3. Section 4 deals with current status, potentials, and significance of waqf in Bangladesh. Different viable methods for financing waqf estates are explored in Sect. 5. Section 6 is devoted to analyze challenges faced by waqf in Bangladesh while Sect. 7 contains policy directors in addressing challenges. Finally, concluding remarks are made in Sect. 8.

2   RESEARCH METHODOLOGY

The key objectives of the paper include (i) to examine current status of waqf and its immense potentials for achieving socio-economic development in Bangladesh; (ii) to analyze viable methods of financing waqf properties; (iii) to investigate challenges faced by waqf in Bangladesh; and (iv) to recommend policies for making waqf as a viable tool to finance social projects so as to bring sustainable benefits for both Muslim and non-Muslim members of the community.

To attain the objectives of the paper, qualitative research method has been applied. The paper uses required information/data collected from secondary sources. It reviews literatures, reports, and Web sites and collects descriptive data/information to present the theme of the paper. The paper also fills up the research gap related to waqf development and its roles in social development s in Bangladesh as there are lack of quality research works relating to waqf in Bangladesh.

3   LITERATURE REVIEW

This chapter defines concept of waqf, its features, and uses, and it also analyzes different articles focusing its socio-economic roles.

3.1   Concepts of Waqf, Its Features, and Uses

In Arabic language, literally waqaf (awaqf in plural) refers to tying up or dedication. In Islamic jurisprudence, waqaf means philanthropic foundations in which certain property is set aside and preserved for specific charitable purpose. According to Murat Çizakça (1998) "this institution, whereby a privately owned property, corpus, is endowed for a charitable purpose in perpetuity and the revenue generated is spent for this purpose." M. Kahf (2003) defines waqaf as "holding certain property and preserving it for the confined benefit of certain philanthropy and prohibiting any use or disposition of it outside its specific objective." Hassan (2010) mentioned waqf as "a perpetual charity that means holding certain property and preserving it for the confined benefit of certain philanthropic purposes."

Under waqf arrangement, property is endowed for different purposes which meet either individual or religious and social objectives mentioned in the waqf deed subject to certain terms and conditions. Major terms and conditions required for a valid waqf include (i) waqf is made under a permanent arrangement; (ii) it becomes immediately effective and cannot be kept in abeyance; (iii) it is an irrevocable legal contact; and (iv) waqf property can never be confiscated (Banglapedia 2012). Murat Çizakça (1998) mentions that waqf has four major components—the founder, the beneficiaries, the mutawallis (trustees), and the endowed property/capital itself. The founder endows his personal property permanently for the benefit of himself or members of his family or general public or for both. The trustees manage the property. All terms and conditions regarding management and uses of revenue are registered in a deed of endowment submitted to the legal authority.

Waqf may be divided into three types based on beneficiaries such as public waqf, family waqf, and mixed waqf. Public waqf is created for meeting religious or public welfare goals. Family waqf is made for the benefit of the founder himself, his family, or descendants. A mixed waqf is established for satisfying both mass religious or charitable objectives and private purpose of the founder, his family, and descendants.

Waqf may be created based on different types of movable, immovable, and liquid assets. These include land, building, factories, cash, company share, grants for religious and charitable purpose, title to a property which can generate revenue, endowment of profit generated from a property and other types of assets supported by law (Khalid 2011; Budiman 2014).

Though waqf is one kind of sadaqah, it is different from other charitable instruments of Islam such as zakat, compulsory levy, and sadaqah in general. Islam has made zakat mandatory for wealthy Muslim and has fixed its eight head of expenditures. Waqf is a voluntary endowment and its head of expenditures is not fixed and it may be used to attain any social objective as determined by the founder of waqf. Ordinary sadaqah is made by transferring substance with profit. To the contrary, waqf allows retainment of substance and permits use of profit for welfare of the beneficiaries. Though waqf and trust have similarities in providing charitable services, there are specific differences between the two. Under waqf, ownership of property goes to Almighty Allah while it is vested in trustee under a trust. In case of waqf, endowment must be perpetual, irrevocable, or inalienable or made with a pious or religious motive, it is not necessary in case of a trust (Mannan 2005).

Waqf made enormous contributions to the welfare of Muslim societies during the glorious period of Islamic civilization (Çizakça 2000). M. Kahf (2003) mentions that waqf can provide vital services/utilities among the general people, the poor, and the needy in particular. These services include offering education and health services, building of bridges, parks, roads, dams, conducting research, undertaking steps for caring of animals and protecting environment and lending to small business. Mannan (2005) focuses on five key areas in which waqf played significant roles in Muslim communities. These include (i) promotion of Islamic values; (ii) promoting education and research; (iii) supporting development of medical science; (iv) supporting development of art and architecture; and (v) helping recovery of Islamic values from colonialism. It is clear that waqf can greatly contribute to offer valuable services in religious and socio-economic fields of Muslim societies as it did in the past.

3.2   Review of Articles/Papers

There are growing numbers of literatures on waqf in order to use it as a tool for financing social projects toward realization of social goals of Islam (Maqasid al Shariah).

Çizakça (1998) analyzes that waqf can contribute to the modern economies of Muslim countries as it has done in the past. As waqf has offered all the essential services in the Muslim countries throughout history, the author argues that if modernized successfully, waqf can curb public expenditure and ensure other benefits with reducing interest burden and even it can make an eventual elimination of riba.

H. Ahmed (2007) studies the sustainability and operational issues of Microfinance Finance Institution (MFI) based on waqf property. The author opines that waqf-based MFI can offer micro-financial services among the poor and it can help create wealth for them. The author mentions that MFI can reduce operational cost and increase the institutional viability.

Sadeq (2005) highlights importance of waqf including its statistics in Bangladesh. The author mentions that there are 8000 educational institutions and more than 123,000 mosques that are established by waqf institutions in Bangladesh. He recommends that other than religious and educational sector cash waqf fund may be utilized for all socio-economic purposes.

Ibrahim et al. (2013) explain cash waqf concept and its implementation around the world. The benefits of cash waqf are that people from all levels can contribute money. However, in implementation of cash waqf there are certain legal constraints—inalienability and perpetuity. For this reason, waqf properties cannot be used as collateral by the waqf institutions. In such situation, a variety of cash waqf is developed and practiced in Muslim majority countries like Egypt, Kuwait, Malaysia, Indonesia, and Bangladesh. Cash waqf has many benefits including financing small- and medium-sized enterprises (SMEs), settling bad debts, and assisting education.

Masoud Ahmad (2015a) opines that microcredit and safety net programs around the world are not successful in poverty eradication and reduction in unequal income distribution. Therefore, waqf other than zakah can be considered as alternate choice in providing basic needs of the poor people—lodging, education, health, etc. at free of charge by the waqf institutions. However, such institutions in Bangladesh are not growing much to meet the basic needs of the poor due to some problems such as highly centralized Waqf administration and its unskilled man power, absence of organizational and administrative competency, mismanagement and misuse of waqf properties and lack of social awareness. His recommendations for the development of waqf properties include formulating of new waqf Act, conducting census on waqf estates on regular basis, recovering illegal occupied waqf estates, arranging training for employees, and preparing guidelines for waqf-based Islamic microfinance institutions.

M. A. Haneef et al. (2015) attempt to formulate an integrated waqf-based Islamic microfinance (IsMF) model (IWIMM) in order to alleviate poverty in Bangladesh. The authors opine that poverty alleviation can be possible in Bangladesh by making integration of the six constructs developed for the model as there exist significant relationships among the constructs. On the other hand, K. M. Hassanain (2015), examines three models for poverty alleviation which include waqf-based Islamic Microfinance Institutions, a Model of Zakah and Awaqf-based MF Organizations and an Integrated Awaqf and Zakah Model of Microfinance.

M. Ahmad (2015b) explores the nature and potentials of cash waqf as an alternative of riba-based financing in helping poor segment of the society. He views that cash waqf-based institutions can replace microfinance banks and prospective Muslim donors will be inspired to donate these institutions with a view to eradicating poverty at the grassroots level. Collection of fund through issuance of shares may be another way of enhancing credit by these institutions. The author also highlighted the associated risks in cash waqf-based institutions such as default in payment by the borrowing poor, potential moral hazards by the managers, lack of resilience in many Muslim countries. He mentions that default loans can be averted by providing loans to those who have received entrepreneurial training, selecting appropriate business for the grass roots by the cash waqf institution, mandatory saving scheme, regular assessment of business performance of the grass roots, and mandatory takaful policy.

Rashid identifies six issues which retard the development of waqf properties and their proper utilization. These include lack of effective administrative policy for waqf properties, lack of public participation, lack of family waqf, wastage of waqf income, costly mode of recovery of encroached waqf properties and underdeveloped waqf properties. For the removal of these barriers for development of waqf property, he recommends effective waqf management, a survey needed in countries with difficulty to get adequate data, formulation of effective Waqf administration policy, encouragement of well-organized family awaqf with strong supervision, establishment of waqf tribunals for aversion of wastage of waqf income, emphasis on recovering encroached waqf properties by litigation, proper upkeep of waqf property and ensuring collection and distribution of waqf income among the beneficiaries.

Thoarlim et al. (2017) highlight the current situation and potentials of waqf properties for welfare-oriented development and benefits of unprivileged people in Bangladesh. The authors raise six features of cash waqf as liquidity, immediate usufruct, mobility, benefit, affordability, and convenience. They reveal that waqf properties in Bangladesh remain unutilized or giving no yield. They give a brief description of current practices of cash waqf in Bangladesh along with other countries like Indonesia, Singapore, Bahrain, Kuwait, Malaysia, and Turkey. They suggest that Bangladesh needs to reform and develop waqf institution and to bring good governance in Waqf administration for the benefits of unprivileged sections of population.

4   Current Status, Potentials, and Significance of Waqf in Bangladesh

As a Muslim majority country in South Asia, Bangladesh has a rich collection of waqf estates. Preaching Islam in the country by a group of Shahabis after its advent in Arab and later Sufi saints and Muslim rule in Bengal during 1205–1757 have played significant roles to develop waqf estates in Bangladesh. During British regime (1758–1947), waqf estates were dormant. After the end of Pakistani rule (1947–1971), the opportunities were created for using waqf as a tool in promoting socio-economic development of the country. During different periods, a large number of waqf estates were created to provide religious services through mosques and support education, orphanages, hospitals, and other social establishments. Contribution of waqf to the education sector alone is significant. More than 8000 educational institutions are being run under waqf arrangement. Besides, there are more than 123,000 mosques imparting religious education which includes secular education as well.

4.1   Current Status of Waqf in Bangladesh

Most of Bangladesh's waqf estates are unlisted. According to the latest data published in the Citizen's Charter of Waqf administration, Bangladesh has 21,953 registered waqf estates; out of them 17,563 are public waqf estates (lillah waqf) and 4390 are family waqf estates (awaladi estates). In addition, 139,256 waqf estates have been identified as unlisted (Annual Report, Waqf administration, Bangladesh).

Waqf estates are classified by principle of beneficiary (Census of Waqf Estate 1986). There are five broad categories of beneficiaries, viz. general public, heirs, religious institutions, educational institutions, and others. A waqf estate may have more than one beneficiary. The major beneficiaries of the waqf estates are the religious institutions (93.5%) followed by the general public (22.2%).

There are five categories of waqf estates from viewpoints of management such as managed by heirs, managed by trustee boards, managed by a committee, managed by government officials, and managed by others (Census of Waqf Estate 1986). A waqf estate is managed by only one of the five arrangements. It appears that most awaqf are managed by the local committees/Motowallis (92.5%) and a small number is managed by trustee boards (0.7%).

There are three broad sources of income—land, other immovable property, and other sources (Census of Waqf Estate 1986). There are 8 categories of income by using land, viz. agricultural land, garden/orchards, pond/tank, mosque or place of performance of salat, Idgah/open space, graveyard/dargah, madrasa/school and use for other purposes. There are 8 such categories of income by using other property than land use, viz. house, factories, other immovable property, public subscription/donation, donation in kind, government grants, investment/share/etc. and other sources. In recent times, cash waqf is gaining popularity in Bangladesh.

Most of the waqf estates are unproductive. If properly developed and managed, these neglected assets can generate revenues for supporting social projects.

4.2   Regulation and Supervision of Waqf Estates

Now Waqf administration Bangladesh, an autonomous organization under Ministry of Religious Affairs run, controls and looks after the issues of waqf estates in Bangladesh in order to manage waqf properties properly toward achieving social and religious welfare. It works under the Waqf Ordinance, 1962 and the waqfs (Transfer and Development of Property) Special Provisions Act, 2013. Its head office is situated in Dhaka and it has 38 regional offices all over the country. The chief of Waqf administration is known as "Waqf Administrator." The key functions of the Waqf administration, Bangladesh include enlisting unlisted waqf estates, employment of mutawalli in listed and unlisted waqf estates, collecting subscriptions from listed waqf estates, and recovering waqf estates from illegal occupations.

4.3   Potentials of Waqf Development in Bangladesh

Bangladesh has enormous potentials using waqf as a tool for attaining socio-economic developments in Bangladesh.

Development of Existing Waqf Estates
There are bright prospects for increasing the number of waqf estates to promote the socio-economic conditions of the people, the needy, and poor people in particular. As market price of waqf lands has increased manyfold following population growth and scarcity of land, if properly managed and structured, existing waqf estates may be viable sources of revenues to support social development projects.

Growing Income of Middle Class
Bangladesh has an expanding middle class with growing per capita income. Proper motivational programs may induce them to create waqf.

Expanding Corporate Sector
There are better chances of corporate waqf in Bangladesh as her economy is transferring from an agrarian economy to an industrial one. Now industrial sector accounts for 31.5% share of GDP (Bangladesh Bank 2016a). Hamdard Laboratories (waqf) Bangladesh has already set an example of well-managed corporate waqf.

Great Potentials of Cash Waqf
There are great potentials of cash waqf in Bangladesh. Nine Islamic banks have already introduced cash waqf certificates worth BDT 1050 million.[2] Other Islamic banks may follow the same path. Now Islamic banks offer financial services among 17 million clients (Bangladesh Bank 2016b). If proper awareness is created by Islamic banks, number of cash waqf will increase manyfold.

Bright Prospect of Remittance Waqf
Bangladesh's annual remittances stood USD 12.77 billion in FY17 (Bangladesh Bank 2016c). As Islamic banks bring one-third of total remittances, they can introduce remittance waqf among remitters.

Potentials of Micro-Waqf
Micro-waqf may blossom among low-income people as Bangladeshi people are pious, liberal, and sympatric. Both Islamic banks and MFIs may introduce micro-waqf-based products.

---

[2] Data collected from concerned banks.

4.4   Significance of Waqf Development in Bangladesh

Waqf estates played significant role in Islamic societies all over the world throughout the history by offering essential social services and meeting needs of the poor people (Çizakça 2000). Waqf can be used as a tool for generating revenue for social welfare of the people, needy people in particular (Budiman 2014). Similarly, if structured and modernized properly, waqf can also emerge as an effective tool for promoting the socio-economic status of the people in Bangladesh including attaining SDGs.

Reducing Poverty and Achieving Sustainable Development Goals
Bangladesh with limited resource has made progress in poverty reduction following 6 plus GDP growth based on solid improvements in agriculture and export-oriented RMG industries, implementation of large social safety net program, massive inflows of foreign remittances, and wide expansion of microfinance. Despite such progress in poverty, 24.3% people out of the 160 million still live in poverty and 12.9% people live in extreme poverty (HIES 2016). In addition, Gini coefficient in case of income inequality is also high in Bangladesh which is 0.483 in 2016 (HIES 2016). Bangladesh has set targets in cutting poverty rate and inequality further. With 193 UN member countries, she has also adopted 2030 Agenda for SDGs comprising 17 goals. Among 17 goals, end in poverty tops the list, goal 2 denotes no hunger, and goal 10 focuses on reducing inequalities. To attain these goals, government, private, and social sector in Bangladesh have adopted concerted efforts which include increasing GDP rate over 8%, enhancing social safety programs, increasing investment in infrastructures, and boosting private and social sector investment (Planning Commission 2016). Bangladesh faces challenges in financing projects related to achieving those goals.

Waqf has the capability to supplement budget for attaining goal 1, goal 2, and goal 10 by mobilization and investment of charitable funds. To this end, waqf-based microfinance model can assist in reducing poverty and inequality. Mohamed Aslam Haneef et al. (2015) and K. M. Hassanain (2015) tested integrated waqf-based Islamic microfinance model. They found significant results indicating that poverty alleviation is made possible by use of integrated waqf-based Islamic microfinance.

Promoting Financial Inclusion

A good number of empirical literatures exhibit that financial development and improved access to finance in a country referred to as financial inclusion contribute to growth by augmenting saving-investment process (Honohan 2004; Levine 2005; Beck and De la Torre 2006; Beck et al. 2004, 2007; World Bank 2007). However, both collateral-based conventional banking system and collateral-free microfinance have been failed to provide necessary financial services to unbanked poor people in Muslim majority countries. The conventional banking system does not offer financial services to poor people due to lack of suitable collateral and greater operational costs generating from credit assessment, monitoring and enforcement of law in case of default. Though the conventional microfinance has some economic and social impacts on the lives of millions of the poor, it could not prove suitable and effective for all the poor, hard-core poor in particular because of high rate of interest, absence of interest-free product, lack of product diversity, paucity of adequate funds, and absence of private sector participation (Iqbal 2015).

Given this, Islamic microfinance can use waqf and other Islamic instruments such as zakat, sadaqah, and qardhasana in promoting financial inclusion in Bangladesh (Table 1). It is clear from the table that Islamic microfinance can serve all categories of poor with redistribution and risk sharing tools of Islam.

Reducing Public Expenditure

Implementation of social projects by waqf can reduce public expenditure and government involvement in the economy (Çizakça 1998; Khalid 2011; Budiman 2014). As a developing country, Bangladesh can reduce public expenditure and participation in the economy by using waqf toward promoting social projects such as poverty alleviation, education, and health services. In adopting such approach, she can lessen pressure on budget, release more funds for development of physical infrastructures, and cut the level of deficit financing based on borrowing funds from banking and non-banking system. This would also help in crowding in more funds accelerating investment in the private sector, contain inflation and reduce government involvement in the economy aiming at avoiding wastages of public resources. It may be mentioned here that budget deficit was 5.0% of GDP in Bangladesh during FY2015–2016 (Bangladesh Bank 2016a).

Table 1   Tools for financial inclusion under Islamic microfinance

Level of poverty	Name of tool	
	Redistribution tool	Risk sharing tool
Extreme Poverty (below poverty line)	Charity-based microfinance model (zakat, sadaqah, and waqf based)	Collective risk sharing through collective support during crisis
Poverty (above poverty line)	Charity-based microfinance model (zakat, waqf, and qard-e-hasan based)	Profit-based microfinance model (Mudarabah, Musharakah) with micro-Takaful
Low income[a]	Charity-based microfinance model (waqf and qard-e-hasan based)	Profit-based microfinance model (Mudarabah, Musharakah) with micro-Takaful

Source Adopted from Z. Iqbal (2015)
[a]If needed, other Islamic financing tools such as murabaha, muajjal, Istisna, salam, and ijara may be used in promoting income

Distribution of Income and Wealth

Promoting waqf can act as a tool of just distribution of income and wealth by transferring fund from waqf institution to meet the demands of needy and destitute people of the society. Bangladesh can use waqf as policy tool to reduce present high level of income inequality (Gini coefficient 0.458). Waqf institutions can support the poor people by transferring revenue generated from them and hence they can work as a vehicle of just distribution of income and wealth in the Muslim communities. Rich people can undertake the assistance of a well-managed waqf in donating their assets among the right beneficiaries. Salman Ahmed Shaikh et al. (2017) show that waqf is more effective in serving all needy people as its heads of expenditures are not fixed like zakat.

Permanent Social Security

Waqf can provide permanent security services as it has perpetuity character. Waqf has flexibility in using fund as compared to zakat. In zakat, funds are required to use among specific categories of recipient mentioned in the Holy Quran. Under waqf, funds can be employed to offer multidimensional welfare services among both Muslim and non-Muslim people.

Transforming Social Capital

M. Woolcock and D. Narayan (2000) opine that societies having diverse stock of social networks can address poverty and vulnerability effectively.

Waqf can transform social capital into social infrastructure by establishing education and training centers and providing health services. Obaidullah (2008) and Haneef et al. (2014) emphasize on the need of training facilities for promoting micro-enterprises. Waqf can work as permanent source for supporting education, training and health services that would enhance income-generating potentials of beneficiaries.

Developing an Inclusive Economy
Inclusive growth depends on economic growth and its distribution. Growth needs to be inclusive to be sustainable and effective in reducing poverty (Anand et al. 2014). Among determinants of inclusive growth, education, fixed investment, and infrastructure are considered vital as sources of inclusive growth. Waqf can assist for developing an inclusive economy in Bangladesh by supporting the poor in availing education, health, and other social services and financing rural physical infrastructures such as roads, bridges, and culvert. The integration of waqf with other charitable instruments of Islam such as zakat and sadaqah may be emerged as a viable platform for financing social and physical infrastructure projects viz-a-viz financing by public and private sector for attaining inclusive economy in which every member of the society will be benefited and none will be left out.

5   Methods of Financing Waqf Properties

It is now imperative to assess different methods of developing and financing waqf properties in Bangladesh as revenue from waqf is insufficient in most cases to run its operation and assist the beneficiaries. Bangladesh has great potentials to revitalize waqf estates, particularly philanthropic estates to generate revenues for supporting social prospects. To this end, we would focus on major modes of financing for development of waqf estates by reviewing key literatures on waqf development.

5.1   Al-Hukr (Indefinite Lease)

A hukr developed by Hanafi Jurists is a classical method for financing for development of waqf estates. According to Obaidullah (2012), a hukr involves an indefinite lease of the waqf assets against payment of a large rental upfront that is almost equal to the market value of the asset, and periodic (annual) rentals that is quite insignificant. The lessee can use own funds for developing property at his risks. In exchange, he enjoys right over the property for a long period which can be transferred and inherited (Mohammad and Sabit 2006).

5.2   Al-Ijarahtain (Dual Lease)

Al-Ijarahtain is another classical mode for financing development of waqf estates. It is a long lease contract in which rent is comprised of two parts, one big lump sum advance for the construction of waqf property and the second part is small periodic (annual) payment (Mustafa and Ogunbado). Like hukr, it requires the lesser to make larger payment up front that is almost equal to the value of the waqf assets including small annual rentals. However, the initial larger payment is invested by the waqf management to increase the value of the asset. In this case, renovated high-value assets remain the rightful asset of waqf but in case of hukr, the waqf does not invest in assets and the lessee does so and own what it invests (Obaidullah 2012).

Both modes hukr and Al-Ijarahtain have become inoperative in modern days due to problems created from indefinite period of lease, fraudulent act of tenant, and fear of extinction of waqf estates. Hukr was disallowed by the laws enacted during the 1950s and 1960s in Egypt, Syria, Iraq, Jordan, Libya, etc. due to its pronounced negative effect on awaqf (Obaidullah 2012). M. T. Sabit et al. (2005) argue that under ijaratain, the waqf beneficiaries may not substantially benefit from either the rental income or the advanced amount.

5.3   Mursad Loan

Mursad loan denotes loan made to the waqf management by a lender to develop a waqf asset. The asset is given on lease to the lender for a period deemed long enough to assure the lender of the definite possibility of repayment of the loan. Once the loan is repaid, the lease comes to an end. Historically, it is widely practiced in Syria during the eighteenth and nineteenth centuries (Obaidullah 2012).

Like hukr and Al-Ijarahtain, mursad loan has lost its applicability in modern days owing to problems of long lease. In a long lease, neither the lessee takes proper care of the property nor does the waqf institution. The waqf property suffers due to this dual apathy. Hence, mursad loan should be avoided as far as possible, as it tends to favor the lender more at the expense of the waqf institution (Mustafa and Ogunbado 2015).

5.4   Istisna

Istisna is a contract executed between a buyer and a seller under which the seller pledges to manufacture and supply certain goods according to specification of the buyer. Istisna-Ijarah a modern financing tool widely used in construction sector may be used in developing waqf estates for generating ample revenues for supporting the beneficiaries. Istisna may be used (1) between waqf and developer; (2) between waqf and a financer; and (3) between financer and developer for the development of waqf land (Mohammad and Sabit 2006).

Under Istisna arrangement, the waqf management can enter into an agreement with developers to promote waqf property with an agreed price and deliver after an agreed period of time. The waqf management makes payment of price in installment over the contract period or in a full at the end of the period. The banks or other financial institutions may involve in Istisna by allowing the job of development to a third party under a parallel Istisna arrangement.

5.5   Diminishing Musharakah

In Islamic finance, musharakah is a financing tool in partnership business in which every partner has to provide more or less equity funds in this partnership business. One special type of musharakah is the diminishing musharakah that may be used as an effective tool in promoting waqf property. In a diminishing musharakah, financer's share in the equity declines through periodic return of capital, the share of the waqf in the project gradually increases over time, and finally, whole ownership of the developed assets goes to waqf management after payment of all installments is made.

The mode is widely used by Islamic banks including IDB to finance the development of waqf properties. Under diminishing musharakah, the waqf as a legal entity and an Islamic bank as a financier can develop properties on a pre-agreed profit sharing ratio. The waqf provides land alone and the bank provides funds for development of the property. The revenue from the project is divided into two parts: one, to pay for the costs provided by the bank, and the other portion is shared by the bank and the waqf institution as profit. The waqf returns its full ownership after returning of all capital to the bank.

5.6   Build-Operate-Transfer (BOT)

BOT model is widely used in financing large infrastructure projects by private firms. It may be an ideal model to develop large waqf projects such as building universities, hospitals, and other social projects. Large projects need massive capital which calls for involvement of multiple parties including investor community. Tabung Haji Malaysia has built a RM 150 million commercial building for the Federal Territory Islamic Religious Council in Kuala Lumpur under a waqf land development project (Obaidullah 2012).

5.7   Cash Waqf

Cash waqf is a unique innovation in waqf literature that has opened the new window of making movable property waqf against the popular perception that waqf can be made only using immovable property like building and land. Çizakça (2004) defines cash waqf as "a charitable endowment established with cash capital." The author also mentions that cash constitutes the nature of capital in case of cash waqf while real estate is the capital in real estate waqf. Under cash waqf, the income generated out of the investment of cash is then used for welfare of the community as mentioned in the waqf deed.

In today's Muslim world, cash waqf has gained popularity as one of the most effective mechanisms in realizing the socio-economic and welfare objectives. During the Ottoman Empire, cash waqf was used in the beginning of fifteenth century and it gained huge popularity all over the empire by the end of sixteenth century (Çizakça 2004). Now cash waqf is widely practiced in many Muslin countries like Kuwait, Oman, UAE, Saudi Arab, Malaysia, Indonesia, and Bangladesh (Ahmad 2015b).

5.8   Corporate Waqf

Corporate waqf is another institutional innovation in waqf literature to revitalize the powerful Islamic waqf institution by sustainable corporate activities. It can be used to mobilize funds for attaining higher GDP growth of Muslim countries, combating poverty and empowering the

Ummah in the long run (Hashim 2015). Corporate waqfs need to be fully business-driven, corporate-structured, and entrepreneur-led at all times for attaining success. The contemporary corporate waqf has been practiced in a number of Muslim countries, namely Turkey, Malaysia, Bangladesh, India, and Pakistan (Ramli and Jalil 2013).

Tan Sri Muhammad Ali Hashim (2015) mentioned that Johor Corporation of Malaysia has set an example of a successful corporate waqf by establishing "Waqaf An-Nur Corporation Berhad (WANCorp)." Hamdard Laboratories (WAQF) Bangladesh is another bright example of a successful corporate waqf that provides a wide range of services including health and education services.[3]

5.9 Issuance of Sukuk

Issuance of sukuk may be another option in financing waqf properties. Sukuk meaning "legal instrument," "deed," or "check" in Arabic language mainly refers to the Islamic Shariah-compliant equivalent of interest-bearing conventional bond. Sukuk can be defined as the real asset-backed security which embodies the claim on the revenue generated from the underlying asset as well as the ownership of the asset. Conventional bond is a debt instrument which has a contractual debt obligation for a specified period of time with a fixed or floating interest rate whereas sukuk is an equity instrument having no interest or any debt obligation.

Under this option, a waqf institution appoints a project management company to issue sukuk certificate to investors and sale proceeds are used by the said company to develop waqf property for generating rentals. Sukuk holders are entitled to receive profits generated from the waqf property. In case of issuance of Ijarah sukuk, the steps are as follows (Obaidullah 2012):

   i. Project company creates SPV (Special Purpose Vehicle);
   ii. It transfers the developed facility or asset to SPV;
  iii. SPV issues sukūk to investors against these assets;
   iv. SPV collects funds from investors;
   v. SPV pays to project company the sale price of asset;
   vi. Project company takes asset on ijārah;

---

[3]Website of Hamdard (www.hamdard.com.bd).

vii. SPV receives ijārah rentals by company in future; and
viii. SPV passes on ijārah rentals to investors after deducting muḍārib share or management expenses.

The assets revert back to the project company at the end of ijarah period, and the waqf gets the property back after the concession period.

6   Challenges for Developing Waqf in Bangladesh

Bangladesh confronts some challenges for developing waqf properties.

Low Public Awareness on Great Potentials of Waqf: In Bangladesh, most people think that waqf is meant for endowment for religious purpose only; it has no social development goal. This means that there is low public awareness regarding great potentials of waqf that can meet up both religious purpose and assist for attaining charitable objectives toward social development such as poverty alleviation and improvements in education and health services.

Inadequate Man power of Waqf Administration: The Waqf administration has shortage of man power in regulating and supervising waqf estates in Bangladesh. There are only 111 officers and staff in Waqf administration that is inadequate to manage more than 100,000 waqf estates.

Absence of Proper database and documentation of waqf estates: There is no updated database and proper documentation of waqf estates in Bangladesh. Updated database needs to adopt proper planning for developing waqf estates.

Lack of Accountability of Mutawallis: Mutawalli is empowered in running waqf estates and maintaining its income and expenditure accounts. In most cases, lack of integrity, accountability, and qualification of the mutawallis stands in the way of developing waqf estates in Bangladesh.

Misuse and Illegal Occupation of waqf properties: M. Ahmad (2015a) mentions that many of the awaqf properties are illegally occupied by private individuals, organizations, groups, or even by government agency.

Want of Funding the Waqf Estates: Now waqf cannot play its due roles in Bangladesh due to lack of funding the waqf estates for their upkeep, maintenance, renovation, and capacity building for addressing social problems like paucity of education and health services.

Lack of Professional Management and Innovative Ideas: The existing man power both in Waqf administration and field management (at mutawallis' level) lacks in professional and technical expertise in running, managing, and developing waqf estates.

7   RECOMMENDATIONS

Bangladesh needs some concrete steps in promoting and expanding waqf estates.

Strengthening Waqf Administration: The Waqf administration needs to be strengthened in regulating and supervising waqf estates in Bangladesh so that it can play its due role to promote waqf estates. Some measures are required to be undertaken such as recruitment proper number of man power, total automation of all operations and uploading updated list of waqf estates, quarterly report on developments of waqf estates, quality local and foreign publication on waqf and procedures for forming new waqf estates in the Waqf administration's Web site. The Waqf administration also needs to upgrade database and recordings documents of waqf estates. It is also necessary to strengthen its Legal Wing to recover waqf estates from illegal occupation and settle other cases relating to waqf estates.

Creating Public Awareness on Great Potentials of Waqf: There lacks awareness among Muslim population and policy makers on how great is the potential of promoting social development in Bangladesh. To create awareness, Waqf administration the regulatory body for overseeing the waqf estates needs to arrange dialogues among Islamic scholars, waqf researchers, benevolent Muslim, private corporate firms having charitable wings, policy makers and Islamic banks/NGOs. Annual waqf fair/seminar may be arranged to motive people to create waqf estates.

Ensuring Accountability and Efficiency of Mutawalli: Mutawalli (trustee/nazir) plays vital roles in managing waqf estates and maintaining its income and expenditure accounts. As preservation and smooth development of waqf estates depend on integrity, accountability, and efficiency of the mutawallis, there should have clear and transparent guidelines on criterion on appointment of qualified mutawalli, their duties/responsibilities and remuneration and transparent reporting of financial assets and transactions. Mutawalli needs to be educated and professionally efficient to preserve, protect, and develop the estates in order to sustain the welfare for the beneficiaries.

Choosing Viable Modes for Funding the Waqf Estates: Waqf has potential in promoting socio-economic developments in Bangladesh like other Muslim countries all over the world. To use waqf as a policy instrument, viable funding options are required for generating revenues to support social services like education and health care. Bangladesh has already included 8 (eight) options (clause 14) in the waqf (Transfer and Development of Property) Special Provisions Act, 2013 to develop waqf properties. These options include developing waqf properties through investment made by (i) Waqf administration; (ii) waqf itself; (iii) grants by the government; (iv) availing loan from banks/financial institutions; (v) receiving advance from shopkeepers; (vi) sale proceeds of shops/flat/commercial space; (vii) money received from developers; and (viii) money received from foreign state/organization subject to the approval of the Government.

In the light of the above-mentioned options, Bangladesh may use some financing options such as Istisna-Ijarah, diminishing Musharakah, Build-Operate-Transfer (BOT), cash waqf, Corporate waqf, and Issuance of Sukuk. These options are already analyzed in sect. 4.

Formation of Shariah Board: There should have a Shariah Board at Waqf administration comprising Islamic Jurists, waqf experts, investment bankers, representatives from Government and waqf estates. The Board will advise the Waqf administration on Shariah rules in regulating and managing of waqf estates including developing waqf estates.

Integration of Waqf with Zakat and Microfinance: The effort to integrate waqf with zakat and Microfinance for poverty alleviation in Muslim communities increased in recent times (Haneef et al. 2014 and 2015). The integration has become imperative because it can address extreme as well as moderate poverty effectively. Waqf and zakat-based microfinance can serve both extreme and moderate poor effectively by using both nonprofit and profit-based financing modes.

Collaboration with International Intuition and Countries: Bangladesh can share experiences with international institution such as Islamic Development Bank and waqf rich countries such as Turkey, Egypt, KSA, Sudan, Malaysia, and Indonesia in order to promote waqf properties toward social developments. Islamic Development Bank may provide technical and financial assistance for developing waqf properties in Bangladesh.

Setting up Training and Research Academy for Promoting Waqf properties: It is an urgent need to establish a Training and Research Academy at Waqf administration for promoting waqf properties in Bangladesh. The proposed academy will perform four jobs mainly. Firstly, the Academy would impart training to man power working in Waqf administration and field management (at waqf's level) for promoting professional and technical expertise in running, managing, and developing waqf estates. Secondly, it would upgrade database of waqf properties and conduct periodical survey regularly. Thirdly, the Academy would conduct research on key issues relating to smooth management and development of waqf properties and finally, it would publish research reports, quarterly and annual reports and other related papers/articles in the Web site of the Waqf administration. In establishing the academy, the Waqf administration can avail funds from Islamic banks under CSR programs.

8   Concluding Remarks

Though Bangladesh has achieved success in poverty alleviation, one quarter of the population of 160 million still live in poverty and 12.9% live in extreme poverty. Reducing poverty, extreme poverty in particular, she needs concerted efforts made by private and public sector with voluntary sector. Given this, waqf as a potential voluntary institution can also supplement the implementation of programs for SDGs by financing programs for poverty alleviation and social projects on health and education. To this end, necessary steps are required to revive existing waqf estates and create new waqf estates motivating benevolent people. To use waqf as a policy instrument for social development effectively, Bangladesh needs to adopt urgent steps such as strengthening Waqf administration, making mutawali accountable, promoting professional management, ensuring viable modes of funding the waqf estates, formation of Shariah Board, integration of waqf with zakat and microfinance, sharing experiences with waqf rich countries, and formation of a training and research academy. Islamic banks with 17 million account holders need to play significant roles for promoting waqf estates in Bangladesh that will help to attain the goals of Shariah (Maqasid al Shariah).

REFERENCES

Ahmad, M. (2015a). Role of Waqf in Sustainable Economic Development and Poverty Alleviation: Bangladesh Perspective. *Journal of Law, Policy & Globalization, 42,* 118.

Ahmad, M. (2015b). Cash Waqf: Historical Evolution, Nature and Role as an Alternative to Riba-Based Financing for the Grass Root. *Journal of Islamic Finance, 4*(1), 63–74.

Ahmed, H. (2004). *Role of Zakah and Awqaf in Poverty Alleviation.* Jeddah: Islamic Development Bank, Islamic Research and Training Institute.

Ahmed, H. (2007). *Waqf-Based Microfinance: Realizing the Social Role of Islamic Finance.* World Bank.

Anand, R., Tulin, V., & Kumar, N. (2014). *India: Defining and Explaining Inclusive Growth and Poverty Reduction* (Working Paper WP/14/63). Washington, DC: International Monetary Fund.

Asutay, M. (2007). Conceptualisation of the Second Best Solution in Overcoming the Social Failure of Islamic Finance: Examining the Overpowering of Homoislamicus by Homoeconomicus. *IIUM Journal of Economics and Management, 15*(2), 167–195.

Asutay, M., & Zaman, N. (2009). Divergence Between Aspirations and Realities of Islamic Economics: A Political Economy Approach to Bridging the Divide. *IIUM Journal of Economics and Management, 17*(1), 73–96.

Ayub, M. (2007). *Understanding Islamic Finance.* West Sussex, UK: Wiley.

Bangladesh Bank. (2016a). *Annual Report, 2015–16.* Dhaka: Bangladesh Bank.

Bangladesh Bank. (2016b, January–March). *Scheduled Bank Statistics.* Dhaka: Bangladesh Bank.

Bangladesh Bank. (2016c). *Website of Bangladesh Bank.* Dhaka: Bangladesh Bank.

Banglapedia. (2012). *The National Encyclopedia of Bangladesh.*

Beck, T., & De la Torre, A. (2006). *The Basic Analytics of Access to Financial Services* (Vol. 4026). World Bank Publications.

Beck, T., Demirgüç-Kunt, A., & Levine, R. (2004). *Finance, Inequality, and Poverty: Cross-Country Evidence* (No. w10979). National Bureau of Economic Research.

Beck, T., Demirgüç-Kunt, A., & Levine, R. (2007). Finance, Inequality, and the Poor. *Journal of Economic Growth, 12,* 27–49.

Budiman, M. A. (2014, June). The Significance of Waqf for Economic Development. *Journal Equilibrium, 2*(1), 19–34.

Census of Waqf Estate. (1986). *Bangladesh Bureau of Statistics.* Census of Waqf Estate.

Chapra, M. U. (2008). Ibn Khaldun's Theory of Development: Does It Help Explain the Low Performance of the Present-Day Muslim World? *The Journal of Socio-Economics, 37*(2), 836–863.

Çizakça, M. (1998). Awqaf in History and Its Implications for Modern Islamic Economies. *Islamic Economic Studies, 6*(1), 43–70.

Çizakça, M. (2000). *A History of Philanthropic Foundations: The Islamic World from the Seventh Century to the Present* (pp. 2–10). Istanbul: Boğaziçi University Press.

Çizakça, M. (2004). *Incorporated Cash Waqfs and Mudaraba, Islamic Non-Bank Financial Instruments from the Past to the Future* (MPRA Paper 25336). University Library of Munich, Germany.

GIFR. (2017). *Global Islamic Finance Report.*

Haneef, M. A., Muhammad, A. D., Pramanik, A. H., & Mohammed, M. O. (2014). Integrated Waqf Based Islamic Microfinance Model (IWIMM) for Poverty Alleviation in OIC Member Countries. *Middle-East Journal of Scientific Research, 19*(2), 286–298.

Haneef, M. A., Pramanik, A. H., Mohammed, M. O., Bin Amin, M. F., & Muhammad, A. D. (2015). Integration of Waqf-Islamic Microfinance Model for Poverty Reduction: The Case of Bangladesh. *International Journal of Islamic and Middle Eastern Finance and Management, 8*(2), 246–270.

Hashim, T. S. M. A. (2015). *Corporate Waqf: A Proposal for Corporate Reform to Bridge Divides and Uphold Economic Justice* (WIEF-UiTM Occasional Papers) (2nd ed.).

Hassan, M. K. (2010). An Integrated Poverty Alleviation Model Combining Zakat, Awqaf and Micro-Finance. In *Seventh International Conference— The Tawhidic Epistemology: Zakat and Waqf Economy* (pp. 261–281). Bangi: Malaysia.

Hassanain, K. M. (2015). Integrating Zakah, Awqaf and IMF for Poverty Alleviation: Three Models of Islamic Micro Finance. *Journal of Economic and Social Thought, 2*(3), 193–211.

HIES. (2016). *Household Income and Expenditure Survey.* Bangladesh Bureau of Statistics.

Honohan, P. (2004). *Financial Development, Growth and Poverty: How Close Are the Links?* (pp. 1–37). Basingstoke: Palgrave Macmillan.

Ibrahim, H., Amir, A., & Masron, T. A. (2013). Cash Waqf: An Innovative Instrument for Economic Development. *International Review of Social Sciences and Humanities, 6*(1), 1–7.

Iqbal, Z. (2015). Islamic Finance: Financial Inclusion as a Core Concept. In *Islamic Finance for Asia: Development, Prospects, and Inclusive Growth, ADB and IFSB.*

Kahf, M. (2003). The Role of Waqf in Improving the Ummah Welfare. In *International Seminar on Waqf as a Private Legal Body* (pp. 6–7). Medan, Sumatera Utara, Indonesia: Islamic University of North Sumatra.

Kahf, M. (2008). Role of Zakah and Awqaf in Reducing Poverty: A Proposed Institutional Setting Within the Spirit of Shari'ah. *Thoughts on Economics, 18*(3), 40–67.

Khalid, R. S. (2011). Certain Legal and Administrative Measures for the Revival and Better Management of Awqaf. *Islamic Economic Studies, 19*(1), 1–40.

Levine, R. (2005). Finance and Growth: Theory and Evidence. In P. Aghion & S. Durlauf (Eds.), *Handbook of Economic Growth*. Amsterdam, The Netherlands: Elsevier Science.

Mannan, M. A. (2005). The Role of Waqf in Improving the Ummah Welfare. *Presentation at the International Seminar on Islamic Economics as Solution* (pp. 18–19). Jakarta Medan, Indonesia: Indonesian Association of Islamic Economists and Muamalat Institute.

Mohammad, M. T. S. H., & Sabit, M. T. (2006). *Innovative Modes of Financing the Development of Waqf Property*. Paper at Konvensyen Wakaf Kebangsaan.

Mustafa, O., & Ogunbado, A. F. (2015). Examining the Traditional Waqf-Based Financing Methods and Their Implications on Socio-Economic Development. *IOSR Journal of Business and Management (IOSR-JBM), 17*(2), 119–125.

Obaidullah, M. (2008). *Role of Microfinance in Poverty Alleviation: Lessons from Experiences in Selected IDB Member Countries*. Jeddah, Saudi Arabia: Islamic Development Bank.

Obaidullah, M. (2012). *Training Manual on Awqāf Development and Management*. Jeddah, KSA: Islamic Research and Training Institute (IRTI), IDB.

Planning Commission. (2016). *SDGs Financing Strategy: Bangladesh Perspective*. Dhaka: General Economic Division, Planning Commission, Ministry of Planning, Government of Bangladesh.

Ramli, A. M., & Jalil, A. (2013). Corporate Waqf Model and Its Distinctive Features: The Future of Islamic Philanthropy. In *World Universities Islamic Philanthropy Conference*. Kuala Lumpur: Menara Bank Islam.

Sabit, M. T., Hamid, A., & Omar, I. (2005). *An Ideal Financial Mechanism for the Development of the Islamic Trust Properties in Malaysia*. Johor Bahru, Malaysia: University Technology Malaysia.

Sadeq, A. M. (2002). Waqf, Perpetual Charity and Poverty Alleviation. *International Journal of Social Economics, 29*(1/2), 135–151.

Sadeq, A. M. (2005). Awqaf in Bangladesh. In S. K. Rashid (Ed.), *Awqaf Experiences in South Asia* (p. 161). New Delhi: Institute of Objective Studies.

Shaikh, S. A., Ismail, A. G., & Mohd Shafiai, M. H. (2017). Application of Waqf for Social and Development Finance. *ISRA International Journal of Islamic Finance, 9*(1), 5–14.

Shirazi, N. S., Obaidullah, M., & Haneef, M. A. (2013). *Integration of Waqf and Islamic Microfinance for Poverty Reduction: Case of Pakistan.* Jeddah, KSA: Research and Training Institute (IRTI), IDB.

Siddiqi, M. N. (2006). Islamic Banking and Finance in Theory and Practice: A Survey of State of the Art. *Islamic Economics Studies, 13*(2), 1–48.

Thoarlim, A., Rahman, M., & Yanya, A. (2017). Cash Waqf in Bangladesh and the Need for Innovative Approach Towards Awqaf: Lessons from Selected Countries. *International Journal of Academic Research in Business and Social Sciences, 7*(4), 151–169.

Woolcock, M., & Narayan, D. (2000). Social Capital: Implications for Development Theory, Research, and Policy. *The World Bank Research Observer, 15*(2), 225–249.

World Bank. (2007). *Finance for All: Policies and Pitfalls in Expanding Access.* Washington, DC: World Bank.

CHAPTER 8

Cash Waqf Deposit Product: An Innovative Instrument of Islamic Banks for Socio-Economic Development in Bangladesh

M. Mizanur Rahman and M. Nurul Islam Sohel

1 Introduction

There is no direct injunction in the Quran about waqf. However, there is a hadith reported by Ibn Umar, whereby Umar Ibn Al Khattab acquired a piece of land in Khyber and went to Prophet (saw) and sought advice regarding the land. The Prophet (saw) advised that the land should be made inalienable and the profit given to charity. This implies that in Islam, land was the first waqf. The mosque of Quba' in Medina, which exists until today, was the first mosque in Islamic history that was waqf oriented. Others using waqf land include the Al-Azhar University in Egypt, the University of Cordova Spain, and the Al Noori Hospital in Damascus (Ahmad Zaki et al. 2006).

Philanthropic waqf was started during the era of Prophet (saw) in Medina when the inflow of immigrant has caused for scarce of

M. Mizanur Rahman (✉) · M. Nurul Islam Sohel
Islami Bank Training and Research Academy (IBTRA), Dhaka, Bangladesh

© The Author(s) 2019
K. M. Ali et al. (eds.), *Revitalization of Waqf for Socio-Economic Development, Volume I*,
https://doi.org/10.1007/978-3-030-18445-2_8

water supply. This has caused for expensive price of water in Medina. After that, Prophet (saw) called anyone of his companion to purchase the Bir' Ruma and declared it for waqf. Caliph Uthman volunteers himself and buys the well and declares it as waqf for the Medina societies (Allah et al. 2014).

The above-mentioned Hadith implies that cash waqf is permitted in Islam. Additionally, the non-cash waqf institutions face numerous and of enormous challenges. Of the problems, highly centralized Waqf administration, inadequate manpower, organizational and administrative incompetency, operational inefficiency and problem of waqf disputes, unregistered waqf properties, lack of integrity and knowledge of the mutawallis, illegal occupation and misappropriation of waqf properties and having no Shariah and advisory board, are mentionable.

However, due to wrong perception among Muslims that waqf endowment can be made only through land and not in cash. Therefore, many Muslim did not get a chance to participate in waqf endowment. They believe that only land can fulfill the conditions of waqf (perpetuity, irrevocability, and inalienability) (Aziz et al. 2013). An individual endows usually when he/she feels of giving and donating his/her property as goodwill, while cash waqf and infaq (donate) have no specific time to implement. It means that he/she is free from any obligations to perform this social service (Yusof et al. 2014).

Therefore, instead of waqf land, the other prominent and potential waqf are a cash waqf, which has developed considerably since the time of Prophet (saw). cash waqf has become increasingly well known due to its flexibility, which allows distribution of the waqf's potential benefit to the poor anywhere (Mannan 1998).

1.1   Cash Waqf

Cash waqf can be defined as the donation of an amount of money by a founder and the dedication of its usufruct in perpetuity for the prescribed purpose (Mohsin 2008). According to history, cash waqf already started during the time of Prophet (saw), in that the Prophet's companion was reputed to have used waqf to donate their farmland for development purposes. The revenue from the land would be solely used for the sake of the development of society. Consequently, cash waqf is targeted to become an effective option for poverty alleviation programs, especially in Muslim countries.

The fund from cash waqf payers will be collected by fund managers and the money will be invested in any Shariah-based investment opportunities (Hoseini 2010). Cash waqf is seen as an alternative to achieve modern macroeconomics development which can reduce government spending, government's reliance on debt and budget deficit, and finance development projects (Mohamad 2012). It is a religious endowment by using cash collected in a trust fund under the management of the superintendent entrusted to manage this endowment for the welfare and benefit of the Muslims (Konsep Wakaf Tunai 2016).

After gaining the profit from the investment, it can be allocated for poor families and also can be channeled through educational and cultural development. Then, waqf funds can provide health center and providing reasonable price for medicines with appropriate quality (Masyita et al. 2005). From the economic perspective, waqf also can be used as a tool to create economic effect or social benefit multiplier effect (Adam and Lahsasna 2013). However, cash waqf is not practiced aggressively nowadays due to debatable element in terms of its perpetuity and inalienability (Ibrahim et al. 2013).

Alternatively, in modern times, a cash waqf can also be established with the shares of incorporated joint-stock companies. Imam Zufar, who had approved of the cash waqf for the first time, had envisaged that the corpus should be invested through mudarabah.

Although the origins of cash waqf can be traced back to ancient Mesopotamia, Greece, and the Roman Empire, their full development and maturity in the Islamic world had to wait until the sixteenth century, when they became the most popular form of philanthropy among the Ottomans. This popularity did not fail to trigger opposition among the learned circles. The basic argument of those, who opposed the cash waqf, was based on a seemingly powerful point: Once endowed, the corpus of a waqf belongs to Allah. But while investing the corpus of a cash waqf, whether in the form of a mudarabah or simple loaning, the cash endowed is inevitably distributed to the borrowers. But what belongs to Allah, the opposition argued, cannot be distributed to third persons (Cizakca 2010).

The cash waqf controversy lasted throughout the sixteenth and seventeenth centuries without conclusion. Apparently, notwithstanding the controversy, based on Abu'l-Su'ud's fatwa and supported by the Ottoman sultans' orders, these waqf continued to flourish. Nowadays, cash waqf, quasi-cash waqf, or mixed cash real estate waqf exist in various forms of development and sophistication, in Turkey, Iran, Egypt, Sudan, India, Pakistan, Bangladesh, Malaysia, and Singapore (Cizakca 2010).

1.2   Waqf Literature Review

In Islamic history, the first religious waqf is the mosque of Quba' which is located in Medina (Yusof et al. 2014). Originally, cash waqf was found back to ancient of Mesopotamia, Greece, and Roman Empire, where they had to wait until sixteenth century for their full development and maturity in Islamic world, when among the Ottomans they became the most popular form of philanthropy (Cizakca 2004).

The University of Al-Azhar is one of the examples of waqf. It was founded in Cairo in 972 and was financed by its waqf revenues until the government of Muhammad Ali in Egypt took control over the waqf in 1812. Parallel to the development of the trust in common law countries, a remarkably similar structure developed in the Islamic world—the waqf developed, thrived, and then declined. Recently, the emergence of great wealth in Islamic countries and the Islamic tradition of philanthropy have resulted in the revival of interest in the structure of the waqf and increased sources being held on terms that seek to comply with the requirements of Islamic law (Stibbard, Russell and Bromley, 2012).

The profit of waqf fund can be allocated for poor "Family Rehabilitation" by enhancing poor people's welfare and can be apportioned through educational and cultural development. It is a new dimension in the mobilization of waqf fund for educational development such as by funding relevant research, supplying free books, and improving educational programmes. Then, waqf funds can provide health and sanitation for poor people by establishing health care center and providing reasonable quality medicines (Masyita et al. 2005). From the economic perspective, waqf is a tool to create economic effect or social benefit multiplier effect (Adam and Lahsasna 2013). Nowadays, technological innovation making cash waqf more user-friendly and easier by sending SMS using mobile phone that are implemented by Bank Islam and Maybank through Yayasan Restu Waqf and Maybank Waqf (Ibrahim et al. 2013).

In the contemporary context, cash waqf seems to be one of the most preferable methods for endowment in perpetuity, because of its liquid nature. This is arguably because cash is free to endow, easy to manage, more practical to distribute its benefits among the wider sections of beneficiaries and easy to utilize for beneficiary's day-to-day needs (Abdullah Nadwi and Kroessin 2013). Imam Az-Zuhri ruled that for the sake of Islamic purposes, the welfare of society and development of the Ummah, waqf in the form of dinar (money) is allowed (Ibrahim et al. 2013). The ruling has made by the National Council, which permitted the cash waqf practices, and it was followed by several states in their respective Islamic Council (Osman et al. 2012).

Cash waqf is mainly to devote or dedicate a certain portion of one's money toward legitimate ends of helping the poor and the needy as well as to bring about positive change in the society. It is further argued that in order to achieve this feat it is essential to develop a strategic plan toward utilizing the philanthropic waqf for maqasid-based legislative strategies.

Pitchay et al. (2014) investigated the priority of cash waqf donors in Malaysia. The findings show that the donors are acquainted and prefer to invest their donations in education, health, masjid and madrasa, social care and welfare, trade and commerce, environment, infrastructure and art, as well as culture and heritage.

The waqf bank can be applied as the bank of the poor. It can be permissible in Islam based on validity of cash waqf and the need of waqf, its beneficiaries as well as the society. But, if there is favorable, political will institution of waqf through waqf bank contributes to society greatly. The institutions of waqf have the unrealized potential to establish a waqf Bank.

Syed Adwam Wafa (2010) explains that the impact of developing waqf for education in Malaysia not only promoting the significant rule of waqf toward the country, but also will be impact to (1) promoting the third sector of Islamic economic, (2) establishing economic activities through several projects and business, (3) complementing the royal aid development, benevolent, and educational programs, and (4) promoting the oneness of society.

Several authors analyzed socio-economic profile and explored potential expenditure options of the waqf institutions in Bangladesh. It is recommended that some potential expenditure options, supervisory investment institutions, insurance (takaful) and microfinance to provide financing and loans to the needy. They realized waqf institutions as social institutions instead of religious one. So that, Islam does not only encourage the waqf institutions to build mosques or orphanages but authorizes them accomplishing the total development in terms of their social, cultural, and economic viability and religious, moral and spiritual supremacy.

The focus of economic growth in the conventional economic system lacks a sense of justice and equality. Doubtless, justice and equality are reflections of Maqasid al Shariah.

Cash waqf is the latest product in the realm of our banking sector particularly in Islamic economics and finance. Cash waqf provides a unique opportunity for making investment in different religious, educational, and social services. Savings made from earning by the well-off and the rich people of the society can be utilized by purchasing cash waqf Certificate. Income earned from there will be spent for different purposes like the purposes of the waqf properties itself (Mannan 2014).

Sadeq (2005) expressed that in Bangladesh 8000 educational institution and more than 123,000 mosques are based on waqf. Other than religious and educational sector cash waqf fund may be utilized for all socio-economic purpose. Sadeq (2002) also discussed the potential role of the institution of waqf in poverty alleviation, particularly in the developing world. He attempted to define a new approach to poverty analysis and suggests a way to make the role of waqf more effective in the poverty alleviation and socio-economic development of a resource-poor country.

Mohsin (2008) add for investing in cash waqf, the contract of mudarabah is allowed in order to generate the funding. There is a source of social fund that is economically and politically free of charge, which is cash waqf under the Islamic socio-economic concept. Cash waqf is a special charitable endowment fund, is expected to become one of the instruments for the property improvement programs worldwide mostly in Islamic countries (Aziz 2013).

Microcredit and Safety Net Program insufficient for poverty alleviation, and on the other hand, these steps fueled income inequality and argued waqf as tool for poverty alleviation and reducing income inequalities along with zakat. So, if we really want to do something for the needy and poor, we have to revive this much needed institutions where at present waqf-based institutions are not growing at a considerable level. Therefore, starting a worldwide waqf movement is indispensable.

The above-reviewed literature shows that the idea of cash waqf is not anything new though its practice is not that old and not even that much. The implementation of this cash waqf has attracted many researchers to study the potential and impacts of this instrument. In 1998, Professor Mannan has promoted cash waqf through SIBL. This bank produces cash waqf certificates to collect funds from waqif and distribute the gains of the managed funds among the deserving persons or beneficiaries. Cash waqf certificates were the first in banking history whereby the certificate provided an opportunity for Muslims in Bangladesh to invest in religious, educational, or other social development.

The banking industry in Bangladesh has continued using cash waqf as its investment product, especially through the Islamic Bank Bangladesh Limited (IBBL), which offers a cash waqf product known as Mudarabah Waqf Cash Deposit Account (MWCDA) The investment is used to generate the cash waqf funds for the welfare of Muslims in Bangladesh. Till now, six Islamic banks out of eight and six conventional banks in Bangladesh are practicing this instrument for social development and some banks are on pipeline.

However, there is a limited study that focuses on the contribution of social development, that is why this study was undertaken to assess the growth and contribution of cash waqf in Bangladeshi socio-economic development and also to sort out the challenges and to project the potentials of cash waqf in Bangladesh. This study is also targeted to develop a microfinance-based cash waqf product proposal, as Islamic microfinance is a very strong instrument of IBBL for rural poverty alleviation in Bangladesh.

This paper is divided into five sections. After this introduction along with the literature review, the second section is research methodology of the study. Third section provides brief understanding on cash waqf, while fourth section discusses cash waqf deposit product in Bangladesh. Fifth section discusses the cash waqf deposit product for socio-economic development in Bangladesh. Section six proposes an integrated approach of cash waqf and Islamic microfinance for poverty alleviation. Section seven discusses the implication of cash waqf toward Muslim society. The last section has concluded paper with some recommendations.

2   RESEARCH METHODOLOGY

The research methodologies applied in the research were quantitative and qualitative as well. In executing this research, a combination of fieldwork and library research was conducted. Thus, both primary and secondary data were collected and used. Some cases were also studied and some brief information on a few clients is presented.

Data were gathered from a wide variety of sources through fieldwork, such as interviewing selected key officials, waqifs and beneficiaries; authors of waqf literature on Bangladesh and media reporters and journalists who have reported on various aspects of waqf, individual mutawalli of various waqf estates as well as some beneficiaries. The result of this data is obtained from the field research whereby the researchers, and from documentation research refers to reading material in relation to cash waqf practices have been presented. The data obtained from the sources stated above will be reviewed and used as guidelines for the construction of cash waqf.

3   THEORETICAL UNDERPINNING OF CASH WAQF

3.1   Cash Waqf

Cash waqf has been defined by many scholars, from that it can be said that cash waqf is a charitable endowment established with cash capital permanently dedicated and privately (Cizakca 2010) owned by a Muslim, or a corporate body governed according to Shariah with perpetual dedication of its usufruct to be spent on any purpose recognized by Shariah.

3.2   The Application of Cash Waqf as Modern Instruments

The economic meltdown and financial difficulties of the twenty-first century have led to demands for the restructuring of waqf institutions across Muslim countries in order to introduce and create movable property such of cash waqf in its comprehensive method and strategy. The modern models for the creation of cash waqf have been in place and practiced in Muslim countries such as waqf shares model, corporate cash waqf model, deposit product model, waqf mutual fund model and wakala waqf fund are discussed in this section.

Waqf Shares Model

Waqf shares model is a system which is known as a public waqf and is practiced and well known in countries like Malaysia, Sudan, Kuwait, and UK (Magda Ismail 2008). In this model, the fund provider will purchase shares from reputable and recognized religious institutions at an agreed amount. The price can range in any amount and the fund provider will receive a cash waqf certificate to indicate that the buyer has purchased waqf shares. The waqf shares will then later be donated to the endowed institution that will act as a mutawalli to manage the accumulated funds. The total amount of accumulated funds is channeled to charitable activities and events as stipulated by the concerned institution such as construction, renovation of mosques, establishment of schools or school renovation, economic and social development and other useful and devotional activities in the interest of needy people in the nation.

Corporate Cash Waqf Model

The corporate cash waqf model has been developed and practiced in Malaysia in Kumpulan an-Nur (1998), in Turkey in Sabanci Foundation (1974), in Pakistan in the Hamdard Foundation (1953), and in South Africa in the National Waqf Foundation (2000). The fund provider of the corporate cash waqf model can be an individual or corporate body. In this corporate, cash waqf model the individual or corporate body concerned channels their dividends to associated waqf institutions as their cash waqf. The role of the associated waqf institution is to act as the mutawalli who will manage the venture and invest the accumulated monies into profitable transactions in the interest of the needy. At the end of the contract or business, the profit is used for charitable projects (Magda Ismail 2008).

The Waqf Mutual Fund Model

The waqf mutual fund model is a system where the fund provider will contribute cash money to mutual funds and they will stipulate that a certain percentage of his return (e.g., 60%) will go to his personal earnings and the rest of the percentages (say 40%) of her returns will directly go to waqf for charitable activities. The waqf endowment will act as the mutawalli to manage the 40% contributed by the fund provider and invest the money in profitable investments for the benefit of the needy (Magda Ismail 2008).

Wakala with Waqf Funds Model

In this system of the wakala with waqf funds model, the donor/shareholder makes initial donation to create waqf funds. The amount is based on the specifications of Shariah experts. Later, the shareholder will lose his ownership right while the donated amount becomes the property of the waqf endowment. The waqf endowment has the right to develop rules and regulation on how to spend, develop, and invest the donated money. The reputable company will manage the accumulated funds as the administrator and deposit the funds while the donation donated as takaful would be combined together for the investment and the total profit will be deposited again with whole fund. In this system, the donor is the beneficiary of the waqf fund. The waqf endowments should consist of a team of capable people with the experience and skill to optimize donated funds, as the more the waqf invests is lucrative investments, business, and transactions, the more the profit would be realized. Also, the more the waqf institution has enough funds, the more waqf is capable of helping the needy.

The Cash Waqf Deposit Product Model

In Bangladesh, cash waqf deposit model has been developed by Professor Abdul Mannan in 1997 and launched in 1998 and since then this product has been practiced in SIBL and later IBBL and four more Islamic banks have also started practicing this product. The procedure for the deposit product model is that the fund provider will deposit money directly into cash waqf in a specific account in a specific bank. The fund provider would be given the list or name of beneficiaries where he will choose the beneficiaries. The bank will later act as a mutawalli and invest the deposited money into a mudarabah contract and the accumulated gain will be used for the needy. It is the duty of the waqf endowment management to consciously plan the type of lucrative transactions and business the waqf institution wants to venture into. The feasibility of proposed ventures should be studied and examined properly in order to meet the demands of applicant who are in serious need.

4   CASH WAQF DEPOSIT PRODUCT DEVELOPMENT IN BANGLADESH

According to 1986 census of waqf estate, there are 150,593 waqf estates in Bangladesh including 1400 estates around different *mazars*, having multipurpose uses. Of the total waqf estates, 97,046 are registered, 45,607 are verbal, and the rest 7940 are waqf by tradition. Out of these large waqf estates, only 13,200 waqf estates are under the administrative control of Waqf Administrator and of which 10,683 waqf estates are of mixed nature. The annual income of the waqf estates is Tk. 906 million and expenditure Tk. 856 million. The net collection is Tk. 50 million only.

Although waqf management and development have been a big concern for the Muslim scholars since long, the phenomenon of corruption in the waqf management can be found throughout history through misuse, mismanagement, looting, encroachment, and unlawful seizure of waqf properties. Bangladesh is no exception to this case. Most of the waqf properties in Bangladesh, registered or unregistered, are neglected and sloppily maintained, underdeveloped and are devoid of any dynamic futuristic developmental plan. Some of these valuable waqf properties, especially the lands, are being leased out with nominal charges or sold out for insignificant prices.

The problem the waqf institutions faces in the country are also numerous and of enormous magnitude, which are: inadequate manpower, occupation and misappropriation of waqf properties, subscriptions remaining unrealized, uncollected arrears, violation of the waqf Ordinance 1962, personal use of the waqf compensation money, etc. Against this backdrop, the trend of waqf endowments in Bangladesh is pathetically negative at present.

There is no dearth of laws in Bangladesh for managing and administering waqf properties. The waqf laws emerged at different stages initiated by the British in 1894. But over the decades, no policy was formulated for ensuring sustainable good governance and better management of such a huge size of waqf properties which could have, like in the past, contributed to the dissemination of Islamic education, development of Islamic science, spread of Islamic culture, and extension of social welfare services.

Considering the above-mentioned problems in handling the waqf entities, Professor Mannan in 1997 has socialized cash waqf in

Bangladesh through SIBL. This bank issues cash waqf certificates to collect funds from the rich and distributes the gains of the managed funds among the poor. Later, 5 more Islamic banks have introduced this model and since development of this cash waqf system it has been becoming increasingly popular, particularly because of its flexibility which allows distribution of the waqfs' potential benefits to the poor.

Some well-to-do persons pooled their funds to jointly create cash waqf to set up a number of private universities in the wake of the enactment of the Private University Act, 1992. Among others, there is one organization, which is partially created by cash waqf, namely the Social Science Institute (SSI). In this way, the cash waqf has added a new dimension to the activities of charity in Bangladesh.

To modernize and to popularize this cash waqf model, the fund accumulation of a cash waqf project could be realized through setting up of three instruments: Cash and E-Waqf Fund, per-square feet value certificate and the issuance of sukuk. These instruments provide an opportunity for the donors to dedicate their wealth for waqf purposes. Cash and E-Waqf Fund is considered as the easiest means for the public to join the waqf scheme because they are only obliged to donate their money in cash or deduct from their bank account via E-Waqf facility. This model may contribute to popularizing the role of waqf in the country including cash waqf which can be instrumental in transferring savings of the rich to the members of the public in financing various religious, educational, and social services in the country. Cash waqf can also work as a supplement to the financing of various social investment projects.

4.1   Objectives of Cash Waqf Deposit Product

The general objectives of the cash waqf deposit model are to mobilize deposit through banking channel and utilize the returns of the deposit to different charity directly by the bank or by the depositors. The more specific objectives are to:

a. provide banking services as facilitator to create cash waqf and to assist in the assist in mobilization of social savings by creating cash waqf with a view to commemorate alive or deceased parents, children and to strengthen the integration of the family relationship of the well-off people and the rich;
b. manage waqf through banking channel;

c. increase social investment and to transform the social savings into capital;

d. benefit the general public specially the poor sections of the people out of the resources of the rich;

e. create awareness among the rich regarding their social responsibilities to the society;

f. assist in developing Social Capital Market;

g. assist in overall development efforts of the country and to make a unique integration between social security and social peace.

4.2 Guidelines of Governing the Operations of Cash Waqf Deposit Product

The guidelines governing the operation of the cash waqf are as follows:

a. Cash waqf shall be accepted as endowment in conformity with the Shariah. The bank will manage the waqf on behalf of the waqif;

b. Waqf are done in perpetuity and account shall be opened in the title given by the waqif;

c. Waqif will have the liberty to choose the purpose to be served, either from the list of 32 purposes identified by bank or any other purpose permitted by the Shariah;

d. Cash waqf amount will earn profit at the highest rate time to time offered by the bank;

e. The waqf amount will remain intact and only the profit amount will be spent for the purpose(s) specified by the waqif. The unspent profit amount will automatically be added to waqf amount and earn profit to grow over time;

f. Waqif may also instruct the bank to spend the entire profit amount for the purpose specified by him/her.

g. Waqif will have the opportunity to create cash waqf at a time. Otherwise, waqif may declare the amount intended to build up and may start with a minimum deposit of Tk. 1000/= one thousand only. The subsequent deposits shall also be made in thousand or in multiples of thousand;

h. Waqif shall also have the right to give standing instruction to the bank for regular realization of cash waqf at a rate specified by him/her from any other a/c maintained with bank;

i. Cash waqf shall be accepted in specified endowment receipt voucher and a certificate for the entire amount shall be issued as and when the declared amount is built;

j. The principles and Shariah-based rules of cash waqf account are subject to amendment and review from time to time.

4.3   The Modus Operandi of the Cash Waqf Deposit Product

The cash waqf deposit product model is a waqf bank model commonly uses by most of the Islamic banks in Bangladesh. The permissibility of cash waqf can be extended to waqf bank for several reasons: (i) waqf issues are rational, (ii) the utility of a Waqf Bank, and (iii) compliance of the structure and operation of a waqf. Thus, the establishment of waqf bank could be allowed for the benefit of waqf, its beneficiaries, and also public interest, as long as it is not against Shariah principles. The function of cash waqf can be the function of a waqf bank through loans to the needy, and investment on mudarabah, musharakah, and ijarah. If a wider application is given to the idea, a waqf bank can use such cash waqf for the same purposes (Mohammad 2011).

In doing so, the mechanism of this figure is: First, an Islamic bank will act as a trustee for cash waqf. It will supervise and monitor the collection of waqf fund, investment, and distribution of profit to the charity activities. Although the Islamic bank will monitor all activities of waqf, actual financing, investment and profit distribution will be done under proper management of its cash waqf windows. If in the future the windows activities expanded in a large extent, then it would be operated as a separate waqf Bank.

Second, the cash waqf model can be used to raise cash waqf fund. It requires diverse techniques because different al-waqif prefers dissimilar way of cash waqf endowment. The techniques as follows: (i) endowment of shares as cash waqf, (ii) cash waqf by other institutions from their parts of dividend, (iii) waqf certificate, (iv) waqf insurance, (v) temporary waqf, (vi) deposit without share of profit, and (vii) e-waqf.

Third, in term of investment, the use of cash waqf fund is the best Islamic mode of financing, such as musharakah, diminishing musharakah and mudarabah, or a combination of both two.

In doing so, waqf fund should be used to finance pious people and other Islamic Financial Institutions (IFI's), basically for two reasons.

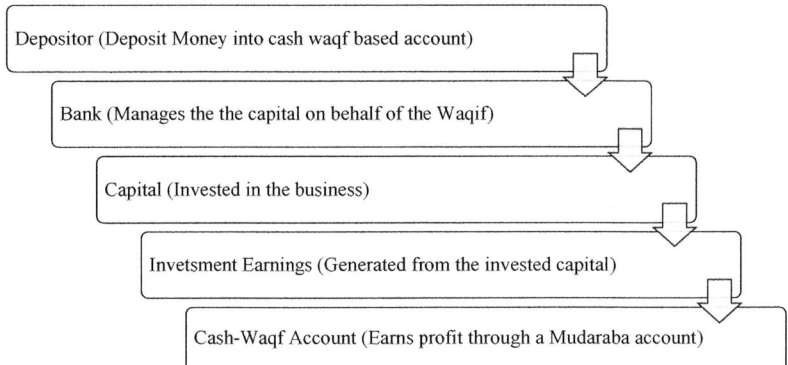

Fig. 1   Deposit product model (Public waqf)

Firstly, al-waqif donates money not only to help poor people but also to get reward hereafter or to satisfy Allah, and secondly, honesty is very important for successful musharakah and mudarabah contract. The investment can be invested through waqf land developments, microfinance, SME loan, portfolio investment in IFI's securities.

Fourth, the profit distribution should be distributed according to the donor's will. However, if he assigns the responsibility to the bank, then it can be distributed in three ways: (i) to charities such as mosque, madrasa, poor, social activities, training of youth, marriage for poor girl religious education, etc., (ii) to management includes maintenance, managerial expenses, and future development and capital enhancement, and (iii) to marketing because when there is any natural disaster or illness, etc. then through publicity by television, radio, or newspaper, it is always easy to raise donated fund. The procedure of deposit product model (Fig. 1) is as follows:

- The fund providers' deposits money with cash waqf-based account in the bank;
- While depositing the money, the founder will be given a list of the beneficiaries whereby he can choose or specify his/her beneficiaries;
- The bank will act as a mutawalli and will invest the capital through mudarabah contract;

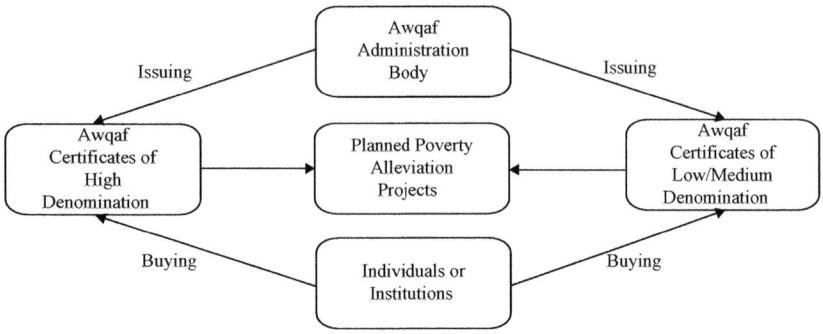

Fig. 2   Cash waqf certificate developed by SIBL, Bangladesh

- Revenue generated will be channeled to charitable purposes, specified by the founder.

4.4   Cash Waqf Certificate Scheme

The fund established through cash waqf will be invested which will ensure social security for the poor and social peace for the rich. Eventually, cash waqf would create a bridge of mutual care and compassion between the rich and the poor, thereby, contributing to the process of social harmony and cooperation. To stimulate this system, it is interesting to report that Social Investment Bank introduced Cash Waqf Certificate (Fig. 2) on experimental basis in December 1997, and it was formally launched on January 12, 1998. The fact of the matter is that Cash Waqf Certificate Scheme is likely to bring about wide-ranging economic and social benefits to the society as a whole. It appears that the cash waqf certificate scheme, introduced by SIBL offers a unique opportunity at the institutional level to drive social benefits and divine blessing for life here and hereafter.

Table 1 Purpose of cash waqf fund utilization of Islamic banks in Bangladesh

Thirty-Two purposes for utilization of cash waqf			
Family empowerment	*Education and culture*	*Health and sanitation*	*Social utility services*
Uplift of absolute poor	Education of orphans Educational development Providing informal education	Villages health care and sanitation	Settling disputes Legal aid to deserving women
Rehabilitating handicapped	Physical education		Arranging dowryless marriages
Rehabilitating beggars	Supporting local culture and heritage Conducting Dawah activities	Supplying pure drinking water	Public transportation and plantation Assistance to non-Muslims
Rehabilitation of destitute women	Supporting vocational education Education in neglected area	Establishing hospitals, clinics, etc.	Public utility services Mosque development Projects
Uplift urban slum Dwellers	Financing educational institutions Educating deserving descendants Projects for memory of father/mother Establishing educational chair	Research in health sector	Graveyard development projects Edgah development projects

5   Cash Waqf Deposit Product for Socio-Economic Development in Bangladesh

Cash waqf is a unique product developed in our banking sector particularly in Islamic banking and finance sector, and it provides opportunity for making investment in different religious, educational, and social services. Six Islamic banks, out of eight, in Bangladesh have so far introduced this cash waqf deposit product in the name of MWCDA with aim in helping the destitute and hapless people of the society. Waqf, a perpetual endowment, by the well-off and the rich people of the society and the income generated from waqf may be spent for different benevolent purposes.

Islamic banks collect waqf deposits as perpetual endowment on mudarabah principle from the rich people and manage the fund on behalf of the Waqif, who will have the right to create cash waqf at a time or client may start with a minimum deposit of Tk. 10,000 and the subsequent deposit shall also be made in thousand or in multiple of thousand Taka. The account can be opened in foreign currency. Any bona fide adult citizen of Bangladesh with sound mind may open this account with any of the bank with a title selected by the Waqif.

The Waqif have the right to choose the purposes to be served either from the list or any other purposes permitted by the Shariah. Bank will spend the fund in the following (Table 1) purposes:

(i) Family Rehabilitation

This cash waqf scheme has target to improve the conditions of poor, living below the poverty line by rehabilitating physical handicapped and disadvantaged group of people, beggars, destitute women, and up-lift of urban slum dwellers.

(ii) Education and Culture

Provide education of orphans, i.e., supplying books/clothes free of cost, expansion, and development of proper education for skill development, informal education facilities for children at home, physical education, and sports facilities, supporting to Islamic culture and heritage and art promotion, supporting education of deserving students in the form of scholarship, supporting vocational education in general, supporting education to inaccessible and neglected area, financing specific madrasa, school, and college, etc. of a particular area, educating deserving dependants, and supporting any project in the area of education, research.

(iii) Health and Sanitation

Cash waqf provides health care and sanitation, supplying arranging of pure drinking water to households, schools, mosques, slums, etc. in the villages, and also establishing hospitals, clinics, health care programs especially for the poor, health research grant and research in particular disease.

(iv) Social Utility Services

Settling disputes, providing legal aid to deserving men/women to establish their lawful rights, assist in arranging dowry-free marriage to poor girls, maintenance of public roads, and tree plantation in the village/ road sides, to rehabilitate the reverted Muslims, providing assistance to peace-loving non-Muslims and solving their problems, creating social awareness to prohibit gambling and other social vices, such as, thieving and other anti-social activities, construction, installation, and development of public utility services, maintenance of a specific mosque, graveyard, and *eidgah*, etc.

(v) Infrastructure Development

Poverty alleviation and economic development require necessary physical facilities and basic utilities. Access roads, irrigation dams, flood control devices, and utilities are essential for implementing any poverty alleviation and development plan in many developing and low-income countries. These are high-priority poverty alleviation and development needs of a typical poor country. It is neither possible for the public sector to provide these goods and services adequately, nor viable for the private sector to deliver them. The institution of waqf may be appropriately applied to finance such projects. Thus, in the new approach to poverty alleviation, the institution of waqf can be made an important instrument to alleviate poverty in a sustainable way. It will increase capabilities of the poor to upgrade their economic conditions, rather than depending on short-lived redistributive charities.

The thirty-two purposes for utilization of cash waqf fund, as indicated below shows the diverse areas of investment by Social Investment Bank Limited. Five more Islamic banks, including Islami Bank Bangladesh Limited has adopted similar model perhaps for utilization of cash waqf fund. Although this is not exhaustive, these social investment activities will create a base for perpetual social capital and help developing credit program that reinforces family values and stimulate social and moral foundation a caring society.

Table 2 Cash waqf account, deposit and profit distribution of IBBL since 2004–2016

Year	MWCD accounts		Deposit (in million Tk.)		Profit		Profit distribution (in million Tk.)	
	Number	Change	Amount	Change	Rate (In %)	Million Tk.	By bank	By client
2004	5		1.25		9.51	0.005	0	0.005
2005	32	27	8.61	7.36	11.22	0.27	0	0.27
2006	90	58	51.43	42.82	11.69	1.48	0.01	1.47
2007	169	79	80.01	28.58	10.77	5.57	0.03	5.54
2008	371	202	108.40	28.39	10.35	8.83	0.07	8.76
2009	578	207	159.81	51.41	10.09	13.66	0.08	13.58
2010	879	301	204.00	44.19	9.60	17.03	0.28	16.75
2011	1403	524	261.00	57.00	10.06	24.55	0.33	24.22
2012	18,815	17,412	367.00	106.00	11.97	34.31	0.49	33.82
2013	22,092	3277	435.99	68.99	11.33	38.98	0.66	38.32
2014	25,123	3031	533.00	97.01	10.63	43.01	1.92	41.09
2015	25,976	853	658.51	125.51	9.33	42.86	1.23	41.63
2016	27,073	1097	752.60	94.09	8.57	30.99	1.35	29.64

Source Islami bank own data source

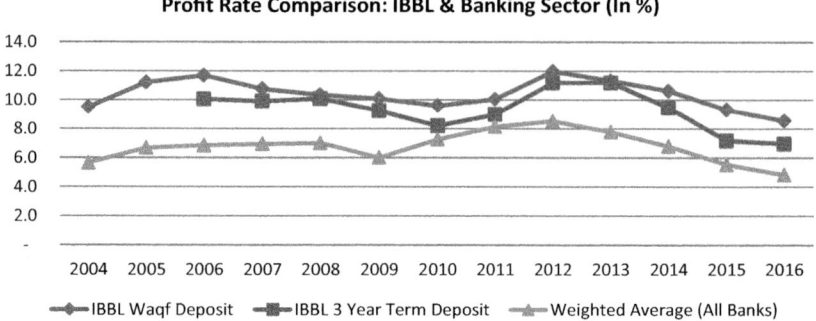

Fig. 3 Profit rate comparison between cash waqf and weighted average of other product

Waqf certificates of different denominations could be issued to raise the cash waqf, so that several individuals or institutions may buy them and finance the development projects. Besides, cash waqf could be encouraged among people through building confidence on management.

5.1 Growth of Cash Waqf Accounts, Deposit, and Profit Distribution of IBBL

Although cash waqf idea was developed in Bangladesh in 1997, IBBL has incepted this idea in 2004. Since then this instrument started growing sharply. Table 2 shows the growth trend of account opening, cumulative deposit along with the actual increase of deposit amount over the year. The table also shows the accrued total profit distribution along with the distribution of waqf profit by the client and bank itself. Growth trend shows that in near future this endeavor will significantly contribute to Bangladesh economic development and the poverty alleviation of the Bangladeshi poor.

It may be mentioned here that Islamic banking is not merely a profit-making institution rather it is welfare-oriented banking. Therefore, to encourage mobilizing cash waqf fund for socio-economic development of the country, Islamic bank has given highest weightage for cash waqf profit distribution. Figure 3 shows that the rate of profit of the cash waqf deposit is much higher than country's weighted average profit rate, while it is also higher than three years term deposit profit rate of IBBL.

5.2 Opportunities of Cash Waqf Development Through Islamic Banks in Bangladesh

SIBL in the process of organizing Social Capital Market operations in the voluntary sector of the bank had, for the first time in the history, introduced "Cash Waqf Certificate" scheme in 1997. It also aims at empowering the family of the rich for the sake of social investment and welfare. Cash waqf can be instrumental in transferring savings of the rich to those entrepreneurs and members of the public in financing various religious, educational, and social services in Bangladesh. Cash waqf can work as supplement to the financing of various social investments projects undertaken by Islamic Banks which can eventually emerge as Waqf Bank. Even today, cash waqf, in Bangladesh, is extremely important in terms of mobilization of fund for the development of waqf properties.

The successful implementation of Cash Waqf Certificate Scheme by SIBL showing impressive growth of accounts and deposits encouraged the IBBL to introduce MWCDA in 2003. Following the similar rules and regulations as adopted by SIBL with an exception that IBBL requires minimum of Tk. 50,000/ as initial deposit whereas SIBL requires Tk. 1000 as initial cash waqf. Later, IBBL has also reduced its minimum requirements. The main justification of smaller initial deposit is to encourage larger number of people to participate in creating Social Capital Market on national scale. The whole spirit of cash waqf fund mobilization is to involve largest number of people in a society for building social infrastructure as well as generating social awareness for creating a caring society. It is to be mentioned that as of June 2017, Islamic Banks (including Islamic Branches and Windows) in Bangladesh having over 1112 branches account for at least 23% of the total deposits, 24% of investment, 31% of inward foreign remittance and around 20% of assets in the entire banking sector (DIBB 2017).

The Al-Arafah Islami Bank, another Islamic Bank of Bangladesh, introduced the cash waqf exactly in terms of SIBL in 2004. Later, 3 more Islamic banks, namely Shahjalal Islami Bank, First Security Islami Bank, Exim Islami Bank have introduced the cash waqf product.

Besides, six conventional banks having Islamic banking operations also introduced cash waqf deposit products. Prime Bank has Mudarabah Cash Waqf Deposit Scheme undertaking through Islamic banking branches. The installment size is BDT 10,000 and it's multiple. Profit under this scheme shall be payable to the respective sector/institution/project/

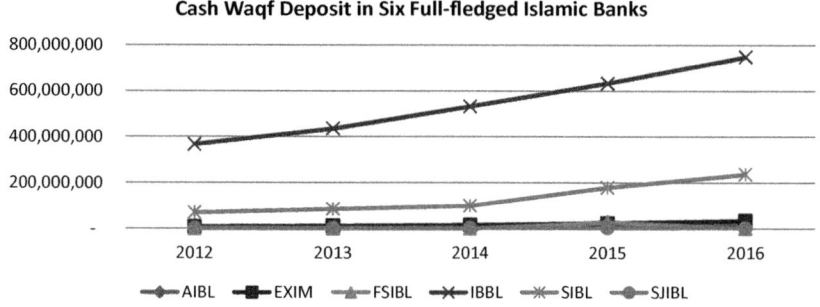

Fig. 4   Growth of cash waqf deposits of full-fledged Islamic banks since 2012–2016 (*Data Source* Annual reports of respective banks)

person determined by the waqf on annual basis. AB Bank, Southeast Bank, Bank Asia, Trust Bank, and Agrani Bank have cash waqf deposit schemes under their Islamic Branches/Windows. The donors can open the waqf cash account by depositing a fixed amount or by contributing a minimum amount every month which they will not be allowed to withdraw. The bank normally invests those deposits in Shariah-compliant investment options and distributes the profit to beneficiaries either by donors or according to their list.

The use of bank as an agent to collect cash waqf is quite a common practice in several Muslim countries. Aziz et al. (2013) investigated the relationship between the level of income and method of contribution and appointment of Islamic Waqf Bank as an agent in collecting waqf fund. They found a strong tendency that the Islamic Waqf bank's operation will run effectively with proper contribution method and appointment of Islamic Waqf bank as an agent in collecting the cash waqf fund. Therefore, the use of Islamic bank be the starting point in developing Islamic Waqf banks, for cash waqf collection purposes in Bangladesh.

Since its inception the cash waqf deposit product the growth is very much encouraging, indeed as indicated in Fig. 4. Deposit growth of all the six Islamic banks is positive, while the deposit growth of IBBL and SIBL is significantly positive and growing sharply in recent years.

5.3   Top Clients of Cash Waqf and Two Cases of IBBL

Case 1: Laila Bilkis and Abu Tayeb
Mr. Mohammad Abu Tayeb and his wife Mrs. Laila Bilkis are jointly operating a Mudarabah Cash Waqf Account with Islami Bank Bangladesh Ltd (IBBL). They are the inhabitants of Monsha village of Potia thana under Chittagong district. Their philanthropic activities started fifty years ago. They mainly work for the unprivileged poor children to meet their educational needs. With a view to addressing those needs, they targeted educational institutions and orphanages located in their native village. Education is one of the most basic needs of human being. The more a nation is educated, the more the nation is self-reliant.

Keeping that view in mind, they are working for the children living below the poverty line. The institutions getting donation from them are located at Monsha village. These institutions are—Monsha High School and College, Monsha Islamia Senior Madrasa, and Monsha Eatimkhana.

These three institutions are housed in the same complex. They play a vital role for the development of poor students of that locality. Among these institutions, Monsha High School and College is a seventy-year-old educational institution. Mr. Abu Tabyeb and his spouse Mrs. Laila Bilkis have been donating to these institutions for fifty years. A significant number of students in the village have been studying in Monsha High School and College. Most of the students are from poor families.

Like any other villages in our country, the children from the poor families in Monsha village had to provide financial support to their parents. So, the parents having no choice instead of sending their children to educational institutions rather send them to different workplaces for earning their livelihood. Although some of them are admitted to the village school, after few years they have to leave education. This lack of continuity of education stands on the way to improve their living condition. Considering this matter with utmost importance and empathy Mr. Abu Tayeb and his better half Mrs. Laila Bilkis decided to help them by providing educational facilities. For this purpose, they opened a mudarabah cash waqf account with Anderkilla Branch of IBBL. They donate entire monthly profit of the waqf deposit with IBBL. For utilizing the fund properly, they formed a committee in the respective institutions. At present, they donate approximately BDT 160,000.00 per month which is used solely to bear educational expenses of 105 students of Monsha High School and College, salary of 10 teachers of the same institutions and all living cost of 35 orphans living in the orphanage. They desire to expand this welfare activity so that poorer and more unprivileged can get benefit for the long term and receive proper education in their childhood.

Case 2: Fayzunnessa-Ahmed Foundation
Fayzunnessa-Ahmed Foundation is operated by Mr. Rizwan Ahmed and Mr. Shamsuddin Ahmed. It has been maintaining two mudarabah cash waqf accounts with IBBL since 2012. They established 02 (Two) institutions to provide better education facility to the poor children. One is a school named "FA Multilingual Elementary School" and another one is a madrasa named "Madrasa-e-Darul Arkam Kawmi Madrasa." "FA Multilingual Elementary School" was established in December 2014 in Paschimpara village under Gazipur district. The school follows National

curriculum of text book board. Although medium of education is Bangla, equal importance is given on teaching English and Arabic language too. At present, there are 161 students from playgroup to class 05 (five) and 10 (ten) teachers and staffs. There is also a computer lab to promote computer literacy among the students and a language club to develop language efficiency in both Bengali and English. The foundation provides BDT 45,000.00 per month from the profit of the waqf account to meet monthly expenditures. As their monthly expenditure is BDT 100,000.00, they must depend on other funding sources for additional fund. "Agami" a USA-based charitable organization visited the school recently and gave assurance to donate fund to this school. They have plan to extend education from class five to class seven which has already been approved by the Education Board, hopefully they will admit students in these classes from the next year.

"Madrasa-e-Darul Arkam Kawmi Madrasa" was established in 2009 in Hospital Road, Basurhat, Noakhali. It is mainly a kawmi madrasa. The specialty of this madrasa is that the students are provided both general and religious education. There are 250 students from nursery to six and 15 teachers and staffs. Fayzunnessa-Ahmed Foundation donates approximately BDT 85,000.00 monthly, and the madrasa has monthly income of BDT 100,000.00 although their monthly requirement as expenditure is BDT 245,000.00. So, they have to depend on another donation too. They also get fund from different sources as zakat, fetra, and other charitable organizations. Their future plan is to extend classes to Kamil.

Beside the above mentioned two cases some brief information of some top ranked clients are presented in Table 3, which implies a very positive potential of cash waqf for socio-economic development of the country.

6 Proposed Integrated Approach of Cash Waqf and Islamic Microfinance

Waqf plays a significant role in the Muslims history since its emergence in more than a millennium in the Arabian Peninsula. Recently, the voluntary and charitable acts such as waqf, zakat, and sadaqah receive much more attention than ever before as a result of increasing inequality and extreme poverty in the Muslim world. The inequality gap and poverty level necessitate the need to explore waqf resources as way of reducing the inequality and reduction of poverty in Muslims communities. It is in this regard, Muhammad Ali (2011), President of Islamic Development

Table 3 Brief information of top waqf beneficiaries of IBBL

Client's (Waqf) Name	Fayzunness-Ahmed Foundation	Fayzunness-Ahmed Foundation	Mawlana Abdur Rashid Memorial Waqf Fund	Laila Bilkis and Md. Abu Tayeb	Mohammad Azizul Haque	Kamalapur Eateemkhana and Islami complex
Beneficiary institution	FA Multilingual elementary school	Madrasa-e-Darul Arkam Kawmi Madrasa	Ashrafia Sheba complex	Monsha High School and College, Monsha Islamia Senior Madrasa, and Monsha Eatimkhana	Uttar Guzara Baitul Ulum Senior Madrasa	Kamalapur Eateemkhana and Islami complex
Type	School	Madrasa and School	Multi Services	School, madrasa and orphanage	Madrasa	Madrasa
Address	Pashchimpara, Purba Chandra, Shafipur, Gazipur	Hospital Road, Basurhat, Noakhali	Kapasia, Gazipur	Monsha, Kusumpura, Patia, Chittagong	Monday, Rauzan, Chittagong	East Kamalapur, Morshedabad, Dasar, Madaripur
Class	Play—Class V	Nursery—Class V	School: up to class 10 Madrasa: up to Dawra-e-Hadith	N/A	Up to Dakhil	
No. of student/beneficiary	161	250	400	Beneficiary: Students: 105 Orphans: 35	300	150
No. of teacher and staff	13	15	33	N/A	08	
Monthly waqf profit (Approx)	Tk. 45,000	Tk. 85,000	Tk. 100,000	Tk. 160,000	Tk. 60,000	Tk. 70,000

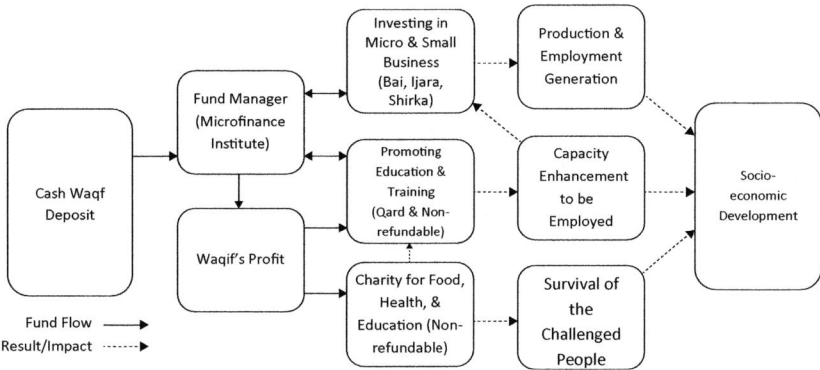

Fig. 5 Proposed integrated cash waqf and Islamic microfinance framework

Bank (IDB), asserts that "Socio-economic justice and equitable distribution of income and wealth are among the paramount goals of the Islamic economy."

For sustainable socio-economic development in Bangladesh, an integrated cash waqf-based Islamic microfinance model can be developed that complies with Shariah and aims at reducing poverty, enhancing the material-well-being and empowering the poor members of the society. The utilization of the cash waqf proceeds will be a catalyst for using the Islamic microfinance to fight poverty. In addition, microfinance institutions as fund managers of the cash waqf have the potential of utilizing the waqf proceeds for the genuine socio-economic development of the poor in their respective communities.

The Fund Manager being the Islamic Microfinance Institute in this proposed model will deploy the majority portion of cash waqf deposit in micro- and small business as per Shariah-compliant mechanisms and modes like bai, ijara, and shirka (Fig. 5).

The waqf fund will provide the needy and suitable citizens with access to credit through Murabaha financing by purchasing the required item and selling it to the needy based on deferred payment. The profit margin added to the deferred payment will be lower than the financing rate quoted by Islamic banks. The lower profit margin is based on charity to lower the burden of repayment on the beneficiary and to distinguish it from the credit services provided by banks.

Mudarabah financing can be used to provide capital to less privilege citizens who desire to start a business venture to support themselves.

Mudarabah financing by the waqf fund may generally involve the contribution of capital by the waqf endowment acting as Rabbul Mal to the needy (as the mudarib) to set up and run a small business, with the intention of establishing financial security and independence for them. The profit may be shared on a pre-agreed ration between the waqf fund and the beneficiary. The waqf fund may then gradually sell back its share in the partnership to the less privilege, until the waqf fund completely exits from the partnership, giving 100% ownership to the beneficiary. The waqf fund can exit the partnership only after the fund has obtained a return on its capital investment and additional profit to ensure sustainability of the waqf fund, which will go toward helping other recipients across the nation.

In cases where the needy citizens have a small amount of capital in their possession to contribute toward a business activity, but which is insufficient to start up a business, then a musharakah partnership can be established with the waqf funds, whereby the waqf fund contributes a determined amount of capital toward the business and the needy applicant contributes some capital to the partnership. The profit from the business venture will then be shared based on the ratio of capital contribution.

Those investments targeting the bottom of the pyramid in productive sectors will create employment opportunities and boost the economy. Subsequently, these production and employment generation will result in socio-economic development of the country.

A portion of the cash waqf deposit would be deployed in promoting higher education and vocational training on qard basis charging only a nominal fee without any mark up or profit. This investment will enhance the capacity of the human resources who will be employed in the productive sectors contributing to the overall development of the economy.

Another portion of the waqif's profit generated from the deployment of the cash waqf deposit would be invested in higher education and training purposes on non-refundable basis as required.

Some of the waqif's profit would also be given as charity for food and health care purposes for the physically and mentally challenged people which will help them survive in the society with care, love, and harmony. Rest of the waqf profit would be spent for primary education purposes targeting the extreme poor of the society. Having support for primary education the students will be able to ready themselves for further higher education. Thus, the financially excluded people will be able to join the mainstream economy creating a win-win and balanced growth momentum.

7   Implication of Cash Waqf Toward Country's Economic Development

While the millions of waqf spanning the world are varied, the majority fall into the five basic categories of food, housing, health, education, and religion. In a civilization, where health, education, and welfare are effectively managed through endowment and donations, waqf will give a huge impact on society's survival. This had been proven during the Ottoman Empire. The funds may also be used to alleviate poverty among Muslims (Sadeq 2002), especially since many Muslim countries are still fighting poverty such as in Indonesia and Bangladesh. Based on the 2005 Statistics Central Bureau's data, there were about 40 million Indonesians living below the poverty line. Waqf may help to narrow the gaps in Muslim communities, especially in education due to its significance in our lives. In addition, it will improve the socio-economic level among the Ummah. Moreover, investments done using the waqf funds will enhance the total permanent equity ownership of Muslims.

The results of waqf can be expressed to humanitarian projects, cultural, economic, health, education, and training, and much other social welfare. There are many instances of benefices use in the fields of health, treatment, education, and training. In many Islamic countries have been doing many considerable parts of a development activities based on sources and dedicated assets (Sadeq 2002).

  i. Training courses such as primary schools and secondary schools and established colleges and higher education centers (e.g., in Bangladesh more than 8000 of educational institution on the basis of waqf have been established).

ii. Building Houses and taking care of orphan centers which kept the children and people without shelter and give those living facilities and free education.

iii. Almost most of the mosques in Bangladesh are as cultural and public centers offer social services to Muslims and about 120 thousand mosques have been established through waqf and educational activities in the mosques would be presented for free. In addition, in rural Bangladesh, mosques and Islamic teachings educational schools would be managed based on benefices.

iv. Clinics and health centers are examples of the charity activities based on sources of benefices. The Hamdard Foundation based on herbal medicine in Karachi that is successful model using the capacity of aid and people's benefices. Also, this clinic financially supported from the University of Karachi and relief aid workers in Pakistan, India, and Bangladesh and give medical services at the disposal of the vulnerable.

In addition to these, waqf can be more effective in eliminating poverty programs and realizing comprehensive methods. In the past, benefits had been used to construction and equipping the shrine, maintenance, and established training centers and the fields of health and treatment, preparing food for poor, but now waqf in addition cases can be use of drinking water supply for urban or rural areas, city protection, pay taxes of neighbors, supply of food for children, etc. In recent years, cash waqf in many Islamic societies is more common and some of the Muslim capitalists, give specific funds in cash as loan to applicants in return the loans will be used for social services for vulnerable strata.

8   Conclusion

Study suggests that there is a considerable mismanagement and misuse of waqf properties, despite their contribution to social development. Cash waqf is a potential instrument to develop and expand Muslim economy. The availability of funds is significant to establish a well financial sector. Thus, it is relevant with the implementation of cash waqf in order to have wider sources of fund in line with the main objective of Islamic economic. To achieve the development of modern macroeconomic and well-being, the cash waqf is needed.

The Mudarabah Cash instrument of Islamic Banking and the Cash Waqf Certificate Scheme developed by Social Investment Bank of Bangladesh is an epoch-making event. As this cash waqf is generally managed by the Bank, it has its transparency, liquidity, and accountability, it is a perpetual deposit and its profit can be invested in a wide spectrum of social investment. Besides the 32 areas identified by several Islamic Banks in Bangladesh, the Waqif or subscriber can select one or more sectors according to his wishes in conformity with Shariah. Money for cash waqf can be deposited at a lump sum or by installment. Bank shall manage cash waqf on behalf of the Waqif. This ensures appropriate utilization of the fund of the Waqif in terms of its goals and objectives.

Bank's 32 sectors of investment include diverse social investment activities having enduring value which in its ultimate analysis will create a base for perpetual social capital and help developing credit program that reinforces family values and stimulates caring society. The Holy Quran has emphasized the virtues of charity in life on earth and life hereafter. The Cash Waqf Certificate offers an opportunity to get the divine blessing and to have a rewarding social and spiritual experience and internal peace. Viewed from this perspective, it becomes social and moral imperative on the part of the well-to-do to come forward and investment under Cash Waqf Certificate Scheme for his own benefit indeed. This will certainly pave the way for a new dimension of social development. Cash waqf fund can be spent for the welfare of non-Muslim also, thereby paving the way of serving the humanity at large.

Cash waqf mudarabah deposit product and cash waqf certificate can easily connect individual initiates of different Muslim countries and Muslim minorities in non-Muslim countries at the local national and global scale and open great prospects, possibilities, and potentialities for greater variety of pluralism in the expression Muslim solidarity and reconstitution of socio-economic infrastructure of Islamic Ummah. We should work for establishment of World Social Bank for managing this fund. Different banks of Bangladesh and banks across the world can draw policy and work together to make the cash waqf initiative a successful model to alleviate poverty of the Muslim world.

REFERENCES

Abdullah Nadwi, M., & Kroessin, M. (2013). Cash Waqf: Exploring Concepts, Jurisprudential Boundaries and Applicability to Contemporary Islamic Microfinance.

Adam, S., & Lahsasna, A. (2013). *Cash Endowment as Source of Fund in Islamic Micro-Financing*. In 4th International Conference on Business and Economic Research (4th ICBER 2013).

Ahmad Zaki Hj Abd Latiff, Che Zuina Ismail, & Norzaidi Mohd Daud. (2006). *Pengurusan Harta Wakaf Dan Potensinya Ke Arah Kemajuan Pendidikan Umat Islam di Malaysia* (Kertas Kerja Konvensyen Wakaf 2006 di Hotel Legend, Kuala Lumpur, 12–14 September 2006).

Allah, M. A., Kameel Mydin, A., & Yusuf, S. M. (2014). Factors Influencing the Behavioral Intentions of Muslim Employees to Contribute to Cash-Waqf Through Salary Deductions. *Islamic Economics, 28*(1), 57–90 (January 2015).

Aziz, M. R. A., Johari, F., & Yusof, M. A. (2013). Cash Waqf models for financing in education. *The 5th Islamic Economic System Conference* (iECONS2013).

Cizakca, M. (2004). Incorporated Cash Waqfs and Mudaraba, Islamic Non-Bank Financial Instruments from the Past to the Future.

Cizakca, M. (2010). *Incorporated Cash Waqfs and Mudaraba, Islamic Non-bank Financial Instruments from the Past to the Future* (MPRA Paper). http://mpra.ub.unimuenchen.de/25336.

Developments of Islamic Banking in Bangladesh (DIBB). (2017, April–June). Islamic Banking Cell, Research Department, Bangladesh Bank.

Hoseini, M. K. (2010). *Cash-Waqf: A New Financial Instrument for Financing Issues: An Analysis of Structure and Islamic Justification of Its Commercialization*. Imam Sadiq University.

Ibrahim, H., Amir, A., & Masron, T. A. (2013). Cash Waqf: An Innovative Instrument for Economic Development. *International Review of Social Sciences and Humanities, 6*(1), 1–7.

Konsep Wakaf Tunai. (2016). *Majlis Agama Islam Negeri Johor*. Retreived April 26, 2016, from, http://www.maij.gov.my/?page_id=439.

Magda Ismail, A. M. (2008, July 28–29). *Cash Waqf a New Financial Product Model Aspects of Shariah Principles on ITS Commercialization*. This Paper Is Presented at Islamic Banking, Accounting and Finance Conference (iBAF 2008), organized by Faculty of Economics and Muamalat, Universiti Sains Islam Malaysia, The Legend Hotel, Kuala Lumpur 2008.

Mannan, M. A. (1998). Cash-waqf Certificate Global Opportunities for Developing the Social Capital Market in 21st-Century Voluntary-sector Banking. The Third Harvard University Forum on Islamic Finance: Local Challenges, Global Opportunities (pp. 243–256). Cambridge, MA: Center for Middle Eastern Studies, Harvard University.

Mannan, M. A. (2014). *Waqf Development: Bangladesh Experience Local Challenge and Global Opportunity* (pp. 1–36). Kuala Lumpur: The International Waqf Seminar.

Masyita, D., Tasrif, M., & Telaga, A. S. (2005, July 17–21). A Dynamic Model for Cash Waqf Management as One of the Alternative Instruments for The Poverty Alleviation in Indonesia. *The 23rd International Conference of The System Dynamics Society Massachussets Institute of Technology (MIT)*, Boston.

Mohamad, M. H. (2012). *Wakaf tunai: Pendekatan terbaik untuk mewakafkan harta masa kini.* Berita Harian.

Mohammad, M. T. S. H. (2008). *Sustaining the Means of Sustainability: The Need for Accepting Wakaf (Waqf) Assets in Malaysian Property Market.* A Paper Presented in the 14 Annual Conference of the Pacific Rim Real Estate Society, Kuala Lumpur, Malaysia.

Mohammad, M. T. S. H. (2011). Towards an Islamic Social (Waqf) Bank. *International Journal of Trade, Economics and Finance, 2*(5).

Osman, A. F., Htay, S. N. N., & Mohammed, M. O. (2012). *Determinants of Cash Waqf Giving in Malaysia: Survey of Selected Works.* Retrieved on June 17, 2014, from, http://irep.iium.edu.my/28284/1/DETERMINANTS_OF_CASH_WAQF_GIVING_IN_MALAYSIA.pdf.

Pitchay, A. A., Mydin Meera, A. K., & Saleem, M. Y. (2014). Priority of Waqf Development among Malaysian Cash Waqf Donors: An AHP Approach. *Journal of Islamic Finance, 3*(1), 13–22. http://doi.org/2289-2117(O)/2289-2109(P).

Sadeq, A. M. (2005). Awqaf in Bangladesh. In Rashid S. Khalid (Ed.), *Waqf Experience in South Asia.*

Sadeq, M. A. H. (2002). Waqf, Perpetual Charity and Poverty Alleviation. *International Journal of Social Economics, 29*(1/2), 135–151, https://doi.org/10.1108/03068290210413038.

Stibbard, P., Russell, Q. D., & Bromley, B. (2012). Understanding the Waqf in the World of Trust. *Trust and Trustee, 18*(8), 785–810.

Syed Adwam Wafa, S. M. G. (2010). Development of Waqfs for Education in Malaysia. *A Working Paper Presented in 7th International Conference—The Tawhidi Epistemology: Zakat and Waqf Economy*, Bangi.

Yusof, M. F. M., Yusof, M. F. M., Hasarudin, M. H., & Romli, N. (2014). Cash Waqf and Infaq: A Proposed E-Philanthropy in Malaysia. *Jurnal Kemanusiaan Bil, 22*, 1; and their Accounting Practices, http://journal.mufad.org/.

CHAPTER 9

Can We Combine Sukuk and Waqf? A Case Study of Indonesia

Murniati Mukhlisin and Rifka Mustafida

1 Introduction

According to the Indonesian Statistics, there were 207.17 million Indonesian Muslims in 2010 (BPS 2010). The number tells us that there is a great potential to develop waqf asset and cash waqf. Referring to the total population of Muslims in Indonesia and a level of their income, Indonesian Waqf Board (*Badan Wakaf Indonesia*/BWI) estimated the potential of waqf in Indonesia could be around Rp 20 billion per year (BWI 2009). Based on empirical data expressed by Çizakca (1998),

Thank you to all reviewers and participants of Research Workshop on Revival of Waqf for Socio Economic Development for their valuable comments. The workshop was organized by IRTI-IDB and Islami Bank Bangladesh Limited in Dhaka, Bangladesh, 4–5 November 2017. We are also indebted to Eri Hariyanto and Anita Priantina for their constructive suggestions.

M. Mukhlisin (✉)
Islamic Accounting Department, STEI Tazkia, Bogor, Indonesia
e-mail: murniati@tazkia.ac.id

R. Mustafida
LPPM Tazkia, Bogor, Indonesia

© The Author(s) 2019
K. M. Ali et al. (eds.), *Revitalization of Waqf for Socio-Economic Development, Volume I*,
https://doi.org/10.1007/978-3-030-18445-2_9

169

development of productive waqf assets has solved several economic problems such as unemployment and poverty. In Turkey, the ratio of people working at the waqf system increased to 12.68% in 1931 from 0.76% in the 1990s. The system of waqf has become one of the largest sources of employment in the Republic of Turkey at that time. However, in practice, according to Ahmed (2009), waqf assets in many Muslim countries mostly are not productive. The management of waqf in Indonesia is still very traditional and the waqf assets have not been managed productively even many endowment assets are idle (Bayinah 2012). Referring to the results of the survey conducted by State Islamic University (UIN) Syarif Hidayatullah 74% of the Manager of waqf (nadzir) cannot manage waqf asset productively (Juwaini 2009).

According to Khan (2010), waqf is one of the instruments for reducing poverty. Waqf aims to promote social and economic justice thus requires optimal management strategy in the development of waqf asset (Ahmed 2009). Kahf (1998) reveals that it consumes lots of time to review and redefine the concept of waqf as holding property and prevent the resulting consumption of action benefit continuously. The waqf has the same character in terms of its sources that are generally from the people who can afford for the benefit of the poor. Yet many institutions that are engaged in this field do not manage it properly and effectively. According to Sadeq (2002), there should be improvement in waqf institutions such as the availability of professional human resources and the productivity of the waqf assets. It could be a business that is capable of creating great opportunities for employment in the local communities and eventually would reduce poverty. However, one of the constraints to develop endowment asset is due to the lack of investment resources. So one of the solutions to address such matters is with the integration between waqf and sukuk (Ahmed 2009).

According to the OJK (2015), the highest growth in sukuk instruments occurs in Sharia government bonds or sukuk (*Surat Berharga Syariah Negara/SBSN*). In the last five years, the country experienced fast growth of sukuk subscription. In the year 2014, there are 16 sukuk issuances of the country with as many as 42 outstanding amount sukuk. As for the value in the year 2014, the sukuk issuance reached Rp 206.1 billion increased from 169.29 billion in 2013 (OJK 2015).

With the rapid growth of sukuk in Indonesia, this is momentum for the issuance of sukuk based on waqf assets in Indonesia. Sukuk based on waqf asset in other countries has been well developed, for instance in Singapore, sukuk is formulated using musyarakah contract based on waqf asset. According to Saad et al. (2013) financing, the development of the waqf assets in Singapore is carried out through a joint venture mechanism with Baitulmal and issuance of sukuk musyarakah based on endowments. According to Kamsani and Leung (2004) asset manager of waqf institutions in Singapore has several strategies: (1) update waqf asset with potential income in the form of rent, (2) the development of waqf assets with higher development value, and (3) the migration of assets which replaces the waqf assets of low-value assets with high value of endowments.

According to the results of the interview with Interviewee I-01, currently, the waqf institution do not have experience in the issuance of Shariah bond. Then for the solution, the issuance of sukuk based on waqf assets in Indonesia can be issued through the Ministry of Finance—Republic of Indonesia in cooperation with the Ministry of Religious Affairs (MRA) and Waqf—Republic of Indonesia. At this time according to Kemenkeu (2010), there are three contracts used in the issuance of Islamic Securities, i.e., Ijarah sale and lease back, asset to be leased, and Ijarah Al Khadamat. The contract of the sukuk Ijarah will use asset to be leased scheme for the construction project on the ground of the waqf land.

The waqf project financed by the sukuk could be a hospital, school, office, or other business premise that serves as a public service agency. Public service agencies in practice also potentially have the advantage over businesses. With the potential development of waqf assets through sukuk, therefore, this study discusses benefits, opportunity, cost, and risk of implementation of sukuk based on waqf assets in Indonesia with the asset to be leased scheme using the method of Analytic Network Process (ANP). From the background of the research, there are some issues to be discussed in this research, including:

1. To what extent does benefit, opportunity, cost, and risk respond to the issuance of waqf-based sukuk if implemented in Indonesia?
2. From the four aspects, which aspect would become the priority?

The remainder of this paper is organized as follows. Section 2 proposes analysis of benefits, opportunities, costs, and risks (BOCR) as research methodology, Sect. 3 presents analysis, and Sect. 4 provides conclusion and recommendation for future research.

2   ANP, BOCR, AND WAQF RESEARCH

This section discusses sources and methods of data collection, ANP method, BOCR analysis, research stages, and data processing.

2.1   Sources and Methods of Data Collection

This research employs primary and secondary data. Primary data obtained from filling up questionnaires by seven experts consist of regulators and practitioners (see Appendix 1). Researchers obtain secondary data that comes from various literatures. Primary data obtained through: (1) In-depth interview, namely the interview conducted in great depth to trawl the details of data about the object of the problems discussed in this study. From the results of the interviews, the authors obtained data about the factors that influence the implementation of sukuk waqf in Indonesia. (2) Survey of Shariah economic experts and practitioners, namely data collection, which has been exposed to Islamic economists and practitioners of sukuk in Indonesia. From the survey, the authors obtained data for quantitative analysis from the in-depth interview.

2.2   General Description of the Method of Analytic Network Process (ANP)

According to Saaty and Vargas (2006), ANP is the general theory of relative measurement, which is used to lower the priority of the composite ratio-scale measurement. It then reflects the individual relief of the influence of the elements interacting in regard to the criteria of control. ANP is a new approach in the decision-making process without making assumptions. In accordance with the principles of nature, the main function of the AHP/ANP is complexity structuring, measurements, and synthesis. Complexity Structuring, i.e., by means of hierarchical complexity into a homogeneous cluster-cluster of factors. Priority-scale ratio used on each methodology with the structure, so that the priority of any element of the hierarchy can be determined by multiplying the priority of the elements on the level with the main element of the priority. Synthesis is made with two formulas one multiplicative and additive subtractive that can give rise to negative overall priorities. Synthesized results of the alternatives for each of the four control benefits (B), opportunities (O), costs (C), and risks (R) merits are combined, along traditional benefit to cost ratio analysis used in economics, to obtain a ratio outcome by taking the quotient of the benefits times the opportunities to the costs times the risks for each alternative (BO/CR), then normalizing the results over all the alternatives to determine the best outcome (see Appendix 2).

2.3   The Analysis of Benefits, Opportunities, Costs, Risks (BOCR)

According to Saaty and Vargas (2006) on the research with the network connection between BOCR benefit, opportunity, cost, and risk are affected by common factors. Analysis of benefits, opportunities, cost, risk (BOCR) is an analysis of the determination of priorities based on the results of the calculation of the desired criteria as the advantages (benefits) and unwanted as the criteria weights (cost). In addition, there are also the criteria based on events in the future, which may occur as a positive thing (opportunity) and things that can lead to negative risk (risk). Saaty and Vargas (2006) also outline the results of a number of alternatives are prioritized, obtained from three results, the general conditions (standard condition) obtained from the calculation of the standard B/C, Pessimistic $B/(C \times R)$, and Realistic $(B \times O)/(C \times R)$. The best alternative is selected with a high value of realistic alternative selected and considered decision that determined from the other alternative.

2.4   Research Stages

This study consists of four stages of research: pre-research stage, data collection, data processing, and interpretation of the results. The first stage starts from the formulation of the problem and the determination of research objectives and then proceeds with composing data collection. The second stage in this study is by conducting field studies to the place of research that aims to ensure the availability of data, which is in this research, primary data, and secondary data. The primary data are data obtained from the first source through interviews and questionnaires. While the secondary data obtained from library materials related to research, such as Indonesian Waqf Board (BWI), Directorate of Islamic Finance DJPPR Ministry of Finance (MoF)—Republic of Indonesia, and MRA—Republic of Indonesia. The next stage is data processing using some appropriate methods. The last step is the interpretation of the results of data processing. The final stage of this study can be used as a basis of conclusions and suggestions.

2.5   Data Processing

The data and information on the opinions represented by the experts and practitioners are arranged in the form of a skeleton model. If the results of the questionnaire about opinions have been collected, the next step is processing the data using Microsoft Excel and "Super Decision" software. The questionnaire is processed into a form comparison (pair-wise comparison), both between elements in the cluster and between clusters, to find out which of the greater influence is seen from one side.

To facilitate the authors in obtaining questionnaires data derived from the questions, as well as to maintain the level of consistency, the authors follow the model of comparison questionnaires that have been modified by Ascarya (2005) in the form of tables and re-modify the matrix form, making it easier for respondents in understanding the problem. This question in the form of a matrix is used as the second interview tool. Meanwhile, to answer the respondent's questions comes with a description of the scale/rating to be used and the ANP network of the issues raised.

The data are then processed through Microsoft Excel and for the results of the quantification results; the next step is to calculate the rater agreement and geometric mean. First, calculate the rater agreement. Rater agreement is a measure that shows the level of respondent's suitability $(R1 - Rn)$ to a problem in one cluster. The tool used to measure the rater agreement is Kendall's coefficient of concordance (W: $0 < W < 1$). $W = 1$ indicates perfect conformity (Ascarya 2005). Second, calculate the mean geometry. This measure is used to identify individual assessments of respondents and for opinions on a single group of respondents. Geometric mean is a type of average calculation that shows a certain tendency or value. The last stage is the choice of the main alternatives used. According to Saaty and Vargas (2006), the formula used is the multiplication formula with the marginal cost/benefit analysis and is generally used to determine the short term, and the negative formula additive = this formula is usually used to determine the long term by the formula $bB + oO - cC - rR$ and (2). A short-term decision-making is done by the formula BO/CR and to determine long-term priorities using the formula $bB + oO + c(1 - C) + r(1 - R)$.

3   PROBLEM COMPLEXITY

Several results from the data tests are presented below: decomposition, geometric mean and rater agreement, and cluster opportunity.

3.1   Decomposition

The purpose of conducting this stage is to anticipate, analyze, and structure the problem complexity into the network of benefit, opportunity, cost, and risk of application of sovereign sukuk issuance based on waqf assets. This composition is from literature review and interview; as one of the stages in ANP benefit, opportunity, cost, and risk (BOCR). All benefit, opportunity, cost, and risk (BOCR) elements in this study are divided into two perspectives, namely: (i) Issuer, the sukuk waqf publisher, in this case is the MoF in cooperation with the MRA and Waqf Board of Indonesia and (ii) Investors, i.e., individuals or companies that buy sukuk waqf. Aspect of publishers and investors is used because of the results of literature review and interviews of respondents, the decomposition.

Benefit
This cluster contains all aspects that can provide short-term benefits or advantages for both the issuer and the investor. Benefit in this cluster is divided into two criteria, the benefit for issuer and benefit for the investor.

Benefit for Issuer
a. Alternative financing Kahf (1998) documented that one solution to financing the development of waqf assets is to issue sukuk. Sukuk as an alternative financing for society and institution in accordance with Islamic law that responds to the needs of the community to utilize waqf assets. The issuance of sukuk waqf by the MoF in cooperation with BWI becomes a source of financing to encourage the development of the waqf sector more rapidly (Interviewee I-03, I-04).

b. Profit According to Omar and Rahman (2013), the issuance of sukuk waqf is a way for waqf asset managers to benefit from waqf assets that will be distributed to the community, for example, the advantage of obtaining large funds in a relatively quick and simple way, an advantage when objects built on waqf assets generate profits, and benefits because reward payments can be set at a certain time period.

c. *Increase type of sukuk Waqf* According to interviews with Interviewee I-01, the issuance of sukuk waqf will become a new form of waqf circulating in the society. So that it will improve, develop, and deepen Islamic financial market in Indonesia. A depth of the Shariah financial market is indicated by a large number of instruments, large transaction volumes, transaction frequency, and number of market participants.

Benefit for Investors

a. *Alternative Investment for Investors* According to Alqahtani (2012), sukuk is an alternative investment for society that complies with Shariah law. According to the Kemenkeu (2010), Shariah government bond guaranteed by the National Council of Ulama/*MUI* in accordance with Shariah principles, as well as safe and free from prohibition by Shariah, such as usury, gharar, and maysir.

b. *Involvement of Investors in the Development of Waqf Asset and Government Projects* According to Hanefah et al. (2006), the sukuk waqf investor is actively involved in the development of waqf asset that will ultimately enhance the self-reliance of the people. In addition, investors also will participate in waqf sukuk projects of the government.

c. *Capital Gain or Profit* According to Omar and Rahman (2013), issuance of sukuk waqf is a way for investors to get profit from investment products that comply with Shariah law.

Opportunity
This cluster contains any profitable opportunities in the future as a result of the issuance of sukuk as productive financing on the waqf assets.

Opportunity for Issuer

a. *Enhancing public welfare* According to Hassan and Shahid (2010), the issuance of sukuk waqf as opportunities for waqf asset to assume the role of distributing wealth and will ultimately reduce the economic gap. Sukuk issuance later will boost the economy of the parties involved in the construction of waqf project. According to Çizakca (1998), productive waqf asset management will create jobs. The research of the waqf system is one of the instrument's field works in Turkey in 1931. When sukuk waqf develops over time then the built assets will become public welfare, public facilities, and public intellect (Maqashid Sharia) (Interviewee I-04).

b. Reduce government expenditure devoted to social fund According to Çizakca (1998), productive management of waqf also will reduce the government budget to social fund. It is due to the need for social funds and social services that can be fulfilled by the profit of the productive waqf.

c. Social infrastructure service providers According to Interviewee I-01, the sukuk waqf issuance used for the development of waqf asset will be able to provide services of social infrastructure in Indonesia.

Opportunity for Investors
a. Role in developing Islamic finance According to Interviewee I-01, the issuance of sukuk waqf can develop Islamic finance, which means that the investor of sukuk waqf would indirectly play a role in developing Islamic finance.

b. Participate in improving the welfare of society The investors might get involved in sukuk waqf to empowering Muslims (Hanefah et al. 2006). In addition, according to Çizakca (1998), waqf can enhance the welfare of society, because the proceeds from the productive waqf are for society's social fund. With total assets of very large endowments would impact to reduction of poverty.

c. The odds get higher return One of the advantages of investing in Islamic government bond is a competitive yield. It is considering to the higher return trend from other financial products.

Cost
This cluster contains about any aspect that may result in a short-term loss or load when sukuk waqf is implemented.

Cost for the Issuer

a. It has not been regulated of waqf assets as the underlying asset According to Hassan and Shahid (2010), cost of issuance of sukuk waqf is currently absent in the government regulations. The issuance of sukuk waqf in Indonesia is still facing some constraints such as the problem of underlying sukuk assets on how to make it Shariah compliance (Interviewee I-01). This one was caused by a Shariah law-related waqf asset that the underlying assets of sukuk is still debated and examined more profoundly.

b. Management of the waqf assets is not professional According to Hassan and Shahid (2010), one of the costs of sukuk waqf issuance is unprofessional waqf asset managers who tend to neglect the rules to manage waqf asset, lack of honesty and integrity in the waqf asset management. In addition, according to Interviewee I-01, the absence of risk management standardization of waqf will be another cost for developing waqf assets.

c. Issuance of sukuk is still very costly Sukuk as Islamic financial instrument has not been much known what more this new form of sukuk waqf. According to Ismal et al. (2015), the secondary market is still relatively underdeveloped such as bond markets. That is because the socialization and education regarding sukuk in the society is still very poor. As a result, the cost of issuance of sukuk is always high. Issuing sukuk waqf could have a similar pattern because due to the need for a massive socialization to increase investor's appetite toward sukuk waqf.

Cost for Investors

a. Less liquid sukuk market Secondary market of the sukuk in Indonesia is not liquid (Wahyuni 2014). This is because sukuk portfolios are still very limited with market share is still below 5%. Furthermore, majority of sukuk investors tend to hold the sukuk to maturity that results to less movement in the secondary market.

b. Return a smaller rise in interest rates occur when the SBI Islamic government bond or SBSN has a fixed return. According to Nasrullah (2015), sukuk yield in Indonesia still benchmarks to the conventional sukuk rate. As a result, the relationship between instruments and interest rates in Indonesia is negative, where if the interest rates increase then investment instruments demand such as stocks, bonds, which mean also sukuk would decline. That is because interest rates are expected to rise following Bank of Indonesia policy because the Fed has a trend to increase the rate. Based on the research of Andrian and Lestari (2013), if interest rate of the Fed hikes, it would affect the increase in BI rate.

c. The potential for lower capital gains or even loss According to Rinaldhy (2015), if Indonesia sukuk waqf is not traded in the secondary market then the potential to get capital gains would disappear. However, if it is traded in the secondary market, the sukuk market must have sufficient liquidity otherwise the opportunity of capital gain would be low. This is one of the main constraints for the investors who chose to invest in this instrument.

Risk
The risk includes all aspects that could result to long-term loss both for the issuer and investor. They are referred as issuer risk and investor risk.

Risk for Issuer
a. Waqf assets dispute According to Interviewee I-01, there should not be a dispute regarding the ownership status of the waqf asset. The waqf assets must have an official certificate endorsed by BWI so that it cannot be claimed by other parties.

b. Default project The issuance of sukuk waqf could result to contract party default, for instance, if the developer fails to carry out the waqf project properly, it would hinder the waqf asset development (Interviewee I-01).

c. Costs of sukuk waqf There is a financial risk in sukuk waqf issuance, for instance, the cost of sukuk issuance is higher than the proceeds of sukuk. The cost of sukuk issuance should commensurate with the results of the sale of sukuk waqf (Interviewee I-02).

Risk for Investors
a. The risk of payment failure This type of risk is the same with sukuk in general; one of the risks in sukuk issuance is the risk of payment failure (Interviewee I-01). When the project is not profitable then it would cause the SPV fail to pay the return to sukuk waqf investors.

b. Market risk This risk is associated with the fall in the price of sukuk in the secondary market. According to Tariq (2004), sukuk price could be lower than the original purchase in the secondary market.

c. Inflation risk Inflation risk is associated with the rising inflation that could tamper value of the waqf assets. It could happen because Islamic government bond with asset to be leased scheme tends to have a fixed rate of return (Tariq 2004).

Alternative
The next cluster is an alternative or strategy. The issuance of sukuk based on waqf in Indonesia is still at the early stage, thus it requires cluster strategies that serve as advice to stakeholders in the issuance of sukuk. This cluster contains all about sukuk waqf issuance strategy when it comes to the implementation.

Regulation

MoF should first enact relevant regulation with regard to the sukuk waqf issuance such as regulation regarding the underlying asset. The Act No. 41 Year 2004 and Government Decree No. 42 Year 2006 regarding the implementation of Act No. 41 Year 2004 spells out that *nadzir* has duty to manage waqf asset productively. In addition, the management of the waqf asset should be in accordance with Shariah principles. From the interview with the Head of Waqf Directorate, MRA, the designated *nadzir* should use a sharing scheme with the *waqif* over the benefits derived from the assets.

In general, waqf assets can generate benefits to support poverty reduction programs. There is *waqif* who give away the waqf assets to be used in the economic and social fields with expectation to support the economic well-being of the community. It is also possible that waqf mosque can generate economic benefits too, for instance, to rent out a mosque space for training purposes. Viewed from the legislation side, it is very possible that waqf asset can be considered as an underlying asset as a base for sukuk issuance.

Partnership

Forming a partnership with several institutions is required to support the issuance of sukuk based waqf. That is because BWI does not yet have an experience related to issuance of sukuk waqf. Such partnerships can be formed between BWI with MRA, MoF, Financial Services Authority, and National Shariah Council—Indonesian Council of Ulama.

Education
The issuance of sukuk waqf would expand the education area on waqf because there is no yet expert in the area. Eventually, it would improve the quality of human resources through waqf education. The education program will range from trainings, seminars to discussions, supported by the three agencies; BWI, MRA, and MoF.

3.2   *Results of the Geometric Mean and Rater Agreement*

BOCR model

Results obtained from the value of the geometric mean or average value of the respondents. There are four aspects of this research methodology, i.e., benefit, opportunity, cost, and risk. Calculation of the geometric mean of the results obtained is a priority aspect of Benefit with a value of 0.467. The second priority aspect is opportunity, followed by cost and risk as the third and fourth priority. The value of the rater agreement (*W*) or the value of agreement of the respondent is 0.693, see Fig. 1.

Cluster benefit

Results from data processing show that top priority falls on the alternative to raise funds with a value of 0.251. That is because the primary purpose of sukuk waqf issuance is to meet the needs of the development of waqf asset. The second priority is an alternative investment for investors with

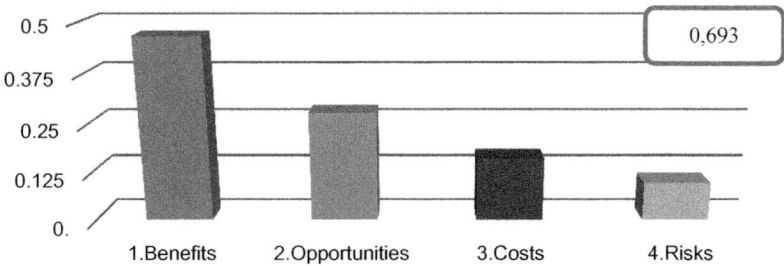

Fig. 1 Poll's result of BOCR model (*Source* Processed data [Authors, 2018])

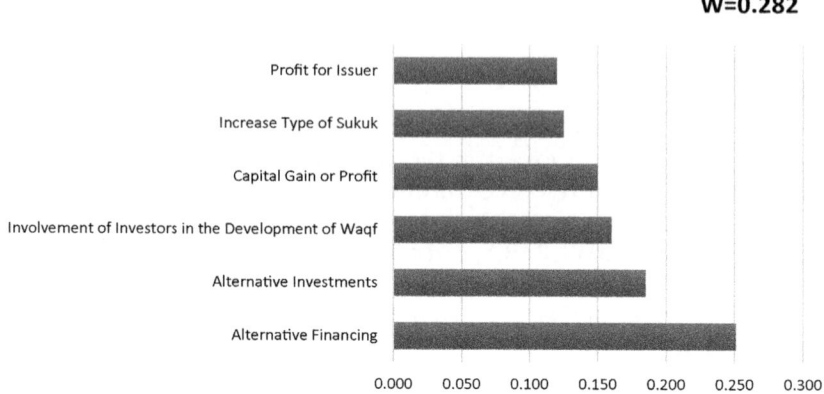

Fig. 2   Result of *geometric mean cluster benefit* (*Source* Processed data [Authors, 2018])

value of 0.185, while the third priority is profit for investor with value of 0.160. The value of rater agreement (*W*) produced of 0.282, see Fig. 2.

Cluster opportunity

On the Cluster, the result that becomes the top priority was instrumental in Islamic finance with value of 0.225. That is because the issuance of Sharia government bond based on waqf has high chance to develop financial instruments, in particular, the Islamic sukuk with different types of underlying asset. The second priority is to participate in public welfare increases with the value of the third priority is 0.208, while social infrastructure service providers is placed at the third priority, with value of 0.203. As a whole, the value of rater agreement (*W*) produced 0.602, see Fig. 3.

Cluster cost

On the Cluster, the result that becomes the top priority is the management of waqf asset that has not been professional with value of 0.189. Unprofessional waqf management will be obstacles for the issuance of sukuk waqf in particular on the determination of waqf asset that will become the underlying asset. The second priority is low liquidity of sukuk market with value of 0.178, while the third priority is a smaller return than the SBI with value of 0.178. Overall, the value of rater agreement (*W*) is 0.499, see Fig. 4.

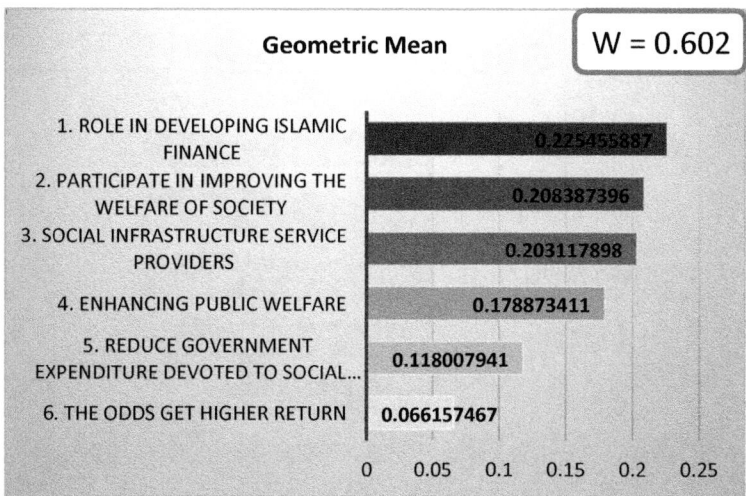

Fig. 3 Result of *geometric mean cluster opportunity* (*Source* Processed data [Authors, 2018])

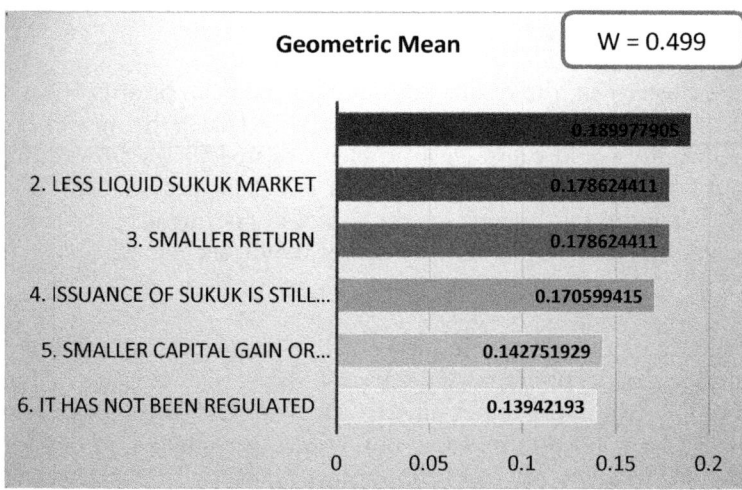

Fig. 4 Result of *geometric mean cluster cost* (*Source* Processed data [Authors, 2018])

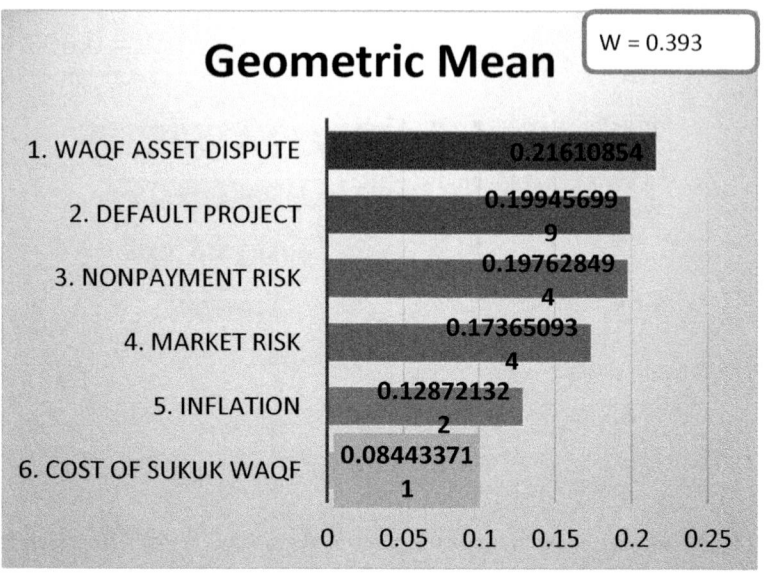

Fig. 5 Result of *geometric mean cluster risk* (*Source* Processed data [Authors, 2018])

Cluster risk

On the cluster risk, the results released that the main priority is with the value of endowments assets dispute is 0.216. That is because the waqf assets dispute would cause legal problems related to asset ownership of the waqf assets. The second risk priority is default project with value of 0.199, while the third priority is the risk of nonpayment by value 0.197. In general, the value of rater agreement is 0.393, see Fig. 5.

BOCR overall

The results of the geometric mean of the elements in the entire cluster benefit, opportunity, cost, and risk show that alternative financing becomes the most important element with the top priority value is 0.062. The second priority value of 0.056 is instrumental in developing Islamic finance. The results of the geometric mean in the cluster benefit put the alternative together and show fund as a priority. On the cluster opportunity that becomes the top priority is instrumental in developing Islamic finance with value of 0.056, while the top priority at cluster cost

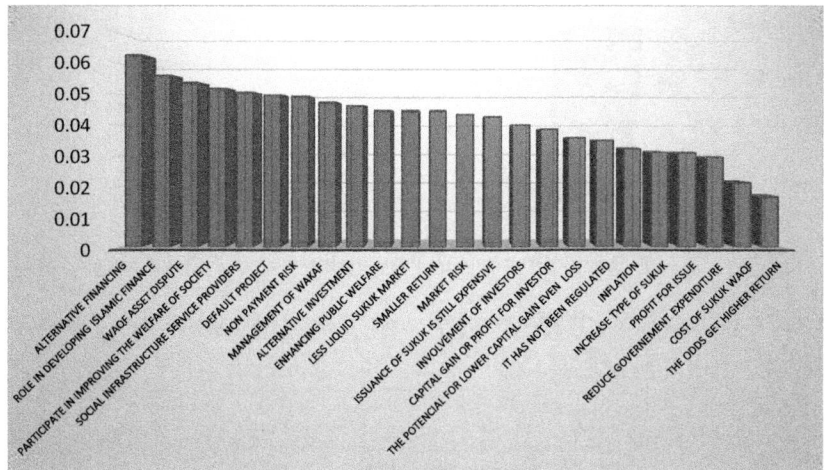

Fig. 6 Result of *geometric mean all cluster* (*Source* Processed data [Authors, 2018])

is a waqf asset management professional with a value of 0.047. On cluster risk, the element becomes the top priority is the risk of project default with a value of 0.049, see Fig. 6.

Alternative cluster

There are three alternatives or strategies in issuing sukuk based on waqf assets, i.e., assets-related waqf regulation with waqf asset as the underlying assets, partnership agencies, and sukuk education. From the results of the rater agreement, it shows that the most important alternative is regulation. Regulation is vital in the issuance of sukuk waqf, given the fact that the government regulation is the legal basis for the issuance of sovereign sukuk. While the second and third alternatives are partnership and education, respectively, see Fig. 7.

BOCR synthesis results

From the ANP results, there are three parts of the resulting decision: (1) scoring system, (2) merits of BOCR decision as consideration of making decisions, and (3) hierarchy or network linkages, facts (objective) that make an alternative decision is more desirable than the other (Saaty 2001). After modeling and assessment phases of the ANP is completed

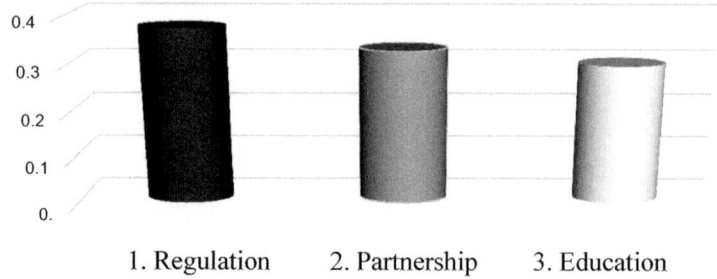

1. Regulation   2. Partnership   3. Education

Fig. 7 Poll's result of *BOCR alternative* (*Source* Processed data [Authors, 2018])

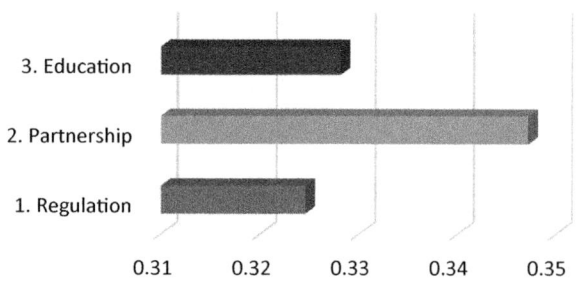

Fig. 8 Short-term priorities according to the overall respondents (*Source* Processed data [Authors, 2018])

then the value of the results obtained from the pairwise comparison of BOCR criteria produce a short-term strategy and policy in the long term that can be seen in Figs. 8 and 9.

From the figures, it can be concluded that the main priority in the short term is a partnership with the other institutions. That is because BWI is not able to issue its own sukuk (Interviewee I-01). Therefore, it requires a cooperation among several related agencies such as Ministry of Finance, MRA, and BWI in issuing sukuk waqf assets in Indonesia. The second priority falls under further education regarding sukuk and waqf. The third priority is related to regulation of the sukuk waqf.

The main priority of the alternatives in the long term is a partnership with the other institutions. That is because the partnership with BWI,

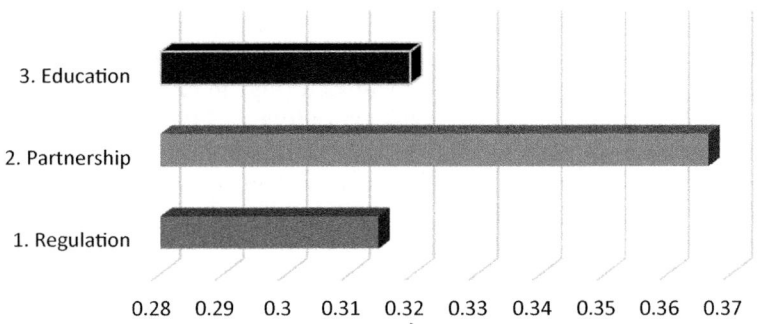

Fig. 9 Long-term priorities according to the overall respondents (*Source* Processed data [Authors, 2018])

MRA, and MoF will take place in the long term when it comes to maturity of the sukuk wakaf. SBSN reaches its maturity in the span of two years and a half to twenty-five years. The second priority is education, whereas the third priority is regulation. From these results, it can be concluded that in the short-term or the long-term priority of the alternatives show the same results. They also show that the partnership is the most important strategy in sukuk waqf issuance, see Fig. 9.

4   Ready to Launch Sukuk Waqf?

Based on the results above, it can be concluded that the issuance of the country's asset-based sukuk waqf in Indonesia will bring benefit, opportunity, cost, and risk as follows.

From the aspect of the benefit, opportunity, cost, and risk above according to the respondents namely experts, practitioners and regulators, benefit and opportunity is more important aspect than cost and risk. In the cluster benefit, the top priority is to fund the development of waqf asset. In cluster opportunity, the main priority is instrumental in developing Islamic finance, while in cluster cost, the top priority is a improfessional waqf assets management. In cluster risk, the top priority is dispute in waqf asset ownership. Priority strategy both in the short term and long term is partnership, that is between MoF, MRA, and BWI.

For opportunity side, sukuk waqf could reduce government spending for providing social facilities for the people hence the government indirectly would be able to reduce its government debt. According to MoF and Bank of Indonesia, Indonesia's external debt at the end of Q2/2017 amounted to USD 335.3 billion or grew at 2.9% year on year with the main concentration on financial, manufacturing, mining, and electricity, gas and water supply sectors (Bank of Indonesia 2017). The shares of these four sectors to total private sector external debt reached 76.6% that could be reduced by increasing the issuance of government sukuk.

Shariah government bonds or sukuk (Surat, Berharga, Syariah, Negara/SBSN) are government securities issued based on Islamic principles as evidence for the inclusion of both SBSN assets denominated in rupiah and foreign currencies. As per June 2017, domestic SBSN reached up to USD 57.854 million increased from USD 21.772 million in 2010 that indicates the need for SBSN increased over time (Bank of Indonesia 2017). Therefore, it is timely to develop waqf assets in Indonesia as a source of financing for the government in particular with the purpose to provide welfare of the people.

Recommendation and future research

Following the results of the research that has been described, then the researchers advise the following factors to the stakeholders. For regulators, issuance of Sharia government bond based on waqf asset by the MoF has benefit and opportunity higher than cost and risk to the government, investors, and the public. Alternative or recommended strategies for sukuk waqf issuers in Indonesia is a partnership between Directorate of Islamic Financing DJPPR MoF of the Republic of Indonesia, MRA and BWI. In addition, there should be a set of regulations to support the issuance of sukuk waqf. The last priority is education for all stakeholders involved in the process of issuance of sukuk waqf. For academics, there should be more research in the area of Shariah-compliant investment instruments particularly sukuk. Specific topic that could be taken into consideration is structure to the issuance of sukuk waqf. For public, especially Muslims in Indonesia, it is timely to increase awareness in Islamic finance and promote investment habit, especially in Shariah government bond.

This paper entails further research that is to continue exploring the opportunity to use waqf as government's source of financing that eventually could reduce the government debt, especially in the waqf governance mechanism. The importance of waqf utilization is on its asset safeguarding where the value of the assets cannot be reduced and its purpose is entirely for the welfare of the public.

Appendix 1

Interviewee	Institution	Duration (minutes)	Total
I-01	Bank of Indonesia	60	1 person
I-02	Ministry of Finance	60	2 persons
I-03	Indonesian Waqf Agency	60	2 persons
I-04	Ministry of Religious Affairs	60	2 persons

Appendix 2

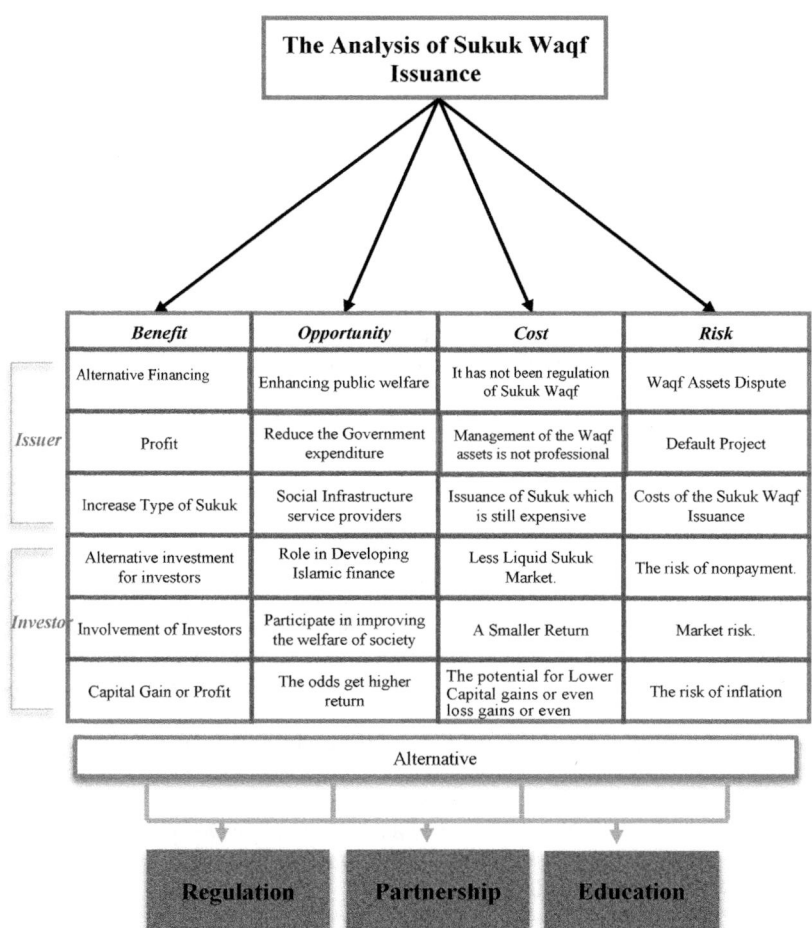

REFERENCES

Ahmed, H. (2009). *Integrating Wakaf and Financial Sector.* Working Paper Presented at Durham University Business School, United Kingdom.

Alqahtani, D. S. (2012). Redefining Sukuk as an Investment Instrument, Not Debt One. *The Journal of Investing Winter, 21*(4).

Andrian, T., & Lestari, T. P. (2013, October). Analysis of the Impact of the Fed's Target Rate Against Bank Indonesia Monetary Policies. *Jurnal Dinamika Ekonomi & Bisnis, 10*(2).

Ascarya. (2005). *Analytic Network Process (ANP): A New Approach of Qualitative Studies, Center for Education and Studies of Central Bank.* Jakarta: Bank of Indonesia.

Bank of Indonesia. (2017). *External Debt Statistics of Indonesia 2017,* Available Online at http://www.bi.go.id/en/iru/economic-data/external-debt/Documents/SULNI-Aug-150817.pdf. Accessed 11 September 2017.

Bayinah, A. N. (2012). *Exploring and Empowering Waqf Investment Toward an Acceleration of Economic Development in Indonesia.* 12th Annual International Conference on Islamic Studies.

BPS. (2010). *Population Data by Region and Religion Embraced.* Social and Population Census Data, http://sp2010.bps.go.id/index.php/site/tabel.

BWI. (2009). *The Potential of Waqf Money Reaches 20 Billion Per Annum,* Article 2014. The Waqf Land Data of Indonesia.

Çizakca, M. (1998, November). Awqaf in History and Its Implications Untuk Modern Islamic Economies. *Journal Islamic Economic Studies, 6*(1), http://www.irti.org/English/Research/Documents/IES/124.pdf.

Hanefah, M. M., Jalil, A., Ramli, A. M., Sabri, H., Nawai, N., & Shahwan, N. (2006). *Financing the Development of Waqf Property: The Experience of Malaysia and Singapore.* Jurnal Fakultas Ekonomi dan Muamalat Universiti Sains Islam Malaysia.

Hassan, A., & Shahid, M. A. (2010). *Management and Development of the Awqaf Assets.* Seventh International Conference—The Tawhidi Epistemology: Zakat and Waqf Economy, Bangi 2010 (pp. 309–328).

Ismal, R., Muljawan, D., Chalid, M. R., Kashoogie, J., & Sastrosuwito, S. (2015). Awqaf Linked Sukuk to Support the Economic Development Awqaf Linked Sukuk to Support the Economic Development. *Occasional Paper Bank Indonesia, 1,* 1–29.

Juwaini, A. (2009, October 28). *The Direction of Development of Waqf in Indonesia.* Seminar on Quo Vadis Wakaf Indonesia Jakarta, a Tube of Waqf Indonesia, The University of Al Azhar Indonesia.

Kahf, M. (1998, March 2–4). *Financing The Development of Awqaf Property.* Paper Prepared Untuk the Seminar on Development Awqaf Organized by IRTI Kuala Lumpur Malaysia.

Kamsani, F. R. B., & Leung, D. T. Z. D. T. (2004). *Wakaf Rejuvenation and Islamic Financing: Singapore's Experience*. Presentation at the Islamic Real Estate Untukum, London.

Kemenkeu. (2010). *To Know the Sukuk*. Directorate General of Management of Risk Financing and the Ministry of Finance of the Republic of Indonesia.

Khan, F. (2010). Wakaf: An Instrument of Poverty Alleviation-Bangladesh Perspective. *Proceedings of Seventh Conference The Tawhidic Epistemilogy: Zakah and Wakaf Economy*. University Kebangsaan Malaysia.

Ministry of Religious Affairs. (2004). *Undang-Undang No 41 Tahun 2004 Tentang Wakaf*. 2006. *Peraturan Pemerintah Republik Indonesia Nomor 42 Tahun 2006 Tentang Pelaksanaan Undang-Undang Nomor 41 Tahun 2004 Tentang Wakaf*.

Nasrullah, A. (2015, September). *Studi Surat Berharga Negara: Analysis Komparatif Sukuk Negara Dengan Obligasi Negara Dalam Pembiayaan Defisit Negara APBN*. Jurnal Lentera: Kajian Keagamaan dan Teknologi.

OJK. (2015). *Sharia Capital Market Roadmap 2015–2019 Islamic Capital Markets Directorate*. The Financial Services Authority.

Omar, H. H., & Rahman, A. A. (2013). The Application of Sukuk in Sustaining the Wakaf Asset: Experience of Selected Wakaf Trustee. *Shariah Journal, 21*(2), 89–116.

Peraturan Pemerintah Nomor 23 Tahun 2005 Tentang Badan Layanan Umum.

Rinaldhy, M. A. (2015). *Study of Application of Sukuk as Alternative Sources of Financing of the State*. Malang: Jurnal Ilmiah Universitas Brawijaya.

Saad, N. M., Kassim, S., & Hamid, Z. (2013). Involvement of Corporate Entities in Waqaf Management: Experiences of Malaysia and Singapore. *Asian Economic and Financial Review, 3*(6), 736–748.

Saaty, T. L. (2001). *Theory and Applications of the Analytic Network Process: Benefit, Opportunity, Cost and Risk*. Pittsburgh: Springer.

Saaty, T. L., & Vargas, L. G. (2006). *Decision Making with the Analytic Network Process: Benefits, Opportunities, Costs and Risk*. Pittsburgh: Springer.

Sadeq, A. H. M. (2002). Waqf, Perpetual Charity and Poverty Allevation. *International Journal of Social Economics, 29*(1/2), 135–151.

Tariq, A. A. (2004). *Managing Financial Risks of Sukuk Structures*. A Dissertation Submitted in Partial Fulfilment of the Requirements Untuk the Degree of Masters of Science at Loughborough University, United Kingdom.

Undang-Undang Nomor 19 Tahun 2008 Tentang Surat Berharga Syariah Negara.

Wahyuni, Y. S. (2014). *The Analysis of the Yield and Risk Comparisons of Sukuk by Using the Market Price and the Reasonable Price (A Case Study on Sukuk Issued in Indonesia Period 2009–2011)*. Unpublished thesis, Universitas Indonesia, Depok.

CHAPTER 10

Opportunities and Challenges of *Waqf* in Bangladesh: The Way Forward for Socio-Economic Development

Abu Umar Faruq Ahmad and Mohd Fazlul Karim

1 INTRODUCTION

1.1 *Meaning and Origins of* Waqf

Waqf is older and much established philanthropic vehicle compared to *zakah* in Islam. At least four significant differences exist between these two charitable instruments of Islam. First, while *zakah* falls under the category of contemporary charity, *waqf* is voluntary in nature. Second,

A. U. F. Ahmad (✉)
Islamic Economics Institute, King Abdulaziz University,
Jeddah, Kingdom of Saudi Arabia

Islamic Cooperative Finance Australia Ltd,
Parramatta, NSW, Australia

Islamic Bank of Australia Project,
Auburn, NSW, Australia

M. F. Karim
GPLLM Faculty of Law, University of Toronto, Toronto, ON, Canada

© The Author(s) 2019   193
K. M. Ali et al. (eds.), *Revitalization of Waqf
for Socio-Economic Development, Volume I*,
https://doi.org/10.1007/978-3-030-18445-2_10

waqf involves using one's wealth for religious purpose over and above the minimum and obligated threshold of *zakah*. Third, *waqf* falls under a specific form of *sadaqah*[1] termed as *sadqah jarriyah*[2]. Last but not least, *waqf* extends the role of *zakah,* which ensures the flow of cash fund to those in need.

The term "*waqf*" is derived from the Arabic root verb "*waqafa*" literally, "cause to stop, immobilise" or "come to a standstill" (Oxford Dictionaries). In Islamic Law, *waqf* refers to a voluntary and perpetual dedication of one's wealth or a portion of it, in cash or kind, and its disbursement for Sharī'ah compliant projects. The classical Muslim jurists defined the term *waqf* according to their own understandings. However, all four Sunni *fiqhi* schools of thought hold the same idea in their definitions of *waqf,* i.e., the corpus of the *waqf* or its value must remain intact, become restricted on a perpetual basis, and be used for general charitable purposes in which the beneficiaries are the public or the poor.

Some contemporary scholars defined *waqf* as holding certain property and preserving it for the confined benefit of certain philanthropy and prohibiting any use or disposition of it outside its specific objective. The Wakf Act 1954 of India defines *waqf* as, "Wakf means the permanent dedication by a person professing the Islam, of any movable or immovable property for any purpose recognised by Muslim Law as religious, pious, or charitable" (LII of India). The legal instrument constituting a *waqf* binds three parties: a donor, a manager, and beneficiaries. The donor passes assets to *waqf,* and it becomes the responsibility of *waqf* manager to look after the assets and direct the benefits of those assets to poor and needy as per the direction of the donor.

The origin of *waqf* remains contentious and cannot be tranced to any single source (Cizakca 2000). There were claims that the concept of *waqf* was found in earlier human civilization such as Mesopotamia, Greece, and Macedonia, as similar structures have existed during the times of various ancient civilizations of Persia, Egyptian, Turkish, Byzantine, and Roman Empires (Cizakca 2000). *Waqf* to be originated

---

[1] *Sadaqah* means charity.

[2] *Sadqah jarriyah* refers to ongoing charity that accumulates even after the death of a Muslim.

in the era of Muhammad (p.b.u.h) rather than a later stage of Islamic history and provides evidence that Europeans were exposed to *waqf* in Jerusalem. The following narrative of events by Ibn Sa'ad provides evidence of *waqf* practiced by Prophet Muhammad (*sallallahu 'alaihi wasallam*):

> Umar got some land at Khaybar and went to the prophet and have him command in it. He said, 'I got land in Khaybar and I did not get any property dearer to me than it. What do you command me to do with it?' He said, 'If you wish, make it a waqf and give it as sadaqah.' Umar gave it as sadaqah.... the first sadaqah given in Islam were the fruits of the sadaqah of Umar Ibn Al Khattab.

1.2 Waqf *Institutions in Bangladesh: The Regulatory Framework*

Bangladesh, according to most recent data, has a population of over 160 million, 87% of which is Muslim, being the fourth largest Muslim population and the third largest Muslim majority country in the world after Indonesia and Pakistan. *Waqf*, as a religious charitable institution, has been in existence in this South Asian Muslim country for centuries. Bangladeshi Muslims have high regard for religious activities and thus have a rich tradition of establishing *waqf* for various types of religious, educational, and social welfare purposes. *Waqf* properties in Bangladesh consist of mosques, *madrasas* (religious schools), *eidgahs*,[3] graveyards, pharmaceuticals, cultivable agricultural lands, barren lands, forests, hillocks, and urban lands. There are a lot of urban real estates in the major cities such as the capital city of Dhaka and the port city of Chittagong. Such *waqf* estates include, for instance, Baitul Mukarram (the national mosque) Complex in the capital city and the Andarkilla Shahi Jame Masjid Complex in the commercial city of Chittagong. Both the estates have huge shopping complexes which are let out in consideration of rents. Besides, there are real estates in the form of residential buildings that are mostly used by the descendant beneficiaries of the *waqif*'s. *Dargah*s and *mazars*[4] constitute a big portion of the *waqf* estates in Bangladesh. Most

---

[3] Large open fields designed and dedicated for congregational *Eid* prayers.

[4] *Dargahs* and *Mazars* are the shrines of great Islamic personalities.

of these estates are recognized as *waqf* by long user.[5] Such estates include, for instance, Shah Jalal and Shah Poran's *mazars* in the northeastern district of Sylhet. These estates earn a huge income, albeit, without any apparent investment. The main sources of income for these estates are various kinds of offerings, *hadiyyahs* (gifts and presents), and consecration of charities made. Usually people believe that if they would go to such *mazars* and *dargahs*, Allah would grant them with special blessings through those saints who are buried in those *mazars*. To achieve these special blessings, they also offer valuables such as livestock and domestic animals, poultries and vegetables, and money in cash and jewelry to their graves. These offerings come in enormous volume particularly during the annual celebration of '*urs mahfil*[6] which is held on a regular basis.

As far as registration with the Office of the *Waqf* Administrator (OWA) is concerned, *waqf* properties in Bangladesh can be categorized into three broad categories. First, *waqf* that is registered with OWA; second, *waqf* that is created as private trusts and is not listed in the OWA in the Ministry of Religious Affairs; and third, *waqf* that is managed by *mutawallis* or committees without registering with OWA. Only *waqf* properties that fall under the first category fall under the *waqf* administrative system of the government. Since *waqf* properties under the second and third categories are not registered, they are not under the direct control of the Office of the *waqf* Administrator as the OWA is not directly involved in various types of dealings, decision-making, and day-to-day activities of these two categories of *waqf* estates.

Recent years have also seen the emergence of a new trend, which is relatively new in Bangladesh, of making *waqf* of money in cash or better known as cash *waqf*. It is encouraging to note that in Bangladesh, a couple of private banks have pioneered in introducing cash *waqf*. Dedicating intellectual properties as *waqf* is another interesting development in Bangladesh that has been found to be in practice recently. Some Islamic scholars have initiated this noble tradition by dedicating the copyrights of the religious books that they have either themselves authored or they have translated other great Islamic scholars' works.

---

[5]Where there is no formal deed on the *waqf* estate but the owner of the estate has for long allowed the estate to be used for some religious or charitable purposes, such *awaqf* are known as *waqf* by user.

[6]A huge annual anniversary get-together of the followers and devotees to commemorate the saints.

2 GENESIS OF *WAQF* LAWS
AND REGULATIONS IN BANGLADESH

During the British occupation, *waqf* estates used to be administered under Muslim personal law (Shariah) dealing with fundamental aspects of *waqf*. The Chief Qadi of a District used to be the guardian of *waqf* estates in the district of his jurisdiction. However, the District Chief Judge did not have proper control and constructive, well-articulated mechanism to supervise and manage the *waqf* estates. In the absence of a governing legislative guidelines, particularly on *Waqf Ahli* (family *waqf*), the Privy Council held in the case of *Abul Fata Mohamed Ishak vs Rusomoy Dhur Chowdhury*[7] that the dedication of property by way of *waqf* for family settlement was invalid. This controversial judgment given in this landmark case created widespread discontentment among Muslim community all over the Indian subcontinent.[8] Consequently, the *waqf* Validating Act of 1913 was enacted, of which the main objective was to remove the disability created by the decision of the Privy Council. This Act paved the way for the Muslims to make settlement of their property by *waqf* in favor of their families, children, and descendants. This was how *awaqf* properties in Bangladesh (the then Bengal) started to come under government supervision.

However, it was not possible in the then Bengal to make provisions for financing the *Waqf* administration from public exchequer and as such for the first time the government passed a special enactment in 1934, known as the *waqf* Act of Bengal 1934 for supervision and protection of the *waqf* estates through a statutory autonomous organization headed by an officer designated as *waqf* Commissioner of Bengal. The Bengal *Waqf* Act 1934 made the way to meet the expenditure incurred by the *Waqf* administration by collecting contributions from the net income of the *waqf* estates.[9] One of the main objectives of the Act was to safeguard the *waqf* estates from mismanagement, misappropriation, and indiscriminate acts of the *mutawallis* concerning administration of *waqf* estates.

---

[7] 23 November 1894, PCJ on Appeals from India, 572; ILR 22 Cal. 619, 68.

[8] The judgment given by the Privy Council, being the highest court of law sitting in London, used to be binding on all the Courts in the then British Empire, including India.

[9] *Management and Development of Awaqf Properties,* Proceedings of the Seminar Held in 1984, edited by Dr. Hasmet Basar, pp. 81–85.

After Pakistan was created in 1947, the Bengal *Waqf* Act of 1934 was adopted for East Pakistan (now Bangladesh) and was followed in administering the *waqf*. Then in 1962, the *Waqf* Ordinance of 1962 was enacted without repealing the Bengal *Waqf* Act of 1934 and to date the status of the Act so remains. Section 103 of the *Waqf* Ordinance 1962, however, provides that this Ordinance shall have effect notwithstanding anything inconsistent therewith contained in any document, decree or order of any Court, deed, enactment other than this Ordinance. Therefore, by virtue of Section 103, the provisions of the Ordinance shall prevail over the Bengal *Waqf* Act of 1934 in the event of any provision thereof comes in clash with the Ordinance. Some of the major changes that the Ordinance brought about include: firstly, that a uniform rate of *waqf* contribution was fixed for the first time. And secondly, that the very post of the *Waqf* Commissioner was re-designated as *Waqf* Administrator giving him some quasi-judicial and administrative powers.

Bangladesh became an independent state in 1971 and the *Waqf* Ordinance 1962 which governed *waqf* in the then East Pakistan was adapted and retained by the government of Bangladesh as such in accordance with Article 5 of the Adaptation of Existing Bangladesh Laws (PO 48) of 1972.[10]

3   The Present Legal and Administrative Structure of *Waqf* Administration in Bangladesh

Initially, the *waqf* sector in Bangladesh used to be under the Ministry of Education. Then in 1972, it was brought under the Ministry of Land Reforms and Land Administration. Currently, *waqf* affairs in Bangladesh are governed under the Ministry of Religious Affairs. By virtue of Section 7 of the *Waqfs* Ordinance 1962,[11] the government appoints an Administrator of *waqfs*[12] for a five year term who must be a Muslim.[13] The Ordinance also provides for a *Waqf* Committee,[14] to

---

[10] This Article required that the word "Bangladesh" shall replace the words "East Pakistan" throughout.

[11] Herein after may be mentioned as the Ordinance.

[12] Herein after may be cited as the Administrator.

[13] See Section 7, subsection 2 and 3. Waqfs Ordinance, 1962.

[14] See Sections 19–25, ibid.

assist the Administrator. There are also provisions in the Ordinance for Deputy and Assistant Administrators[15] the government may, in consultation with the Administrator, appoint as may be deemed necessary. In pursuance to this, the Administrator of *waqf* is assisted by two Deputy Administrators, six Assistant Administrators, eighteen *Waqf* Supervisors, eighteen *Waqf* Auditors, and fifty-four other staff members.[16] That brings the total number of staff to ninety-eight. The Office of the Administrator of *waqf* is located in the capital city of Dhaka, as it is specifically required and provided for in Section 12 of the Ordinance. Apart from the Office of the Administrator in Dhaka, there are four divisional offices and 24 district level offices. This brings the total number of offices to twenty-nine that are dealing with *waqf* affairs throughout the country.[17] However, the *Waqf* administration in Bangladesh is highly centralized. The divisional and district level officers do not have power to make decisions and pass order. The power to make decisions and to give orders lies solely with the Administrator sitting at the Headquarter in Dhaka. At present, however, the *waqf* sector in Bangladesh is governed under the *Waqf* Ordinance 1 of 1962 which is the sole legislation in force in the country.

In accordance with Section 47 of the Ordinance, all *waqf* whether existing or created after the commencement of the Ordinance are to be enrolled at the office of the Administrator. Once an application for the enrollment of a *waqf* is received, the Administrator of *waqf* processes the applications by examining the *waqf* deed, account, and objects. The application for enrollment may be made by the *waqif* (the settlor), *mutawalli* (manager), or the *waqf* committees. Although such enrollment is required and compulsory by virtue of this section, and the Ordinance prescribes penalty for those *mutawallis* who fail to enroll their *awaqf* with the *waqf* office, many *mutawallis*, however, do not enroll and somehow escape punishment. The estates that are not enrolled are managed by the *mutawallis* according to the provisions of the *waqf* deed.

[15] See Section 13, ibid.

[16] Sadequr Rahman, *Waqf Shompotti Proshonge* (An Appraisal of *Waqf* Properties) an Article Published in Six Installments from 17 June 2003 to 24 June 2003 in the Daily Sangram (a Bengali News Paper Published Daily from Dhaka), http://www.dailysangram.com.

[17] Ibid.

4   THE KEY BARRIERS TO THE DEVELOPMENT
OF *AWAQF* IN BANGLADESH

Waqf sector in the country represents an underdeveloped, underutilized segment of the national asset, which is waiting for proper and better utilization. The problems, which the *waqf* institutions face in the country, are numerous and of enormous magnitude. Some of the major problems that the *waqf* sector is currently facing in Bangladesh are as follows:

4.1   *Inadequate Manpower*

As cited earlier, compared to the magnitude of the total number of *waqf* estates, a very small number of officials are managing the *waqf* sector. Only 98 officers and employees are managing nearly 100,000 *waqf* estates of the whole country. For proper administration and management of such a huge number of *waqf* estates scattered all over the country, the *waqf* sector needs a sizable number of qualified staff. Bangladesh has 64 administrative districts. Due to lack of manpower, only 29 districts offices are managing *waqf* estates of all 64 districts. These district offices have only one supervisor to cover nearly 800 *waqf* estates. If and when he goes to audit or inspect a *waqf* estate, the office of the supervisor remains closed. The divisional offices of Dhaka, Khulna, Rajshahi, and Chittagong divisions have been brought under direct control of the Headquarter, again, due to lack of manpower.[18]

4.2   *Unregistered* Waqf *Properties*

Although Section 47 of the Ordinance requires that "all waqfs existing at or created after the commencement of this Ordinance shall be enrolled at the office of the Administrator," more than one-third of the total *waqf* properties in Bangladesh remains unregistered. According to the Census of *waqf*, out of 150,593 *waqf* estates in the country, only 97,046 are registered, 45,607 are verbal, and the rest 7940 are *waqf* by tradition. These shows as many as 53,547 *waqf* estates are not registered. The reason for not enrolling the *waqf* estates is not known. However, it could

---

[18] Md. Azharul Islam, *Waqf Mosjid, Mondir O Majar Bebosthapona Proshongay* (On the Management of Waqf Mosques, Temples and Tombs), Office of the Administrator of Waqfs, Dhaka, n.d., pp. 4–6.

be due to various factors. First, the existence of the *Waqf* administration is not known to many people particularly in the rural areas. Second, there might be a deliberate attempt not to register to evade being controlled by the *Waqf* administration. Third, to evade payment of 5% levy as this payment is imposed upon all registered *waqf* estates. As such, the *Waqf* administration has no control whatsoever over these estates.[19] This is a very disappointing state of affairs which must be addressed seriously. Bringing these estates under the direct control of the office of the Administrator would, among many other benefits, definitely increase the *waqf* income in the country.

4.3   Illegal Occupation and Misappropriation of Waqf Properties

Many of the *waqf* properties are illegally occupied by private individuals and or organization and groups or even by government agency. It has been reported, just to mention one prominent example, that the country's Police Headquarter in Dhaka stands on a *waqf* land.[20] This area (that the Police HQ occupies) is in the heart of the capital city. It could be developed into huge profit earning business enterprise. Many *waqf* properties are underutilized such as being leased at a very low rental rate while many others are being misappropriated.[21]

There are innumerable cases of neglect and encroachments and illegal occupations. There is hardly any machinery to detect this and to recover the property in and outside the courts of law. No social pressure exists for such recoveries. Adequate and competent staff are lacking and as a result the single *Waqf* Committee for the whole country cannot make frequent and thorough inspections to prevent the mismanagement of *waqf* properties. The 5% contribution from *waqf* income which is diverted toward the Committee has not benefited the country very much. Nearly, the whole amount is spent in administration. Nor is the contribution realized effectively and very large realizable balances are reported to have accumulated. Therefore, it can be said to the minimum

[19] A. H. M. Sadeq, op.cit. p. 166.

[20] Sadequr Rahman, op.cit.

[21] For details of such misappropriation see "in Pursuit of Power: Local Elites and Union-Level Governance in Rural Northwestern Bangladesh", Care Bangladesh. August 2002, p. 17.

that the *Waqf* Committee of Bangladesh have not delivered any good for the country and so is the case with the *mutawallis*.

4.4   Uncollected Arrears

The recovery of arrears of contribution is another inherent problem. The Ordinance makes this recovery under its S.71. Moreover, it provides a punitive method of realizing contribution. But, despite these provisions, huge amounts of arrears have piled up during recent years. In order to put the finances of the *Waqf* Committee on an even keel, it is necessary that unpaid contributions shall be speedily recovered. In this respect, the experiences faced and procedure adopted under the Indian *Waqf* Acts 1995 may be taken into consideration.

4.5   Operational Inefficiency and Problem of Waqf Disputes

Hundreds of *waqf* related disputes are adjudicated by the various Courts and the *Waqf* Administrator's office.[22] This number is increasing everyday. The *Waqf* Administrator performs quasi-judicial functions. Disputes related to illegal possession or transfer of *waqf* estates, misappropriation, improper management, and so on are referred to the *Waqf* Administrator. He conducts the hearings like a Judge and delivers judgment, which is binding unless it is overruled by an Appeal Court. In cases of illegal possession or transfer a *waqf* property, or illegal interference in the management of *waqf* estates, *Waqf* Administrator enforces his order with the help of the local administration of the government at the district level. However, as mentioned above, compared to the total number of *waqf* estates in the country, a very small number of officials are managing the *waqf* sector and as such the *Waqf* administration in is overburdened not only with a large number of cases but also many other relevant matters that require due attention. This results in slow and inefficient operation.[23]

The statutory set up of *Waqf* administration in Bangladesh is empowered to look after *waqf* and to administer *waqf*. But in many instances, *mutawallis* bring the *waqf* cases to the Court where every trick is employed to get them decided in accordance with the convenience of

---

[22] Ibid.

[23] Office of the Administrator of Waqfs, Dhaka, "Bangladesh Sharkar Kortrik Gothito Waqf Komitir 20–04–95 Tarikhey Onushtitabya Prothom Shobhar Karjopotro". pp. 7–9.

parties. The Courts do not have the means to make proper investigation into the affairs of *waqf* estates and go by records that are tempered, and evidences given by hired witnesses. The *Waqf* administration is thus side-lined. However, sadly enough, the *waqf* administration is also accused of giving less than impartial and just decisions, and complaints of bribery against the *waqf* officials are not uncommon. In many cases, the integrity of the *waqf* officials is questioned. The statutory checks imposed to check corrupt practices are found to be inadequate, and the amount of autonomy granted to the *Waqf* administration is one of the causes of cover-ups.

4.6   Absence of Provisions in the Waqfs Ordinance 1962 Relating to the Development of Waqf

The *Waqfs* Ordinance 1962 contains no provision concerning the development of *waqf* properties. This is a stagnant situation due to which many of the *waqf* properties are not utilized fully or remain idle. Those estates that are in use are underutilized, i.e., they are not developed to their optimum level. The Indian *Waqf* Act 1995, for instance, regards the issue of development of *waqf* properties as a function of the *Waqf* Board of every state in India to undertake the development of *awqaf*. Section 32 of the Indian *Waqf* Act 1995 provides in its subsections (4) to (6) as follows:

> (4) Where the Board is satisfied that any waqf land, which is a waqf property, offers a feasible potential for development as a shopping center, market, housing flats and the like it may serve upon the mutawalli of the concerned waqf a notice requiring him within such time, but not less than sixty days, as may be specified in the notice, to convey its decision whether he is willing to execute the development works specified in the notice.
>   (5) On consideration of the reply, if any, received to the notice issued under subsection (4) the board, if it is satisfied that the mutawalli is not willing or is not capable of executing the works required to be executed in terms of the notice, it may, with the prior approval of the Government take over the property, clear it of any building or structure thereon, which, in the opinion of the Board is necessary for execution of the works and execute such works from waqf funds or from the finances which may be raised on the security of the properties of the waqf concerned and control and manage the properties till such time as all expenses incurred by the

Board under this section together with interest thereon the expenditure on maintenance of such works and other legitimate changes incurred on the property are recovered from the income derived from the property: Provided that the Board shall compensate annually the mutawalli of the concerned waqf to the extent of the average annual net income derived from the property during the three years immediately preceding the taking over of the property by the Board.

(6) After all the expenses as enumerated in subsection (5) have been recouped from the income of the developed properties, the developed properties shall be handed over to mutawalli of the concerned waqf.

The absence of a similar provision in the *Waqf* Ordinance 1962 is a serious lacking and an impediment to the development of *waqf*. Many *waqf* estates in Bangladesh have a lot of potentials to be developed into shopping and housing complexes, office and residential buildings that may bring in large amounts of income. Likewise, unused cultivable lands may be brought under cultivation and dairy farming. *Waqf* estates that are in the hilly areas like Chittagong and Sylhet could be used for tea plantation, while those in the costal areas could be utilized for fishery and salt industries. The income generated from these projects could then be utilized for the benefit of *waqf* beneficiaries and thus for the benefit of the *ummah* at large.

4.7   Integrity of the Mutawallis and Their Qualifications

Cases of dishonesty on the part of some *mutawallis* are not uncommon.[24] Dishonesty may be in the form of incorrect accounts of income, fabrication of bogus vouchers for amounts not spent, subscription not accounted for, illegal alienation of *waqf* properties, rents at high rates realized from the tenants but receipts for lower amounts issued and the balance pocketed as black money, and so on. The Ordinance has a number of provisions to prevent such occurrences. For instance, a *mutawalli* is debarred from making compromise in any suit or proceedings in respect of any *waqf* property without the Administrator's approval and the sanction of the trying court.[25] But very often these statutory checks

---

[24] For details please see, for instance, the case of Hafiz Mohamed Fateh v Swarup Chand HUkum Chand. AIR, 1948, PC 76.

[25] See sections 60–80 of the Ordinance.

prove inadequate.[26] The ordinance provides for the imposition of fines on an erring *mutawalli*. It is, however, to be noted that the Ordinance has given the power of imposing fines to the courts of law,[27] acting upon a complaint made by the Administrator. Thus, in every case of default by a *mutawalli*, they have to knock at the door of a court where the process of complaints, countercomplaints, and explanations generally consume much time and money. This is why more often than not; the authorities prefer not to make use of the penal provisions. Many *waqf* estates are headed by *mutawallis* who are near illiterate or not educated enough to keep and maintain accounts of income and expenditure. This sometimes may open the door for corruption.[28]

4.8 Unauthorized Alienation

The Ordinance debars *mutawallis* from transferring in any way immovable *waqf* property over a specified period of time without the previous sanction of the Administrator. As to the recovery of such property, the Administrator may institute a suit or proceeding in a court under S–83 of the Ordinance, which provides:

> If there is no mutawalli or the mutawalli refuses or neglect to act in the matter, within a reasonable time, the Administrator may, in his own name, institute a suit or proceeding in a court against a stranger to the waqf or any other person (a) for the establishment if right, title and interest in a waqf property, or (b) for confirmation of possession in a waqf property, or (c) for the recovery of any waqf property wrongfully possessed, alienated or leased. or (d) for having any waqf property discharged of an encumbrance or obligation wrongfully created, or (e) for the recovery of any money belonging to waqf, or (f) for any other relief in the interest of a waqf he may consider necessary.

Moreover, the general procedure which is usually followed appears to be that, in case the *mutawalli* or the stranger defies this provision, the Administrator may send a requisition to the Deputy Commissioner within whose jurisdiction the property is situated to obtain and deliver

---

[26] Sadequr Rahman, op.cit.

[27] See for details, section 61(1) of the Ordinance.

[28] A. H. M. Sadeq, op.cit.

possession of the property to him. On receipt of such requisition, the Deputy Commissioner shall take action. Any person aggrieved by the order of the Deputy Commissioner may prefer an appeal to the District Judge within whose jurisdiction the property is situated. The decision of the District Judge or when there is an appeal, the decision of the High Court shall be final. Surely, the above procedure involves delay and costs. Therefore, a tribunal could be set up to handle these matters more efficiently.

4.9   Personal Use of Waqf's Compensation Money

Complaints are often heard that the compensation money derived from the acquisition of *waqf* properties is kept for the personal use of the officials. The Ordinance provides that where any *waqf* property is acquired under the Land Acquisition Act, 1894, (Act I of 1894) or any other law for the time being in force, the compensation money payable for such property shall be paid to the Administrator and shall be kept in deposit in the *waqf* fund till it is invested for the purposes stated in subsection (3) of section 74.[29] This provision should be reviewed and amended to prevent possible corrupt practices on the part of the Administrator. Such amendment will surely build public confidence in *Waqf* administration in Bangladesh and ensure that the *waqf* institutions are above corruptions and irregularities.

4.10   Lack of Progressive and Innovative Ideas

It is sadly observed that progressive and innovative ideas for the development and extension of *waqf* properties are not much in evidence, neither from public nor from private sector. The great majority of *mutawallis* and managers do not think in terms of suitably adjusting the objects of the *waqf* in these changing times. *Mutawallis*, even those who are known and believed to be honest, have no concept of property maintenance and development. The idea of investment in man, that is, upgrading of Muslim human capital through education and training has not been given any attention. Most *waqf* deeds do not have a built-in provision for maintaining property.

---

[29] Section 85 of the Ordinance.

The above mentioned sad state of affairs raise doubts about the efficacy of the existing *waqf* legislation, the *Waqf* administration which operates under it, and the way in which the management of *waqf* properties is handled. The problems mentioned above are deep rooted. The *Waqf* administration is far from being satisfactory and efficient. If the Ordinance was enacted to eradicate the evils tormenting the holy purpose of the *waqf* institution in Bangladesh, it has failed to achieve its purpose. The Ordinance in the present circumstances is not potential enough to become the model *waqf* legislation in Bangladesh. It must be replaced by a new one. In this respect, a legal and administrative analysis is necessary.

5 THE PROSPECTS OF UTILIZING THE POTENTIAL OF *WAQF* IN BANGLADESH

Waqf properties in Bangladesh have immense potential of being developed into income earning ventures generating enough income to support social welfare programs in the area of education, health, and social sectors, thereby reducing the expenditure of the government in these areas. It is estimated that proper development of *waqf* estates could generate an income of at least one hundred million Taka[30] a year, which could meet part of socio-economic needs of the Muslims.[31] This is a substantial amount of income, not worth ignoring, particularly for a populous third world country like Bangladesh.

5.1 Waqf *Income and the Program for Community Development and Eradication of Poverty*

History tells us that *waqf* played the role side by side with the Islamic State to fund important community and state services. *Waqf* sector in Bangladesh can play similar role in contributing to the social and community development of the rural population of Bangladesh. *Awaqf* as an institution may mobilize community capital and provide *qard-e-hasan* which may be used to establish projects such as Islamic microlending and microfinancing on *mudarabah* or *musharakah* basis. There can be established self-reliance programs; imarets and skills training centers;

---

[30] The Bangladesh currency is called Taka. US$1 = 70 Taka (approximately).
[31] Sadequr Rahman, op.cit.

small business and bursary grants; youth development and activity programs; student exchange programs; training; general education and awareness programs, e.g., aids/drugs; dedicated women institutions; literacy and *da'awah* programs; township *masjid*s and *madrasas*, community empowerment; poverty alleviation, and related programs; and in fact any imaginable programme that could further Muslim interests in the country could be implemented and supported.

Several case studies, past and present, suggest that income from *waqf* investments and properties is used for a variety of purposes provided that these are Sharī'ah compliant. Examples of uses include: payment of teachers salaries; provision of free food; assistance to *hajis*; provision of students' tuition fees; fully paid hospitals and free medical services; publishing literature; schools and guilds for skills training; free trading market; centers for learning the art of recitation of the Holy Quran; supporting *masjid* and *madrasa; da'awah*; art and culture; research; seminars and conferences; assistance to needy traders; helping to start up enterprises and establishing factories.

6   Suggestions, Recommendations, and Plans for Action

There appears a clear need to refurbish and review the whole *waqf* sector in Bangladesh. The socio-economic role that *waqf* can play in the betterment of Muslim society is very significant. Therefore, in order to revitalize *waqf* and to make it more relevant to the overall development process in Bangladesh, we would like to recommend the followings:

6.1   Need for a New Waqf Act

A fresh *Waqf* Act is the need of the day in Bangladesh. The existing "*Waqfs* Ordinance of 1962" emerged as a poorly drafted piece of legislation in the face of the present-day needs. Many of its important provisions are poorly drafted. The machinery of administration it laid down in those days of Pakistan Martial law is now incompatible in the new framework of Bangladesh.[32]

---

[32] The Ordinance originated during Martial Law. It came into force on January 19, 1962 when there was no Parliament. Pakistan's 1962 Constitution was promulgated on March 1, 1962. East Pakistan became independent Bangladesh in 1971.

A resolution was adopted at a recently held seminar on "*Awaqf Experiences In South Asia*"[33] in New Delhi, where it was resolved, with regard to Bangladesh, that the implementation of *Waqfs* Ordinance 1962 without repealing the Bengal *Waqf* Act 1934 has brought uncertainty to the law of *waqf* and that the enactment of a new *waqf* law is necessary. Another resolution specifically highlighted the need for amending Sect. 86 of the *Waqfs* Ordinance 1962 which empowers the Administrator to realize from an individual *waqf* all costs and legal expenses incurred by the Administrator.[34] This, again, shows the need of a thorough and critical appraisal of all the laws applicable to *waqf* in Bangladesh to evaluate their appropriateness of meeting the current need of effective *waqf* management.

As mentioned earlier that *waqf* plays an important role in the religious and socio-economic development of the Muslims. The vast resources of *waqf* can, in theory, become a strong instrument not only for the preservation of religious, charitable and philanthropic institutions but also for the educational and economic boost up of the community. It is of utmost importance that *waqf* should be maintained properly. So, the need of a pragmatic and empirical approach in the area of *waqf* is obvious. The Ordinance cannot fulfill this task in today's changed situation, it has become ineffective. Hence, an ideal Act is essential.

6.2 Development of Urban Waqf and Issuance of Waqf Bond

The urban *waqf* properties situated in busy commercial areas possess immense potentials for development. There is no scheme to develop these properties. These properties being more secure, financing may be easily available. It seems to be the need of the hour that the government should have on contract basis the services of some consultant engineer to help in developing these *waqf* properties. In order to remove the hesitation on the part of financing institutions to advance money on the security of *waqf* property (because of its inalienability), a suitable clause may be added to the future *Waqf* Act. The procurement of necessary finances for such ventures could be negotiated by the Administrator with various

---

[33] Held in May 1999, jointly organised by the Institute of Objective Studies, New Delhi, the Islamic Development Bank, Jeddah, the Kuwait *Awaqf* Public Foundation, Kuwait and *Ta'awun* Trust, New Delhi.

[34] Resolution No. 17 and 18 of above mentioned seminar.

banking institutions locally and internationally. Moreover, the *Waqf* administration should be empowered to issue bonds and debentures for making available necessary finances. This venture may attain a bright prospect. Therefore, adequate attention must be paid to the development of urban *waqf* properties.

6.3   Collaboration with Other Countries

In Bangladesh, what really remains to be done in this important and interesting area is to undertake collaboration and comparative study of *Waqf* administration with countries where an administrative setup for *waqf* exists. Such countries include almost all the Middle Eastern countries, Malaysia and Indonesia just to name a few. Among countries where Muslims are minorities, India and Singapore have made considerable development in *waqf* sector. Obviously, such a study would go a long way toward the betterment of *Waqf* administration in Bangladesh.

6.4   Establishment of National Waqf Advisory Board (NAWAB)

Bangladesh should establish a National *Waqf* Advisory Board (NAWAB) that would work in collaboration with the *Waqf* administration. It may serve as a think tank and a key driving force that would have, *inter alia*, the following strategic functions:

- To establish branches of NAWAB in District and *Thana* (Sub-District) level. Its aim, among others; would be to encourage, attract, and strive to solicit every able Muslim to create *waqf*;
- To provide consulting services to the *Waqf* administration and its various chapters;
- To help establish various community development projects and institutions that would be supported primarily from *waqf* revenues and resources;
- To promote and establish stronger cooperation and coordination with Islamic NGOs and financial institutions nationally and internationally in order to find and determine common and innovative ways of finance for better utilization of *waqf*;
- To establish cooperation and collaboration with World *Waqf* Foundation (WWF) established by the Islamic Development Bank (IDB).

It is an admitted fact, that in order to improve the situation, there must be a *Waqf* Administrator competent to perform all functions entrusted to him. Government should nominate experts in law, finance, and administration as member of NAWAB to help the Administrator. The body will advise in matters such as compromising suits by or against *mutawallis* and appoint *mutawallis* in cases where *mutawalli*ship is in dispute or no suitable person is available according to the *waqf* deed.

6.5   Education and Training for **Mutawallis**

The *mutawallis* have to be educated and adequately trained. The objective of such training would be to equip them with proper knowledge and guidelines for productive utilization the *waqf* properties. The training should also serve them to realize that they are holding a trust and they must exhibit a high standard of trustworthiness. This can be achieved by holding regular training camps at the district and divisional levels. Booklets and brochures containing instructive material can be issued by the *Waqf* Administrator's Office and distributed free to the *mutawallis*.

6.6   Increasing Staff Benefit

Social security, adequate salary, and other benefit for the staff are not available and this substandard situation fails to attract young talented persons to this sector. There is no Insurance Scheme which can help the employees in different situation in their career.

6.7   Waqf Tribunal

Waqf disputes and their resolution are another area that must be improved. If litigation and litigation alone is the mode of resolving such disputes, it is wastage of time, money, and vital *waqf* resources. Therefore, establishing *Waqf* Tribunals would be a huge step forward in dispute resolution of *waqf*. Such tribunals, for instance, are operating in India and have been found to be effective. It may be made mandatory for the disputing parties who must go to the *Waqf* Tribunal for mediation and arbitration before the dispute may be taken to a court of law. Then, *waqf* institutions must be exempted from paying court fees and registration charges, and preferably, any legal action against a religious or charitable *waqf* may be defended at the cost of the state, because the state is the custodian of public interest, and the *waqf* is a public matter. Only cases relating to family *waqf* need to be defended by the beneficiaries themselves, as it is their private matter.

7   SUMMARY AND CONCLUSION

As mentioned earlier, Bangladesh has a huge wealth of *waqf* properties that could be utilized to bring out the poor segment of the population out of the ocean of poverty. And this can be done by bringing in the necessary changes in the administration of *waqf* in order to make it suitable to the present-day need. Empowering the poor through *waqf* based on various Islamic finances, and not by donation grants, thereby making the poor segments of the society an integral part of the development process should be the primary goal of the *Waqf* administration in the country. Bangladesh should set up its strategic goals with top priority given to *waqf* development in the country and arrange and organize institutions that will serve those goals. *Waqf* as a deeply rooted Shariah institution offers a built-in developmental and empowerment tool. It is indeed a vehicle explicitly designed in the Shariah to pursue noble and creative goals and to elicit goodwill and positive tendencies within the community. The benefits of *waqf* projects are far reaching. The challenge for Bangladesh thus is to pursue the establishment of *waqf* related institutions as outlined above to serve the greater *ummah* and promote and protect the cause of Islam.

REFERENCES

A Brief Outline of Waqf in Bangladesh, Office of the Administrator of *Waqfs* (Dhaka, n.d.) The *Waqf* Ordinance I of 1962, Government of the Peoples Republic of Bangladesh. *Report on the Census of Waqf Estates 1986, 1987*, Bangladesh Bureau of Statistics, Government of Bangladesh.

Cizakca, M. (2000). *A history of Philanthropic Foundations: The Islamic World from the seventh century to the present*. Istanbul: Bogazici University Press.

PART II

Waqf Management and Poverty Alleviation

CHAPTER 11

Integration of Zakat and Awaqf for Poverty Alleviation and Development

Abdul Awal Miah

1 INTRODUCTION

Although the UN-sponsored SDGs can be seen as a clear reflection of the world's concern for many an issue of socio-economic under-development prevailing in the under-developed, developing and even the developed countries, and the associated sufferings of human beings and societies, mankind is yet to envision a realistic and achievable solution that could render the civilizations optimistic about their future. In this regard, Islam does have an answer that yet needs to be properly explored. The answer does not only involve quality and expertise in working out necessary and effective provisions out of the guidelines available in Islamic Shariah but also the commitment and sincerity required for the purpose of translating them into reality. Appropriate technology and universal morality must be blended and fused together as inputs to obtain the much desired output, that is, balanced socio-economic development. Clearly enough, one input separated from the other will, certainly, produce something else than

A. A. Miah (✉)
WMIP (World Bank funded water management project),
Washington, D.C., Bangladesh

Asian Development Bank, Dhaka, Bangladesh

© The Author(s) 2019   215
K. M. Ali et al. (eds.), *Revitalization of Waqf
for Socio-Economic Development, Volume I*,
https://doi.org/10.1007/978-3-030-18445-2_11

mankind is in need of. The magic/mystery, therefore, lies in the effective application of Islamic financial provisions and tools blended with universal Islamic morality and moral values.

Following half a century of intensive practices and experiments, recent development and progress in Islamic banking and finance have proved its ability to provide a complement to the conventional system evident through the resilience of Islamic finance during the recent past financial crisis (2007–2009). The United Nations' paradigm shift to Sustainable Development Goals (SDGs) is another avenue that paves the way for Islamic finance to excel since its models focus on the societal well-being and environmental protections through Maqasid Shariah realization. In this regard, an efficient waqf management can help to preserve valuables in the form of either cash or non-cash fixed asset earned from voluntary but permanent distribution of wealth in an Islamic society. A waqf institution transforms this value to enhance socio-economic contributions of Muslims and Islamic entities in a Shariah-compliant way. The importance of waqf can be understood from its role as a voluntary contribution, a sustainable development institution, and an effective socio-economic development tool. And, zakat, another tool of Islamic finance, together with waqf can form a wonderful matching in the efforts directed toward achieving the desired socio-economic development.

1.1   Definition of Basic Human Needs: Conventional Concept

Proper understanding of basic human needs and poverty arousing out of the shortfall is a prerequisite for being able to present an appropriate model for socio-economic development. A traditional list of immediate basic needs includes food and water, shelter, clothing, sanitation, education, and health care. The basic needs approach has been described as consumption oriented, giving the impression that poverty elimination is all too easy. Amartya Sen has, however, focused on 'capabilities' rather than consumption (en.wikipedia.org/wiki/basic_needs).

Basic needs consist of adequate food, shelter, and clothing plus some household equipment and furniture. They also include essential services provided by and for the community at large such as safe drinking water, sanitation, health, and education (Inc. US Legal 2017). Max-Neef classifies the fundamental human needs as subsistence, protection, affection, understanding, participation, leisure, creation, identity, and freedom needs. Needs are also defined according to the existential categories of being, having, doing, and interacting (Salado and Nilchiani 2013).

1.2 Definition of Human Needs: Islamic Perspective

Alongside conventional definitions, there are Islamic definitions on poverty and human needs as well, and the most prominent of them is known as categorization of human needs. Emphasizing the poverty alleviation issue, Islamic scholars like Imam Sabith and Imam Ghazali in their works entitled 'Al-Muaffaqat' and 'Al-Mustashfa' have ventured to classify human needs as Zaruriat (i.e., essential needs) comprising those survival requirements, firm belief (Yaqin), knowledge and wisdom, physical needs (food, clothing, shelter, etc.), sex and procreation, freedom, transport, and environmental needs without which human life faces deadlock; Haziat (i.e., beneficial needs) including civic amenities like electricity, gas, telephone, etc., and gifts of science such as medical treatment, assistive devices, etc.; and Tahsaniat (i.e., aesthetic needs) including home decoration materials, fashion, design, architectural beauty, gardening, games and sports, and so on.

1.3 Definition and Significance of Zakat

Zakat, that is, divinely ordained poor tax, has been defined by Allah SWT in the Holy Quran. Zakat is a monetary obligation bounden upon those among the believers who are wealthy and affluent. It is a kind of tax to be levied upon the surplus money and other assets of the rich people. Al-Quran says: "Alms are for the poor and the needy, and those employed to administer (the funds); for those whose hearts have been (recently) reconciled (to Truth); for those in bondage and in debt; in the cause of Allah; and for the wayfarer: (thus is it) ordained by Allah, and Allah is full of knowledge and wisdom" (Sura 9: Al-Tawba, ayat 60).

This verse has identified the following eight categories of Muslims to be the proper recipients of zakat:

1. *Al-Fuqarā'*, the poor: That is, those living without means of livelihood, such as beggars;
2. *Al-Masākīn*, the needy: That is, those who cannot meet their basic needs and are shy of begging;

3. *Al-Āmilīyn 'Alihā*: That is, zakat collectors, either salaried or volunteers;
4. *Al-Mu'allafatu Qulūbuhum*: That is, to persuade those sympathetic to or expected to convert to Islam, recent converts to Islam, and potential allies in the cause of Islam;
5. *Fir-Riqāb*: That is, to free from slavery or servitude; slaves of Muslims who have or intend to free from their master by means of a *kitabah* contract;
6. *Al-Ghārimīn*: That is, those who have incurred overwhelming debts while attempting to satisfy their basic needs, debtors who in pursuit of a worthy goal incurred a debt;
7. *Fī Sabīlillāh*: That is, those fighting for a religious cause or a cause of God or for Jihad in the way of Allah by means of pen, word, or sword, or for Islamic warriors who fight against the unbelievers but are not salaried soldiers;
8. *Ibnu Al-Sabīl*: That is, wayfarers, stranded travelers, travelers who are traveling with a worthy goal but cannot reach their destination without financial assistance.

1.4   Significance of Awaqf

In Arabic language, waqf literally means to stop, contain, or preserve. In Islamic terms, waqf refers to a religious endowment, i.e., a voluntary and irrevocable dedication of one's wealth or a portion of it in cash or kind (such as a house or a garden), and its disbursement for Shariah-compliant projects (such as mosques or religious schools). Waqf is a permanent donation. Once a waqf is created, it can never be donated as a gift, inherited, or sold. Disbursement of its returns is done in accordance with the endower's wishes (awaqf.ae).

Awaqf or endowment (Arabic: وقف), also known as habous or *mortmain* property, is an inalienable charitable endowment under Islamic law, which typically involves donating a building, plot of land, or other assets for Muslim religious or charitable purposes with no intention of reclaiming the assets. The donated assets may be held by a charitable trust. The person making such dedication is known as *waqif*, a donor. In Ottoman Turkish law, and later under the British Mandate of Palestine, the *waqf* was defined as usufruct state land (or property) of which the state revenues are assured to pious foundations. Although based on several hadiths and presenting elements similar to practices from pre-Islamic cultures, it seems that the specific full-fledged Islamic legal form of endowment called *waqf* dates from the ninth century CE (Wikipedia). Hundreds of thousands of charitable institutions like mosques, madrasas, graveyards, etc., have developed throughout India and elsewhere in the world with waqf fund. Recognizing the immensely beneficial contribution of such institutions, the British government passed the first piece of legislation in the British Parliament in 1905 entitled: the Mohammedan and Hindu Endowments Ordinance (MHEO) of 1905, designed to administer religious endowments of non-Christian communities in the Straits Settlements (SS) allowing the formation of a permanent board, the Mohammedan and Hindu Endowments Board (MHEB), in each of the three settlements of Singapore, Penang, and Malacca (Sinha 2017).

1.5   Significance of Conventional Microfinance

"Microcredit, or microfinance, is banking the unbankables, bringing credit, savings and other essential financial services within the reach of millions of people who are too poor to be served by regular banks, in most cases because they are unable to offer sufficient collateral. In general, banks are for people with money, not for people without" (Gert van Maanen, *Microcredit: Sound Business or Development Instrument*, Oikocredit, 2004). Microfinance and microcredit are generally regarded as synonymous in concept and practice. "(Microcredit) is based on the premise that the poor have skills which remain unutilized or underutilized. It is definitely not the lack of skills which make poor people poor....charity is not the answer to poverty. It only helps poverty to continue. It creates dependency and takes away the individual's initiative to break through the wall of poverty. Unleashing of energy and creativity in each human being is the answer to poverty" (Muhammad Yunus, *Expanding Microcredit Outreach to Reach the Millennium Development Goals*, International Seminar on Attacking Poverty with Microcredit, Dhaka, Bangladesh, January, 2003).

Microfinance has emerged as an industry throughout the world, originating from Bangladesh. It has been widely known as the vehicle of poverty alleviation, that is, development in the developing world. Conventional microfinance is interest based. This interest is termed within the industry as service charge. It is highly appreciated as a collateral-free loan for the poor. Although microfinance has been recognized by the United Nations (UN) and International Monetary Fund (IMF) as one of the important instruments of poverty eradication, it has been perceived that the traditional microfinance cannot play opposite role to alleviate such poverty for its scopes and limitations (Khan and Obaidullah 2014).

1.6   Poverty Alleviation and Islamic Microfinance

Islamic microfinance is an effective alternative to traditional system of microfinance for reaching the poor, raising their living standards, creating jobs, boosting demand for other goods and services, contributing to economic growth, and alleviating poverty (Khan and Obaidullah 2014).

Unique Position of Bangladesh in Microfinance
Bangladesh being the breeding ground and champion of microfinance in the world and hence credited as the capital of world microfinance industry has all potentials to make meaningful contribution to these great IDB initiatives toward improving the socio-economic condition of the people of the developing countries of the world. The world can benefit from the valuable experience that Bangladesh gathered through planning and implementing hundreds and thousands of microfinance projects in Bangladesh as well as elsewhere in the world. This workshop will also find special meaning in exploring waqf regulation in IDB member and non-Muslim majority countries, its modernization and relationship to Shariah, stacking the performance of waqf activities in IDB member Muslim countries/jurisdictions, offering activity- and time-wise distribution of waqf resource management in member countries, understanding the antecedents and consequences of waqf assets (both physical and cash) in member countries, understanding the strategies and models to promote waqf-related activities for greater socio-economic development, enhancing good governance practices through the formulation of informed policies for waqf projects in the country, and understanding the confluence of waqf, zakat, charity, Islamic microfinance, impacting socio-economic development of member countries during the course of the workshop in Bangladesh.

Islamic Modes of Microfinance

The word "Modes" literally means "methods," or in other words, it refers to systematic and detailed rules, stipulations, and steps to be followed for accomplishing a specific thing. The thing that needs to be accomplished in this context is, however, the subject matter of each of the said modes, i.e., any of the different types of investment activities (trade, manufacturing, agriculture, agriculture production, etc.) using *Shariah expressions Murabaha, Mudarabah, Musharakah, Ijarah, Istisna, Bai-Muajjal,* etc. The word "Finance" in one of its different meanings refers to the supply of money capital or credit, provided by either a person (household) or an organization (private or public—financial or non-financial). The word "Islamic" is inserted in the above expression to restrict the type of rules that can govern different modes of finance to the *Shariah* rules. A complete definition for the term "Islamic Modes of Finance" may be given as follows:

> The systematic and detailed Shariah rules that govern the contractual relationship of an investment activity that can be applied for attracting money capital. (Fahmy and Sarkar 1997)

A few Shariah-compliant modes of transactions that can be applied while operating Islamic microfinance include:

Bai-Murabaha: "*Bai-Murabaha*" means sale for an agreed upon profit. *Bai-Murabaha* may be defined as a contract between a buyer and a seller under which the seller sells certain specific goods permissible under Islamic Shariah and the law of the land to the buyer at a cost plus an agreed upon profit payable today or on some date in the future in lump sum or by installments.

Musharakah: The word *musharakah* is derived from the Arabic word Sharikah meaning partnership. Islamic jurists point out that the legality and permissibility of *musharakah* are based on the injunctions of the Quran, Sunnah, and Ijma (consensus) of the scholars.

Mudarabah: The term *mudarabah* refers to a contract between two parties in which one party supplies capital to the other party for the purpose of engaging in a business activity with the understanding that any profits will be shared in a mutually agreed upon.

Bai-Salam: *Bai-Salam* is a term used to define a sale in which the buyer makes advance payment, but the delivery is delayed until sometime in the future. Usually, the seller is an individual or business and the buyer is the IMFI. The seller receives advance payment in exchange for the obligation to deliver the commodity at some later date. He benefits from the Salam sale by locking in a price for his commodity, thereby allowing him to cover his financial needs whether they are personal expenses, family expenses, or business expenses.

Istisna Sale: The Istisna sale is a contract in which the price is paid in advance at the time of the contract and the object of sale is manufactured and delivered later. The majority of the jurists consider Istisna as one of the divisions of Salam.

Qard al-Hassan: *Qard al-Hassan* is a contract in which one of the parties (the lender) places into the ownership of the other party (the borrower) a definite parcel of his property, in exchange nothing more than the eventual return of something in the same value of the property loan. The Faisal Islamic Bank of Egypt provides interest-free benevolent loans to the holders of investment and current accounts, in accordance with the conditions set forth by its board of directors. The banks also grant benevolent loans to other individuals under conditions decreed by its board. On the other hand, the Jordan Islamic Law authorizes it to give "benevolent loans" (*Qard al-Hassan*) for productive purposes in various fields to enable the beneficiaries to start independent lives or to raise their incomes and standard of living (ibid., pp. 49–50).

Bai-Muajjal: The term "Bai" means purchase and sale and the word "Ajal" means a fixed time or a fixed period. "Bai-Muajjal" is a sale for which payment is made at a future fixed date or within a fixed period. In short, it is a sale on credit. The Bai-Muajjal may be defined as a contract between a buyer and a seller under which the seller sells certain specific goods, permissible under Shariah and law of the country, to the buyer at an agreed fixed price payable at a certain fixed future date in lump sum or in fixed installments.

1.7   Poverty Situation in the World and in Bangladesh

In the World

Two-thirds of the incomes derived from the present economic and financial activities go to only 20% rich people while only 5% income goes to 20% poor people. Four hundred million poor people have as low income as less than a dollar. Overall, 80% of the people in the world have less than 10-dollar income per day. (Shah 2017). According to UNICEF, 25,000 children die every day due to poverty; 29% children are born with malnutrition, mostly from South Asia and Sahara region of Africa. Out of 6.5 billion people of the world, 1.00 billion live in rich countries that enjoy 76% of GNP. On the other hand, 2.5 billion people of low-income countries enjoy only 3.3% of GNP.

In Bangladesh

Bangladesh is one of the poorest countries in the world in terms of income and other social and economic indicators. In 1990, approximately 58.5% of the population lived below the poverty line, which gradually improved to 40% in 2005. Even today, about 18% of the population lives in absolute poverty who suffer from food insecurity coupled with illiteracy, lack of proper health, and sanitation facilities.

2   ROLE OF ZAKAT FOR POVERTY ALLEVIATION

Zakat is a divinely ordained Islamic Shariah provision for eliminating poverty from the society through creating wealth distribution mechanisms as opposed to wealth accumulation. It is very simply an inbuilt right of the poor and needy of the society in the wealth of the rich. It is unique in a financial system that fixes rights of certain categories of community members that lag behind in resources in the surplus money and/or wealth of rich people. It is not an optional act of almsgiving to the beggars of the givers' choice but compulsory duty upon the surplus asset holders to surrender fixed portion of their money to the official collectors. According to the **Holy Quran (Surah Al-Tawba)**, there are eight categories of people (*asnaf*) who qualify to benefit from *zakat* funds. To put in the words of the Holy Quran:

Certainly, the alms are for the poor and the needy, and those employed to administer the (funds); for those whose hearts have been (recently) reconciled (to Truth); for those in bondage and in debt; in the cause of Allah; and for the wayfarer: (thus is it) ordained by Allah, and Allah is full of knowledge and wisdom. (Sura: Al-Tawba, ayat 60)

It is evident from the verse that a special provision of charity called zakat has been created in Islamic financial systems to address the need of eight types of people in special situation. These can be summarized as below:

2.1 Zakat provides survival needs to the extremely poor, destitute, homeless, provision-less, for example, the beggars living under poverty line, say having less than a dollar income per day. This is free charity to enable them to meet their basic needs, that is, expenses of food, clothing, housing/shelter, education, health care, etc., and survive. These people comprise the most bottom section in the society usually skipped by microfinance program due to their inability to enter into any regular financial activity and to repay the collateral-free loan under microfinance.

2.2 Zakat provides subsistence needs to the needy people who cannot earn bare subsistence income but living under poverty line slightly above the extremely poor. This is free charity to enable them to meet their basic needs and thereby survive without begging. These people comprise the bottom section in the society often covered under microfinance program but their incomes are not always sufficient enough to maintain an honorable life.

2.3 Zakat provides money for repayment of loan to the debtors/loanees who are unable to pay back the money taken as loan for legitimate purpose of meeting the lawful expenses.

2.4 Zakat provides money to create employment for the zakat collectors who may be salaried staff or volunteers.

2.5 Zakat provides money for achieving freedom (salvation from servitude) to those unfortunate slave people who have been leading the life of servitude. Islamic Shariah provision of zakat seeks to gradually eliminate slavery from the society. People in prison and suffering from undue penance can also be assisted under this provision to appoint lawyer or otherwise free themselves from such unfortunate situation.

2.6 Zakat provides assurance for new/potential Muslims by bearing any potential risks for them so as to attract their hearts and encourage them to embrace Islam without fear or danger.

2.7 Zakat fund provides travel costs to those stranded travelers who cannot reach destination for want of money to pay for their travel costs. Such people in awkward/embarrassing situation will be assisted, poor or rich alike.

2.8 Zakat fund provides money for protection of citizens from enemies by financing Jihad in the way of Allah (En.wikipedia.org).

2.9 Bangladesh Context Zakat has immense potential in implementing poverty alleviation projects and making substantial contribution to government's poverty alleviation initiatives, especially taken under Ministry of Industries **(GoB, PRSP-II).** If zakat fund is collected and managed properly, it can be used to create a pool of funds, which can be used in financing development activities and can replace government expenditures (*Dr Kabir Hasan, Professor at New Orleans University, USA*). In Bangladesh, zakat funds could have contributed up to 21% of the ADP in 1983–1984 and up to 43% in 2004–2005. There were immense scopes in Bangladesh to explore zakat fund that remains unexplored. The Bangladesh Zakat Board data show that out of the 42 commercial banks, 14 had collected Tk 60.3m during FY2012–13 as zakat but the Board distributed only Tk 2m. The remaining 28 commercial banks did not collect any money for the Zakat Board although they opened separate accounts and collected over Tk 10m each. These banks, however, did not disclose how they spent the funds (Kallol 2017). That means the potential of zakat is not yet properly taped or organized in Bangladesh.

3   ROLE OF AWAQF FOR POVERTY ALLEVIATION

3.1   Introduction

Waqf/Islamic endowment can be defined as dedication of property through will or otherwise by a person for pious, religious, and charitable purposes. Waqf plays a paramount role in general, and in needy societies or in unforeseen circumstances in particular. It aids in the development process by helping the needy and establishing mosques and social welfare institutions such as schools, health care centers, and centers for people with special needs (YouTube 2014). Waqf is a form of charity for the sake of Allah. It is lawful because it aids in the sustainable development. It also seeks to empower the Muslim society. Waqf is a beautiful loan to Allah—Exalted—Who shall reward the endower granted it is done with pure intention.

Waqf comprises three components such as the endower/Waif, the endowment (waqf), and the beneficiary. The endower must confirm his/her decision to grant an endowment and designate its beneficiary either verbally or in writing. One can also have a tangible evidence on his/her endowments such as a built mosque or cemetery. Endowment must be granted with full determination and as a final decision; in other words, a promissory and conditional endowments are not accepted. Further, endowment is irrevocable and for an unlimited time. Most scholars agree that endowment cannot be valid for a limited period. The Maliki school of thought, however, is the only one that accepts the limited time endowment. The endower must be an adult with free will. His/her decision to grant an endowment must be a personal one, i.e., is not imposed on him/her by anyone. Endowment funds or assets must be in compliance with Shariah.

Endowment can be either in cash or in kind such as estates and stocks. Since an endowment is a continuous charity (Sadaqah Jariyah), it must be permanent and non-perishable. Therefore, food cannot be endowed. Moreover, the endowment can be a part of an undivided joint estate granted its percentage is known (such as 25% of the estate). Endower has the right to increase his waqf with time by additional funds or in kind. The beneficiary can be an individual(s) or an institution(s) which is awarded the income generated from investing the waqf. Waqf must also be designated to Shariah-compliant deeds or people such as printing the Holy Quran, or helping the needy, the poor, the relatives... (Awaqf.ae 2017).

3.2 Waqf Is Charitable by Nature

Unlike microfinance, waqf is charitable in nature. Likewise, waqf plays a paramount role in general, and in needy societies or in unforeseen circumstances in particular just as zakat does. It aids in the development process by helping the needy and establishing mosques and social welfare institutions such as schools, health care centers, and centers for people with special needs. People are driven to perform good deeds by human nature or for religious, social, family-related, and other reasons. The majority of Islamic scholars agree that waqf is a Shariah-compliant charity.

3.3 Waqf Fulfills Needs of the Backward Sections

Waqf is purely a charitable endowment usually dedicated for the welfare of the backward sections of the society including the poor and needy, orphan boys and girls, widows, PWDs, old-age people. The endower dedicates a waqf to his family, children, relatives, or others. Upon the death of the beneficiaries, this waqf may be transformed into a charitable one at the endower's request. The endowment is designated to help the poor, orphans, and widows and for any other charitable causes. This waqf is a combination of both family and charitable awaqf.

3.4 Waqf for Common Good and Development Needs

Waqf/Islamic endowment is dedication of property through will or otherwise by a person for pious, religious, and charitable purposes (YouTube 2014). Waqf plays a paramount role in general, and in needy societies or in unforeseen circumstances in particular. It aids in the development process by helping the needy and establishing mosques and social welfare institutions such as schools, health care centers, and centers for people with special needs. The endowment is designated to help the poor, orphans, and widows and for any other charitable causes. This waqf is a combination of both family and charitable awaqf. Endower is permitted to earn the whole or some of the income generated by the waqf during his/her life. Upon one's death, the income will be spent on the beneficiary designated by the endower (Tahir and Haji Mohammad 2013).

4   Zakat and Awaqf as Complementary Tools for Poverty Alleviation

As financial tools/sources for poverty alleviation, zakat and awaqf are complementary to each other. Awaqf complements zakat mainly by taking up the responsibility to fulfill the need for asset and infrastructure building of the institution, while zakat fulfilling the instant needs of the poor. A detailed list of complementary role of the two Islamic financial tools is presented in the foregoing section.

4.1   Comparative Features of Zakat and Waqf

Sl	Zakat	Waqf	Remarks
1	Mostly cash fund and fast and instant in nature	Mostly reserved asset and slow in nature	Zakat envisages short-term planning while
2	Limited by time (maximum one year)	Not limited by time	waqf is mostly medium and long-term
3	Fulfills only survival needs	Can fulfill survival as well as other developmental needs	Zakat is wholly dedicated to the extremely poor while awaqf supports
4	Covers certain specific category of people only	Fulfills both individual and collective needs of community members	organization's sustainability aspects
5	Addresses mostly personal needs	Addresses mostly institutional/collective needs	
6	Zakat is mandatory	Not mandatory, rather mostly charitable	
7	Certain rates on the specific asset are applicable/fixed	Unlimited in nature: Whole or part of an asset can be an endowment	
8	Mostly seasonal in nature	All year round	
9	Handed over to a person forever	Not handed over to any person, rather to society collectively	
10	Zakat is a one-time gift/charity to be consumed/used by a single person/family	Waqf is a permanent asset to be perpetually administered by an administrator	
11	Zakat forms mostly a cash fund for instant distribution	Waqf is mostly an asset for planned use	

4.2 Comparative Advantages/Limitations of Zakat and Awaqf

Sl	Zakat	Waqf	Remarks
1	Zakat fund must be distributed among persons falling within eight fixed categories	Waqf is open for any deserving individual or collective body/organization in the society	Use of waqf fund needs medium-and/or long-term planning While Zakat is purely short term
2	Zakat must be distributed within Shariah stipulated time (maximum one year)	Not limited by time, can be held for longer periods, if necessary	
3	Zakat fund is consumed by the receiver only	Benefits of waqf fund can be consumed by wide range of beneficiaries including the endower himself/herself and/or his/her family members	
4	Management of Zakat fund requires light monitoring	Awaqf fund management involves strong monitoring system	Accounts close annually
5	Zakat is an annual program	Awaqf is perennial	Accounts continue for unlimited period of time

5 Integrated Approach of Zakat and Awqf as Poverty Alleviation Tools

It is observed that awaqf- and zakat-based charitable poverty alleviation programs are not so significant and popular, neither in Bangladesh, nor elsewhere in the world, while microfinance programs are like giants in fund size as well as in amounts for capital investment. Microfinance is for the unbankables who lack collateral and security for loan. Microfinance industry in Bangladesh earned a very good name not only in Bangladesh but also elsewhere in the world mainly due to making capital available within the reach of the poor who have no access to bank capital for want of collateral but are being criticized for high interest rate on loans, over-indebtedness of the borrowers. Likewise, Islamic microfinance has already earned good name for comparatively low service charge but has been facing challenges of sustainability of the IsMFIs. It has been observed that conventional microfinance was too expensive

(8–100%), while Islamic products were relatively cheap (4–18%) but can still be called expensive. The cost of Islamic microfinance (IsMFIs) varies between as low as 1.5–4% in Malaysia and 5–17% in Pakistan and Malaysia (Tahir and Haji Mohammad 2013). Islamic microfinance has all potentials to emerge as an ideal microfinance industry once awaqf and other forms of Islamic charities are combined together. Conventional microfinance has been designed and standing on commercial basis thus earning bad reputation of being exploiters/usurpers while Islamic microfinance must primarily be charity based and not commercial in nature. Comparative advantages of zakat and awaqf combined are only too clear as evident from the following sections.

5.1   Develop Ideal Islamic Microfinance

Ideal Islamic microfinance free from being commercial and exploiters is achievable through the utilization of zakat, sadaqah, and awaqf funds and other properties to complement the usual loan fund. The use of zakat for Qard al-Hassan fund, for the benefit of the extremely poor when they are unable to make their timely payments or for the development project of community. waqf projects are a continuing charity with long-lasting positive effect and generous outcome. "Indeed, the men who practice charity and the women who practice charity and [they who] have loaned Allah a goodly loan - it will be multiplied for them, and they will have a noble reward" (Al Hadid:18). Writing off loans when necessary and the occasional subsidy should come from the zakat and other disposable charitable funds. Sometimes, it is necessary to offer consolidated or parallel credits (re-payable and not so), subsidize the Qard al-Hassan/beautiful loan and micro-ventures for the poor with normal commercial products, reducing cost of operational capital by integrating loans to micro-enterprises with provision of goods and business premises and by using trade, credit, and leasing contracts for such deals, and stratify the amount of service charges according to the income of the borrower and not benchmarking the rate of profit on loans with the market rate. It is possible to introduce all these beneficial provisions only through integration of zakat, awaqf, sadaqah, and other sources of charity fund in the process of implementing poverty alleviation programs and projects. Thus, an ideal Islamic microfinance developed through the integration of awaqf and zakat can serve not only as a better alternative to conventional microfinance but also to separate awaqf- and zakat-based charitable services to the poor.

5.2   Develop Strong and Sustainable IsMFIs

Unlike conventional microfinance, the IsMFIs deal with charity funds that do not earn them any profit. They also earn less from their investment as microfinance due to lower profit rate realized from their beneficiaries. Zakat includes provision for staff salaries but not other overhead costs. Thus, they have to find alternative sources of fund like awaqf, sadaqah, etc., to cover administrative and overhead costs. A strong organization is known by the quality and quantity of its man, money, and material. Role of awaqf is, therefore, highly significant in building strong and sustainable organizations rich with expert manpower, formidable fund, and appropriate technology so that they can offer better and continued services to the poor until the target of their socio-economic development is achieved.

5.3   Use of Appropriate Technology

In order for the development work to go smoothly and productivity to be increased significantly, especially in agriculture and SME sectors, use of machines and equipment is a must. Very often, these involve capital expenditure of huge amount which is not usually available to an IsMFI working with charitable fund like zakat. The possibility of poverty alleviation and socio-economic development of the poor masses largely depends on the availability of appropriate technology for ensuring high productivity. Countries like Bangladesh that are not industrially developed must pursue promotion of SME and agriculture alongside full-fledged use of ICT. These are some of the requirements that call for building strong funds through integration of awaqf, zakat, sadaqah, and other charity funds. This strategy is suitable for increasing productivity of the assets of awaqf organization as well that will increase income which will, ultimately, benefit the poor more than ever.

5.4   Investment for Earning Profit

Business initiatives with profit earning motif are essential for attaining organizational sustainability. The conventional microfinance does not only disburse loans on high interest rates, but also use their fund randomly for the purpose of running business enterprises. While zakat has

Table 1 Contribution of awaqf and zakat in integrated initiatives

Sl	Sectors of intervention	Awaqf	Zakat	Remarks
1	Distribution of charity money to extremely poor for fulfilling immediate survival needs (food, clothing, shelter, etc.)	Income derived from Awaqf asset distributed among poor and extremely poor	Zakat money (cash/kind) distributed among extremely poor	Awaqf proceeds can be distributed among non-poor as well
2	Disbursement of investment money for microfinance/SME as loan to borrowers	Awaqf money can be distributed on long-term basis	Zakat money can be distributed under certain conditions	Need strong monitoring in case of Awaqf and light monitoring in case of zakat
3	Purchase of machinery and equipment (power tiller, sewing machine, vehicles, fan, AC, furniture, etc.)	Awaqf fund is open and participates fully	Zakat participates under certain conditions	
4	Cost of training and training materials	Awaqf participates fully	Zakat participates under certain conditions	
5	Cost of staff salary and benefits	Awaqf participates	Zakat participates with full responsibility for Zakat staff	Zakat can spend 1/8th of the total Zakat collected
6	Other overhead costs (conveyance, house rent, communications, entertainment, repair and maintenance, etc.)	Awaqf participates	Zakat participated under certain conditions	
7	Cost of development initiatives/needs (education, health care, sanitation, etc.)	Awaqf participates	Zakat participates under certain conditions	
8	Sustainability of IsMFIs: business investment/initiatives for income/profit earning	Awaqf money is available	Zakat money isn't available	
9	Infrastructure building (hospital, clinic, madrasa, school, college and universities, bridge/culvert, orphanage, training institute, production center, etc.)	Awaqf meets construction/establishment costs	Zakat meets running/operating costs	

no scopes for such commercial initiatives, awaqf does often have huge idle amounts to be invested in profitable concerns. So, integration of awaqf and zakat is very likely to strengthen program side as well as organizational sustainability through pursuing development orientation in designing programs and projects.

5.5   Addressing Development Needs

Besides charity-based welfare activities of zakat and awaqf funds, the poor also need institutional services like education, health care, orphanage, old-age home, public toilet, bathroom, etc. In such cases, zakat can meet operating cost while awaqf can meet construction/establishment costs.

5.6   Contribution of Awaqf and Zakat

In an integrated initiative for poverty alleviation, both zakat and awaqf amply contribute to achieving the socio-economic development targets. Table 1 shows how these two Islamic tools jointly perform.

6   CZM Model Operating in Bangladesh

Since inception in 2008, Center for Zakat Management (CZM), a faith-based welfare organization pioneering institutionalization of zakat, has been working for the poor and extremely poor in Bangladesh by means of mobilizing and distributing mainly zakat in larger volume and also awaqf in smaller volume and implementing a number of charity as well as development programs to this end. Over the last nine years of program period (2008–2016), CZM achieved considerable success in poverty alleviation and socio-economic development of the poor through the utilization of zakat as well as awaqf funds charitably as well as with development orientation. CZM designs its intervention in such a way that is suitable for addressing the survival, emergency, and development needs of the zakat right holders covered under its different programs. Although CZM's success and achievement are quite appreciable, they are not as remarkable as they could be if funds beyond zakat like awaqf and sadaqah could be fully integrated with zakat. The following shows some of CZM's achievement.

6.1   Achievements (Cumulative)

CZM program interventions have already marked tangible changes in different aspects of the life of the beneficiaries, especially in terms of income earning, capital accumulation, quality of housing, landholding, asset building, food intake, indebtedness, financial empowerment, market access, poverty status, and so on. Income of the beneficiaries increased 80% over the last five years. They accumulated capital at about 50%, while 7.7% of the beneficiaries improved the quality of their house from thatched house to tin-shed with brick floor. Likewise, protein intake (fish/meat/milk, etc.) improved significantly. Landholding increased from 2.88 to 3.91 decimals per family. Other asset buildings in which CZM beneficiaries have marked changes include: Fishing net ownership increased from 55 to 100%, boat ownership increased from 18% to 100%, livestock ownership increased from 30 to 50%, various home appliances ownership increased from 30 to 40% to about 80–90%. On the other hand, indebtedness of the beneficiaries especially on NGOs and money lenders reduced significantly, in fact, to about zero level. As far as poverty level is concerned, 66% of the beneficiaries have surplus income today whereas earlier 22% used to suffer from chronic deficit and 47% occasional deficit (Rahman 2014).

A total of BDT 500 million has been mobilized by CZM including 450m zakat and 50m from other sources.

Table 2 shows some achievements of the CZM in terms of coverage and distribution of zakat.

6.2   Operational Strategies of Major Interventions

CZM follows definite strategies for its program interventions. Strategies for the largest program, that is, Jeebika (livelihood), are the most clearly chalked out ones. Zakat money is transferred to zakat right holders organized under groups (grassroots organizations—GROs) which is in turn invested by the beneficiaries in the GROs following the Islamic mode of investments, such as *Mudarabah*, *Musharakah*, and *Bai-Muajjal*. GROs follow the basics of *Bai-Muajjal* system for investment. Capital equity of a GRO under CZM livelihood (Jeebika) program consists of the amount of capital transferred, group savings and group profit. CZM programs are community based and their operational modes involve the following common strategies:

Table 2 Program overview 2016, CZM

Sl	Title of program	Achievement				Remarks
		Beneficiary coverage (No.)	Institutions built	Geographical coverage (district)	Amount transferred (BDT)	
1	Jeebika: Livelihood and Human Development Program	43,000 population 10,340 families	305 GROs	20 out of 64	160,000,000	1. An integrated program includes health care, education, and disaster relief services 2. Total revolved amount including transferred invested in 9 trades including small business, cottage industry, beef fattening, dairy, poultry farm, bamboo and cane works, fish farming, rickshaw/van, sewing and embroidery, etc.
2	Ferdousi: Women and Child Welfare Program	75,000 population 16,000 families Female 72% Child 13% Male 15%	600 Women groups 350 Adolescent groups 33 centers	27	18,000,000	100% safe delivery, 100% breast feeding, 75% malnutrition reduced, 80% infectious disease reduced, high incidence of disease reduced from 61% to 27%, child mortality rate reduced to 0%, hygienic sanitation, awareness of pregnant mother care 87%, 100% zakat right holders received health services, child immunization 100%

(continued)

Table 2 (continued)

Sl	Title of program	Achievement				Remarks
		Beneficiary coverage (No.)	Institutions built	Geographical coverage (district)	Amount transferred (BDT)	
3	Gulbagicha: Pre-primary Education Program	32,265	Total 1120 centers	20	53,000,000	• Contribute to education for all (EFA) of Sustainable Development Goal (SDG) • Targeted to poor and marginalized children • Focused on urban slum area and hard to reach area • Provide nutritious food support • Provide religious and moral education
4	Genius: Students Scholarship Program	Total 2191 Current 1832	8 divisions	29 Public Universities and 27 Medical Colleges	82,000,000	• In 2017, All Public Universities and Govt. Medical Colleges is being Covered
5	Naipunna Bikash: Vocational Training and Employment Program	Total 1757	3 Centers 1 vocational 1 school 10 trades	03	22,000,000	• 3–4 month Vocational training • Trades: welding and fabrication, electric and solar, driving, dress making, plumbing, and machineries

Table 2 (continued)

Sl	Title of program	Achievement				Remarks
		Beneficiary coverage (No.)	Institutions built	Geographical coverage (district)	Amount transferred (BDT)	
6	Insaniat: Emergency Humanitarian Assistance Program	25,000 Beneficiaries			42,000,000	Supported emergency medical treatment, loan repayment difficulties, house reappearing & livelihood, food, assistance for education, winter cloth distribution, emergency response for flood victim, Qurbani meat distribution
7	Zakat Awareness Building	294 Donors donate CZM zakat fund				As a strategy of creating awareness on zakat, motivating donors, and collection of zakat: • Seminar on zakat organized • Round table organized • Annual zakat Fair organized

- Target beneficiaries are selected using participatory selection method.
- Selected members are formed into community groups (grassroots organizations—GROs).
- Provide skill development training to the GRO members on business development issues considering experience and market profitability using the community funds made up of each individual's share of money in the group fund.
- Capital is transferred to the GROs for conducting income generation activities by the group members.
- Provide support services such as pre-primary education, life skill education, primary health care service, and referral service for critical and emergency patients, pregnant mothers and lactating mothers, and humanitarian assistance to disaster victims.
- Provide marketing services for selling products and services of the GRO members.
- Establish a central association of all the GROs (called Jeebika Unnayan Kendra—JUK) for promoting cooperative and collective investment with their ownership (CZM AnnRep2016/2015).

6.3   Planning

CZM works on the basis of annual planning formulated through consultation with all level staff in a participatory manner. Annual plan envisages all important issues including zakat awareness building, zakat collection, distribution, program expansion, monitoring and evaluation, and so on. Usually, zakat collection and related activities are launched in a well-prepared condition on the eve of Ramadan. Although zakat collection continues round the year, most of the amounts are collected during or immediately after Ramadan. Special campaign is organized for the purpose of collection of zakat.

6.4   Zakat Fair, Seminar, Round Table

Every year, zakat Fair is organized as part of creation of zakat awareness among the wealthy class and collection of zakat from them. Participants in the events are motivated to deposit and/or make commitment for donation of zakat to the CZM. Besides zakat Fairs, seminars and round table discussion meetings are also organized for the same purpose.

6.5 Integrity with the SDGs

CZM designs its programs in line with the global approach of development as far as possible. CZM does also work with a partner of Bangladesh government in implementing the UN-sponsored SDGs. In pursuance of the concept of global partnership, CZM works with a number of corporate business partners and other local partners that support CZM in implementing its program interventions (CZM AnnRep2016; Table 3).

6.6 Rationale of Integrating Awaqf and Zakat

Although successes and achievements of CZM in terms of mobilization of zakat and awaqf funds, beneficiary and program coverage, partnership with corporate donors, reduction in sufferings and poverty of its beneficiaries, and some other indicators of socio-economic development are remarkable, its challenges and limitations are also visible that

Table 3 CZM Annual Report 2016

SDGs	CZM program	Volume of work
Goal-1: No poverty	Jeebika Program	25 projects
Goal-2: No hunger	Jeebika Program	25 project
Goal-3: Good health and well being	Jeebika Program and Ferdousi	31 primary health care centers
Goal-4: Quality education	Jeebika Program and Gulbagicha, Genius Program	25 project, 121 education center, scholarship to all public university, engineering college, and medical college
Goal-6: Clean water and sanitation	Jeebika Program and Ferdousi	25 project and 31 health care centers
Goal-11: Sustainable cities and community	Jeebika Program, Gulbagicha Program, Naipunna Bikash	25 project, 40 center in Dhaka city, 5 centers for youth development
Goal-12: Responsible consumption and production	Jeebika Program	25 projects
Goal-13: Climate action	Jeebika Program and Insaniat Program	25 projects and this year support more than 12,000 people
Goal-17: Partnership for the goal	Jeebika Program, Ferdousi Program and Gulbagicha Program	Works with over 20 corporate partners and 7 local partners that support these programs

necessitate integration of the two Shariah-approved tools for poverty alleviation. The rationale for integration may be presented in the following manner:

Lack of Infrastructure

Office: CZM has no central office space of its own which is a cause of various inconveniences. The organization needs to establish its regional, branch, and program offices to be able to coordinate, monitor, and supervise its activities in a better way.

Service Centers: CZM runs a number of health centers, primary schools, etc., and is able to run more such institutions providing running cost from its zakat fund, but it is difficult to construct buildings to house such programs from zakat fund. Availability of support from other funds like awaqf, sadaqah would remove this barrier and CZM could expand its services to reach more and more zakat right holders and other poor beneficiaries.

Profit Earning Ventures/Businesses/Investments

As a charitable organization with development orientation, CZM needs to develop a formidable size of fund to be able to address any need of the poor masses, often with unforeseen costs. This is normally not possible with only zakat fund that has its own limitations. This is possible if some additional fund can be mobilized and invested in profitable businesses.

Supplementary Income Earning Structure

CZM can offer training services on a wide range of zakat, awaqf, sadaqah, and other Shariah-related topics around the year and create awareness among the educated people and professionals regarding Islamic Shariah-approved financial provisions and tools and modes. Such services can be provided at cost-effective rates. This will earn CZM some additional funds for re-investment and earning profit. Such a center must be well equipped to attract potential trainees and their authorities.

Ambulance/Vehicles for Efficient Service

For offering effective health care services, importance of ambulance can hardly be exaggerated. For better coordination and monitoring purposes, frequent field visits have no alternative. Overall, an equipped office with improved working condition increases productivity manifold. These are such heads of expenditure that are difficult to be covered with zakat fund. Awaqf, sadaqah, and other charitable funds can complement zakat fund to enable a big organization like CZM to function better with wider and more effective service coverage.

Appropriate ICT
The world is, in fact, totally ICT based today. CZM needs to be ICT based too. This calls for extra expenditure which is a burden for a zakat-based organization like CZM. In order to arrange necessary ICT equipment for CZM, support of other fund is needed.

7 Conclusion

It is apparent from the above discussion that there are immense potentials of integrated zakat and awaqf for socio-economic development in Bangladesh as well as elsewhere in the world. Isolated approaches of zakat and awaqf are weak, inadequate, and limited by a number of factors and hindered by numerous challenges. Once these two Shariah provisions are integrated, all barriers are removed and the integrated approach is a powerful one in being able to deal with poverty and under-development with strong hands. It ensures meeting instant survival needs of the extremely poor and medium- and long-term development needs of the poor and non-poor alike under the leadership of strong and sustainable organization. The CZM model is just an emerging one and needs to be strengthened through complete and effective integration of zakat and awaqf in the greater interest of the poor.

References

Awqaf.ae. (2017). *General Authority of Islamic Affairs and Endowments—UAE—AWQAF*. Available at: http://www.awqaf.ae/Waqf.aspx?Lang=EN&-SectionID=13&RefID=857. Accessed 18 September 2017.

En.wikipedia.org. (2017a). *Waqf*. Available at: http://en.wikipedia.org/wiki/Waqf. Accessed 18 September 2017.

En.wikipedia.org. (2017b). *Zakat*. Available at: http://en.wikipedia.org/wiki/Zakat. Accessed 18 September 2017.

Fahmy, H. K., & Sarker, A. A. (1997). Islamic Modes of Finance and Financial Instruments for Resource Mobilization: A Survey. In A. Ahmed & T. Khan (Eds.), *Islamic Financial Instruments for Public Sector Resource Mobilization*. Jeddah, KSA: IDB/IRTI.

Inc. US Legal. (2017). *Basic Needs Law and Legal Definition.* Available at: https://definitions.uslegal.com/b/basic-needs/. Accessed 18 September 2017.

Kallol, A. (2017). *Zakat Fund Runs Dry | Dhaka Tribune.* Archive.dhakatribune.com. Available at: http://archive.dhakatribune.com/bangladesh/2013/jul/31/zakat-fund-runs-dry. Accessed 18 September 2017.

Khan, A. B., & Obaidullah, M. (2014). Poverty Alleviation: A Comparative Study of Traditional and Islamic Microfinance with Special Reference to Zakat and Waqf. In *7th International Conference on "Development of Social Enterprunership and Social Business for Eradication of Extreme Poverty and Street Begging".* Chittagong, Bangladeesh, Volume: International Islamic University Chittagong. Available at: https://www.researchgate.net/profile/Dr_Muhammad_Obaidullah/publication/270103836_POVERTY_ALLEVIATION_A_COMPARATIVE_STUDY_OF_TRADITIONAL_AND_ISLAMIC_MICROFINANCE_WITH_SPECIAL_REFERENCE_TO_ZAKAT_AND_WAQF/links/54a013df0cf257a636021425/POVERTY-ALLEVIATION-A-COMPARATIVE-STUDY-OF-TRADITIONAL-AND-ISLAMIC-MICROFINANCE-WITH-SPECIAL-REFERENCE-TO-ZAKAT-AND-WAQF.pdf. Accessed 18 September 2017.

Microfinance & Microcredit. (2017). *The Definition of Microfinance—Microfinance and Microcredit.* Available at: http://www.microfinanceinfo.com/the-definition-of-microfinance. Accessed 18 September 2017.

Rahman, H. (2014). *Zakat for Sustainable Livelihoods: Innovations in Financial Empowerment.* Dhaka: Power and Participation Research Centre (PPRC).

Salado, A., & Nilchiani, R. (2013). *A Categorization Model of Requirements Based on Max-Neef's Model of Human Needs.* Wiley Online Library. Available at: http://www.academia.edu/4674776/A_Categorization_Model_of_Requirements_Based_on_Max-Neefs_Model_of_Human_Needs. Accessed 18 September 2017.

Shah, A. (2017). *Poverty Facts and Stats—Global Issues.* Globalissues.org. Available at: http://www.globalissues.org/article/26/poverty-facts-and-stats. Accessed 18 September 2017.

Sinha, V. (2017). *The Mohammedan and Hindu Endowments Ordinance, 1905: Recourse to Legislation.* Springer Link. Available at: https://link.springer.com/chapter/10.1007/978-94-007-0887-7_4. Accessed 18 September 2017.

Tahir, M., & Haji Mohammad, S. (2013). *Integration of Waqf, Zakat, Sadaqat, in Islamic Microfinance.* Academia.edu. Available at: http://www.academia.edu/9832350/Integration_of_Waqf_Zakat_Sadaqat_in_Islamic_Microfinance. Accessed 18 September 2017.

YouTube. (2014). *Zakat (Charity) and Waqf (Islamic Endowment).* Available at: http://www.youtube.com/watch?v=1d-enf5mudc. Accessed 18 September 2017.

CHAPTER 12

Waqf Resource Mobilization for Poverty Alleviation Based on Maqasid Framework

Khalifa M. Ali Hassanain

1 Introduction

In Arabic language, the word waqf or Habs means preventing something from movement. In *Shariah* terminology, waqf refers to making a property invulnerable to any disposition that leads to transfer of ownership and donating the usufruct of that property to beneficiaries (AAOIFI 2017).

Waqf funds/assets must have a well-defined purpose and these funds/assets cannot be used for any purpose other than what was already stipulated. Its main underlying purpose is to benefit the mankind as a whole.

Generally, waqf is divided into two kinds, namely *waqf 'amm* (general) and waqf *khas* (specific). It can also be classified as public and private, respectively, as pointed out by Hasan (2010). The former refers to the dedication of waqf assets for the benefit of the society at large while the latter refers to the dedication of waqf assets for designated purposes or for the benefits to be enjoyed by certain beneficiaries named by the person who gives the waqf.

K. M. A. Hassanain (✉)
Islamic Research and Training Institute,
Islamic Development Bank, Jeddah, Saudi Arabia
e-mail: khalifaali@isdb.org

© The Author(s) 2019   243
K. M. Ali et al. (eds.), *Revitalization of Waqf
for Socio-Economic Development, Volume I*,
https://doi.org/10.1007/978-3-030-18445-2_12

According to Zuki (2012), waqf institutions play a pivotal role in enhancing social welfare. He asserts that the management for waqf institutions need to be improved and equipped with modern approaches in order to ensure that better and efficient services are provided to the community. It is understood that public services for Muslims can be provided through waqf system. Waqf is seen as the medium for equal distribution and reduces inequity in the society. It is agreed that waqf is the platform to support the above-mentioned activities, i.e., religious and benevolent purposes. However, over the years, the scope has been expanded suitably to the current development and situation.

Kahf (2007) proposes that the purpose of waqf should cover anything related to social welfare activities encompassing various sectors. These include sectors which the government has a direct responsibility to administer such as national defense system, education system, and health institutions.

It should be noted that waqf departs from profit-driven goal theme held by other sectors such as the financial sector. Nevertheless, it does not mean such sectors would not be able to contribute positively to economic development. In fact, as mentioned by Imtiaz (2009) many scholars continue to advocate that waqf is able to alleviate poverty and eventually elevate the socio-economic level of society.

Kahf (1999) highlights that waqf institutions are regarded as separate legal entities but require having a management to ensure that the waqf can provide benefits for the society in an efficient manner and it could be viable concurrently. Hence, it is perceived that a good and effective management is an essential element to substantiate the role of waqf in socio-economic development. It is maintained that the sustainability of waqf institutions greatly depends on robust and prudent management and administration. Consequently, the discharge of duties and responsibilities by waqf managements is certainly crucial.

2   Significance of Poverty Alleviation in IsDB Member Countries

Poverty alleviation is one of the core objectives of IsDB and was emphasized as a key strategic thrust of the bank in its 1440H vision. Following the "Makkah Declaration" by the Third Extraordinary

Session of the Islamic Summit of Dhul Qadah 1426, the IsDB established the Islamic Solidarity Fund for Development (ISFD) to enhance its poverty alleviation efforts. The ISFD, which has a target of $10 billion, shall operate as waqf and income resulting therefrom to be used for financing projects aimed at reducing poverty in IsDB member countries. The fund formally started operation on 1 Muharram 1429H (January 10, 2008).

ISFD capital commitments currently (2017) stand at US$2.68 billion, contributed by 48 member countries (US$1.68 billion) and the IsDB (US$1.0 billion). This represents 26.8% of the approved target capital of US$10 billion. Paid-in capital currently stands at US$2.532 billion (ISFD 2017). The operations and investment activities are done in a *Shariah*-compliant manner particularly governed by the rulings and principles of Islamic Awaqf (Trusts). The operations financing is from two main sources of fund, i.e., the ISFD income and IsDB waqf Fund for ISFD Grant Assistance Operations.

The fund must be on concessional terms to the member countries while preserving its long-term sustainability. The income, on the other hand, consists of ISFD Liquid Funds and its unutilized earnings, which are invested in *Shariah*-compliant placements, for instance, investments made based on the modus operandi of Commodity Murabahah or Tawarruq. The ISFD net income in 1437H (2016) was US$87.67 million, compared to US$63.04 million in 1436H, an increase of 25% (ISFD 2017).

In spite of the achievements of the ISFD as reflected in various projects, it is believed that there are still lessons that can be learnt from the recent replenishment experiences of similar MDBs, and this also includes ensuring horizontal communication with IsDB donors. Keeping open the channels of communication and interaction with the well-connected multilateral network of senior officials will enable the bank to better understand the motives behind donors' aid allocation decisions. A study by David Dollar (2004) suggested poverty and good governance as main drivers behind donors' aid decisions, and this may be considered by the ISFD in its mobilization approaches. In the following deliberation, experiences of other MDBs are drawn upon to explore the prospects of the global waqf fund.

3   INTERDEPENDENCE OF *MAQASID AL SHARIAH* WITH IDA
    FUNDS IN POVERTY ALLEVIATION

Poverty is a grave situation for any entity. It is even worse when countries fall under the poverty line. If countries fall under this line, they may acquire funds by several methods. The first method is by requesting funds from IDA. The IDA is an organization that entirely focuses on poverty-stricken countries. The success stories of IDA are vast, and some of the IsDB member countries that IDA assisted so far are Afghanistan, Yemen, Somalia, and Sudan. IDA specializes in assisting countries with extreme unforeseen climatic changes, gender inequality, fragility, conflict, war, violence, job creation, economic transformation, and the like. Today, IDA has been able to reach out to at least 76 countries and participate in 912 projects in about 10,996 various locations across the world.

Today, there are 75 countries eligible for borrowing funds from IDA. Among the 75 countries, 29 IsDB member countries are eligible for donorship under the IDA scheme (Table 1).

Like all institutions, IDA too has eligibility criteria. The primary requirement for any country is that eligible nations should be under the poverty line. There are numerous ways in which poverty for any country is calculated. Poverty can be defined as gross national income (GNI) per capita income below the net income. This figure is updated annually, and at times, new criterion is added based on immediate requirement. Additionally, the other required criteria are the level of creditworthiness for a country to borrow based on market value. Once these prerequisites are satisfied and complied with, it is up to IDA to decide and determine the amount of disposable funds allotted to each country and this is done through a series of mathematical calculations on an annual basis. This calculation is called Performance-Based Allocation (PBA). In addition, there is another formula that is incorporated into PBA and that is Country Policy and Institutional Assessment (CPIA). These two formulas are correlated. However, it is PBA that determines the level of donor's contribution as it evaluates the level of need versus a nation's potential benefit to receiving donorship. CPIA, on the other hand, defines the current sound of a country's current policy and institutional framework which deals with monitoring the country's performance versus the rate of poverty reduction. Just like PBA, there is no fixed standard of formula or a precise method of calculation for CPIA. It is also revised annually based on revisions and implementations of new policies.

Table 1 IDB member countries eligible for IDA

IDB member country	IDA eligible
Uganda	IsDB eligible
Guyana	
Mozambique	
Gambia	
Mali	
Burkina Faso	
Kyrgyz Republic	
Guinea	
Pakistan	
Benin	
Bangladesh	
Cameroon	
Sierra Leone	
Afghanistan	
Togo	
Nigeria	
Uzbekistan	
Tajikistan	
Cote D'Ivoire	
Syria	
Niger	
Guinea-Bissau	
Djibouti	
Mauritania	
Chad	
Yemen	
Comoros	
Sudan	
Somalia	

Source List extracted from IDA site

The study examines the country's performance by adding an additional component to determine how well the country is doing based on MSCI (*Maqasid al Shariah* composite index). Therefore, it is best to note that PBA is never fixed, and it is best to monitor performance and allocation using Result Measurement System (RMS), as this is the main determinant for acquiring and allotting of funds.

4   INTERNATIONAL DEVELOPMENT
ASSOCIATION VERSUS GLOBAL WAQF FUNDS

In the implementation and adoption of IDA, a holistic approach is considered in order to encourage IsDB member countries to pool in more donors which would eventually assist in contributing toward the global waqf fund with the incorporation of *Maqasid al Shariah*.

Maqasid al Shariah-based Development Index (MSDI) is a tool used for measuring human development. The tool offers a very comprehensive solution in line with the teachings of Islam. Moreover, this index assists in policy making to help provide easily relatable results to Muslim communities at large. This combination of acceptance, understanding, and ease of communication is very important in developing the will for action toward betterment in society.

5   RANKING OF IsDB MEMBER
COUNTRIES—*MAQASID AL SHARIAH* COMPOSITE INDEX

To rank IsDB member countries in terms of *Maqasid al Shariah* composite index, we review and use the results derived from several studies that generated indices for measuring achievements in terms of adherence to *Maqasid al Shariah*.

We use the findings and average rankings from the following studies (Nizam and Larbani 2017) (AMIR-UD-DIN 2014, November), (Shaikh 2017), (Anto 2009), (Ramli et al. 2015), and (Bedoui 2014) to generate average ranking of IsDB member countries based on adherence to *Maqasid al Shariah* (see Table 2).

Based on Table 2, Qatar, Kuwait, Jordan, Tunisia, and Turkey ranked the highest in terms of the Islamic human development index. While countries performing lower on the MSCI table are Comoros, Djibouti, Somalia, Togo, Ivory Coast, and Guinea-Bissau. The results indicate that UAE, Bahrain, Kuwait, Malaysia, Brunei, and Qatar ranked as the top five, whereas Guyana, Suriname, Palestine, Somalia, and Sudan all ranked the lowest in MSCI Indices.

Table 2 Ranking of IsDB member countries in terms of their MSCI index from various sources

IsDB Member Country	MSCI Source A^a (%)	MSCI r = .25 Source B^b (%)	MSCI r = .50 Source C^c (%)	MSCI r = 1 Source D^d (%)	MSCI Source E^e (%)	MSCI Source F^f (%)	MSCI Source G^g (%)	MSCI Source H^h (%)	MSCI Source I^i (%)	Average score (%)	Ranking
Qatar	59	25	26	26	28	90	63	88	77	54	1
Kuwait	64	25	26	26	26	86	55	65	62	48	2
Jordan	64	26	28	27	NA	69	48	63	56	42	3
Tunisia	62	26	28	28	23	63	48	60	51	43	4
Turkey	65	26	27	27	23	66	50	60	53	44	5
Indonesia	58	23	25	25	20	58	47	57	48	40	6
Saudi Arabia	61	26	28	28	29	72	52	55	57	45	7
Morocco	62	24	25	25	21	52	41	55	48	39	8
Malaysia	68	25	27	27	26	77	62	50	59	47	9
Palestine	66	23	25	26	NA	32	0	56	40	30	10
Libya	62	25	27	27	NA	52	39	50	38	35	11
Iran	62	26	28	28	23	58	31	49	43	39	12
Azerbaijan	57	24	25	23	23	50	40	48	49	38	13
Bangladesh	48	21	21	21	20	43	37	48	40	33	14
Albania	55	22	23	23	28	60	51	45	50	40	15
Egypt	62	25	27	26	19	60	29	46	45	38	16
Uzbekistan	59	22	24	24	14	54	33	44	49	36	17
Pakistan	51	19	20	21	16	47	28	41	39	31	18
Kazakhstan	56	22	24	24	27	60	50	37	54	39	19
Algeria	62	25	27	26	23	59	0	40	44	34	20
Kyrgyz Rep.	59	22	23	23	NA	54	38	36	47	34	21
Iraq	56	22	24	24	28	24	28	35	42	31	22

(continued)

Table 2 (continued)

IsDB Member Country	MSCI Source A (%)	MSCI r=.25 Source B (%)	MSCI r=.50 Source C (%)	MSCI r=1 Source D (%)	MSCI Source E (%)	MSCI Source F (%)	MSCI Source G (%)	MSCI Source H (%)	MSCI Source I (%)	Average score (%)	Ranking
Lebanon	61	25	27	27	18	54	35	33	40	35	23
Yemen	48	19	20	19	3	46	20	34	36	27	24
Burkina Faso	53	17	16	16	NA	29	38	23	32	25	25
Mali	55	18	18	16	4	28	31	20	29	24	26
UAE	68	26	27	27	26	88	61	NA	70	44	27
Bahrain	64	24	25	26	27	78	50	NA	56	39	28
Oman	55	23	25	26	23	67	49	NA	56	36	29
Suriname	53	22	23	24	NA	62	49	NA	60	33	30
Senegal	55	15	20	20	11	31	46	NA	37	26	31
Guyana	54	22	24	24	NA	NA	48	NA	54	25	32
Benin	60	18	18	18	6	35	39	NA	31	25	33
Nigeria	45	18	17	16	−1	35	37	NA	35	23	34
Uganda	51	18	18	18	11	35	35	NA	32	24	35
Tajikistan	62	22	23	23	19	52	29	NA	48	31	36
Mozambique	53	16	15	14	−4	18	38	NA	38	21	37
Niger	55	17	17	17	6	21	36	NA	26	22	38
Cameroon	49	20	21	21	10	38	32	NA	37	25	39
Turkmenistan	57	26	26	24	NA	46	29	NA	39	27	40
Syria	49	26	27	26	27	58	24	NA	45	31	41
Mauritania	52	19	19	20	8	42	27	NA	34	25	42
Sierra Leone	43	19	15	14	5	14	31	NA	27	19	43
Guinea	46	18	18	17	4	30	28	NA	26	21	44
Sudan	45	20	21	21	6	34	25	NA	32	23	45

Table 2 (continued)

IsDB Member Country	MSCI Source A[a] (%)	MSCI r=.25 Source B[b] (%)	MSCI r=.50 Source C[c] (%)	MSCI r=1 Source D[d] (%)	MSCI Source E[e] (%)	MSCI Source F[f] (%)	MSCI Source G[g] (%)	MSCI Source H[h] (%)	MSCI Source I[i] (%)	Average score (%)	Ranking
Afghanistan	51	21	22	22	NA	NA	25	NA	22	18	46
Chad	49	14	14	14	2	18	23	NA	24	18	47
Brunei	61	25	26	27	NA	90	0	NA	74	34	48
Maldives	62	25	27	27	23	58	0	NA	45	30	49
Gabon	50	23	25	25	29	50	0	NA	49	28	50
Gambia	52	19	20	20	7	38	0	NA	39	22	51
Comoros	62	18	18	17	NA	38	0	NA	34	21	52
Djibouti	55	20	20	21	NA	30	0	NA	38	20	53
Somalia	53	16	16	16	NA	37	0	NA	0	15	54
Togo	40	19	19	19	NA	32	0	NA	26	17	55
Cote D'Ivoire	50	16	16	16	NA	23	0	NA	34	17	56
Guinea-Bissau	45	18	17	16	−5	29	0	NA	29	16	57

[a]Nizam and Larbani (2017), [b]AMIR-UD-DIN (November 2014), [c]AMIR-UD-DIN (November 2014), [d]AMIR-UD-DIN (November 2014), [e]Shaikh (2017), [f]ANTO (2009), [g]Ranking Chart of 2015, [h]Ramli et al. (2015), [i]Bedoui (2014)

6   RANKING OF ISDB MEMBER COUNTRIES—HUMAN DEVELOPMENT COMPOSITE INDEX

Several studies measured adherence to *Maqasid al Shariah* in terms of UNDP's HDI, and yet HDI does not still capture the actual dimensions of human development. In the past, HDI was only set to capture GDP per capita and this was not an actual indication of social progression. In recent years, socio-economic indicators were added to portray a better image of HDI. Thus, today HDI mainly focuses on economic growth and gross national product, basic human spending, longevity, etc. Many developing countries realized that actual development is not in the economic growth of the country but in improving the living conditions of the masses. Evidently, a bad income distribution tends to create social problem that would eventually destabilize institutions to reducing human consumption, investments, and growth, hence creating a bad income distribution.

Again, we used seven studies that relied on HDI to assess MSCI, namely (Anto 2009), (Ramli et al. 2015), (Bedoui 2014), (Shaikh 2017), (Nizam and Larbani 2017), (Jatmiko and Hajrina 2015), and (Zuki 2012). Clearly, Qatar, Kuwait, Saudi Arabia, Malaysia, and Turkey ranked the highest in human development index. The countries that ranked the lowest in the HD index were Comoros, Djibouti, Afghanistan, Cote d'Ivoire, Togo, and Somalia. Some of these countries were also among the lowest ranked countries on MSCI index.

It is important to note that some of the sources from which values of HDI and MSCI are extracted are from the same references. For example, for source 5 on MSCI index and source 15 on the HD index (see Tables 3 and 4), the author of that research paper compares the values of HDI and MSCI to determine a ranking score of which is a better performer in terms of which country. Furthermore, the other sources indicate a more independent study whereby the author examines either MSCI or HDI independently.

Finally, in Table 4 and Fig. 1 below we compare the results obtained from all studies.

The countries that equally top both charts were Qatar, Kuwait, and Turkey. Qatar ranks first, Kuwait second, and Turkey fifth. While both MSCI and HDI values for the top-ranking countries are the same, MSCI index for lower ranking countries is different from those on the human development index.

Table 3 Comparing HDI indices from seven sources to determine ranking of IsDB member countries in terms of HDI

IsDB member country	Source A[a] HDI values (%)	Source B[b] HDI values (%)	Source C[c] HDI values (%)	Source D[d] HDI values (%)	Source E[e] HDI values (%)	Source E[f] HDI values (%)	Source F[g] HDI values (%)	Average score[h]	Ranking[j]
Qatar	59	25	28	85	85	83	83	64	1
Kuwait	64	25	26	82	81	84	79	63	2
Saudi Arabia	61	26	29	84	84	77	78	63	3
Malaysia	68	25	26	78	77	80	77	62	4
Turkey	65	26	23	76	76	74	72	59	5
Iran	62	26	23	77	75	73	74	59	6
Lebanon	61	25	18	77	77	78	75	59	7
Albania	55	22	28	73	72	82	75	58	8
Tunisia	62	26	23	72	72	78	71	58	9
Algeria	62	25	23	74	72	75	71	57	10
Kazakhstan	56	22	27	79	76	64	75	57	11
Azerbaijan	57	24	23	75	75	68	73	57	12
Egypt	62	25	19	69	68	72	66	54	13
UAE	68	26	26	84	83	NA	82	52	14
Indonesia	58	23	20	68	68	62	63	52	15
Morocco	62	24	21	63	62	72	59	52	16
Uzbekistan	59	22	14	68	66	65	65	51	17
Bahrain	64	24	27	82	82	NA	80	51	18
Iraq	56	22	28	65	64	62	59	51	19
Oman	55	23	23	79	78	NA	73	48	20
Maldives	62	25	23	71	70	NA	69	46	21
Bangladesh	48	21	20	57	56	62	52	45	22
Pakistan	51	19	16	54	54	58	52	43	23

(continued)

Table 3 (continued)

IsDB member country	Source A[a] HDI values (%)	Source B[b] HDI values (%)	Source C[c] HDI values (%)	Source D[d] HDI values (%)	Source E[e] HDI values (%)	Source E[f] HDI values (%)	Source F[g] HDI values (%)	Average score[h]	Ranking[i]
Syria	49	26	27	59	66	NA	65	42	24
Tajikistan	62	22	19	62	61	NA	62	41	25
Jordan	64	26	NA	42	75	76	NA	40	26
Yemen	48	19	3	50	50	55	46	39	27
Libya	62	25	NA	NA	78	79	NA	35	28
Gabon	50	23	29	68	67	NA	NA	34	29
Palestine	66	23	NA	NA	69	77	NA	34	30
Cameroon	49	20	10	51	50	NA	50	33	31
Mali	55	18	4	42	41	34	34	33	32
Mauritania	52	19	8	51	49	NA	47	32	33
Benin	60	18	6	48	48	NA	44	32	34
Senegal	55	15	11	47	49	NA	47	32	35
Uganda	51	18	11	48	48	NA	46	32	36
Nigeria	45	18	-1	51	50	NA	47	30	37
Kyrgyz Rep.	59	22	NA	NA	63	66	NA	30	38
Sudan	45	20	6	48	47	NA	41	30	39
Guinea	46	18	4	41	39	NA	36	26	40
Sierra Leone	43	19	5	41	37	NA	36	26	41
Niger	55	17	6	35	34	NA	30	25	42
Chad	49	14	2	39	37	NA	34	25	43
Guinea-Bissau	45	18	-5	42	40	NA	36	25	44
Brunei	61	25	NA	NA	85	NA	NA	24	45
Gambia	52	19	7	44	44	NA	NA	24	46
Turkmenistan	57	26	NA	NA	70	NA	NA	22	47

Table 3 (continued)

IsDB member country	Source A[a] HDI values (%)	Source B[b] HDI values (%)	Source C[c] HDI values (%)	Source D[d] HDI values (%)	Source E[e] HDI values (%)	Source F[f] HDI values (%)	Source F[g] HDI values (%)	Average score[h]	Ranking[i]
Burkina Faso	53	17	NA	NA	39	37	NA	21	48
Suriname	53	22	NA	NA	70	NA	NA	21	49
Guyana	54	22	NA	NA	64	NA	NA	20	50
Mozambique	53	16	−4	NA	39	NA	33	20	51
Comoros	62	18	NA	NA	49	NA	NA	18	52
Djibouti	55	20	NA	NA	47	NA	NA	17	53
Afghanistan	51	21	NA	NA	47	NA	NA	17	54
Cote D'Ivoire	50	16	NA	NA	45	NA	NA	16	55
Togo	40	19	NA	NA	47	NA	NA	15	56
Somalia	53	16	NA	NA	NA	NA	NA	10	57

[a]ANTO (2009), [b]Ramli et al. (2015), [c]Bedoui (2014), [d]Shaikh (2017), [e]Nizam and Larbani (2017), [f]Fatmiko and Hajrina (2015), [g]Zuki (2012), [h]Average score from all mentioned sources, [i]Ranking of HD index based on country standards

Table 4   Ranking of MSCI index and HDI of IsDB member countries based on the data from Tables 2 and 3

IsDB member country	Cumulative MSCI score (%)	Ranking MSCI	Cumulative HDI score (%)	Ranking HDI
Qatar	54	1	64	1
Kuwait	48	2	63	2
Jordan	42	3	40	26
Tunisia	43	4	58	9
Turkey	44	5	59	5
Indonesia	40	6	52	15
Saudi Arabia	45	7	63	3
Morocco	39	8	52	16
Malaysia	47	9	62	4
Palestine	30	10	34	30
Libya	35	11	35	28
Iran	39	12	59	6
Azerbaijan	38	13	57	12
Bangladesh	33	14	45	22
Albania	40	15	58	8
Egypt	38	16	54	13
Uzbekistan	36	17	51	17
Pakistan	31	18	43	23
Kazakhstan	39	19	57	11
Algeria	34	20	57	10
Kyrgyz Rep.	34	21	30	38
Iraq	31	22	51	19
Lebanon	35	23	59	7
Yemen	27	24	39	27
Burkina Faso	25	25	21	48
Mali	24	26	33	32
UAE	44	27	52	14
Bahrain	39	28	51	18
Oman	36	29	48	20
Suriname	33	30	21	49
Senegal	26	31	32	35
Guyana	25	32	20	50
Benin	25	33	32	34
Nigeria	23	34	30	37
Uganda	24	35	32	36
Tajikistan	31	36	41	25
Mozambique	21	37	20	51
Niger	22	38	25	42
Cameroon	25	39	33	31

(continued)

Table 4 (continued)

IsDB member country	Cumulative MSCI score (%)	Ranking MSCI	Cumulative HDI score (%)	Ranking HDI
Turkmenistan	27	40	22	47
Syria	31	41	42	24
Mauritania	25	42	32	33
Sierra Leone	19	43	26	41
Guinea	21	44	26	40
Sudan	23	45	30	39
Afghanistan	18	46	17	54
Chad	18	47	12	43
Brunei	34	48	24	45
Maldives	30	49	46	21
Gabon	28	50	34	29
Gambia	22	51	24	46
Comoros	21	52	18	52
Djibouti	20	53	17	53
Somalia	15	54	10	57
Togo	17	55	15	56
Cote D'Ivoire	17	56	16	55
Guinea-Bissau	16	57	25	44

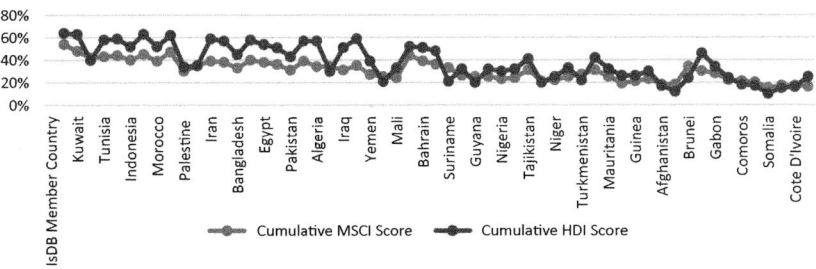

Fig. 1 MSC & HDI score

Even if MSCI is broadly correlated with HDI, much of the divergence is visible at the lower levels of achievement (first rank represents the highest level of development in MSCI). Malaysia ranks 1st in MSCI, but in HDI, it ranks fourth among the countries in the Organisation of Islamic Cooperation (OIC). Sudan and Somalia have performed extraordinarily well in the indicators that are generally not included in the HDI, such as freedom of person and property and adherence to faith and deeds, considered important in Islam. Nigeria presents a reverse case where it ranks 31st in HDI but 53 in MSCI.

7   COMPUTATION FOR CIPA WITH MSCI AT DIFFERING WEIGHTS

The purpose of this study is to use the same transparent method used by other MDBs, namely the IDA methodology, as a base for fund allocation in a global waqf-based fund. The difference is to attempt to factor *Maqasid al Shariah* into measuring individual country performance for fund allocation. To do this, we first must recall the IDA formula:

IDA Allocation

$$= f \left(\text{Country Performance Rating}^{5.0}, \text{Population}^{1.0}, (\text{GNI/Capita})^{-0.125} \right) \quad (1)$$

where the table includes the CPIA Criteria part of the formula

---

A. Economic Management
   1. Macroeconomic Management
   2. Fiscal Policy
   3. Debt Policy

B. Structural Policies
   4. Trade
   5. Financial Sector
   6. Business Regulatory Environment

C. Policies for Social Inclusion
   7. Gender Equality
   8. Equity of Public Resource Use
   9. Building Human Resources
   10. Social Protection and Labor
   11. Policies and Institutions for Environmental Sustainability

D. Public Sector Management and Institutions
   12. Property Rights and Rule-based Governance
   13. Quality of Budgetary and Financial Management
   14. Efficiency of Revenue Mobilization
   15. Quality of Public Administration
   16. Transparency, Accountability, and Corruption in the Public Sector

---

Clearly, the formula is made up of two parts: (i) Country Performance Rating simply to measure county performance relying on indicators based on the above table and (ii) IDA Population[1] * $(GNI/Capita)^{-0.125}$ which determines country need. We use the indices we generated for MSCI to augment the part of the formula that measures performance and to simply create a weighted average of CPR and MSCI for various weights. Below are the resource allocation formulas for all major MDBs highlighting performance and need components and the suggested formula for a global waqf fund.

8 RESOURCE ALLOCATION FORMULAS

African Development Fund

$$\underbrace{(0.7 * \text{CPIA} + 0.3 * \text{PORT}) * (\text{GOV}/3.5) * \text{PCEF})^{\wedge}2}_{\text{Performance}} \underbrace{\text{Pop} * \text{GNI}^{\wedge} - 0.125}_{\text{Needs}}$$

Asian Development Fund

$$\underbrace{(\text{ES\_CPIA } 0.7 * \text{PORT } 0.3 * \text{GOV})^{\wedge}2.0}_{\text{Peformance}} * \underbrace{\text{Pop } 0.6 * \text{GNI}^{\wedge} - 0.25}_{\text{Needs}}$$

International Development Association (IDA)

$$\underbrace{\left((0.24 * \text{CPIA } A - C + 0.68 * \text{CPIA } D + 0.08 * \text{PORT})^{\wedge}2.0\right)}_{\text{Performance}}$$
$$* \underbrace{\text{Pop} * \text{GNI}^{\wedge} - 0.125}_{\text{Needs}}$$

Global Waqf Fund

$$\underbrace{\left((0.24 * \text{CPIA } A - C + 0.68 * \text{CPIA } D + 0.08 * \text{PORT})^{\wedge}2.0\right) * \alpha + \text{MSCI} * \beta}_{\text{Performance}}$$
$$* \underbrace{\text{Pop} * \text{GNI}^{\wedge} - 0.125}_{\text{Needs}}$$

Or simply
$$\underbrace{(\text{CPR} * \alpha + \text{MSCI} * \beta)}_{\text{Performance}} * \underbrace{\text{Pop} * \text{GNI}^{\wedge} - 0.125}_{\text{Needs}}$$

Table 5 Weights

	MSCI weights	HDI weights
1	CPR, .25 α + .75 β	CPR, .25 α + .75 β
2	CPR, .50 α + .50 β	CPR, .50 α + .50 β
3	CPR, .75 α + .25 β	CPR, .75 α + .25 β

Notes

CPIA: Country Policy and Institutional Assessment; ES_CPIA is CPIA clusters A-C;

PORT: Portfolio performance ratings; GOV: Governance rating; Pop: Population; GNI p.c: GNI per capita;

PCEF: Post-Conflict Enhancement Factor;

α and β are the weights for CPR and MSCI respectively where $\alpha + \beta = 1$.

The weights of governance differ across the MDBs—59% for the African Development Fund, 50% for the Asian Development Fund, and 68% for IDA.12 In contrast to IDA and the African Development Fund, the Asian Development Fund does not double count governance. Moreover, the dispersion of country performance ratings also varies across the MDBs, allowing for differences in the way good performers are distinguished from the weaker ones. In addition, the Asian Development Fund uses a smaller exponent on population compared to IDA and the African Development Fund, thus favoring smaller countries. Instead, IDA and the African Development Bank have base allocations that favor small countries. Finally, the African Development Fund includes a Post-Conflict Enhancement Factor (PCEF) in the PBA formula to direct more resources to countries emerging from conflict. IDA directs resources to post-conflict countries using the Post-Conflict Progress Indicators, although the term is not directly built into the PBA formula IDA (2007) (Table 5).

9   Computation for IDA with MSCI and HDI

The major observations from this exercise are that first, as shown in Tables 6–7 and Figs. 2–3, that there seems to be no difference in the impact of using the MSCI or the HDI-based MSCI. The second is that countries performing very low (based on the CPR) tend to do better with higher share of MSCI, and the opposite was true for very high performing countries with two exceptions, Sudan and Guinea-Bissau.

Table 6 CPR & MSCI simulations

Country	CPR	CPR, .75 α + .25 β	CPR, .50 α + .50 β	CPR, .25 α + .75 β
Uganda	1.00	0.810372	0.6207439	0.4311159
Guyana	0.08	0.121145	0.16453	0.207915
Mozambique	1.00	0.8021806	0.6043612	0.4065418
Maldives	0.08	0.1325166	0.1872732	0.2420298
Senegal	1.00	0.8152347	0.6304694	0.4457041
Gambia	1.00	0.8040938	0.6081877	0.4122815
Mali	1.00	0.8108109	0.6216219	0.4324328
Burkina Faso	1.00	0.8120864	0.6241728	0.4362592
Kyrgyz Rep.	0.08	0.1423309	0.2069019	0.2714728
Guinea	1.00	0.8021807	0.6043614	0.4065422
Pakistan	0.08	0.1368204	0.1958808	0.2549413
Benin	1.00	0.8127641	0.6255282	0.4382923
Bangladesh	0.08	0.1412556	0.2047512	0.2682468
Sierra Leone	1.00	0.7966408	0.5932816	0.3899223
Afghanistan	0.08	0.1033519	0.1289439	0.1545358
Togo	1.00	0.7930387	0.5860774	0.3791162
Nigeria	1.00	0.8064254	0.6128508	0.4192762
Uzbekistan	0.08	0.1480464	0.2183328	0.2886193
Tajikistan	0.08	0.1357736	0.1937872	0.2518008
Cote D'Ivoire	1.00	0.7929039	0.5858078	0.3787117
Niger	1.00	0.8041374	0.6082747	0.4124121
Guinea-Bissau	0.33	0.286989	0.2462979	0.2056069
Djibouti	1.00	0.8011108	0.6022216	0.4033323
Mauritania	1.00	0.8113415	0.6226829	0.4340244
Chad	1.00	0.7937957	0.5875914	0.3813871
Yemen	0.08	0.1264424	0.1751247	0.2238071
Comoros	1.00	0.8021212	0.6042424	0.4063637
Sudan	0.33	0.3022276	0.2767753	0.2513229

Table 7 CPR & MSCI (HDI) simulations

Country	CPR	CPR, .75 α + .25 β	CPR, .50 α + .50 β	CPR, .25 α + .75 β
Uganda	1.00	0.810372	0.620744	0.431116
Guyana	0.08	0.121145	0.16453	0.207915
Mozambique	1.00	0.802181	0.604361	0.406542
Maldives	0.08	0.132517	0.187273	0.24203
Senegal	1.00	0.815235	0.630469	0.445704

(continued)

Table 7   (continued)

Country	CPR	CPR, $.75\,\alpha + .25\,\beta$	CPR, $.50\,\alpha + .50\,\beta$	CPR, $.25\,\alpha + .75\,\beta$
Gambia	1.00	0.804094	0.608188	0.412282
Mali	1.00	0.810811	0.621622	0.432433
Burkina Faso	1.00	0.812086	0.624173	0.436259
Kyrgyz Rep.	0.08	0.142331	0.206902	0.271473
Guinea	1.00	0.802181	0.604361	0.406542
Pakistan	0.08	0.13682	0.195881	0.254941
Benin	1.00	0.812764	0.625528	0.438292
Bangladesh	0.08	0.141256	0.204751	0.268247
Sierra Leone	1.00	0.796641	0.593282	0.389922
Afghanistan	0.08	0.103352	0.128944	0.154536
Togo	1.00	0.793039	0.586077	0.379116
Nigeria	1.00	0.806425	0.612851	0.419276
Uzbekistan	0.08	0.148046	0.218333	0.288619
Tajikistan	0.08	0.135774	0.193787	0.251801
Cote D'Ivoire	1.00	0.792904	0.585808	0.378712
Niger	1.00	0.804137	0.608275	0.412412
Guinea-Bissau	0.33	0.286989	0.246298	0.205607
Djibouti	1.00	0.801111	0.602222	0.403332
Mauritania	1.00	0.811341	0.622683	0.434024
Chad	1.00	0.793796	0.587591	0.381387
Yemen	0.08	0.126442	0.175125	0.223807
Comoros	1.00	0.802121	0.604242	0.406364
Sudan	0.33	0.302228	0.276775	0.251323

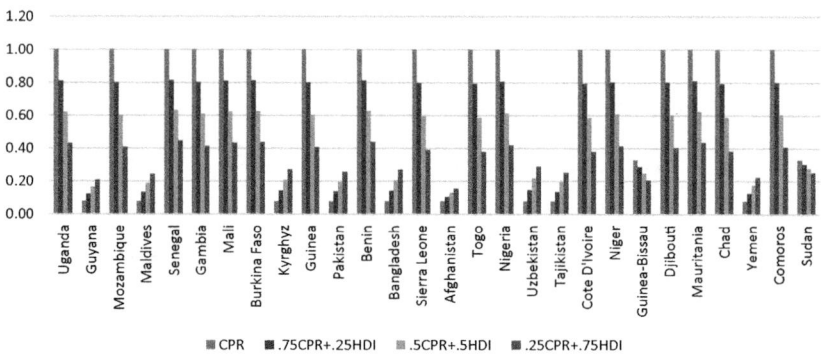

Fig. 2   CPR & MSCI (HDI) simulations

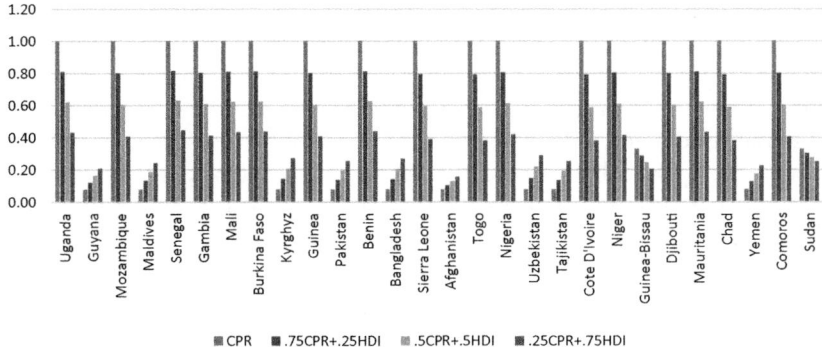

Fig. 3 CPR & MSCI simulations

10 CONCLUSION

The implementation of PBA system to attract more donors in contributing to the global waqf fund could be emulated and implemented in light of *Maqasid al Shariah*. As a holistic system, Islam provides various mechanisms in mobilizing resources and channeling of funds in an equitable manner to all. Apart from zakat, the institution of waqf plays an important role to elevate the overall economic and social development. Over the years, waqf has been a source of financing for various sectors such as administration of schools, mosques, and more. It appears that this institution is highly relevant on the reinforcement to the alleviation of poverty, as essentially the funds are augmented for charitable purposes for a longer period of time (infinity). Interestingly, to suit the contemporary context, there is still a lacuna to explore any tools that are able to increase the participation of donors to the funds that can utilize for waqf purpose.

In our first part of this study (Hassanain 2014, 2016), we concluded that the proposed global fund can be strengthened in many aspects, drawing examples from the conventional development associations. Mechanisms and formulas implemented by various multinational developments associations, i.e., PBA and CPIA, set a good example to emulate, guided by *Maqasid al Shariah*.

Despite the challenges caused by the absence of unique method for calculating Maqasid index over fixed time interval which hoped to eventually disappear, this study shows how we may adjust the IDA formula to generate a more transparent system of fund allocation in a global Islamic waqf-based fund that targets among other things achieving *Maqasid al Shariah*. The process of adjustment needs to be refined further, depending on how the proposed fund management chooses to create the Maqasid index (i.e., what to emphasize in the index and how to combine it with the CPR in light of the discussion in this paper). It is hoped that this transparency will increase the confidence in such a global fund and attract more donors' contributions during replenishments.

Adding the MSCI indices seemed to alter the CPR result, specifically where countries performing very low (based on the CPR) tend to do better with higher share of MSCI. The opposite was also true for very high performing countries; hence, fund allocations can easily be used to achieve the fund objectives which are based on *Maqasid al Shariah*.

References

AAOIFI. (2017). *Shari'ah* (Standard No. 33). Waqf.

AMIR-UD-DIN, R. (2014, November). *Maqāṣid al-Sharī'ah: Are We Measuring the Immeasurable? Islamic Economic Studies, 22*(2), 1–32.

Annual Report on Portfolio Performance: Fiscal Year 2008. (2009, April 22). Quality Assurance Group.

ANTO, M. H. (2009). *Introducing an Islamic Human Development Index (I-HDI) to Measure Development in OIC Countries*. Islamic Finance and Economics International Conference, Langawi.

Bedoui, H. E. (2014). Socio-Economic Development Based on *Maqasid Shari'ah. Seminar on Maqasid Shari'ah Based Socio-Economic Development*.

Dollar, D., & Victoria, V. (2004). *Increasing Selectivity of Foreign Aid, 1984–2002* (Policy Research Working Paper No. 3299). Washington, DC. World Bank.

GNI Per Capita Ranking, Atlas Method and PPP Based. (2017). Retrieved from World Bank Group. https://data.worldbank.org/data-catalog/GNI-per-capita-Atlas-and-PPP-table.

Hasan, M. (2010). *The Effects of the Global Crisis on Islamic and Conventional Banks: A Comparative Study* (IMF Working Paper).

Hassanain, K. M. (2014). *Waqf for Poverty Alleviation: Challenges and Opportunities* (Working Papers 1435-20). The Islamic Research and Teaching Institute (IRTI).

Hassanain, K. M. (2016, December). Waqf for Poverty Alleviation: Challenges and Opportunities. *Journal of Economic and Social Thought, KSP Journals, 3*(4), 509–520.

Hurayra, M. A. (n.d.). *Achievement of Maqasid-al-Shari'ah in Islamic Banking: An Evaluation of Islamic Bank Bangladesh Limited.*

Imtiaz, A. (2009). *Waqf: A Sustainable Development Institution for Muslim Communities.*

International Development Association Resource Mobilization (FRM). (2007, February). *IDA's Performance-Based Allocation System: Options for Simplifying the Formula and Reducing Volatility.*

Islamic Solidarity Fund for Development. (2017). *Progress Report 33rd Meeting of the Follow-Up Committee of the COMCEC.*

Jatmiko, W., & Hajrina, N. (2015). *Between Shari'ah Maqasid Index and Human Development Index: Which One Is Happier?* The First International Conference on Shari'ah Oriented Public Policy in Islamic Economic System, Aceh, Indonesia.

Kahf, M. (1999). *Towards the Revival of Awqaf, a Few Fiqhi Issues to Reconsider.*

Kahf, M. (2007). *The Role of Improving the Ummah Welfare.* The Singapore International Waqf Conference, Singapore.

Nizam, I., & Larbani, M. (2017). A *Maqāsid Al-Shari'ah* Based Composite Index to Measure Socioeconomic Prosperity in OIC Countries. *Roundtable Policy Discussion on Maqasid Shari'ah.*

Ramli, R. M., Ismail, A. G., & Tasrif, M. (2015). *M-Dex Among the Islamic Countries.*

Shaikh, S. A. (2017). Developing an Index of Socio-Economic Development Consistent with Maqāṣid al-Sharī'ah. *Journal of King Abdul Aziz University, Islamic Economics, 30*(1), 117–130.

Zuki, M. S. (2012). Waqf and Its Role in Socio-Economic Development. *SRA International Journal of Islamic Finance, 4*(2), 173–178.

CHAPTER 13

Islamic Microfinance and Rehabilitation Program for the Slum and Floating Population by the Waqf Funds: A Proposal Based on Empirical Evidences for the Muslim Countries

Basharat Hossain

1 Background of the Study

The waqf is an Arabic terminology used in Islam to refer the "religious bequest." This paper presents a model to initiate the Islamic Microfinance program by using the waqf funds for the slum as well as floating people. It should be mentioned that, the concept of modern Microfinance was first introduced by the Nobel Prize laureate economist professor Dr. Muhammad Yunus in 1976 by establishing "Grameen Bank" (Yunus and Jolis 2006). On the contrary, modern Islamic Microfinance started in Iran in 1967. It was known as Qard al-Hassan fund that was used to provide interest-free loans for marriage, providing trousseau, cure diseases, house repairing, educational subsidies, and

B. Hossain (✉)
Department of Business Administration, International Islamic University
Chittagong, Chittagong, Bangladesh

© The Author(s) 2019   267
K. M. Ali et al. (eds.), *Revitalization of Waqf*
for Socio-Economic Development, Volume I,
https://doi.org/10.1007/978-3-030-18445-2_13

subsidies for rural housing and for other needs (Sadegh 2009). However, modern Microfinance is run by the interest or usury, while Islamic Microfinance is based on profit-loss sharing and interest-free loan. This paper presents a model to start the Islamic Microfinance and rehabilitation program by using waqf funds for the slum and floating population in the Muslim countries. This section (introduction) will discuss the concept of waqf, slum, Islamic Microfinance and information on the waqf institution, slum population and coverage's of Islamic Microfinance in Muslim countries.

In addition, Sects. 2 and 3 discuss the objective and methodology of this study. Moreover, the literature review and rationale of the study are presented in Sects. 4 and 5. Finally, Sects. 6 and 7 described the model and conclusion, respectively. Further research scope, reference, and appendix are dealt separately.

1.1   A Discussion on the Concept of Waqf and Waqf Institution in Muslim Countries

Definition, Classifications of Waqf and Its Application
Waqf means "religious bequest", recognized by the Islamic law. Awqaaf is the plural of waqf. It has been used for the establishment and development of religious as well as public institutions such as the building of mosques, madrasa, i.e., religious schools, orphanage centers, hospitals, educational institutions, libraries, inn and houses for disables. Most important features of waqf are that, its benefits are not restricted to the Muslim community alone, but go beyond religious, cultural, racial and sectarian boundaries (Mohammad and Mar Iman 2006).

Basically, there are two types of waqf. General Waqf and Family Waqf. The General waqf is also known as philanthropic or public waqf and the religious waqf-where the usufruct is devoted to the interest of mass people like public hospitals, public bathrooms, mosques, public libraries, books, etc. Helping the needy and poor people is the prime objective of this waqf. Example: Hamdard Laboratories (waqf) Bangladesh

The second type of waqf is Family waqf also known as posterity waqf. In this case, waqf revenues will be spent with the children, or offspring of their family, but they have no rights to sell it. In addition, the family only has rights on the benefits of usufruct but not on the property. Surplus revenue will be distributed to the underprivileged people. Waqf from parents to children and heirs (Habibollah et al. 2010).

Alias (2012) presented another type of waqf is known as cash waqf. That is defined as: "…an endowment of cash by a founder with the intention that the corpus or principal should be managed by a trustee so as to earn an income that could be spent towards righteous purposes as designated by the founder" (Alias 2012).

Waqf Authority and Number of Waqf Institutions in the Muslim Countries It should be mentioned that, most of the waqf institutions are supervised and administered by the Ministry of Religious Affairs of the Muslim countries. The exact data on the waqf asset and institutions are not available for all Muslim countries. However, Table 1 presents the information regarding the waqf authority and number of waqf institutions in the Muslim countries.

1.2 A Discussion on the Concept of Slum, Slum Population, and Urban Population in the Muslim Countries

A slum can be defined as a cluster of housing units or a compact settlement with a minimum of 5–10 households or a mess unit with a minimum of twenty-five members and mostly very poor housing which grow unsystematically in the government owned or private vacant land, very

Table 1 Waqf authority and number of waqf institutions in the Muslim countries

Country	Waqf authority	Number of waqf institutions/value of the waqf asset	Annual contribution to national waqf fund
Bangladesh	Ministry of Religious Affairs	20,536 (2014–2015)	BDT 58.67 million
Pakistan	Ministry of Religious Affairs	–	–
Malaysia	–	9937 hectares of waqf land worth RM1.9 billion	–
Indonesia	Ministry of Religious Affairs	Waqf land 4.2 million meters	–
Turkey	–	9000	
Yemen	Ministry of waqf	10–15% land	–
Jordan	Ministry of waqf	10,000	JOD 0.94 million (1998)

Compiled by the author from GOB (2017) and from other sources

Table 2 The status of slum population and urban poverty in the Muslim countries-2015

Country	Number of slum population (in thousand)	% of total urban population
Afghanistan	5155	62.7
Bangladesh	29,273	55.1
Indonesia	29,212	21.8
Iraq	11,383	47.2
Jordan	808	12.9
Pakistan	32,265	45.5
Saudi Arabia	4384	18.0
Syrian	2429	19.3
Turkey	6578	11.9
Yemen	5166	60.8

Source United Nations Human Settlement Programme (UN-Habitat), Global Urban Indicators Database 2015, computed from country household data using the four components of the slum (improved water, improved sanitation, durable housing and sufficient living area)

high population density and room crowding, very poor environmental services, especially water and sanitation, very low socio-economic status, lack of security of tenure (CUS 2006).

It should be noted that, with the growth of urbanization, the number of slum population increases in the Muslim countries. Actually, it is not urbanization but may be called as slumization. Table 2 shows the latest status of slum population in the Muslim countries. The data reveal that, among the ten countries in Asia, on average, 35.5% of the urban population is living in the slum areas (UN-Habitat 2015).

1.3   Nature, Services, and Status of Islamic Microfinance in the World

Microfinance consists of financial and non-financial services. Financial services are—microcredit, deposits, loans, payment services, money transfers, and insurance products. The non-financial services offer health care services, education, skills and training program, enterprise development, development of self-confidence, marketing and management capabilities, and women empowerment (Ledgerwood 2000).

Nature of Islamic Microfinance
Based on the nature of the services, there are two kinds of services in Islamic Microfinance. The first one is the profitable investment and

second one is nonprofitable (may have some nominal fee) investment. Profitable services mainly concentrated on those Islamic modes of investments that are profitable in nature. For instance, Mudarabah (Trustee Partnership), Musharakah (Equity Partnership), Murabahah (Cost plus Profit), and Bai-Salaam. For example: product sales and transfer such as buying a cow or a house or rickshaw or boat and so more. On the contrary, nonprofitable (may have some nominal fee) services mainly concentrated on the Qard al-Hasan (Benevolent loan) modes of investments. The example is the installation of water tube well, health care services.

Product and Services of Islamic Microfinance
Islamic Microfinance institutions provide both financial and nonfinancial products and services for its members. Table 3 exposes the list of some products and services of Islamic Microfinance institutions.

Sources of Fund in Islamic Microfinance
The main sources of the funds in Islamic Microfinance are the charity, zakat, sadaqah, and waqf.

Islamic Modes of Investment Employed in Islamic Microfinance Industry
The most common Islamic modes of investment employed in Islamic Microfinance industry are Bai-Murabaha, Bai bithaman ajil, Ijara, Bai-Salam, Qard al-Hassan, Mudarabah, and Musharakah.

Table 3 Product and services of Islamic Microfinance

Financial	*Non-financial*
Microcredit	Health service: medical camp, circumcision camp,
Micro savings	medical assistance, welfare gift
Micro-insurance-Takaful	
Small industry: handicraft	Education: award and scholarship, distribution of
	educational materials program, religious education
Quard al-Hasanah	Training
Poultry, /bird and livestock	Environment: nursery/forestry,
fisheries	Plantation program
Agro-based product: crops	–
Relief and rehabilitation	–
Transport buying	–
Housing equipment	–

Source Mannan (2015), compiled by the author

Islamic Microfinance and Its Coverage in the Muslim Countries
The Islamic finance industry has been growing at the 7% rate around the
world and its estimated asset is $2.5 trillion at the end of 2016. There
are more than 300 Islamic financial institutions have been functioning
in the world among these 255 institutions provide Islamic Microfinance
services (CGAP 2017; GIFR 2017; Rashad 2014). The Islamic
Microfinance institutions have been growing at a 20% rate and contributed 1% market share to the total Islamic finance market in the world
(GIFR 2017). Table 4 reveals the latest status of Islamic Microfinance in
the world. It should be mentioned that, unfortunately, there are no latest
compiled statistics and survey report on Islamic Microfinance industry
available in the world. Most of the data are incomplete and insufficient
for research.

Table 4 The status of Islamic Microfinance in the world

Country	Year	No of Islamic MFIs (IMFIs)	No of total MFIs	Share in the market	Name of well-known Islamic MFIs
Afghanistan	2017	1	14	–	FINCA
Bangladesh	2017	8	703	1%	Islami Bank Bangladesh Limited (IBBL), Muslim Aid Bangladesh, Islamic Relief Bangladesh
Indonesia	2007	105	64,000	–	–
Iraq	2017	6	14	10%	Al Takadum,
Pakistan	2017	15	31	0.9%	Akhuwat Islamic Relief Pakistan (IRP)
Yemen	2017	2	12	–	Al-Hudaidah, Al Amal Microfinance Bank
Sudan	2017	7 9 banks	7	–	–
Malaysia	2017	2	–	–	AIM and Bank Rakyat.
Iran	2008	7000	7000	–	Qard al-Hassan
Maldives	2017	1	–	–	
Bahrain	2017	1	2	–	Family Bank
Algeria	2017	1	–	–	

Source Compiled by the authors from MRA (2017), MCI (2017), MICRA (2017), Alshebami and
Rengarajan (2017), and Sadegh (2009)

However, the performance of Islamic Microfinance industry is quite satisfying in the several Muslim countries around the world. For Instance, performance of FINCA in Afghanistan, Islami Bank Bangladesh Limited (IBBL) in Bangladesh, Akhawat and Wasil foundation in Pakistan is well mentionable. The participation of women varies from 60 to 80% and the average recovery rate is 99% (Mannan 2015).

2 Objective

The main objective of this report is to propose a model to initiate the Islamic Microfinance and rehabilitation program by the waqf funds for the slum and the floating population among the Muslim countries.

3 Methodology

This paper has been prepared by collecting both the primary and secondary data. The secondary data were collected on the waqf estate, Islamic Microfinance and slum population of the Muslim countries. Besides, different books, articles, reports, brochures, and newspapers have been reviewed to prepare this report. Primary data: The primary data were collected through a semi-structured questionnaire that comprises both open-ended and closed-ended questions. Data were collected during May-June-2017. Besides, the visiting of the slums, observations, and discussion was also the process of data collection. The main question is: Whether they receive the Islamic Microfinance or not? What is their eagerness to interest-free Microfinance? The report of this survey was not yet published. Secondary data: The secondary data were mainly collected from the Global Islamic Finance Report 2012–2017, Microfinance Regulatory Authority in Bangladesh, Global Urban Indicators Database 2015 by UN-Habitat, Web sites of the government and central bank of different countries.

4 Literature Review

A good number of researches have been done on the waqf, Islamic Microfinance, and slum population separately. This section will describe the related researches conducted on the topic of this paper. Zubair Mughal (2017) discusses the sources of funding for the Islamic Microfinance (IMF) in his article. He proposes to use the waqf fund in Islamic Microfinance. In addition, Alpay and Haneef (2015) in their edited research described an Integrated waqf-based Islamic Microfinance (IWIM) model for poverty reduction in Malaysia, Indonesia, and Bangladesh. Moreover, the opportunities of cash waqf and Islamic Microfinance have been explored in the research of Md. Saad and Anuar (2009) and three models for poverty alleviation integrating zakah, awaqf, and Islamic Microfinance. It should be mentioned that, such kinds of more research are available, but they did not relate the waqf fund with the Islamic Microfinance and slum population. This is the key point of this paper is to present a model for the slum population.

However, this research paper is different from the earlier research in a sense that, it analyzes the latest scenario of the waqf estates and regulators, the slum population in Muslim countries and the status of Islamic Microfinance in the Muslim world. Besides, it proposes a model to start the Islamic Microfinance and rehabilitation program by spending the waqf funds for the slum and floating population in the Muslim countries. This model is a new addition to the earlier research. On the contrary, the earlier research only emphasizes separately on the waqf and Islamic Microfinance. But they had no proposal to use waqf funds for the slum and floating population through the Islamic Microfinance program.

5   Rationale of the Study

5.1   Why Is the Islamic Microfinance?

It should be mentioned that, the global Islamic finance industry has been growing tremendously during the last 40 years. But Islamic Microfinance industry contributes only one percent to the Islamic finance industry. Moreover, about 2420 Microfinance institutions are working in the world, whereas only 255 Islamic Microfinance institutions are working in the world (MIE 2008; CGAP 2017; GIFR 2017). There is very little coverage of Islamic Microfinance industry. Furthermore, conventional- or interest-based Microfinance institutions offer 8–32% interest rate on the microcredit loans while offer only 6–8% interest on savings (Badruddoza 2011). Conversely, Islamic Microfinance institutions only take nominal profit rate (10–12%) and also share the profits as well as losses in their services (Mannan 2015). Besides, Islamic Microfinance institutions also provide the buying and selling the product and services and interest-free loan. The superiority and performance of Islamic Microfinance are beyond question and it provides the maximum welfare for its recipients.

So the level of little coverage and backwardness of Islamic Microfinance institutions deprives the poor Muslim of the world. This is why; this paper proposes to initiate the Microfinance program by the waqf funds.

5.2   Why Is the Slum Population?

The slum is the anomaly of the urbanization. There are about 7.53 billion people are living in the world of which about one-sixth population is living in the slum (worldometers 2017, Murphy 2017). Table 2 depicts the scenario of the slum population among the Muslim countries. It is reported that, about 20–40% potential Muslim borrower are not eager to be the member of the interest-based Microfinance around the world (Rashad 2014). In addition, almost all of the urban poor live in the slum of the cities. It is the matter of great regret that, the combined coverage in rural and urban areas of Islamic Microfinance institutions is very little compared to the conventional Microfinance institutions. More precisely, the coverage in the urban areas is totally dissatisfactory and merely mentionable. This report has been prepared by collecting the primary data on several slums of the Dhaka and Chittagong city of Bangladesh. Table 5 exposes that, among the seven slums and about four hundred respondents, only two respondents in a slum received the Islamic Microfinance services. This is why, this paper suggests to initiate the Islamic Microfinance among the slum population in the Muslim countries.

6   Islamic Microfinance and Rehabilitation Program for the Slum and Floating Population By the Waqf Funds: A Proposal Based on Empirical Evidences for the Muslim Countries

6.1   The Model

This section presents the structure of the model while Sect. 6.2 discusses the implementation method of the model. This paper presents a model

Table 5   The coverage of Islamic MFIs among the slums in Bangladesh

City of Bangladesh	Name of the slum	Slum population	Coverage of total MFIs in the slum	Coverage of Islamic MFIs in the slum
Dhaka city, the capital city	Juraine Rail line slum	5000	3	0
	Gendaria Rail line slum	7000	6	1 (IBBL)
	Kamalapur Rail line slum	10,000	3	0
	Malibag Rail line slum	12,000	4	0
	Khilgaon Rail line slum	500	0	0
	Korail slum	80,000	15	0
Chittagong, the second largest city	Khalpar slum, Bahadda hat	5000	3	0

Source Collected by the author

to initiate the Islamic Microfinance and rehabilitation program for the slum and floating people with the waqf funds. This model suggests the following five stages to execute this model:

Stage-1: Revival and registration of the waqf estate and institution: This stage will ensure the registration of the waqf asset in the respective country.

Stage-2: Fund accumulation: This stage will design the sources and processes of collecting funds from the waqf institutions.

Stage-3: Islamic Microfinance by the waqf fund: This stage will start the Islamic Microfinance program by using the waqf fund.

Stage-4: Rehabilitation of slum people by the waqf fund: This stage will make the plan of rehabilitation and execute the rehabilitation program for the slum and floating population.

Stage-5: Slum people contribute to the society: This stage will introduce the way that may help the slum people to engage and contribute to the society.

6.2   Implementation

This model will be executed by the joint venture of Government and Private Islamic authority. An independent institution (may be called the Waqf Management Authority [WMA]) should be formed by the joint committee from the government of the respective country and the national as well as international Islamic institutions (such as Islamic Development Bank [IDB]). The accumulated fund will be added to the central waqf fund (CWF). The final disbursement and accomplishment will be run by the respective institution—WMA (Fig. 1).

Waqf Management Authority (WMA)
The WMA will be responsible to raise the funds and execute the model. To run the functions smoothly and properly, the national as well as international Islamic institutions and government authority will provide the logistic supports, manpower and also monitor its activities. There are a large number of evidences available on the joint venture project between

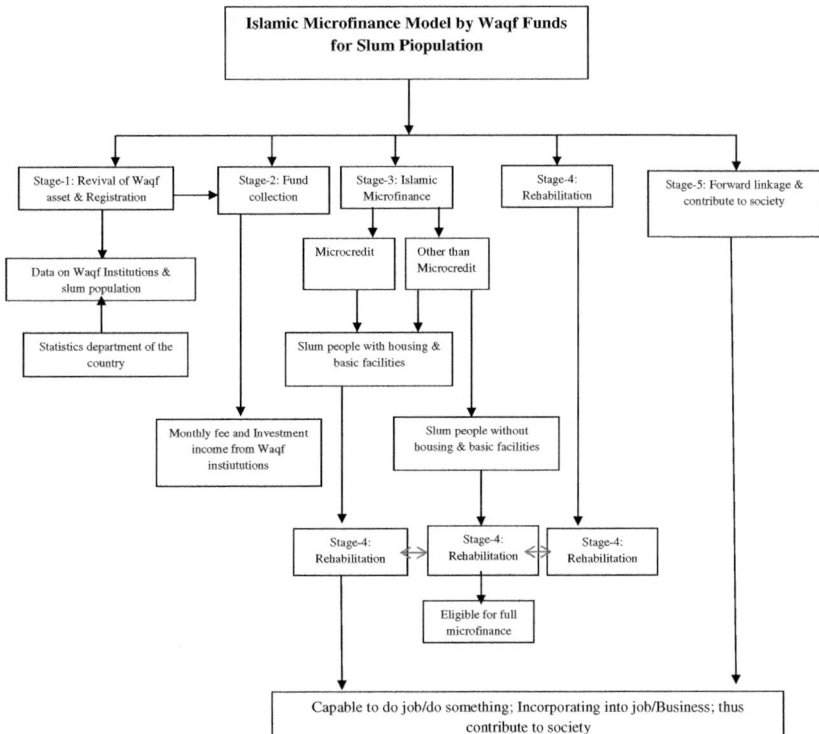

Fig. 1 The schematic presentation of the model

the government and the private authority in different countries. For instance, Private-Public Partnership (PPP) project.

However, this institution will have five departments:

a. Statistics department;
b. Fund accumulation and financing department;
c. Islamic Microfinance department;
d. Rehabilitation department;
e. Public relation and the forward linkage department.

a. Statistics department

The statistics department will fulfill the goal of the first stage. The statistics department will have two functions. The first function is to collect the data on the waqf estates and waqf institutions in the respective country. In most of the countries, Ministry of Religious Affairs collects data and supervises the waqf institutions (Table 1). The second function is to collect the data on the number of slums, slum population, floating population, and landless slum population in the respective country. In addition, it has to collect the data on the number of Microfinance recipients, slum people eager to be the member of Islamic Microfinance institutions, educational and occupational status of the slum people. Usually, the national statistics divisions, waqf authority, and the Microfinance regulatory authority collect and preserve these data. This department may take help from these respective offices. The data on the urban slum population are given in Table 2 (Fig. 2).

b. Fund accumulation and financing department

The fund accumulation department will achieve the objective of the second stage. This department will be responsible to collect the funds from the respective country and international agency. The statistics department will help the fund accumulation department by providing relevant data and information. Funding can be accumulated through integrating income and contributions from the waqf estates and institutions. The details sources of funding are given below (Fig. 3):

Cash waqf (Personal + Institutional): The fund from cash waqf may be collected from the person who is willing to donate his waqf funds. In addition, this fund may be raised by the financial institutions such as the waqf account in Islamic banks, Islamic non-bank financial institutions.

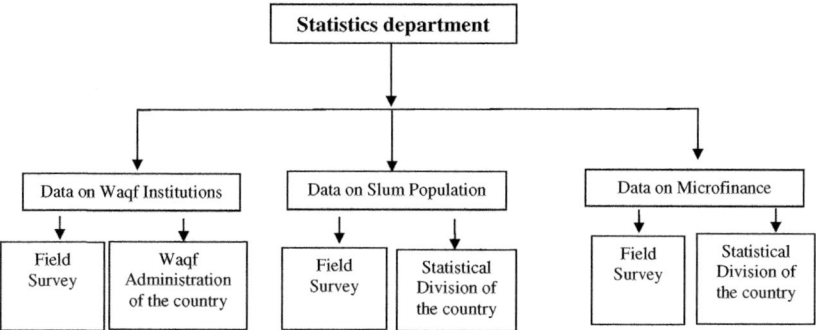

Fig. 2 Fund accumulation and financing department

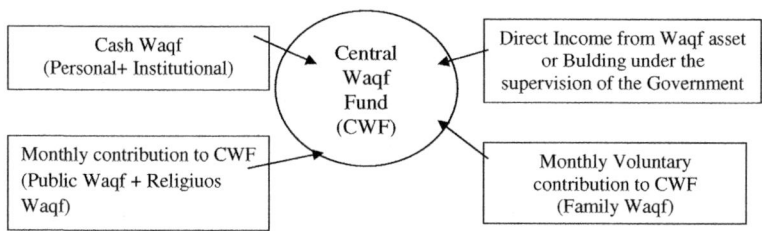

Fig. 3 Central waqf fund

Monthly Contribution to the CWF (Public waqf + Religious Waqf): There is evidence is that; the Waqf administration of Bangladesh imposes the compulsory fee or contribution on the waqf estates and institutions. The yearly contribution is BDT 56.87 million in Bangladesh in 2017. In Bangladesh, about 1.392 million waqf estates are waiting to be registered. Such kind of waqf fee may be introduced to raise the waqf funds for other countries also.

Direct Income from the Waqf Asset or Building: The investment income from the waqf assets under the supervision of the government will also be included in this fund.

Monthly Voluntary Contribution to the CWF (Family Waqf): It should not be wise to impose any fee on the family waqf institutions, but CWF may receive any voluntary donation from the family waqf estates and institutions.

c. Islamic Microfinance department

The Islamic Microfinance department will succeed the goal of the third stage. The key functions of this department are to innovate and execute the Islamic Microfinance services to the slum and floating population. To determine the targeted slum and floating people for Islamic Microfinance program; the nature and characteristics, the housing and residential status of the slum people should be explored. For this purpose, it should be mentioned that, there are two kinds of groups of the slum people. The first group lives in the rented government or private land and they have some facilities of the water, sanitation, and electricity. In contrast, the second group lives in the government vacant land or the land adjacent to the rail line and have no facilities of the water, sanitation, and electricity.

The first group may be qualified for the full pledge Islamic Microfinance services including Microcredit investment. After being the member of Islamic Microfinance, they will be rehabilitated gradually. On the contrary, the second group should be rehabilitated first and then may be the member of the full pledge Islamic Microfinance services including Microcredit investment. But they may be the recipients of services (education, health care, etc.) of Islamic Microfinance other than the Microcredit investment.

In addition, the policy for the second group may also be applied for the floating population who live on the footpath or roadside and rehabilitate them in the same way as mentioned in the first function.

Moreover, the Islamic Microfinance program should provide the primary services of the water, sanitation, education, health care, training, and skill development purposes for the slum and floating population, and then it may offer the microcredit services for the floating population.

d. Rehabilitation department

The rehabilitation department will attain the goal of the fourth stage. The rehabilitation department will have two functions. The first function is to rehabilitate the landless slum people who have lost their houses from river erosion or any other reasons and migrated from the villages. The land for rehabilitation may be acquired or bought by the WMA with the help of the government. The houses will be constructed with the help of the international Islamic institutions under the supervision of WMA. The rehabilitation department will design or form the different family units. Each unit may consist of five families and rehabilitate them gradually. The rehabilitated family will have to pay nominal rent for the housing unit. This rent will be added to the central waqf fund (CWF). The number of the unit and family may be fixed based upon the availability of the fund. Besides, this department will brief them about the future prospect of their life. The second function is to rehabilitate the floating poor who live on the footpath or roadside and rehabilitate them in the same way as mentioned in the first function.

e. Public relation and the forward linkage department

The public relation and the forward linkage department will finally accomplish the goal of the fifth stage. The main function of this department is to make relationship with the several institutions, centers, companies, firms, and industries, where it can incorporate the Microfinance member as a trainee for part-time or full-time job. Besides, it may create linkage with the local and international market and agencies to sell the handicraft products–these are produced by the Microfinance borrowers.

These sectors may include garment industries, security companies, shopping centers, educational institutions, home service companies, financial institutions, small and medium enterprises (SME), non-government organizations (NGOs), and development agencies.

Example of some positions with minimal education is third or fourth class worker such as a peon, bearer, worker in motor repairing and washing center, electronic product making and repair center such as refrigerator, television, computer, mobile servicing, salesmanship, tailoring, etc. Furthermore, affiliations with different institutions will train and make capable the participant for the job and then, he/she will be capable to contribute to the society.

7 Conclusion

Islam has several first-rated charity tools for the poor and public welfare. Besides zakah and sadaqah; waqf is another superb instrument that is considered as religious will-a gift of personal property by will. This paper presented a model to start the Islamic Microfinance and rehabilitation program by spending the waqf funds for the slum and floating population in the Muslim countries. This paper has been prepared by collecting both the primary and the secondary data. This model will be accomplished by launching an independent waqf Management institution by the joint venture of the government of the respective country and the national as well as International Islamic agency such as the Islamic Development Bank (IDB). Likewise, this model will be executed through the five stages; these are the revival and registration of the waqf estate, accumulation of funds, introducing the Islamic Microfinance, rehabilitation for the slum people, and forward linkage that may help the slum people to engage in the job and make contribution to the society. This is the high time to reduce the burden of the slum population among the Muslim countries, because the tremendous growth of the slum population warns the Muslim countries about the future threat. Nevertheless, if we will not take any measures to check it now, it will create a hell for the Muslim and humanity in the near future.

8   Scope for Further Research

The application of the waqf and the Islamic Microfinance is a wide area of research. This paper only discusses the topic that how to use the waqf funds for the slum population. In addition, the waqf estates can also be used for charitable investment fund; it is another strong tool for the sustainable development. There are huge scopes to do the further research on these issues and so more.

Appendix: Islamic Microfinance Institutions in Bangladesh

Islamic Microfinance institutions in Bangladesh	Establishing year
IBBL's Rural Development Scheme (RDS)	1995
Social Islami Bank Limited—Islamic Microfinance	–
Al-Arafah Islami Bank Limited—Islamic Microfinance	–
Muslim Aid Bangladesh	1991
Al Falah A'am Umayan Sangasta (AFAUS)	1989
TMSS Islamic Microfinance (TIMF)	2008
RESCUE started operation in Rangpur district	1991
Noble Foundation and Literary Society, Bogra	–

References

Alias, T. A. (2012). Venture Capital Strategies in Waqf Fund Investment and Spending. *ISRA International Journal of Islamic Finance, 4*(1), 99–126.
Alpay, S., & Haneef, M. (2015). *Integration of Waqf and Islamic Microfinance for Poverty Reduction: Case Studies of Malaysia, Indonesia and Bangladesh.*

Kuala Lumpur: The Statistical, Economic and Social Research and Training Centre for Islamic Countries (SESRIC) and International Islamic University Malaysia (IIUM). Available at https://www.islamicfinance.com/wp-content/uploads/2015/07/Waqf-and-Islamic-Microfinace-for-Povery-Reduction.pdf. Accessed 22 September 2017.

Alshebami, A., & Rengarajan, D. V. (2017). Microfinance Institutions in Yemen, "Hurdles and Remedies". *International Journal of Social Work, 4*(1), 10–21.

Badruddoza, S. (2011). *Microfinance in Bangladesh: Red and Green Lights*. Paper Presented at the Department of International Relations, University of Dhaka. Available at https://www.slideshare.net/badruddoza/Microfinance-in-bangladesh-red-and-green-lights. Accessed 22 September 2017.

CUS. (2006). *Slum of Urban Bangladesh: Mapping and Census 2005* (for USAID), Dhaka: Centre for Urban Studies (CUS), pp. 10–22. Available at https://www.measureevaluation.org/resources/publications/tr-06-35/at_download/document. Accessed 22 September 2017.

GIFR. (2017). *Global Islamic Finance Report (GIFR 2017)*. Available at http://www.gifr.net/publications/gifr2017/intro.pdf. Accessed 22 September 2017.

GOB. (2017). *Annual Report, Office of the Administrator of Waqf, Government of Bangladesh*. Available at http://Waqf.portal.gov.bd/sites/default/files/files/Waqf.portal.gov.bd/annual_reports/0cf9f56e_f404_46c1_b7af_b26652197e9d/7%20years%20Succ.doc...pdf. Accessed 22 September 2017.

Habibollah, S., Hamed, A., & Davoud, N. (2010). Waqf as a Social Entrepreneurship Model in Islam. *International Journal of Business and Management, 5*(7), 179–186.

Ledgerwood, J. (2000). *Microfinance Hand Book: An Institutional and Financial Perspective*. Washington, DC, USA: The International Bank for Reconstruction and Development/The World Bank.

Lend with Care. (2015). *What Is the Difference Between Microfinance and Microcredit?* Available at https://www.lendwithcare.org/info/about_us/about_Microfinance. Accessed 4 May 2017.

Mannan, A. M. (2015). *Islamic Microfinance: Bangladesh Experience*. Islami Bank Bangladesh Limited. Available at www.irti.org/English/.../Islamic%20Microfinance-Bangladesh%20Experience.pdf. Accessed 20 September 2017.

MCI. (2017). *Microfinanceconnect.info; Microfinance Practitioners; A Profile of Our Providers*. Available at http://www.microfinanceconnect.info/microfinanceproviders/institutions. http://www.microfinanceconnect.info/microfinanceproviders/banks. Accessed 22 September 2017.

Md Saad, N., & Azizah, A. (2009). Cash Waqf and Islamic Microfinance: Untapped Economic Opportunities. *Islam and Civilisational Renewal (ICR), 1*(2), 337–354.

MICRA. (2017). *The Microfinance Innovation Center for Resources and Alternatives, About Us*. Available at http://www.micra-indo.org. Accessed 22 September 2017.

Mohamed Ali, K. (2014). *Integrating Zakah, Awqaf and Islamic Microfinance for Poverty Alleviation: Three Models of Islamic Micro Finance* (IRTI Working Paper Series, WP# 1435-19). Available at http://www.irti.org/English/Research/Documents/WP/WP-1435-19.pdf. Accessed 22 September 2017.

Mohammad, M. T. S., & Mar Iman, A. H. (2006). Obstacles of the Current Concept of Waqf to the Development of Waqf Properties and the Recommended Alternative. *Malaysian Journal of Real Estate, 1*(1), 1–95. Available at http://eprints.utm.my/501/1/27-38.pdf. Accessed 25 October 2017.

MRA. (2017). *List of Licensed MFIs as of Sep 12, 2017*. Dhaka, Bangladesh: Microfinance Regulatory Authority. Available at http://mra.gov.bd/index.php?option=com_content&view=article&id=115&Itemid=95. Accessed 22 September 2017.

Murphy, J. (2017). 1 Billion Live in Slums. *CBS News*. Available at https://www.cbsnews.com/news/1-billion-live-in-slums/. Accessed 22 September 2017.

Rashad, D. S. (2014), *New Trends in Global Islamic Microfinance*. Available at www.kantakji.com/strategic.../new-trends-in-global-islamic-Microfinance.aspx?...true. Accessed 22 September 2017.

Sadegh, B. (2009). Islamic Microfinance, Providing Credit to the Poor: A Case Study of Iran. *International Economics Studies, 34*(1), 99–107.

The Consultative Group to Assist the Poor. (CGAP). (2017). *Islamic Microfinance: An Emerging Market Niche*. Available at 470010ENGLISH01PUBLIC10FocusNote149.pdf. Accessed 22 September 2017.

UN-Habitat. (2015). *Global Urban Indicators Database 2015*. United Nations Human Settlement Program (UN-Habitat). Available at https://unhabitat.org/wp-content/uploads/2014/03/Table13.2.3-Proportion-of-urban-population-living-in-slums-and-urban-slum-population-by-country-1990-2014.pdf. Accessed 22 September 2017.

World Bank. (2017). *Global Report on Islamic Finance: A Catalyst for Shared Prosperity?* Washington, DC, USA: World Bank. Available at https://doi.org/10.1596/978-1-4648-0926-2. Accessed 22 September 2017.

Worldometers. (2017). *Current World Population*. Available at http://www.worldometers.info/world-population/. Accessed 22 September 2017.

Yunus, M., & Jolis, A. (2006). *Banker to the Poor: The Autobiography of Muhammad Yunus, Founder of Grameen Bank* (pp. 1–15). London: Oxford University Press.

Zubair Mughal, M. (2017), *Funding Sources for Islamic Microfinance Institutions*. Available at http://www.alhudacibe.com/imhd/news43.php. Accessed 22 September 2017.

CHAPTER 14

The Investment of Waqf Properties and Infrastructure Development

Nosratollah Nafar

1 Introduction

The global development community has emphasized infrastructure development as an important goal in SDGs, with a particular focus on both soft and hard infrastructure. In addition, many developing countries have included infrastructure development as one of the main goals in their national development plans. Developing countries particularly least developed countries (LDCs) are mostly less able to mobilize the required amount of finance to achieve the targets of the 2030 Agenda Meeting the infrastructure needs requires unprecedented investments in areas such as water and sanitation, education, health, energy, transport, as well as telecommunications.

According to UNCTAD (2014), the additional finance required to fund for the infrastructure (physical and social) needs associated with the SDGs for developing countries alone will be at least $2.5 trillion per year. This significant amount must mainly come from domestic resources

N. Nafar (✉)
Country Strategy and Cooperation Department,
Islamic Development Bank, Ankara, Turkey
e-mail: nnafar@isdb.org

© The Author(s) 2019
K. M. Ali et al. (eds.), *Revitalization of Waqf
for Socio-Economic Development, Volume I,*
https://doi.org/10.1007/978-3-030-18445-2_14

285

both public sector and private sector finance and investment. However, the resource-poor developing countries particularly LDCs remain heavily reliant on official development assistance and other sources. In 2014, LDCs received about $41 billion in ODA from OECD donor countries (OECD 2015a), which will not be sufficient to fund the large-scale investments needed in infrastructure sector to achieve the SDGs in these countries. In this context, the key question is how to design a broader set of financing instruments to surge the amount of financing to support infrastructure development particularly in developing countries.

Global community needs to represent new mechanisms to mobilize additional sources of finance, both domestic and international for investments in infrastructure development. In this context, expanding financing, in ways that make sense to each country, will be critical to meet the investment needs of infrastructure effectively. The main objective of this paper is to measure the infrastructure gap and recognize the role of Islamic finance with special focus on waqf in both economic and social infrastructure development. Specifically, the study aims at introducing waqf as an effective financial instrument to support additional funding for infrastructure investment particularly social infrastructure. In spite of the huge potentiality of waqf assets and properties, little has been invested in these assets and properties to support social infrastructure development. Therefore, this study intends to raise public awareness about the significant role of waqf in supporting social infrastructure development.

The paper summarizes some of the key findings in latest studies on the vital role of infrastructure development in long-term economic growth and underlines the massive funding gap that many developing countries face. The paper also explores issues and challenges in financing infrastructure and introduces the Islamic finance as a strong instrument to support infrastructure development in IDB member countries. The rest of the paper is organized as follows: Section 2 deals with definition and initial consideration. Section 3 discusses the impact of infrastructure on SDGs. Section 4 presents the status of infrastructure in developing countries. Section 5 explores the global infrastructure investment gap. Section 6 presents IDB financing modes for infrastructure development. Section 7 presents financing infrastructure development in IDB member countries and related challenges and priorities. Section 8 briefly overviews the role of waqf in supporting social investment. Finally, Sect. 9 offers conclusion and recommendations.

2 DEFINITION/INITIAL CONSIDERATIONS

Infrastructure plays an important role in promoting sustainable growth and development. It refers to all necessary factors for the proper working of the economy (UN 2011). Infrastructure is a complex field with so many different components, but all of them can be categorized into two main types of infrastructures: economic and social infrastructures (Parker 2008; RREEF 2008). Economic infrastructure refers to basic facilities including facilities of telecommunication, electricity, transportation, energy, stations etc. They are commercial in nature and are provided to make the business easier and more profitable. Social infrastructure refers to those facilities that help achieve both various economic activities and certain social objectives (Department of Planning Western Australia 2012). Examples of social infrastructures include education, public health care, sanitation, governance systems, and correctional facilities. Social infrastructure has enormous externalities.

Although infrastructure is split into broad groups of economic and social infrastructure, they are not independent: They support each other, and a weakness in one area will have a negative impact on others. The right mix of two is important to ensure that infrastructure system supports economic growth and poverty alleviation. Therefore, understanding the consequences of the interaction between economic and social infrastructure is fundamental for scaling investments in infrastructure.

Generally, no country has developed without access to well-functioning infrastructure. In fact, the level of infrastructure development determines the pace of economic growth in any country as it provides foundation on which the structure of development and growth can be established.[1] It is worth to mention that a large number of studies suggest that infrastructure development is essential but not enough to boost economic growth and alleviate poverty. For instance, Estache (2006), Romp and De Haan (2007), and Straub (2008) conducted interesting studies at the macroeconomic level to assess the effects of infrastructure on output, growth, productivity, and poverty. They suggest that there

---

[1] According to the World Development Report (1994), one percent increase in the stock of infrastructure is associated with a one percent increase in the GDP across all countries.

should be a set of factors to be considered if investment in infrastructure is to contribute to growth significantly. For example, the economic infrastructure must be combined with the social objectives. This allows the infrastructure system to perform and have the intended impact. Inadequate focus on social infrastructure (health and education) will delay the contribution to growth and poverty alleviation.

3   INFRASTRUCTURE DEVELOPMENT AND SDGs

The Sustainable Development Goals (SDGs) were adopted through wide and extensive consultations with the member countries of the UN in September 2015. The SDGs are composed of 17 goals and 169 targets, which are integrated and inseparable. The SDGs cover a wide range of development issues including poverty, inequality, climate change, health, education, etc. The prominence of SDGs will certainly direct the development plans over the next two decades as they embrace a universal approach to the sustainable development agenda.

While infrastructure outcomes affect a large number of the SDGs, SDG 9 specifically addresses the infrastructure development to promote inclusive and sustainable development. This goal defines infrastructure in a broad sense, including both soft and hard infrastructure, which are essential for fostering economic and social development. As an example for economic infrastructure, target 9.1 reads, "develop quality, reliable, sustainable and resilient infrastructure, including regional and trans-border infrastructure, to support economic development and human well-being, with a focus on affordable and equitable access for all." As an example for social infrastructure, target 9.3 says, "increase the access of small-scale industrial and other enterprises, particularly in developing countries, to financial services including affordable credit and their integration into value chains and markets."

The scale and ambition of SDGs require a revitalized global partnership to ensure its implementation, which can bring huge gains to all countries regardless of their level of income or stage of development. In this context, MDBs made a commitment at the United Nations General Assembly in September 2015 to move beyond business as usual to address development challenges and fully support the successful implementation of the SDGs (United Nations 2015). It is clear that investment in both economic and social infrastructure will be critical for the achievement of these ambitious goals. Whether it is dealing with poverty, investing in water and power, investing in health and education, or improving cities, infrastructure investment is the primary enabler.

4   STATUS OF INFRASTRUCTURE IN DEVELOPING COUNTRIES/MCs

In spite of recognition of significant contribution of infrastructure development in poverty reduction, many developing countries including IDB member countries are facing severe infrastructure deficiency, mainly due to lack of proper investment, significant population growth, and increasing urbanization. About 2.6 billion people live without safe water and electricity. In addition, 2.4 billion people live without sanitation, and more than 1 billion people are without access to an all-weather road or telephone services (Fig. 1).

Access to infrastructure services varies widely across regions. Figure 2 ranks various grouping countries according to the basic infrastructure indicator for the period 2011–2015. Majority of developing countries including IDB member countries are lagging behind the world average.

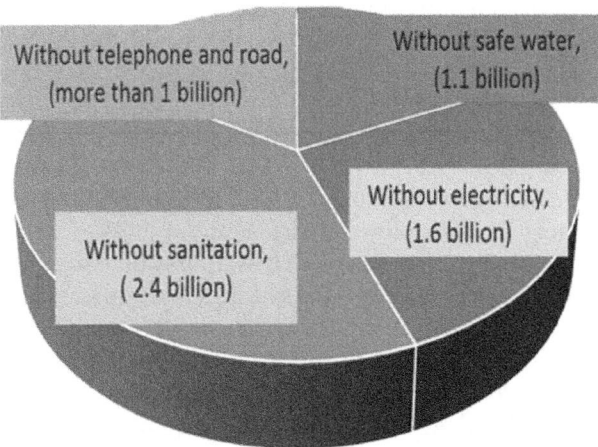

Fig. 1   Status of infrastructure in developing countries (*Source* Infrastructure Development, Atlas of Global Development, World Bank, 2009)

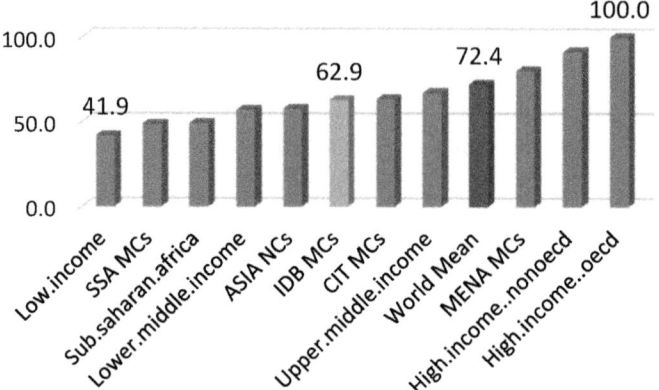

Fig. 2 Basic infrastructure (2011–2015) (*Source* Global Competitivness Report, 2016)

In addition, in many low-income countries the quality of existing infrastructure services is very poor. For example, many people have not accessed to drinkable and safe water. Sanitation facilities are often insufficient, and electricity service is unreliable. Transport services may be lacking, and roads are often in poor condition.

5 Global Investment Gap

The need for infrastructure is significant, particularly in emerging and developing countries. From 2016 through 2030, the global infrastructure demand is estimated at about US$3.7 trillion (5.4% of global GDP) while the supply of new infrastructure is about US$2.7 trillion (4% of global GDP) annually. This means that high infrastructure demand will not be met with current pace of infrastructure investment due to various obstacles, notably the shortage of fiscal space following the global financial crisis and the hesitancy of private sector to put capital to long-term and risky investment particularly in low-income countries. Government budgets are the biggest source of funds, accounting for about three of every four-infrastructure dollars, while the private sector provides the rest. Yet in the aftermath of the financial crisis, governments have seen their fiscal deficits grow and their budgets shrink indicating that that private capital must be mobilized to fill these gaps. However, most

Fig. 3 Annual infrastructure investment by sector and region (*Source* EMCompass Quik Take, International Finance Corporation, April 2016)

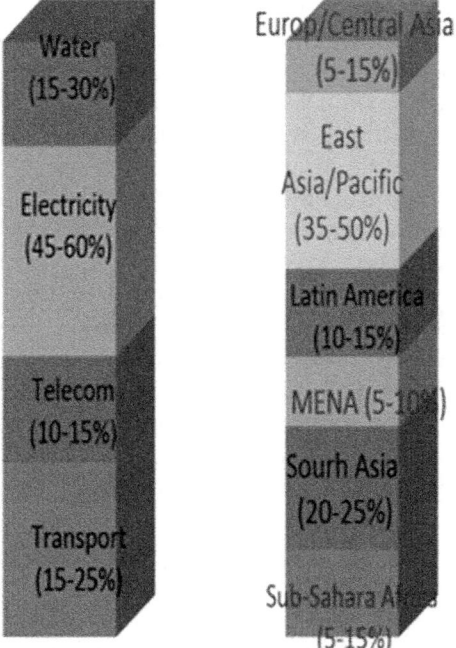

private funding flows to upper-middle-income countries. Therefore, across all sectors of economic and social infrastructure, the global investment gap in infrastructure amounts to at least US$1 trillion per year, which corresponds to about 1.4% of global GDP (World Economic Forum 2014).

In terms of sectors, electricity will require over half of all infrastructure spending. That includes power generation, capacity, and transmission and distribution networks. Water and sanitation will demand about 15 to 30% of the total infrastructure investment (Fig. 3). In Latin America, the telecommunication and electricity sectors are representing about 2.2 and 1.7% of regional GDP, respectively. Transport and water and sanitation need about 1.1 and 0.2% (Perrotti and Sanchez 2011). For MENA region, about USD 106 billion per annum is needed for infrastructure over 2010–2020, representing 6.9% or regional GDP. About 3% of GDP needs to be devoted to capital expansion and additional 4% to operation and maintenance. Of the total investment, transport sector needs about 40% and electricity needs 40%. Water and sanitation needs 5% and ICT sector needs 9% (Estache et al. 2013). Sub-Saharan Africa needs more than US$93 billion to invest in infrastructure sector annually over the next two decades, and traditional financing is providing just less than half of that. This means that the region faces a significant financing gap (about US$50 billion) to fill (Foster and Briceño-Garmendia 2010). As mentioned earlier, government budgets are the biggest source of funds for infrastructure investment in emerging economies. Yet in the aftermath of the financial crisis, governments have seen their fiscal deficits grow and their budgets shrink, increasing the need for private funding. Domestic private sector banks can play a particularly important role, given their ability to assess local project and provide lending in local currency. However, most private funding flows to upper-middle-income countries. The poor condition of basic infrastructure in the region (electricity, water, roads) affects the economic growth significantly and reduces productivity by as much as 40% (Patel 2014).

6   IDB Financing Modes for Infrastructure Development

Infrastructure project financing has traditionally been a key strength of IDBG, and the bank has gone farther than most peer MDBs in prioritizing this area.[2] Generally, the group uses Shariah-compliant instruments to finance projects and operations in member countries. These instruments can be deployed for infrastructure financing. They are robust and easily adaptable to all form of development activities in member countries. Sometimes, the instruments could be combined, and beneficiaries have options to pick and choose what suit them most. The following provides a brief snapshot of the modes of finance based on Islamic values that are being used by IDB to support development in its member countries.

Grants: There are two types of grants: (i) Technical Assistance provided for technical assistance and capacity building activities in IDB's member countries, with special focus on least developed member countries (LDMCs) and (ii) Special Assistance provided for social

---

[2] Almost 80% of requests for IDB financing from member countries are in infrastructure sectors—energy, water, transport, and telecommunication (IDB Annual Report 2014).

projects (schools, hospitals, etc.) particularly in Muslim communities in non-member countries. They are also provided for disaster relief in member countries. Subsequent to approval by IDB and its agreement with the recipient of grant, the recipient signs a contract with a supplier/contractor/consultant to procure the goods/services to whom IDB disburses directly. The supplier/contractor/supplier then delivers the goods/services to the recipient.

Loan: Generally, there are two different types of loans. First, Ordinary Capital Resources Loans classified into 2 types depending on their scope of activities: (a) Ordinary Loans are long-term concessional loans provided for financing development and infrastructure projects and (b) Technical Assistance Loans (with soft terms to assist member countries) in obtaining consultancy services to conduct feasibility and other such studies for major projects. Second, Islamic Solidarity Fund for Development Loans: These are soft-term loans directed at programs for poverty alleviation and microfinance programs in various sectors (education, health, etc.) in the member countries, especially LDMCs. Subsequent to approval of loan by IDB and its agreement with the recipient of grant, the borrower signs a contract with a supplier for procurement of goods/services to whom IDB disburses directly. The borrower repays to IDB the principal loan amount plus service fee. IDB charges the service fee to cover its administrative costs. It ranges from a minimum of 0.75% to a maximum of 2.00% per annum of the principal amount. The loan product is modeled after the Qard al-Hassan contract on which service charge based on actual cost is permissible and does not tantamount to riba. Total value of the projects financed by the bank through loan mode of financing since the inception is $3.36 billion.

Leasing: Under a basic lease contract, the owner of an asset (lessor) sells an asset in exchange for a periodic definite reward (the rent). This product is used to provide for fixed assets and capital equipment (movable assets in certain cases) such as machinery and equipment for projects. The lessee acts as an agent on behalf of IDB, to procure the asset and for the maintenance of the asset. Subsequent to approval of leasing arrangement, IDB appoints the client as its agent, to sign a contract with a supplier to procure the assets and to supervise, monitor, and take delivery of the assets. The client also maintains the assets, takes care of insurance, and repairs in the name of IDB during the lease period. Then, IDB pays the price of the assets directly to the supplier. The client (now the lessee), as IDB agent, takes delivery of the assets from the supplier.

The lessee pays fixed periodical rentals to IDB over the agreed lease period. At the end of the lease period, IDB transfers ownership of the assets to the lessee, as a gift. The calculation of the rental is based on the Capital Cost of IDB, plus a fixed or floating markup. In case of a floating markup, there is a floor and a cap and the rental of the first 6 months is known to the parties. Leasing has accounted for US$9.34 billion as applied mode of financing by the bank since the inception.

Istisna: IDB operates Istisna on a medium to long-term basis, wherein IDB appoints the purchaser (client) as its agent who gets the asset constructed/manufactured. When the asset is constructed/manufactured and accepted by the purchaser, IDB transfers the title of the asset to the purchaser. The purchaser then pays the sale price of the asset in deferred payments. IDB uses this product to finance infrastructure projects and trade in capital goods within and among member countries. The purchaser, as IDB's agent, ensures that until the final acceptance of the asset, it is comprehensively insured with an acceptable Islamic insurance company and that IDB is named as a loss payee under the insurance policies. The bank provided financing under the Istisna mode for the total amount of US$16.3 billion.

Installment Sale: It is a credit sale of an asset, delivered on spot, in which the purchaser can pay the price of the asset at a future date, either in lump sum or in installments. IDB operates installment sale on a medium to long-term basis. Under this arrangement, IDB purchases an asset for its client against a promise by the latter to purchase the asset once it is delivered. IDB appoints the client as its agent, to procure the assets from the supplier and to supervise, monitor, and take delivery of the assets. The client insures the assets in the name of IDB during the transit period. IDB pays the purchase price of the assets directly to the supplier. The purchaser, as IDB agent, takes delivery of the assets from the supplier. Then, upon delivery, IDB sells the assets to the purchaser at sale price on deferred basis. The purchaser pays the sale price to IDB in installments. IDB uses this product to provide for assets such as equipment and machinery for developmental projects. The installment sale agreement provides for the procurement function of the client (as the agent of IDB), the terms and conditions as well as the sale price, tenor of financing, etc. Installment sale mode of financing has been applied by the bank for financing of projects in the amount of US$5.2 billion.

Restricted Mudarabah: It is a variant of Mudarabah that is used by IDB, wherein the Mudarib (the entity) is bound by certain restrictions on the sectors/areas/projects into which it can invest the Mudarabah capital. These restrictions are agreed in advance, which lists the terms and conditions of the operation, the investment plan, profit-sharing ratio, duration, etc. IDB uses this arrangement for investment in specific sector projects such as sustainable agriculture, renewable energy, and youth employment programs. Upon the maturity of the Mudarabah arrangement, the Mudarib will liquidate the assets of the Mudarabah operation. Following the liquidation by the Mudarib, IDB will receive the Mudarabah capital plus IDB's share of profits. If the profit is greater than what was agreed upon, the Mudarib, as an incentive, will retain the excess. The authority and responsibilities of Mudarib include the following: (i) conduct the relevant feasibility studies to determine the financial viability of the projects that will be invested in and ensure that the financing will be used only for *Shariah*-compliant ventures; (ii) invest only in those projects which will return not less than the anticipated profit as mentioned in the agreement; and (iii) submit progress reports to IDB, as and when requested. The Restricted Mudarabah is new instrument and has only been extended for projects with total financing package of US$440 million.

Musharakah (Equity Participation): In its classical form, a musharakah is an arrangement where two or more parties agree to contribute to the capital of the partnership in equal or varying amounts to establish a new project or share in an existing one. IDB uses a variant of this under which it makes strategic long-term investments with the objective to maximize its developmental objectives. These investments are usually in the equity of *Shariah*-compliant industrial, agro-industrial projects, Islamic banks, and financial institutions of its member countries. IDB does not acquire majority or controlling interest in the share capital of a company. Its investments do not exceed one-third of the company's capital and do not provide IDB with control or the ability to exercise any significant influence over the financial and operating policies of such companies. Investments are sold at a time when IDB considers it appropriate.

Blended Finance: In order to help member countries (especially low-income and least developed member countries) overcome their inability to access ordinary financing, the group has developed an innovative financing mechanism called Triple-Win. In this mechanism, the group partners with a member country and a "third party" (usually a philanthropist, multilateral development banks, bilateral donors, etc.) to avail more financial resources for developmental interventions in a social sector. The mechanism allows the group to tap into its ordinary capital resources to augment its concessional pool, thereby extending a large quantum of financing to its member country to support social sector operations. The member country concerned only pays the principal, while the "third party" pays the markup/administrative fee of the loan directly to the group. Thus, member countries who are often constrained by the inability to use non-concessional market resources to finance their social projects in education and health are able to absorb non-concessional financing through Triple-Win mechanism.

This mechanism, which is Shariah-compliant, holds promise for millions of people as more concessionary financing is made available to their governments especially those with more severe development challenges. The responsibility to effectively implement a project under the mechanism lies squarely with the recipient member country government. This enhances national ownership and gives absolute power to beneficiary member country to be in a driver's seat for its development agenda, in line with the aspirations of the Paris Declaration and Development Effectiveness. The mechanism has been piloted for two projects in which the group collaborated with the Bill Gates Foundation and West African Economic and Monetary Union (UEMOA), respectively, to finance national responses to polio eradication in Pakistan and rural water supply and sanitation in eight UEMOA countries.[3] This mechanism of finance (the IDB Triple Win Financing in partnership with Bill & Melinda Gates Foundation) has great potential to bring together development partners to unlock US$2.5 billion of financing on concessional terms to support both soft and hard infrastructure particularly in low-income countries. The bank has also launched its B-Finance resource mobilization initiative (i.e., private sector debt capital flows to support PPP infrastructure projects in MCs) and is actively developing other tools to help IDB expand its intervention within the non-sovereign financing sphere for selected member countries. For instance, the IsDB is working to establish global platforms for crowdsourcing and thus expand its capacity to mobilize resources without increasing its financial liability, especially on knowledge crowdsourcing platforms.

The IsDB and its development cooperation partners have launched a $2.5 billion "Lives and Livelihoods Fund" (LLF), which is the largest development initiative of its kind based in the Middle East serving many

---

[3] Benin, Burkina Faso, Guinea Bissau, Cote d'Ivoire, Mali, Niger, Senegal and Togo.

member countries. The major LLF donors are the Islamic Solidarity Fund for Development (ISFD) of the IsDB, the Bill & Melinda Gates Foundation, and other donors in the GCC countries. By the end of 2016, the fund had raised about $400 million of the targeted $500 million in grant funding. The LLF is a model of Triple-Win mechanism, which in a horizon of five years provides a unique access to finance by pooling together grant resources from regional and international donors, along with IsDB market-based ordinary project financing to offer highly concessional funding that target sub-sectors and project areas that could not be reached before. This mechanism has great potential to bring together development partners to support both soft and hard infrastructure particularly in low-income countries.

A successful experience of partnership with national development banks was built with the Industrial Development Bank of Turkey (TSKB) in the area of renewable energy. IsDB used *Restricted Mudarabah* financing. This approach eliminated the need for IsDB to enter into individual financing agreements for each sub-project being financed. It also gave freedom to TSKB as the local executing agency, for example, to use its own procedures for appraisal, quality assessment and risk assessment, as well as the procurement of goods and services. As a result, $3.8 was mobilized for every dollar invested by IsDB. In order to fully utilize Islamic finance in promoting economic and social infrastructure, IsDB Group is playing an active role in promoting knowledge of stakeholders, including policy makers, investors, and market participants about these type of finance and explore the relevant policy, legal, regulatory, and institutional interventions necessary to expand Islamic financing. The bank is paying special attention to support the efforts of member countries in mainstreaming Islamic finance into their financial systems to enhance productive financial intermediation for engendering new source of finance.

Sukuk: Islamic finance has strong potential in promoting both social and economic infrastructure development. While zakat and awaqf have great potential to support small size and social infrastructure, sukuk (Islamic bonds) can successfully finance large-scale infrastructure (water and sanitation projects, sustainable and affordable energy, transport, roads, and shelter). The global market for sukuk exceeds $100 billion and is estimated to grow by 25–35% per year, mostly are issued in the Malaysian market, Saudi Arabia, and the UAE. A "green sukuk" is also a Shariah-compliant version of a green bond, which can be used to finance renewable energy, low-carbon technologies, and other environmental assets. Eligible assets for Green Sukuk as defined by Climate Bond Standards certification include: solar parks, biogas plants, wind energy, ambitious energy efficiency and renewable transmission and infrastructure, electric vehicles and infrastructure, and light rail. In 2016, the IsDB issued four series of trust certificates (sukuk) under its existing $25 billion medium-term note (MTN) program. The IsDB continues to expand its public–private partnership (PPP) portfolio by actively seeking opportunities to help bridging the infrastructure gap in its member countries. The bank's PPP portfolio is mainly targeting non-sovereign infrastructure projects to promote economic development, job creation, regional integration, and the transfer of skills and expertise to achieve sustainable growth in its member countries.

7   FINANCING INFRASTRUCTURE DEVELOPMENT IN IDB MCs: CHALLENGES AND PRIORITIES

This part evaluates the financial ability of IDB member countries in supporting infrastructure development in line with the 2030 global development agenda. In this view, IDB member countries are grouped in two categories, according to their income level, as per the World Bank classification.

The low-income group consists of low- and lower-middle-income MCs, while the high-income group is composed by high- and upper-middle-income MCs. Most of the IDB member countries are in the first group (34 out of 57 MCs). These countries generally have a weak performance in terms of revenue mobilization, relatively low savings, and limited access to private finance. Other member countries in the upper-middle-income and high-income categories can rely on important public revenues and national savings and have better access to private finance (Table 1).

For the IDB member countries, increasing domestic public resources is essential. At 25%, the average ratio of budget revenue to GDP for IDBC member countries is well below the world average of 28% over the last five years. However, it is well aligned with the average ratios for developing countries. Among member countries, there are marked differences according to the income level. For the low-income

Table 1 IDB member countries: Selected financing indicators (2011–2015)

	I	II	III	IV	V
Domestic financing					
Budget revenue (% of GDP)	27	34.1	15.1	n.a	28
Budget expenditure (% of GDP)	28.4	32.1	21	n.a	30
Gross national savings (% of GDP)	29	34	23	26.2	33
Total investment (% of GDP)	25	26	24	25	32.0
Domestic credit provided by financial sector (% of GDP)	51.07	55	43	168	107.1
Domestic credit to private sector (% of GDP)	45	52	38	122.2	87.0
Market capitalization of listed companies (% of GDP)	43.5	50.3	32.3	75.1	61.7
External financing					
Net ODA received (% of GNI)	0.6	0.4	1.4	0.2	0.6
Debt-service paid (% of GDP)	3.5	4.3	2.3	n.a	2.4
Foreign direct investment, net inflows (% of GDP)	1.9	1.8	2.1	2.7	2.7
Personal remittances, received (% of GDP)	2.1	0.6	4.1	0.7	1.4

Data sources IMF, EIU, and the World Bank
I = IDB-57; II = High- and upper-middle-income IDB-23; III = Low- and lower-middle-income IDB-34; IV = World; V = Developing countries; VI = Developing countries excluding. China and India

group, the average ratio is relatively weak (15%), over fifty percent lower than the average ratio for the high-income group (31%). In low-income countries, tax bases tend to be quite narrow, reflecting the smaller share of the formal sector in employment and business activity. Large informal economies and agricultural sectors are rarely taxed (World Bank 2013). This situation is compound by weak administrative capacity. For the IDB low-income group, specific efforts are hence needed to enhance administrative capacity and broaden the tax base. For all member countries, improving the management of natural resources and further combating illicit financial flows can improve the efficiency of revenue collection. Strengthening public expenditure and investment management can also help limit waste and graft and improve the quality of public expenditure, including through better selection, design, and management of public investment projects. Reforms in subsidy regime and procurement in particular can increase public expenditure efficiency and create more fiscal space to support large-scale investment.

Developing the domestic financial sector is a key challenge for IDB MCs. In IDB member countries as a group, national savings as a percentage of GDP stand at nearly 30% and total investment is below 26% of GDP over the last five years. This indicates that IDB member countries need to find proper ways and means to channel idle domestic savings into investments effectively. In this respect, the financial sector can make an important contribution by increasing the savings rate and the availability of savings for investment. As in other developing countries, the financial system in IDB MCs is dominated by the banking sector. Nonetheless, domestic credit ratios for IDB member countries are markedly low, compared to the world average, and even to developing countries averages. While the average ratio of domestic credit to GDP is below 48% for MCs, the world average is 164%. Stock markets are at an early stage of development in most of the IDB member countries, especially the low-income MCs, and the related data are weak. In terms of market capitalization, the average ratio for IDB member countries stands at 43.5% of GDP over 2010–2014. Over the same period, the average ratio for developing countries is around 62%. IDB member countries need to expand the financial sector and diversify their products to (i) meet the needs of all segments of the economy and (ii) move from being just credit providers toward becoming more holistic financial services providers. In this context, policy makers in IDB member countries need to put more effort on developing more diversified financial system, where banks and capital markets complement each other to enhance the efficiency of capital allocation. The challenge, therefore, is to strike a right balance between financial policies, measures, and investments in activities that target both hard and soft infrastructure.

External sources of financing can be further mobilized through enhanced policies and institutional framework. ODA remains important for provisioning the delivery of the post-2015 development agenda, particularly in low-income IDB member countries. Net ODA received in IDB member countries represented 1% of GDP on average over the last five years, and for the IDB low-income group, the average ratio was 1.6%, against 0.7% for developing countries (excluding China and India). In contrast, the debt-service paid represented 3.5% of GDP on average for IDB MCs, despite the fact that debt relief initiatives have substantially lowered the stock of external debt and related debt services requirements. With respect to FDI inflows, there is not a marked difference between the two IDB income groups. FDI stands at 2.4% in 57 IDB member countries, 2.5% in the low-income group, and 2.3% of GDP in the high-income group over 2010–2014. However, IDB countries as a group lag behind the developing country average, which is around 3.5%. Finally, remittances are a key source of funds for the IDB countries. On average, IDB member countries received the equivalent of 2.1% of GDP, and the group of low- and lower-middle IDB member countries received 4.1% of GDP. For many low-income member countries, remittances are the key part of international capital flows and sometimes are important than FDI and foreign aid. The dependence of these countries on remittances has sharply increased over the past decade. Channeling these resources to more productive investment can therefore provide a critical contribution to supporting the achievement of SDGs. Overall, attracting more private capital to complement scarce public resources calls for further improvement of the investment climate and business regulation.

Promoting new and innovative sources of finance with a special focus on blended finance is the way forward. Given the limited financial resources of the public sector finding, finding new ways to attract private sector financing to support long-term investments is critical. At national level, the institutional investors such as mutual funds, insurance companies, and pension funds have great potential to support infrastructure development. At the OIC level, there is a huge amount of Sovereign Wealth Funds (SWF) particularly in oil exporting countries. However, the challenge is how to direct these funds toward productive investments in other member countries to support the achievement of development objectives with rational economic returns. PPPs can be an effective model for financing large-scale investments, particularly in low-income member countries. The success of effective implementation of PPP requires improved governance and stronger institutions to build new forms of public–private dialogue to strengthen the voice of the private sector in designing and developing national economic strategies. In this context, IDB member countries need to formulate a clear policy framework that define the roles, responsibilities, and potential gains of private sector firms; design a transparent and competitive procurement framework; and increase the capacity of both private banks and the public sector in designing mutually beneficial framework agreements for infrastructure PPPs.

Mainstreaming Islamic finance into the financial system will improve resources mobilization. Islamic finance has strong potential in promoting both social and economic infrastructure development. While zakat and awaqf have great potential to support small size and social infrastructure, sukuk (Islamic bonds) can successfully finance large-scale infrastructure such as energy, transport, roads, and shelter. In order to fully utilize Islamic finance in promoting economic and social infra-structure, IDBG need to play an active role in promoting knowledge of its member countries about these types of finance and explore the rel-evant policy, legal, regulatory, and institutional interventions necessary to expand Islamic financing. Specifically, the bank needs to pay special attention to support the efforts of member countries in mainstreaming Islamic finance into their financial systems to enhance productive finan-cial intermediation for engendering new source of finance. Three key priority areas are to (i) strengthen infrastructure building blocks of the Islamic financial services industry; (ii) accelerate the implementation of Shariah and prudential standards and rules to facilitate the creation of a more stable, efficient, and internationally integrated Islamic financial ser-vices industry; and (iii) create a common platform for the regulators of the Islamic financial services industry to enhance constructive dialogue.

8   WAQF AND SOCIAL INVESTMENT GAP

Given the significant financial needs to support both economic and social infrastructure, it is vital to explore new financing mechanisms to comple-ment the traditional financing. As a system, Islamic finance helps stimu-late economic activity and entrepreneurship toward inclusive economic development, financial and social stability, and comprehensive human development.[4]

Traditionally, Islamic finance possesses models for solidarity-based financing with important features of social sustainability. For example, zakat, waqf, and sadqaat have played dynamic role in alleviating pov-erty and have helped the society to move to wider social and financial inclusion. Particularly, waqf funds have played an important role in the provision of social infrastructure such as education, hospitals, as well as economic infrastructure such as roads and bridges. (Sadeq 2002). It has

---

[4]According to the most recent World Islamic Banking Competitiveness Report, global Islamic banking industry assets amounted to USD \$2 trillion in 2014, growing at a rate of approximately 20%, and have the potentiality to cater the most of the banking and finance needs of modern economies.

been argued that the entire health, education, and welfare budget during the Osman Caliphate based in Istanbul came from its charitable foundations (Cizakca 2004). Historically, education has been the second largest recipient of waqf revenues after religious matters, which was its original purpose. Since the beginning of Islam, education has been financed by waqf and other voluntary aids. The third big beneficiary of waqf is the category of health services.[5] Of course, the social welfare role of waqf institutions depends on their type and size. waqf can be established in many forms depending on its purpose or nature of its outcome.[6] Interestingly, all forms could significantly support economic and social infrastructure development thus fulfill the society's needs adequately. The instrument of awaqf is ideal for generating sufficient income-earning opportunities and ensuring a flow of resources to support the provision of both quantity and quality of social infrastructure (education, sanitation, health care) and other social goods. The role of waqf has been great in countries with high levels of financial and social exclusion as it can play a critical role in protecting vulnerable against many hazards such as unemployment, hunger, illness, and other disasters. It is also worth to mention that they are not restricted to the Muslim community and can be shared beyond religious, cultural, racial, and sectarian boundaries.

Unfortunately, large portion of waqf properties in most Muslim countries is not being used for socio-economic development purposes.[7] For example, Kahf (1989) estimates the potentiality of zakat revenue between 0.9 and 7.5% of GDP in different countries. The average of the lower and higher ranges equals 1.8 and 4.3% of GDP. The effective way of using zakat and waqf can enhance productive capacities of the society. In this context, Cizakca (2004) proposes a model to use cash waqf for providing microfinance to low skilled labor force. Elgari also suggests establishing a nonprofit financial intermediary to provide interest-free loans (qard hassan) to the poor who are mostly excluded from

---

[5] The Shishli Children Hospital in Istanbul founded in 1898 is one of the examples of the health Waqf. Many educational services, which are financed by the Turkish government budget, were financed by waqf foundations existed during the Ottoman era.

[6] On the basis of its purpose, waqf can be classified into waqf ahli (waqf zhurri), waqf khayri, waqf al-sabil, and waqf al-awaridh.

[7] For example, IRTI & TR (2013) report that Indonesia has 1400 sq. km of waqf land valued at US$60 billion. If these assets yield a return of 5% per annum, then US$3 billion could be used for various socio-economic purposes.

financial systems. Financial inclusion is a very vital factor in the process of inclusive development. Available data show that most of Muslim countries lag behind other emerging economies with only 27% of financial inclusion. Cost, religious belief, distance, and documentation requirements are among important obstacles. The issue of financial inclusion can also be addressed through specific Islamic redistributive channels (zakat, sadaqah, qard-e-hasan, and awaqf).

Given the significant potentiality of waqf funds in financing social and economic infrastructure, many attempts have been made to revive waqf institutions in recent years. For example, a number of IDB member countries such as Lebanon, Turkey, Jordan, Sudan, Morocco, Qatar, Kuwait, Malaysia, Iran, Brunei, and Algeria have taken significant steps to revive and develop the properties of waqf. They have ratified new laws of awaqf which help recovering, preserving, and developing several awaqf properties to support the needs of their economy. In line with the efforts of these countries and expand the usage of waqf in other Islamic countries, there is a need to enhance waqf mechanism by adopting an innovative element to support many socio-economic activities in the process of inclusive economic development. To do so, a holistic approach should be developed to achieve harmonization and coordination of rules and principles between various waqf institutions at national, regional, and global levels. Using the results of other studies, there are three major constraints which hinder the effectiveness of waqf funds in line with the current and emerging financial needs of IDB member countries. They are (i) inadequate awareness about the role of waqf in addressing socio-economic difficulties in many IDB member countries; (ii) insufficient widely accepted Shariah-compliant products to integrate these Islamic redistributive institutions (i.e., waqf and zakat) to inclusive development; and (iii) lack of innovative products to use waqf funds under certain programs such as Poverty Entrepreneurship Schemes that can be used for creating employment opportunities. In this context, creating a diverse range of financial services for using waqf and zakat resources through competition and innovation is essential.

Central banks or monetary authorities shall play critical role in mobilizing resources generated by waqf endowments. Specifically, they can develop a supportive legal and regulatory framework (as in the case of Indonesia) and "proactive" policy targets on usage, access, and quality, the three main dimensions of effective usage of waqf and zakat. Formalizing and standardizing of these instruments will improve the efficiency and facilitate the achievement of inclusive development. Using the results of other studies, the experience of Malaysia, Indonesia, and Bangladesh shows that there is strong indication that waqf can be a viable alternative model for supporting social infrastructure (health and education). However, there are variations in the selected countries in terms of funding and implementing agencies for supporting socio-economic programs. For example, in Malaysia, even the implementing agencies are very much government-backed or government-assisted, whereas in Bangladesh. Non-governmental organizations (NGOs) are playing a leading role in this context.

9   Summary and Conclusion

Approximately 50% of population in member countries lacks access to basic infrastructure, which isolates communities, prevents access to health care, education, and jobs, and impedes economic growth. Most of the countries in sub-Saharan Africa are underdeveloped, mainly due to the region's deep infrastructure deficit. It is estimated that the infrastructure need in sub-Saharan Africa is more than US$93 billion annually over the next two decades and only less than half of that will be provided using the traditional ways of financing thus leaving a significant gap of more than US$50 billion to fill. The poor state of infrastructure in sub-Saharan Africa negatively affects economic growth and reduces productivity by as much as 40% every year.

Given the large scale of financial needs to support both economic and social infrastructure, the key question is how to design a broader set of financing instruments to increase the amount of financing for infrastructure development in ways that make sense to each country. As a system, Islamic finance has strong potential in promoting both social and economic infrastructure development. While zakat and awaqf have great potential to support small size and social infrastructure, sukuk (Islamic bonds) can successfully finance large-scale infrastructure (energy, transport, roads, and shelter). Islamic redistributive instruments such as zakat, waqf (endowment), and sadaqah (charity) have played significant part in alleviating poverty and helped the society to move to more social and financial inclusion. Particularly, waqf funds have played an important role in the provision of both economic and social infrastructure. Historically, education and health have been the second and third largest receivers of waqf revenues after religious matters, which was the original purpose of waqf.

Unfortunately, large pool of waqf assets in most Muslim countries are dormant and not being used for socio-economic development purposes properly. The effective way of using zakat and waqf can enhance productive capacities of the society and provide interest-free loans (qard hassan) to the poor who are mostly excluded from financial systems. Available data on the usage and access of financial services by individuals and companies show that most of OIC member countries lag behind other emerging economies with only 27% of financial inclusion. Cost, religious belief, distance, and documentation requirements are among important obstacles. The issue of financial inclusion can also be addressed through specific Islamic redistributive channels (zakat, sadaqah, Qard al-Hassan, and awaqf). Given the significant potentiality of waqf funds in financing social and economic infrastructure, a number of IDB member countries such as Lebanon, Turkey, Jordan, Sudan, Morocco, Qatar, Kuwait, Malaysia, Iran, Brunei, and Algeria have taken significant steps to revive and develop the properties of waqf. They have ratified new laws of awaqf which help recovering, preserving, and developing several awaqf properties to support the needs of their economy.

Using the results of other studies, there are three major constraints, which hinder the effectiveness of waqf funds in line with the current and emerging financial needs of IDB member countries. They are (i) inadequate awareness about the role of waqf in addressing socio-economic difficulties in many IDB member countries; (ii) insufficient widely accepted Shariah-compliant products to integrate these Islamic redistributive institutions (i.e., waqf and zakat) to inclusive development; and (iii) lack of innovative products to use waqf funds under certain programs such as Poverty Entrepreneurship Schemes that can be used for creating employment opportunities.

At the country level, governments need to play critical role in mobilizing resources generated by waqf endowments. Specifically, they should develop a supportive legal and regulatory framework and "proactive" policy targets on usage, access, and quality, the three main dimensions of effective usage of waqf and zakat. Formalizing and standardizing of these instruments will improve the efficiency and facilitate the achievement of inclusive development. As the experience of Malaysia, Indonesia, and Bangladesh shows, there is strong indication that waqf can be a viable alternative model for supporting social infrastructure (health and education). However, there are variations in these countries in terms of funding and implementing agencies for supporting socio-economic programs. For example, in Malaysia, even the implementing agencies are very much government-backed or government-assisted, whereas in Bangladesh. NGOs are playing a leading role.

At the IDBG level, the bank needs to play more active role in supporting the efforts of its member countries to explore the relevant policy, legal, regulatory, and institutional interventions necessary to expand the role of Islamic redistributive institutions in engendering new source of finance for socio-economic infrastructure development. In this context, three key priority areas are to (i) create a common platform to enhance the dialogue among member countries to with the aim of promoting knowledge and increasing awareness on the role of waqf in socio-economic infrastructure development; (ii) identify successful case studies and good Islamic redistributive income practices anywhere in the world and have exchange of visits and technical cooperation among member countries in the form of reverse linkage initiative; and (iii) support creating widely accepted Shariah-compliant products related to Islamic redistributive institutions including waqf and zakat to support inclusive development.

REFERENCES

Cizakca, M. (2004). *Cash Waqf Models for Financing in Education*. The Fifth Islamic Economic System Conference, Kuala Lumpur.

Department of Planning Western Australia. (2012). *Role of Social Infrastructure in Local and Regional Economic Development*.

Estache, A. (2006). *Infrastructure: A Survey of Recent and Upcoming Issues*. Washington, DC: World Bank.

Estache, A., Ianchovichina, E., Bacon, R., & Salamon, I. (2013). *Infrastructure and Employment Creation in the Middle East and North Africa*. Washington, DC: World Bank.

Foster, V., & Briceño-Garmendia, C. (2010). *Africa's Infrastructure: A Time for Transformation*. Washington, DC: World Bank.

Kahf, M. (1989). Zakat: Unresolved Issues in the Contemporary Fiqh. *IIUM Journal of Economics and Management, 2*(1), 1–22.

OECD. (2015a). *Fostering Investment in Infrastructure: Lessons Learned from OECD Investment Policy Reviews*. Paris: OECD.

Parker, G. (2008, July). *Investing in Asian Infrastructure: The S&P Asia Infrastructure Index*. http://www2.standardandpoors.com/spf/pdf/index/Investing_Asian_Infrastructure_0708.pdf.

Patel, P. (2014). *Regional Infrastructure in Sub-Saharan Africa: Challenges and Opportunities*. Washington, DC: World Bank.

Perrotti, D., & Sánchez, R. J. (2011). *La brecha de infraestructura en América Latina y el Caribe* (Recursos naturales e Infraestructura Series No. 153). Chile: United Nations Publication.

Romp, W., & De Haan, J. (2007). Public Capital and Economic Growth: A Critical Survey. *Perspektiven der Wirtschaftspolitik, 8*(s1), pp. 6–52, 20.

RREEF. (2008). *China Infrastructure Investment RREEF Research London*. London: RREEF.

Sadeq, A. (2002). Waqf, Perpetual Charity and Poverty Alleviation. *International Journal of Social Economics, 29*(1–2), pp. 135–151.

Straub, S. (2008). *Infrastructure and Growth in Developing Countries: Recent Advances and Research Challenges* (Policy Research Working Paper No. 4460). World Bank.

UNCTAD. (2014). *World Investment Report.*

United Nations. (2011). *Infrastructure for Economic Development and Poverty Reduction in Africa*. The Global Urban Economic Dialogue Series. Nairobi: Human Settlements Programme.

United Nations. (2015). *Transforming Our World: The 2030 Agenda for Sustainable Development.*

World Bank Group. (2013). *Financing for Development Post 2015*. Washington, DC: World Bank.

World Economic Forum. (2014). *The Global Infrastructure Gap*. http://reports.weforum.org.

Yagan, Zuhdi (1388H). *Al-Waqf fi Al-Shari`h Al-Islamiyyah wa Al-Qanun, Dar Al-Nahdah Al-'Arabiyyah*. Beirut.

INDEX

Printed by Printforce, the Netherlands